W9-DFF-239

Robert Louis Stevenson

THE SCOTTISH STORIES
AND ESSAYS

Robert Louis Stevenson

THE SCOTTISH STORIES
AND ESSAYS

∗

Edited by
KENNETH GELDER

Edinburgh University Press

HIGHLAND PARK PUBLIC LIBRARY

© Kenneth Gelder 1989
Edinburgh University Press
22 George Square, Edinburgh

Set in Linotron Goudy
by Koinonia, Bury, and
printed in Great Britain by
Redwood Burn Limited,
Trowbridge, Wilts

British Library Cataloguing
  in Publication Data
Stevenson, Robert Louis,
  1850-1894
The Scottish stories and essays.
I. Title   II. Gelder, Kenneth
828'.809
ISBN 0 85224 591 2
ISBN 0 85224 592 0 pbk

List of Contents

✳

I INTRODUCTION

II STORIES

III ESSAYS

IV APPENDIX

V EXPLANATORY NOTES

VI REFERENCES

VII GLOSSARY

Acknowledgements

✳

I would like to thank, especially, Dr Donald Low of Stirling University for his enthusiasm and support over the last few years: no postgraduate student could ask for a better supervisor. Thanks also to Dr Ian Campbell of Edinburgh University and Professor John MacQueen from the School of Scottish Studies at Edinburgh for help when needed in tracking down some of the allusions. Thanks as well to Dr Graham Tulloch of Flinders University, Adelaide.

I am grateful for permission to publish 'The Plague-Cellar' from Princeton University Library and Mr Alan Osbourne.

Most of all, thanks to my wife Hannah.

I   INTRODUCTION

❋

The fortune of a tale lies not alone in the skill of him that
writes, but as much, perhaps, in the inherited
experience of him who reads
Pastoral

The several collections of Stevenson's short stories to appear over
the last few years have, if anything, drawn attention to the miscellaneous character of his writing.[1] These collections have either
presented Stevenson's non-Scottish stories alone (his South
Pacific writing, for example), or have placed Scottish stories
alongside the non-Scottish (South Pacific, English, European
fables like 'Olalla', and so on). Certainly the variety of Stevenson's
writing needs to be underscored: recent attention has rightly been
given to his South Pacific material,[2] to show him off, rightly again,
as one of the few Victorian writers to understand properly (as
properly as was possible at the time) South Pacific cultures and
the ways in which western imperialism had affected those cultures.
But one consequence of underscoring Stevenson's 'other' writing
or of representing the miscellaneous character of that writing, is
that his specifically Scottish work doesn't get the attention it
deserves.

   In fact Stevenson's reputation as a Scottish writer, among
earlier twentieth century critics especially, has not been good. C.
M. Grieve (Hugh MacDiarmid) launched a passing attack on
Stevenson while praising Sir Walter Scott's 'Wandering Willie's
Tale' from *Redgauntlet* (1824) – 'a masterpiece of prose. . . which
one must go back to the seventeenth century to parallel' – and
Carlyle's 'struggle' between his native Scots and the dominance
of the English language (Grieve 1926, p. 119). Yet Stevenson also
shows symptoms of that 'struggle', as will be suggested below: in
some of the Scottish stories he *did* write, Stevenson drew attention
to the differences between Scots and English, linguistically and
culturally. Moreover, Stevenson's 'The Tale of Tod Lapraik'

(included here) directly alludes to and is comparable in many ways to Scott's 'Wandering Willie's Tale' (see 'The Tale of Tod Lapraik', note 7); it is not impossible to see Stevenson as operating *within* a tradition of writing in Scots established by the Scott MacDiarmid had praised. More importantly, this story and others by Stevenson return for their inspiration *to* the 17th century, so highly regarded by MacDiarmid, as will also be shown below.

Stevenson's reputation as a Scottish writer has also been attacked by less actively nationalist critics. In his revised *The Scots Literary Tradition*, the Leavisite critic John Speirs remarks on the 'inconsistency' of including George Douglas Brown's *The House with the Green Shutters* (1901) while omitting altogether the novels of Scott. Although he too admires 'Wandering Willie's Tale', he argues that a 'Scott and Stevenson phase' must be grown out of; and he notes somewhat dismissively that he first wrote *The Scots Literary Tradition* 'at a time when Stevenson (not to speak of Barrie and John Buchan) continued to be overestimated as representing "the line of Scott" with the added attraction of "style"' (Speirs 1962, p. 19). Certainly Stevenson *was* operating very much within a literary tradition prescribed by Scott, for better or worse. But like Scott again, his stories in Scots and some of his Scottish characters complicate the issue and call for some kind of reassessment of Stevenson's own Scottishness. This collection brings together for the first time all the available Scottish stories by Stevenson, firstly for the pleasure of reading, but secondly so that questions about Stevenson's Scottishness may be raised and addressed. I have also included those essays by Stevenson that deal with specifically Scottish subjects, not least because the essays often directly relate to the stories. Of course, the placing of stories alongside non-fiction that relates to or provides a context for those stories is itself in 'the line of Scott', whose novels contained extensive explanatory notes full of related facts, anecdotes and background material: indeed, both writers tended to blur the none-too-solid boundaries *between* story and fact, fiction and history.

For Speirs, 'the line of Scott' seems to have more or less described how certain nineteenth-century Scottish novels, under Scott's influence, had slipped into the somewhat 'debased' or juvenile literary mode of romance. Certain novels by Stevenson, *Catriona* (1893) in particular, were very much a part of the romance mode as Scott had presented it. In Stevenson's well-known essay 'A Gossip on Romance', Scott's novels are discussed at some mode as Scott had presented it. In Stevenson's well-known essay 'A Gossip on Romance', Scott's novels are discussed at some length, and Stevenson calls him 'out and away the king of the romantics' (*Memories and Portraits*, xxix, p. 129). Of course, Stevenson was influenced by other writers using the romance mode elsewhere, especially in France. Alexandre Dumas, *père*, was a particular favourite and Stevenson had also written an essay on Dumas's romantic novel *Vicomte de Bragelonne* (1843), 'A Gossip on a Novel of Dumas's'. But Scott was certainly the dominant influence on Stevenson's *Scottish* fiction in terms of his use of the romance mode. Shorter Scottish stories by Stevenson like 'The Pavilion on the Links' and 'The Merry Men' clearly owe much to Scott. They are, loosely, romantic adventure stories told by narrators who, in temperament and background, are very much like the narrators of, say, *Rob Roy* (1817) or *Redgauntlet*. Frank Cassilis in 'The Pavilion on the Links' is in rivalry against a character called Northmour in a way that recalls the Lowlander/Highlander juxtaposition common to Scott's novels. Both Cassilis and Charles Darnaway, the narrator of 'The Merry Men', are solitary, drifting, yet moralising and somewhat bland young men who fall in love with romanticised heroines – again very much like Scott's 'mediocre heroes', as George Lukács called them in his seminal study of Scott (Lukács 1981, p. 32).

Of course as Lukács pointed out, Scott's protagonists, for all their mediocrity, are nevertheless implicated in history and historical struggle. However, in Stevenson's 'The Pavilion on the Links' and 'The Merry Men' – his most Scott-like stories in many ways – history by contrast seems to be more or less absent; the characters seem, even, removed from history, with events taking place in isolated parts of Scotland. Here, history is now replaced by a much less ambitious and more private context, the family. For Stevenson in these stories, the protagonist's family now becomes the primary site for struggle and opposition. And there is at least one difference between the family in Stevenson's Scott-like stories and the family as Scott had represented it in his novels. In Scott's novels, the narrators generally speak fondly of their fathers and uphold the patriarchy (Alan Fairford follows his father's profession in *Redgauntlet*; even the Whig Darsie Latimer comes to admire his Jacobite uncle in this novel); but in Stevenson's 'The Pavilion on the Links' and 'The Merry Men', the patriarchy is always shown to be in decay, both physically and morally. Cassilis's father-in-law or 'uncle' is a swindler, while Darnaway's uncle Gordon is corrupted by the treasures from sunken ships which he hoards on his islands. In both stories, the father-figures are subjected to the criticism and moral upbraiding of the younger narrators, and eventually come to grief as victims of their own degraded lives. The stories end by severing the two generations from one another, even to the extent in 'The Pavilion on the Links' of erasing the father-figure completely from the narrative: just after Mr Huddlestone is killed, there is literally 'no sign of him, nor so much as a trace of blood'.

In Stevenson's 'The Misadventures of John Nicholson', the patriarchy is again severely criticised; but as a comic Christmas story, it offers a final scene of reconciliation between father and son that is more akin to Scott. Old Mr Nicholson is an Edinburgh patriarch from, probably, the mid-1840s. In the story, his intransigence and conservatism are linked to his position as an upholder of the newly-formed Free Church of Scotland. Through Mr Nicholson, the story attacks the Free Church's rigid position on Sabbath-breaking and intemperance and shows the old man as, for a while, incapable of the Christian act of forgiveness. And here, Stevenson's involvement with Scottish cultural history begins to deepen. For old Mr Nicholson, the formation of the Free Church and the events of the Disruption of 1843 are specific to what the story calls the 'tight little theological kingdom of Scotland', incomprehensible to the English beyond the border; indeed, they confirm and secure his position *within* the specifics of Scottish cultural history. His house in stately Randolph Crescent becomes an emblem of that secure position, an emblem of Scotland itself: 'Here, at least, was a citadel unassailable by right-hand defections or left-hand extremes'.

This description of old Mr Nicholson's house is important to notice: Stevenson is in fact paraphrasing a passage from the Covenanter historian Patrick Walker's well-known complaint about 'dissenters' in his *Biographia Presbyteriana* (1827): see 'The Misadventures of John Nicholson', note 6. The Covenanter allusion is significant, since as Drummond and Bulloch (1975, p. 5) note, the newly-formed Free Church actually saw itself as 'the Church of the Reformers and Covenanters, in her rightful freedom'. Old Mr Nicholson's Walker-like position, however, is one that disallows 'Dissenters'; indeed, he fortifies himself in his 'citadel' at Randolph Crescent *against* dissension. Of course, the 'Dissenter' in this story is Mr Nicholson's son John, and the story goes on to show the split between the older generation with its Covenanting traditions and a younger generation for whom those traditions allow no room. In a way, Stevenson may be remarking on his own position in Scotland here, and there are in fact close parallels between his own movements (especially his trip to California) and the 'misadventures' John experiences. The Free Church of Scotland, with the support of patriarchs like old Mr Nicholson, revives a specifically Scottish tradition with Covenanting origins; such a tradition, intransigent and conservative, is ultimately unable to accommodate (or it actually resists accommodating) 'Dissenters' like, perhaps, Stevenson himself.

In his two stories written in Scots, 'Thrawn Janet' and 'The Tale of Tod Lapraik', Stevenson brought the specifics of history back into his writing by actually turning *to* the days of the Covenanters, and it is his fascination with them (partly admiring, partly critical) that seems to me to lie at the base of Stevenson's own Scottishness. In this context, the suggestion that he merely operated in 'the line of Scott' is now too reductive and too dismissive; interestingly, in these two stories in Scots, Stevenson also turned his back on the romance mode that had otherwise dominated his fiction. These stories are now implicated *in* a specific moment of Scottish history. Stevenson drew on Patrick Walker again for his account of the 'outed' Covenanter minister and prophet Alexander Peden, prisoner on the Bass Rock in 'The Tale of Tod Lapraik' (see note 4); while in 'Thrawn Janet', the days of the Persecution in the late 17th century provide an invisible yet still potent historical site for events that take place some thirty years later. Stevenson wrote 'Thrawn Janet' in mid-1881, but there is evidence that he had worked on the story as early as 1868, when he was seventeen, for inclusion in a projected 'Covenanting Story-Book'.[3] By this time, Stevenson had already written his essay 'The Pentland Rising', a bicentennial account of the Pentland insurrection of November 1666 when a small Covenanter army was defeated by the notorious persecutor Sir Thomas Dalyell. Stevenson's biographer J. C. Furnas has noted in passing that the essay consists of 'extracts from. . . Patrick Walker' (Furnas 1952, p. 47); in fact, Walker was not a source for this essay at all, but many other Covenanter historians were, and 'The Pentland Rising' testifies to the depth of Stevenson's interest even at such a young age in the turbulent events at this time. His early and so far uncollected story 'The Plague-Cellar' is also included here and follows on from those events in 'The Pentland Rising', set as it is in Edinburgh in early January 1667 'with the blood of five of the Pentland insurgents' still fresh on the scaffold. The story is sensationalist, but it is important to remember that the Covenanter histories Stevenson drew upon (and immersed himself in) were themselves sensationalist narratives, speaking always from the position of oppressed visionaries at a time when the 'true Kirk' was seen to be at its most persecuted.

It might be useful to provide a brief summary of the background to events in the so-called days of the Persecution. When the Stuart Charles II was restored to the throne in 1660, Presbyterianism in Scotland soon came under attack. As J. M. Reid summarises, 'By its Act Rescissory of 1661 the Scottish Parliament swept away all legislation passed since 1633, when Scotland had Charles I's bishops' (Reid 1960, p. 88). The Act meant a return to episcopacy and in 1662 bishops were formally restored. James Sharp, minister of Crail at this time, was sent down to London to negotiate for Presbyterian uniformity in Scotland, but he returned as the Archbishop of St Andrews and came to preside over the executions of the Pentland Covenanters in Edinburgh in December 1666: Stevenson refers to him a number of times in his Scottish essays, and the mad Covenanter Ravenswood in 'The Plague-Cellar' rightly calls him an 'apostate' (see note 10). Episcopacy soon dominated. As Reid continues,

> patronage was restored and the settling of a minister in his parish had to be approved not by the presbytery but by the bishop. Ministers appointed since 1649 had none of these qualifications. On October 1st, 1662, the Scottish Privy Council, in a drunken session at Glasgow, ordered that ministers in this position who failed to find the backing of a patron and of their bishop during the next month should leave their churches. To the surprise of the Government 274 refused to apply for a bishop's collation and were expelled. Most of them were in the south-western shires where the Protestors, who held most firmly to the Covenants, were strong. (Reid 1960, p. 89).

These ministers were 'outed', their places taken by 'curates' who gave an oath of allegiance to the King and had the support of a bishop. However, when more and more parishioners in some areas began to attend the secret conventicles held by their 'outed' ministers, the govenment raised an army under Sir Thomas Dalyell and the days of the Persecution began in force. Stevenson describes the kinds of harassment to which parishioners in the south-west were subjected in 'The Pentland Rising'; it was sufficient to incite an insurrection, resulting in the Covenanter defeat at Rullion Green in November 1666. There were other famous Covenanter battles throughout the 1670s and 1680s against commanders like Dalyell and John Graham of Claverhouse (see 'Pastoral', note 4), but this turbulent time at last came to an end when James II and the Stuart line was overthrown, and in 1689 the Dutchman William of Orange was crowned King. On 7 June 1690 the Presbyterian Kirk of Scotland was again fully established by law, marking the climax of this long-awaited Glorious Revolution.

As indicated already, the Covenanter historians who documented events at this time wrote from the position of an oppressed, outlawed and radical minority. Their rhetoric was forceful and figurative, and in their accounts of persecutions and martyrdom they constructed a rich and vivid mythology. Stevenson's favourite Covenanter sources included Patrick Walker, Robert Wodrow and James Kirkton. Kirkton was an especial favourite and, like Stevenson's Ephraim Martext in 'The Plague-Cellar', he was an 'outed' Presbyterian minister: he had refused the acts of the Council in 1662, and was outlawed by the Council in 1674 for holding conventicles at Cramond, preaching in secret to those of his own persuasion. The purity of this position contrasted with those ministers like James Sharp who had embraced episcopacy, and Kirkton in his *The Secret and True History of the Church of Scotland, from the restoration to the year 1678* told a number of stories about the grisly fates that befell such 'apostates' who betrayed or compromised the Presbyterian church during the days of the Persecution (his history also contained James Russell's account of Sharp's murder in May 1679). One story involves Edward Thomson, the son of a devout Presbyterian minister. Thomson tries to follow the true Kirk, as his father had, but he later wearies of a life of non-conformity and becomes the 'curate' of Anstruther Easter. Stevenson takes up Kirkton's story of 'curat Thomson' in his essay 'The Coast of Fife': one night, while coming home, the devil passes by him, and soon after (so the mythology surrounding Thomson's death goes) he is taken by the devil for his apostacy. Kirkton's story, paraphrased by Stevenson, shows late 17th century Presbyterian ideology transformed into a basic and effective narrative structure: those who ignore or betray the true cause of Presbyterianism can expect, sooner or later, to be overtaken by the real Enemy of the Kirk himself. This narrative structure is put into practice in Stevenson's two stories written in Scots, 'Thrawn Janet' and 'The Tale of Tod Lapraik'.

In Summer 1871, when he was twenty, Stevenson wrote in a letter to Mrs Churchill Babington about just why he was so interested in the Covenanters and their 'secret histories' and narratives:

> It is a pet idea of mine that one gets more real truth out of one avowed partisan than out of a dozen of your sham impartialists – wolves in sheep's clothing – simpering honesty as they suppress documents. After all what one wants to know is not what people did, but why they did it – or rather, why they *thought* they did it; and to learn that, you should go to the men themselves. Their very falsehood is often more than another man's truth (*Letters*, i, pp. 35-6).

His attraction to Covenanter histories is an attraction to 'partisan' writing, writing that mythologises its radical ideology, its faith and convictions, through narrative. His two stories in Scots show this process at work, and seem to support his claim in a letter to J. M. Barrie in December 1893, 'My style is from the Covenanting writers' (*Letters*, v, p. 93). They are both in fact narrated by 'partisans', supporters of the Kirk and Covenant. Although 'Thrawn Janet' is set in 1712, well after the Glorious Revolution (and after the Union of 1707), the narrator looks longingly back at the 'outed' ministers who preached in secret during the days of the Persecution 'wi' a Bible under their oxter an' a speerit o' prayer in their heart'. Later, he speaks figuratively of the moment 'the blessed licht shone upon the kingdom', the Glorious Revolution of 1689 that returned Presbyterianism to the country. Black Andie Dale, the narrator of 'The Tale of Tod Lapraik', is described by David Balfour (the narrator of *Catriona*, in which the tale appears) as 'a good Whig and Presbyterian; read daily in a pocket Bible, and. . . both eager and able to converse seriously on religion, leaning more than a little towards the Cameronian extremes' (*Catriona*, vii, p. 120). Andie's 'partisan' character fundamentally colours the tale he tells. It is about the fortunes of two of King Charles' soldiers employed to guard Covenanter prisoners on the Bass Rock in the mid-1670s, in the midst of the days of the Persecution. One soldier, Tam Dale, is so influenced by the Covenanter

Alexander Peden that he refuses ever more to 'lift arms against the cause o' Christ': he is, in other words, converted to the Covenanter position, realising at last the error of his ways. The other soldier, Tod Lapraik, undergoes no such conversion. His history as a persecutor of the true Kirk catches up with him, and he suffers an extraordinary and diabolical fate.

Stevenson seems to have been particularly pleased with the Scottishness of, and his use of Scots in, these two stories: as he wrote to Sidney Colvin in April 1893, 'he who can't read Scots can *never* enjoy *Tod Lapraik.* . . *Tod Lapraik* is a piece of living Scots; if I had never writ anything but that and *Thrawn Janet*, still I'd have been a writer' (*Letters*, v, p. 18). Certainly the 'partisan' positions of the narrators of these two stories produce a kind of writing (though both stories are actually spoken) that is recognisably located within a 'living' Scottish Covenanting tradition. Indeed, one of the points of both stories is to show that this tradition *is* still very much alive. Both stories show the lingering effects of the bygone days of the Persecution in the late 17th century on characters who may otherwise have forgotten about them or dismissed them. In 'Thrawn Janet', the naive young Rev. Mr Murdoch Soulis comes to Balweary parish fresh from 'book-learnin'' at Edinburgh University. He considers the days of the Persecution well and truly over, and this upsets the 'auld, concerned, serious men and women' in the parish who still clearly remember those turbulent times. These older folk (the narrator is one of them) consider the new minister to have 'nae *leevin*' experience in religion' (my italics), and, like a kind of cautionary tale, the story provides him with just such a 'leevin' experience' by resurrecting the horrors of those days gone by.

The effects of this on Soulis are quite profound. He changes from a liberal and progressive young minister to 'the man ye ken the day', a 'severe, bleak-faced old man, dreadful to his hearers' who now frightens 'the younger sort' away with his vivid, fundamentalist sermons. He has become, in other words, like the Covenanter ministers he had earlier dismissed. The account of what Soulis is now like is given in English fifty years after the events told in Scots by the old narrator, and the juxtaposition in time and in language produces an ambivalence about Soulis's fate. From the older Covenanter position, the naive young minister has deserved a lesson in Scottish religious 'living' history. But the English introduction suggests that the lesson has a tragic effect,

among other things alienating the minister from a younger generation still keen to come to church. From this English position, a
progressive post-Union liberal minister has been restrained by a
tradition (recalling the description in 'The Misadventures of John
Nicholson') specific to the 'tight little theological kingdom of
Scotland': a young 'Dissenter' has, in other words, been made to
conform to the Scottish traditions of an older generation. And
here is a version of the 'struggle' between two cultures, poignantly
represented through the clash between old and young, traditional
and progressive; and through the use of two opposing languages,
Scots ('living Scots') and English.

The partisan representation of historically-based events in
the two stories in Scots certainly contrasts with Stevenson's other
Scottish stories, 'The Pavilion on the Links' and 'The Merry Men'
especially. Here, the narrators, as 'mediocre heroes' with romantic
inclinations, operate very much within the romance mode mentioned earlier; they may in this sense be in 'the line of Scott',
though not the Scott of 'Wandering Willie's Tale'. But as already
noted, these stories are also less historically specific, less historically implicated than Scott's novels. The stories dissociate themselves from history just as their protagonists dissociate themselves
from Scots. In 'The Merry Men', Charles Darnaway is more or
less totally Anglicised, educated at Edinburgh University: he only
breaks into Scots once, in a moment of distress when declaring
his love for Mary. The story contrasts him with his uncle Gordon
who has a Cameronian background, and in fact Charles distances
himself from his uncle and his uncle's generation by showing him
to be overtaken by a Cameronian-infused self-consuming insanity.
But even Charles is momentarily affected by his uncle's Cameronian superstitions, as is shown when he dives for the sunken Armada
treasures (one of the reasons he visits his uncle on the island in
the first place); even here, the younger generation isn't entirely
free from its own history. Indeed, 'The Merry Men' seems to me
to express the very tension arising from this generational and cul-
tural-linguistic division through its own uncertain literary form.
Unlike 'The Pavilion on the Links', it is not properly *in* the
romance mode: the relationship between Charles and Mary is
hardly central to the story and, in fact, is more or less forgotten
as the story goes on. What replaces it is an account of uncle
Gordon's reactions to the 'black man' from the shipwreck, reactions firmly located within his own Scottishness and the super-

stitions it has generated. As a consequence, the story turns away from the romance mode and towards the kind of Scottish tragedy evoked more succinctly in 'Thrawn Janet' and 'The Tale of Tod Lapraik'. The earlier part of the story seems less historically related but, finally, history catches up and dominates 'The Merry Men'.

'The Merry Men' is actually quite literally in 'the line of Scott', drawing on Scott's descriptions of Sumburgh Roost in *The Pirate* (1822) in its own descriptions of Aros Roost and the ships that come to grief there; Stevenson may even have lifted the title of his story from Scott's introduction to the novel (see 'The Merry Men', note 3). For Stevenson, *The Pirate* was a particular favourite not least because it had evolved out of Scott's famous tour of the northern islands in late Summer 1814 with the lighthouse commissioners, one of whom was Stevenson's grandfather Robert Stevenson. In 1893, Stevenson wrote a short introduction to his grandfather's account of the tour: it is included here for the first time since its publication in *Scribner's Magazine* of that year, and like Stevenson's 'Memoirs of an Islet' (also included here) it is useful to read alongside 'The Merry Men'.

Indeed, all the Scottish essays included here are worth reading alongside the stories, often linking up with them quite specifically. As already noted, Stevenson (like Scott) blurred the boundaries between fiction and fact in his stories. Some of his Covenanter sources have been remarked upon above, and of course the Covenanter historians themselves were adept at fictionalising or mythologising the factual. Stevenson had often planned stories *about* actual Covenanters: he mentions his early attempts at writing a novel on David Hackston of Rathillet, one of James Sharp's murderers, in his essay 'The Coast of Fife' (see notes 20, 22-25). Other stories turned to different sources. 'The Body Snatcher' draws on the actual confession of William Burke printed in the *Edinburgh Evening Courant*, 21 January 1829: this is certainly a very different Scottish Christmas story from his later comic effort, 'The Misadventures of John Nicholson'.

The Scottish essays also show the extent of Stevenson's inclinations towards fiction or myth-making through the representations of his childhood and ancestry. In 'An Old Scots Gardener' and 'Pastoral', he shows how his childhood was coloured by two 'auld, concerned, serious men' who linked him directly to the Covenanting mind. In 'The Manse', Stevenson lists some of his ancestors, making random connections with familiar and less familiar moments in Scottish history home and abroad, opening his background up beyond the 'tight little theological kingdom'. The connections may or may not always be traceable, while at other times they fuse history and fiction together (for example, his connection with 'a daughter of Burns' Dr Smith'): in the essay Stevenson presents himself as a character wandering through his own past, turning recollection into myth or fiction as he goes. 'The Coast of Fife' works in a similar way, scattering recollection, myth and history over the 'kingdom' (as Fife was and is actually called). In this essay in particular, Stevenson shows off his familiarity with Scottish history and literature: the two become, ultimately, hard to distinguish. A nice slip between the two occurs when he mentions Kinghorn in Fife where 'Alexander "brak's neckbane"'. The historical reference here is to Alexander III (see note 8); but the quote comes from Burns' 'Tam o' Shanter. A Tale', 'Whare drunken *Charlie* brak's neck-bane'. The quote bears no relation to the historical event, except insofar as a neck was broken too; in fact, the quote takes us from the east coast to the south-west of Scotland, and to another time altogether. The point is that a familiar historical event has been neatly filtered through a piece of fiction in its recollection.

Like the stories, the Scottish essays show us the places that most interested and fascinated Stevenson: Edinburgh and the nearby Pentland Hills, Wick and Caithness, Fife and St Andrews and Magus Muir, the tiny island Earraid off the south-west tip of Mull on the west coast. All these places are connected to Stevenson's childhood and adolescence, and the essays often develop out of a recollection of his first memories of the place: indeed, the title of the collection in which some of them first appeared, *Memories and Portraits* (1887), underscores their recollective character. His incomplete essay 'A Winter's Walk in Carrick and Galloway' is also presented here, coming from a walking tour of that district in 1876. It is less recollective than other essays, and less inclined towards myth-making: he notes rather severely at one point, 'Maybole is tumbledown and dreary. . . I heard a great deal about drinking, and a great deal about religious revivals: two things in which the Scottish character is emphatic and most unlovely' (perhaps testifying to his own well-to-do Edinburgh background as much as to Maybole itself). But the essay indicates again the depth of Stevenson's interest in and knowledge of Scottish places and their history, and he turns to sources here ranging from old Scottish songs and ballads, to Burns (naturally), to James Paterson's detailed *History of the County of Ayr* (1847). Indeed, all the essays are dense with allusions and references to literary and historical sources: this collection has endeavoured to annotate and explain as many of them as possible, and it is hoped the reader will find these notes useful.

The recollective character of the essays in particular shows how keen Stevenson was to place *himself* within a suitably complex Scottish context, even though he may also have cultivated his own position as a 'Dissenter'. In his unfinished novel *Weir of Hermiston*, Stevenson confidently declared that the differences between the Scots and the English related specifically to the Scots' ability to recollect and respect their own past:

> that is the mark of the Scot of all classes: that he stands in an attitude towards the past unthinkable to Englishmen, and remembers and cherishes the memory of his forebears, good or bad; and there burns alive in him a sense of identity with the dead even to the twentieth generation (*Weir of Hermiston*, xvi, p. 54).

But this unified vision of the 'Scot of all classes' isn't always maintained. In his earlier *Travels with a Donkey in the Cevennes* (1879), Stevenson (paraphrasing Patrick Walker once more) observed a class-based split in the Scots' power of recollection:

> in isolated farms or in the manse, serious Presbyterian people still recall the days of the great persecution, and the graves of local martyrs are still piously regarded. But in towns and among the so-called better classes, I fear these old doings have become an idle tale. . . Nay, at Muirkirk of Glenluce, I found the beadle's wife had not so much as heard of Prophet Peden (*Travels with a Donkey in the Cevennes*, xvii, p. 233).

Ambivalent about 'serious Presbyterian people' and the Covenanter tradition they helped to perpetuate or tried to revive (a position he satirised, as indicated, through old Mr Nicholson in 'The Misadventures of John Nicholson'; see also his remarks above about 'religious revivals' in Maybole), Stevenson nevertheless himself acquiesced in a desire to inform his readers about such 'old doings' in Scotland. His best stories, the two stories he wrote in Scots, actually turn those 'old doings' into a 'leevin' experience', and they are certainly wonderfully evocative. And they indicate that although Stevenson was himself from the 'so-called better classes', he could nevertheless recollect those moments and events in Scottish history that others might have forgotten under the influence of an English language and culture. Perhaps Stevenson was speaking of himself when he noted of his countryman in the essay 'The Foreigner at Home' (where he most directly addressed the issue of Scottishness), 'even though his tongue acquire the Southern knack, he will still have a strong Scots accent of the mind'.

II STORIES

*

The Plague-Cellar[1]

✳

The wind howled chilly and with a mournful cadence through the funnel-like closes, up the winding high street and round the castle rock, raising wavelets on the dull Nor' Loch and shaking from the creaking trees such withered leaves as autumn had not taken long before. The filmy clouds that drifted across the crescent moon, now hid her in their dark embrace, now let a glimmering beam fall with a ghastly pallor on the quaint old town. It was freezing pretty hard; and all the streets were slippery; and the more sheltered corners of the Loch had curdled into watery ice, in spite of the gale. There was good promise of snow, before the dawn.

Therefore it was with little satisfaction that Master Ephraim Martext, outed Minister of the Gospel, drew his door shut after him, and strode down the close. There, he was sheltered; but, next moment, as he entered the Grassmarket, the wind nearly bowled him off his feet, by twitching his cloaking round his sturdy shanks. Master Ephraim drew his refractory garment tighter round his frame, and leant against the blast. At the same moment the moon cleared a cloud, only indeed to pass beneath another; but there was time for one pale and uncertain beam to fall upon that scaffold, which had been stained the day before with the blood of five of the Pentland insurgents.[2]

Master Ephraim's brow darkened. "An evil night," he muttered: "Oh Lord! how long wilt thou delay the day of thy vengeance!"

A few minutes' walk, and he entered the indicated wynd, and stopped at the door. Drawing for the key which had been enclosed in the letter, he inserted it into the lock. With a groan the bolt fell back: with a shriek, the door revolved upon its hinges. Carefully the divine closed it after him; and, then, he turned to examine the scene. A wide lobby, and a princely staircase lay exposed to his eyes, the one paved with large flags, the other bordered with carved oak balustrades, and both begrimed with dirt, draped with cobwebs, and carpeted (sic.) with dust. For a small space round the door, the air and the entry of persons had cleared away the dust; but Martext could see the prints of ascending feet, faithfully preserved in the covering of the stairs. The whole scene was exhibitted (sic.) by the yellow radiance of an oil preserved from strong draughts in a stable lantern, and set upon the first landing. A chill smote on the minister's heart. The wind was rough, and the frost nipped his face and hands shrewdly; but he wished himself out again. "Poor lad!" he thought. "It would be a shame to leave him. Who have a better right to my assistance and ministration than those who have fought for my church. Nevertheless this is an eerie place, and the air is wondrous unwholesome."

Then, he gathered courage and hurried up four flights of steps, to where an open door let a beam of flickering red light fall out upon the topmost landing. He entered. The room was long, low, uncarpetted (sic.), unfurnished. At one end there lay a heap of discoloured, bemired, and blood-stained cloaks, with a brace of pistols, a drawn sabre, and a Bible with a black bullet hole right through the middle of it. Close by, a great wood fire smouldered with a dull red glow, and leapt occasionally into flickering tongues of flame, in a fire-place lined with blue Dutch picture tiles; and even as the flames leapt up, Moses would strike the rock with his uplifted rod, and the fire would curl round the Hebrew boys and their divine companion in the furnance heated seven times, and the imps that circled St. Anthony would toss their deformed arms about and wax and wane changing from squat little Pucks, to colosssal Apollyons; and then the flames sank back; and the pictures became stiff tiles again. In front of the fire stood a tall thin sallow man, of some seven and twenty years of age. His face was worn and haggard; his brow was tied up in a bloodstained napkin; and his eye gleamed with a cold, fierce, feverish light. His clothes were torn, disordered, and muddy. Very strange did he look beside the solid, sensible face and black and seemly garments of the worthy divine.

I shall pass over the first greetings which were like most other first greetings. When he was standing before the fire warming his frost-pained fingers, Master Ephraim began: "Well, Master Ravenswood, and what made you summon me hither? It is a bitter night and a tempestuous: besides it is no great recommendation to the Council to be found with a bluidy rebel and sacrilegious murderer – for so they call you, Master Ravenswood."[3]

"Do you grudge coming?" inquired Ravenswood, in a surly

tone. "There is yet time to go."

"Nay, nay, you mistake me," returned Martext, warmly. "It would not be seemly for an uncle to desert a nephew, nor a minister, one of the defenders of his faith: I only meant to hurry you; for my absence must not be noticed."

"I have more need of you than you think, perhaps. Sometimes, I think I shall go mad, sitting up here alone in the old empty house. Last night man Corsack[4] sat opposite me for an hour with his living eyes glaring strangely from his dead face; and he spoke – he said – Bah! Mister Martext, I wish you to pray with me."

It was an age of superstition: Martext was interested in what he heard. "What did he say – what did he say, Ravenswood?" he asked, in a hoarse whisper.

"It is strange," said the other. "To tell you what he said, I got poor Donald[5] to take the letter to you; and now, when you are here, I dare not speak. I will constrain myself. Listen: you know well enough that my family were among the first to be stricken down by the plague of 1661.[6] My sister, Janet, went into the secret closet on the stair. How she found the spring, Heaven only knows; for when we found her lying, plague stricken, upon the steps without she was only able to say that she had entered the cellar. That night she died. My father determined to penetrate the mystery. With his own hand, he burst the panel in and entered; and, two hours after, an old servant found him lying with the plague mark on him, on the landing at the top of a narrow flight of stairs. Both of them died that evening. Everyone, too, who passed the fatal door, were stricken like those who entered. In alarm, my mother sent for workmen to board the entrance up. The carpenters met the same fate as all the others."

"I have heard all this before, my young friend," said Master Ephraim, observing that the narrator paused; "nor is it altogether without parallel. The Lord had permitted, in his wisdom, that there should be several of these noctious (*sic.*) receptacles of Death. In part of this city, there are more than one, whereof the neighbours live in wholesome dread. But what is all this, Master Ravenswood, to the words of Nielson's ghost?"[7]

"He said words which I may not mention; but he told me to essay the entrance of the Plague Cellar."

"God forbid!"

"I have had other augery," returned Ravenswood, in sepulchral tones, his eyes gleaming with a still wilder fire; "and besides, it is in a glorious cause. He told me, sir, as plainly as a living man could speak that he who entered the Plague Cellar should save our Church from it's (*sic.*) present wretched state."[8]

Any unbiased spectator could have seen that the words of Ravenswood took their birth from fever. The baleful fire in his eyes, the shaking of his emaciated hands, the volubility and wildness of his words all tended to prove the same fact. But in matters of superstition, men gave up their prerogative of common sense in the year 1667. Besides, who is so deaf as he that will not hear. Master Martext wished to believe in the possible renovation of his oppressed Church, and the physical impossibility of the matter did not stick much in his throat.

"A glorious aim, as you say, kinsman," he replied – "a glorious aim. What is the other augery?"

"It is more certain still. You see here my Bible pierced by the bullet of an erastian dragoon. After the vision, I opened it to seek for some divine command. Spared by a miracle from the course of the ball, I found the command: Seek and ye shall find!"[9]

For a long time, the preacher sat brooding over the strange revelations of his companion. At last, he raised his head. "And will you dare?" he asked.

"Dare!" was the only answer: but it was made in a tone so firm and so enthusiastic, that all doubt was stilled in Master Ephraim's mind.

"The Lord God of Isaac and of Israel guide and assist you! I myself will wait on the landing above to catch what you may say, if you are too suddenly smitten. I suppose I also must die; but essay, my son, to close the door when you come out, lest when I pass, I should be rendered incapable of spreading the secret." The minister's heavy face was idealized by his noble determination.

Both rose without a word. Ravenswood went first, his eyes scintillating, his cheeks glowing with a hectic flush. As they passed down the stair, Ravenswood said something so incoherent, that Martext supposed he had not heard distinctly: he was too much excited to think of asking into it's (*sic.*) meaning.

At last the minister paused on the landing, whence he could see distinctly a portion of wainscot where some boards less time-stained than the others led him to believe that the cellar door existed.

Ravenswood continued his descent to a corner of the stair where a large axe was propped against a wall. Three vigorous strokes on the crunching boards, burst in the patched-up entrance. Martext was so pleased that he could not see into the space that lay beyond: he heard Ravenswood give a strange, wild, falsetto laugh which rang hideously through the echoing stair: the sound smote him to the heart: he felt very cold. Ravenswood descended the stair, picked up the lantern, and plunged into the mysterious passage.

For a space all was terribly still. The light, which fell across the stair from the ragged entrance, grew fainter and fainter. Martext, in an agony of fear and excitement, craned forward over the shaking balustrade, the dim light falling with strange effect, on his wrought and eager visage.

Suddenly, that hateful laugh burst forth again louder, wilder, higher, more utterly appalling than before. "Ha-ah!" he yelled. "See! the plague-spots! for the Church! Glory!" And again, the demon laugh echoed strangely out into the stair.

Next instant, a bright light arose in the passage: something highly inflamable, had been lit. The figure of Ravenswood appeared at the entrance, standing out against the light behind. The wild words, the fiendish laugh, the sudden conflagration had all terrified the divine; yet he did not forget his duty to his church.

"Speak," he articulated. "Speak! What have you heard?"

"Ha! Ha! I know you!" replied the madman. "You are Sharpe – Sharpe the apostate![10] Do you think I will tell *you*! Glory! Glory! Ah! apostate, murderer! Where is the pardon! Five men died yesterday! Give me the King's letter of mercy! Give it me!"

And he rushed up towards the other. Martext was rooted to the ground with horror: with eyes protruded, he stood waiting the madman. Then with a long drawn breath, he turned and fled. Up the stair they ran, the dust rising in clouds, the empty vault of the stair echoing to the maniac's howls. Master Ephraim plunged desperately into an open door: the room was pitch dark; he flattened himself against the wall. His pursuer almost touched him, as he passed, feeling in every corner. The moment that the way was clear, Martext dashed forth and ran down the stairs again. He did not know what he was doing: his only object was to escape from the touch of his miserable nephew.

The combustibles in the Plague Cellar had been exceedingly dry surely; for, when Master Ephraim reached that part of the stair in his downward flight, great tongues of flame leapt across the whole path, and curled round the balustrade; while the whole entrance was obscured by pitchy smoke. At no other time would the minister have dared to pass such a barrier. But now, goaded by despair, he plunged through the fire, leapt the remainder of the steps, and fell, half dead with terror, against the massive door.

Recovering his presence of mind and remembering that every minute he might be overtaken and seized, he strove to withdraw the bolt of the lock. What seemed a century elapsed. At last the lock opened. He looked back: Ravenswood, terrified by the flames, was halting irresolutely on the farther side. With a cry of wild joy, Martext rushed out and pulled the great door to behind him, with a loud crash.

The wind blew bitingly up the close: the snow fell thickly around. Through the great fan light over the door shone the red and flickering glow of the conflagration within. The divine fell on his knees on the powdered pavement and thanked God for his escape.

We are glad that we can supplement the above (drawn from the rev. gentleman's own account) with the following particulars from contemporaneous documents.

We find (in Dr Zophar Cant's "Special Judgements and Providences")[11] that, that vessel of God, Ephraim Martext, did linger long in a sore fever, raving much and saying that he was plague stricken in his delerium.

Farther, we read in a personal narrative, that the mansion of the Ravenswoods was reduced on that night to four black and tottering walls. So the mystery of the Plague Cellar was never solved.

The Pavilion on the Links[1]

✳

CHAPTER I

*Tells how I camped in Graden Sea-Wood,
and beheld a light in the Pavilion*

I was a great solitary when I was young. I made it my pride to keep
aloof and suffice for my own entertainment; and I may say that I
had neither friends nor acquaintances until I met that friend who
became my wife and the mother of my children. With one man
only was I on private terms; this was R. Northmour, Esquire, of
Graden Easter, in Scotland. We had met at college; and though
there was not much liking between us nor even much intimacy,
we were so nearly of a humour that we could associate with ease
to both. Misanthropes, we believed ourselves to be; but I have
thought since that we were only sulky fellows. It was scarcely a
companionship, but a coexistence in unsociability. Northmour's
exceptional violence of temper made it no easy affair for him to
keep the peace with anyone but me; and as he respected my silent
ways, and let me come and go as I pleased, I could tolerate his
presence without concern. I think we called each other friends.

When Northmour took his degree and I decided to leave the
university without one, he invited me on a long visit to Graden
Easter; and it was thus that I first became acquainted with the
scene of my adventures. The mansion-house of Graden stood in
a bleak stretch of country some three miles from the shore of the
German Ocean.[2] It was as large as a barrack; and as it had been
built of a soft stone, liable to consume in the eager air of the
seaside, it was damp and draughty within and half ruinous without.
It was impossible for two young men to lodge with comfort in such
a dwelling. But there stood in the northern part of the estate, in
a wilderness of links and blowing sand-hills, and between a plantation and the sea, a small Pavilion or Belvidere, of modern design,
which was exactly suited to our wants; and in this heritage, speak-

ing little, reading much and rarely associating except at meals, Northmour and I spent four tempestuous winter months. I might have stayed longer; but one March night there sprang up between us a dispute, which rendered my departure necessary. Northmour spoke hotly I remember, and I suppose I must have made some tart rejoinder. He leaped from his chair and grappled me; I had to fight, without exaggeration, for my life; and it was only with a great effort that I mastered him, for he was near as strong in body as myself, and seemed filled with the devil. The next morning, we met on our usual terms; but I judged it more delicate to withdraw; nor did he attempt to dissuade me.

It was nine years before I revisited the neighbourhood. I travelled at that time with a tilt cart, a tent, and a cooking- stove, tramping all day beside the waggon, and at night, whenever it was possible, gipsying in a cove of the hills, or by the side of a wood. I believe I visited in this manner most of the wild and desolate regions both in England and Scotland; and, as I had neither friends nor relations, I was troubled with no correspondence, and had nothing in the nature of headquarters, unless it was the office of my solicitors, from whom I drew my income twice a year. It was a life in which I delighted; and I fully thought to have grown old upon the march, and at last died in a ditch.

It was my whole business to find desolate corners, where I could camp without the fear of interruption; and hence, being in another part of the same shire, I bethought me suddenly of the Pavilion on the Links. No thoroughfare passed within three miles of it. The nearest town, and that was but a fisher village, was at a distance of six or seven. For ten miles of length, and from a depth varying from three miles to half a mile, this belt of barren country lay along the sea. The beach, which was the natural approach, was full of quicksands. Indeed I may say there is hardly a better place of concealment in the United Kingdom. I determined to pass a week in the Sea-Wood of Graden Easter, and, making a long stage, reached it about sundown on a wild September day.

The country, I have said, was mixed sand-hill and links; *links* being a Scottish name for sand which has ceased drifting and become more or less solidly covered with turf. The Pavilion stood on an even space; a little behind it, the wood began in a hedge of elders huddled together by the wind; in front, a few tumbled sand-hills stood between it and the sea. An outcropping of rock

had formed a bastion for the sand, so that there was here a promontory in the coast-line between two shallow bays; and just
beyond the tides, the rock again cropped out and formed an islet
of small dimensions but strikingly designed. The quicksands were
of great extent at low water, and had an infamous reputation in
the country. Close in shore, between the islet and the promontory,
it was said they would swallow a man in four minutes and a half;
but there may have been little ground for this precision. The
district was alive with rabbits, and haunted by gulls which made
a continual piping about the pavilion. On summer days the outlook
was bright and even gladsome; but at sundown in September, with
a high wind, and a heavy surf rolling in close along the links, the
place told of nothing but dead mariners and sea disaster. A ship
beating to windward on the horizon, and a huge truncheon of
wreck half buried in the sands at my feet, completed the innuendo
of the scene.[3]

The pavilion – it had been built by the last proprietor, Northmour's uncle, a silly and prodigal virtuoso – presented little signs
of age. It was two storeys in height, Italian in design, surrounded
by a patch of garden in which nothing had prospered but a few
coarse flowers; and looked, with its shuttered windows, not like
a house that had been deserted, but like one that had never been
tenanted by man. Northmour was plainly from home; whether,
as usual, sulking in the cabin of his yacht, or in one of his fitful
and extravagent appearances in the world of society, I had, of
course, no means of guessing. The place had an air of solitude
that daunted even a solitary like myself; the wind cried in the
chimneys with a strange and wailing note; and it was with a sense
of escape, as if I were going indoors, that I turned away and,
driving my cart before me, entered the skirts of the wood.

The Sea-Wood of Graden had been planted to shelter the
cultivated fields behind, and check the encroachments of the
blowing sand. As you advanced into it from coastward, elders were
succeeded by other hardy shrubs; but the timber was all stunted
and bushy; it led a life of conflict; the trees were accustomed to
swing there all night long in fierce winter tempests; and even in
early spring, the leaves were already flying, and autumn was beginning, in this exposed plantation. Inland the ground rose into a
little hill, which, along with the islet, served as a sailing mark for
seamen. When the hill was open of the islet to the north, vessels
must bear well to the eastward to clear Graden Ness and the

Graden Bullers. In the lower ground a streamlet ran among the trees, and, being dammed with leaves and clay of its own carrying, spread out every here and there, and lay in stagnant pools. One or two ruined cottages were dotted about the wood; and, according to Northmour, these were ecclesiastical foundations, and in their time had sheltered pious hermits.

I found a den, or small hollow, where there was a spring of pure water; and there, clearing away the brambles, I pitched the tent and made a fire to cook my supper. My horse I picketed farther in the wood where there was a patch of sward. The banks of the den not only concealed the light of my fire, but sheltered me from the wind, which was cold as well as high.

The life I was leading made me both hardy and frugal. I never drank but water, and rarely ate anything more costly than oatmeal; and I required so little sleep, that, although I rose with the peep of day, I would often lie long awake in the dark or starry watches of the night. Thus in Graden Sea-Wood, although I fell thankfully asleep by eight in the evening I was awake again before eleven with a full possession of my faculties, and no sense of drowsiness or fatigue. I rose and sat by the fire, watching the trees and clouds tumultuously tossing and fleeing overhead, and hearkening to the wind and the rollers along the shore; till at length, growing weary of inaction, I quitted the den, and strolled towards the borders of the wood. A young moon, buried in mist, gave a faint illumination to my steps; and the light grew brighter as I walked forth into the links. At the same moment, the wind, smelling salt of the open ocean and carrying particles of sand, struck me with its full force, so that I had to bow my head.

When I raised it again to look about me, I was aware of a light in the pavilion. It was not stationary; but passed from one window to another, as though some one were reviewing the different apartments with a lamp or candle. I watched it for some seconds in great surprise. When I had arrived in the afternoon the house had been plainly deserted; now it was as plainly occupied. It was my first idea that a gang of thieves might have broken in and be now ransacking Northmour's cupboards, which were many and not ill supplied. But what should bring thieves to Graden Easter? And, again, all the shutters had been thrown open, and it would have been more in the character of such gentry to close them. I dismissed the notion, and fell back upon another. Northmour himself must have arrived, and was now airing and inspecting the pavilion.

I have said that there was no real affection between this man and me; but, had I loved him like a brother, I was then so much more in love with solitude that I should none the less have shunned his company. As it was, I turned and ran for it; and it was with genuine satisfaction that I found myself safely back beside the fire. I had escaped an acquaintance; I should have one more night in comfort. In the morning, I might either slip away before Northmour was abroad, or pay him as short a visit as I chose.

But when morning came, I thought the situation so diverting that I forgot my shyness. Northmour was at my mercy; I arranged a good practical jest, though I knew well that my neighbour was not the man to jest with in security; and, chuckling beforehand over its success, took my place among the elders at the edge of the wood, whence I could command the door of the pavilion. The shutters were all once more closed, which I remember thinking odd; and the house, with its white walls and green venetians, looked spruce and habitable in the morning light. Hour after hour passed, and still no sign of Northmour. I knew him for a sluggard in the morning; but, as it drew on towards noon, I lost my patience. To say the truth, I had promised myself to break my fast in the pavilion, and hunger began to prick me sharply. It was a pity to let the opportunity go by without some cause for mirth; but the grosser appetite prevailed, and I relinquished my jest with regret, and sallied from the wood.

The appearance of the house affected me, as I drew near, with disquietude. It seemed unchanged since last evening; and I had expected it, I scarce knew why, to wear some external signs of habitation. But no: the windows were all closely shuttered, the chimneys breathed no smoke, and the front door itself was closely padlocked. Northmour, therefore, had entered by the back; this was the natural and, indeed, the necessary conclusion; and you may judge of my surprise when, on turning the house, I found the back door similarly secured.

My mind at once reverted to the original theory of thieves; and I blamed myself sharply for my last night's inaction. I examined all the windows on the lower storey, but none of them had been tampered with; I tried the padlocks, but they were both secure. It thus became a problem how the thieves, if thieves they were, had managed to enter the house. They must have got, I reasoned, upon the roof of the outhouse where Northmour used to keep his photographic battery; and from thence, either by the window of the study or that of my old bedroom, completed their burglarious entry.

I followed what I supposed was their example; and, getting on the roof, tried the shutters of each room. Both were secure; but I was not to be beaten; and with a little force, one of them flew open, grazing, as it did so, the back of my hand. I remember, I put the wound to my mouth, and stood for perhaps half a minute licking it like a dog, and mechanically gazing behind me over the waste links and the sea; and, in that space of time, my eye made note of a large schooner yacht some miles to the north-east. Then I threw up the window and climbed in.

I went over the house, and nothing can express my mystifica- tion. There was no sign of disorder, but, on the contrary, the rooms were unusually clean and pleasant. I found fires laid, ready for lighting; three bedrooms prepared with a luxury quite foreign to Northmour's habits, and with water in the ewers and the beds turned down; a table set for three in the dining-room; and an ample supply of cold meats, game, and vegetables on the pantry shelves. There were guests expected, that was plain; but why guests, when Northmour hated society? And, above all, why was the house thus stealthily prepared at dead of night? and why were the shutters closed and the doors padlocked?

I effaced all traces of my visit, and came forth from the window feeling sobered and concerned.

The schooner yacht was still in the same place; and it flashed for a moment through my mind that this might be the *Red Earl* bringing the owner of the pavilion and his guests. But the vessel's head was set the other way.

CHAPTER II

Tells of the nocturnal landing from the yacht

I returned to the den to cook myself a meal, of which I stood in great need, as well as to care for my horse, whom I had somewhat neglected in the morning. From time to time I went down to the edge of the wood; but there was no change in the pavilion, and not a human creature was seen all day upon the links. The schooner in the offing was the one touch of life within my range of vision. She, apparently with no set object, stood off and on or lay to, hour after hour; but as the evening deepened, she drew steadily nearer. I became more convinced that she carried Northmour and his friends, and that they would probably come ashore after dark; not only because that was of a piece with the secrecy of the preparations, but because the tide would not have flowed sufficiently before eleven to cover Graden Floe and the other sea quags that fortified the shore against invaders.

All day the wind had been going down, and the sea along with it; but there was a return towards sunset of the heavy weather of the day before. The night set in pitch dark. The wind came off the sea in squalls, like the firing of a battery of cannon; now and then there was a flaw of rain, and the surf rolled heavier with the rising tide. I was down at my observatory among the elders, when a light was run up to the masthead of the schooner, and showed she was closer in than when I had last seen her by the dying daylight. I concluded that this must be a signal to Northmour's associates on shore; and, stepping forth into the links, looked around me for something in response.

A small footpath ran along the margin of the wood, and formed the most direct communication between the pavilion and the mansion-house; and, as I cast my eyes to that side, I saw a spark of light, not a quarter of a mile away, and rapidly approaching. From its uneven course it appeared to be the light of a lantern carried by a person who followed the windings of the path, and was often staggered and taken aback by the more violent squalls. I concealed myself once more among the elders, and waited eagerly for the newcomer's advance. It proved to be a woman; and, as she passed within half a rod of my ambush, I was able to recognise the features. The deaf and silent old dame, who had nursed Northmour in his childhood, was his associate in this underhand affair.

I followed her at a little distance, taking advantage of the innumerable heights and hollows, concealed by the darkness, and favoured not only by the nurse's deafness, but by the uproar of the wind and surf. She entered the pavilion, and, going at once to the upper storey, opened and set a light in one of the windows that looked towards the sea. Immediately afterwards the light at the schooner's masthead was run down and extinguished. Its purpose had been attained, and those on board were sure that they were expected. The old woman resumed her preparations;

although the other shutters remained closed, I could see a glimmer going to and fro about the house; and a gush of sparks from one chimney after another soon told me that the fires were being kindled.

Northmour and his guests, I was now persuaded, would come ashore as soon as there was water on the floe. It was a wild night for boat service; and I felt some alarm mingle with my curiosity as I reflected on the danger of the landing. My old acquaintance, it was true, was the most eccentric of men; but the present eccentricity was both disquieting and lugubrious to consider. A variety of feelings thus led me towards the beach, where I lay flat on my face in a hollow within six feet of the track that led to the pavilion. Thence, I should have the satisfaction of recognising the arrivals, and, if they should prove to be acquaintances, greeting them as soon as they had landed.

Some time before eleven, while the tide was still dangerously low, a boat's lantern appeared close in shore; and, my attention being thus awakened, I could perceive another still far to seaward, violently tossed, and sometimes hidden by the billows. The weather, which was getting dirtier as the night went on, and the perilous situation of the yacht upon a lee shore, had probably driven them to attempt a landing at the earliest possible moment.

A little afterwards, four yachtsmen carrying a very heavy chest, and guided by a fifth with a lantern, passed close in front of me as I lay, and were admitted to the pavilion by the nurse. They returned to the beach, and passed me a second time with another chest, larger but apparently not so heavy as the first. A third time they made the transit; and on this occasion one of the yachtsmen carried a leather portmanteau, and the others a lady's trunk and carriage bag. My curiosity was sharply excited. If a woman were among the guests of Northmour, it would show a change in his habits and an apostasy from his pet theories of life, well calculated to fill me with surprise. When he and I dwelt there together, the pavilion had been a temple of misogyny. And now, one of the detested sex was to be installed under its roof. I remembered one or two particulars, a few notes of daintiness and almost of coquetry which had struck me the day before as I surveyed the preparations in the house; their purpose was now clear, and I thought myself dull not to have perceived it from the first.

While I was thus reflecting, a second lantern drew near me from the beach. It was carried by a yachtsman whom I had not

yet seen, and who was conducting two other persons to the pavilion. These two persons were unquestionably the guests for whom
the house was made ready; and, straining eye and ear, I set myself
to watch them as they passed. One was an unusually tall man, in
a travelling hat slouched over his eyes, and a highland cape closely
buttoned and turned up so as to conceal his face. You could make
out no more of him that he was, as I have said, unusually tall,
and walked feebly with a heavy stoop. By his side, and either
clinging to him or giving him support – I could not make out
which – was a young, tall, and slender figure of a woman. She
was extremely pale; but in the light of a lantern her face was so
marred by strong and changing shadows, that she might equally
well have been as ugly as sin or as beautiful as I afterwards found
her to be.

When they were just abreast of me, the girl made some remark
which was drowned by the noise of the wind.

"Hush!" said her companion; and there was something in the
tone with which the word was uttered that thrilled and rather
shook my spirits. It seemed to breathe from a bosom labouring
under the deadliest terror; I have never heard another syllable so
expressive; and I still hear it again when I am feverish at night,
and my mind runs upon old times. The man turned towards the
girl as he spoke; I had a glimpse of much red beard and a nose
which seemed to have been broken in youth; and his light eyes
seemed shining in his face with some strong and unpleasant
emotion.

But these two passed on and were admitted in their turn to
the pavilion.

One by one, or in groups, the seamen returned to the beach.
The wind brought me the sound of a rough voice crying, "Shove
off!" Then, after a pause, another lantern drew near. It was Northmour alone.

My wife and I, a man and a woman, have often agreed to
wonder how a person could be, at the same time, so handsome
and so repulsive as Northmour. He had the appearance of a finished
gentleman; his face bore every mark of intelligence and courage;
but you had only to look at him, even in his most amiable moment,
to see that he had the temper of a slaver captain. I never knew a
character that was both explosive and revengeful to the same
degree; he combined the vivacity of the south with the sustained
and deadly hatreds of the north; and both traits were plainly written

on his face, which was a sort of danger signal. In person he was tall, strong, and active; his hair and complexion very dark; his features handsomely designed, but spoiled by a menacing expression.

At that moment he was somewhat paler than by nature; he wore a heavy frown; and his lips worked, and he looked sharply round him as he walked, like a man besieged with apprehensions. And yet I thought he had a look of triumph underlying all, as though he had already done much, and was near the end of an achievement.

Partly from a scruple of delicacy – which I dare say came too late – partly from the pleasure of startling an acquaintance, I desired to make my presence known to him without delay.

I got suddenly to my feet, and stepped forward.

"Northmour!" said I.

I have never had so shocking a surprise in all my days. He leaped on me without a word; something shone in his hand; and he struck for my heart with a dagger. At the same moment I knocked him head over heels. Whether it was my quickness or his uncertainty, I know not; but the blade only grazed my shoulder, while the hilt and his fist struck me violently on the mouth.

I fled, but not far. I had often and often observed the capabilities of the sand-hills for protracted ambush or stealthy advances and retreats; and, not ten yards from the scene of the scuffle, plumped down again upon the grass. The lantern had fallen and gone out. But what was my astonishment to see Northmour slip at a bound into the pavilion, and hear him bar the door behind him with a clang of iron!

He had not pursued me. He had run away. Northmour, whom I knew for the most implacable and daring of men, had run away! I could scarcely believe my reason; and yet in this strange business, where all was incredible, there was nothing to make a work about in an incredibility more or less. For why was the pavilion secretly prepared? Why had Northmour landed with his guests at dead of night, in half a gale of wind, and with the floe scarce covered? Why had he sought to kill me? Had he not recognised my voice? I wondered. And, above all, how had he come to have a dagger ready in his hand? A dagger, or even a sharp knife, seemed out of keeping with the age in which we lived; and a gentleman landing from his yacht on the shore of his own estate, even although it was at night and with some mysterious circumstances, does not usually, as a matter of fact, walk thus prepared for deadly onslaught. The more I reflected, the further I felt at sea. I recapitulated the elements of mystery, counting them on my fingers; the pavilion secretly prepared for guests; the guests landed at the risk of their lives and to the imminent peril of the yacht; the guests, or at least one of them, in undisguised and seemingly causeless terror; Northmour with a naked weapon; Northmour stabbing his most intimate acquaintance at a word; last, and not least strange, Northmour fleeing from the man whom he had sought to murder, and barricading himself, like a hunted creature, behind the door of the pavilion. Here were at least six separate causes for extreme surprise; each part and parcel with the others, and forming all together one consistent story. I felt almost ashamed to believe my own senses.

As I thus stood, transfixed with wonder, I began to grow painfully conscious of the injuries I had received in the scuffle; skulked round among the sand-hills; and, by a devious path, regained the shelter of the wood. On the way, the old nurse passed again within several yards of me, still carrying her lantern on the return journey to the mansion-house of Graden. This made a seventh suspicious feature in the case. Northmour and his guests, it appeared, were to cook and do the cleaning for themselves, while the old woman continued to inhabit the big empty barrack among the policies. There must surely be cause for secrecy when so many inconveniences were confronted to preserve it.

So thinking, I made my way to the den. For greater security, I trod out the embers of the fire, and lit my lantern to examine the wound upon my shoulder. It was a trifling hurt, although it bled somewhat freely, and I dressed it as well as I could (for its position made it difficult to reach) with some rag and cold water from the spring. While I was thus busied, I mentally declared war against Northmour and his mystery. I am not an angry man by nature, and I believe there was more curiosity than resentment in my heart. But war I certainly declared; and, by way of preparation, I got out my revolver, and, having drawn the charges, cleaned and reloaded it with scrupulous care. Next I became preoccupied about my horse. It might break loose, or fall to neighing, and so betray my camp in the Sea-Wood. I determined to rid myself of its neighbourhood; and long before dawn I was leading it over the links in the direction of the fisher village.

CHAPTER III

Tells how I became acquainted with my wife

For two days I skulked round the pavilion, profiting by the uneven surface of the links. I became an adept in the necessary tactics. These low hillocks and shallow dells, running one into another, became a kind of cloak of darkness for my enthralling, but perhaps dishonourable, pursuit. Yet, in spite of this advantage, I could learn but little of Northmour or his guests.

Fresh provisions were brought under cover of darkness by the old woman from the mansion-house. Northmour, and the young lady, sometimes together, but more often singly, would walk for an hour or two at a time on the beach beside the quicksand. I could not but conclude that this promenade was chosen with an eye to secrecy; for the spot was open only to the seaward. But it suited me not less excellently; the highest and most accidented of the sand-hills immediately adjoined; and from these, lying flat in a hollow, I could overlook Northmour or the young lady as they walked.

The tall man seemed to have disappeared. Not only did he never cross the threshold, but he never so much as showed face at a window; or, at least, not so far as I could see; for I dared not creep forward beyond a certain distance in the day, since the upper floor commanded the bottoms of the links; and at night, when I could venture farther, the lower windows were barricaded as if to stand a siege. Sometimes I thought the tall man must be confined to bed, for I remembered the feebleness of his gait; and sometimes I thought he must have gone clear away, and that Northmour and the young lady remained alone together in the pavilion. The idea, even then, displeased me.

Whether or not this pair were man and wife, I had seen abundant reason to doubt the friendliness of their relation. Although I could hear nothing of what they said, and rarely so much as glean a decided expression on the face of either, there was a distance, almost a stiffness, in their bearing which showed them to be either unfamiliar or at enmity. The girl walked faster when she was with Northmour than when she was alone; and I conceived that any inclination between a man and a woman would rather delay than accelerate the step. Moreover, she kept a good yard free of him, and trailed her umbrella, as if it were a barrier, on the side between them. Northmour kept sidling closer; and, as the girl retired from his advance, their course lay at a sort of diagonal across the beach, and would have landed them in the surf had it been long enough continued. But, when this was imminent, the girl would unostentatiously change sides and put Northmour between her and the sea. I watched these manoeuvres, for my part, with high enjoyment and approval, and chuckled to myself at every move.

On the morning of the third day, she walked alone for some time, and I perceived, to my great concern, that she was more than once in tears. You will see that my heart was already interested more than I supposed. She had a firm yet airy motion of the body, and carried her head with unimaginable grace; every step was a thing to look at, and she seemed in my eyes to breathe sweetness and distinction.

The day was so agreeable, being calm and sunshiny, with a tranquil sea, and yet with a healthful piquancy and vigour in the air, that, contrary to custom, she was tempted forth a second time to walk. On this occasion she was accompanied by Northmour, and they had been but a short while on the beach, when I saw him take forcible possession of her hand. She struggled, and uttered a cry that was almost a scream. I sprang to my feet, unmindful of my strange position; but, ere I had taken a step, I saw Northmour bareheaded and bowing very low, as if to apologise; and dropped again at once into my ambush. A few words were interchanged; and then, with another bow, he left the beach to return to the pavilion. He passed not far from me, and I could see him, flushed and lowering, and cutting savagely with his cane among the grass. It was not without satisfaction that I recognised my own handiwork in a great cut under his right eye, and a considerable discolouration round the socket.

For some time the girl remained where he had left her, looking out past the islet and over the bright sea. Then with a start, as one who throws off preoccupation and puts energy again upon its mettle, she broke into a rapid and decisive walk. She had forgotten where she was. And I beheld her walk straight into the borders of the quicksand where it is most abrupt and dangerous. Two or three steps farther and her life would have been in serious jeopardy, when I slid down the face of the sand-hill, which is there precipitous, and, running half-way forward, called her to stop.

She did so, and turned round. There was not a tremor of fear in her behaviour, and she marched directly up to me like a queen. I was barefoot, and clad like a common sailor, save for an Egyptian scarf round my waist; and she probably took me at first for some one from the fisher village, straying after bait. As for her, when I thus saw her face to face, her eyes set steadily and imperiously upon mine, I was filled with admiration and astonishment, and thought her even more beautiful than I had looked to find her. Nor could I think enough of one who, acting with so much boldness, yet preserved a maidenly air that was both quaint and engaging; for my wife kept an old-fashioned precision of manner through all her admirable life – an excellent thing in woman, since it sets another value on her sweet familiarities.

"What does this mean?" she asked.

"You were walking," I told her, "directly into Graden Floe."

"You do not belong to these parts," she said again. "You speak like an educated man."

"I believe I have right to that name," said I, "although in this disguise."

But her woman's eye had already detected the sash.

"Oh!" she said; "your sash betrays you."

"You have said the word *betray*," I resumed. "May I ask you not to betray me? I was obliged to disclose myself in your interest; but if Northmour learned my presence it might be worse than disagreeable for me."

"Do you know," she asked, "to whom you are speaking?"

"Not to Mr. Northmour's wife?" I asked, by way of answer.

She shook her head. All this while she was studying my face with an embarrassing intentness. Then she broke out –

"You have an honest face. Be honest like your face, sir, and tell me what you want and what you are afraid of. Do you think I could hurt you? I believe you have far more power to injure me! And yet you do not look unkind. What do you mean – you, a gentleman – by skulking like a spy about this desolate place? Tell me," she said, "who is it you hate?"

"I hate no one," I answered; "and I fear no one face to face. My name is Cassilis – Frank Cassilis. I lead the life of a vagabond for my own good pleasure. I am one of Northmour's oldest friends; and three nights ago, when I addressed him on these links, he stabbed me in the shoulder with a knife."

"It was you!" she said.

"Why he did so," I continued, disregarding the interruption, "is more than I can guess, and more than I care to know. I have not many friends, nor am I very susceptible to friendship; but no man shall drive me from a place by terror. I had camped in Graden Sea-Wood ere he came; I camp in it still. If you think I mean harm to you or yours, madam, the remedy is in your hand. Tell him that my camp is in the Hemlock Den, and to-night he can stab me in safety while I sleep."

With this I doffed my cap to her, and scrambled up once more among the sand-hills. I do not know why but I felt a prodigious sense of injustice, and felt like a hero and a martyr; while, as a matter of fact, I had not a word to say in my defence, nor so much as one plausible reason to offer for my conduct. I had stayed at Graden out of a curiosity natural enough, but undignified; and though there was another motive growing in along with the first, it was not one which, at that period, I could have properly explained to the lady of my heart.

Certainly, that night, I thought of no one else; and, though her whole conduct and position seemed suspicious, I could not find it in my heart to entertain a doubt of her integrity. I could have staked my life that she was clear of blame, and, though all was dark at present, that the explanation of the mystery would show her part in these events to be both right and needful. It was true, let me cudgel my imagination as I pleased, that I could invent no theory of her relations to Northmour; but I felt none the less sure of my conclusion because it was founded on instinct in place of reason, and as I may say, went to sleep that night with the thought of her under my pillow.

Next day she came out about the same hour alone, and, as soon as the sand-hills concealed her from the pavilion, drew nearer to the edge, and called me by name in guarded tones. I was astonished to observe that she was deadly pale, and seemingly under the influence of strong emotion.

"Mr. Cassilis!" she cried; "Mr. Cassilis!"

I appeared at once, and leaped down upon the beach. A remarkable air of relief overspread her countenance as soon as she saw me.

"Oh!" she cried, with a hoarse sound, like one whose bosom has been lightened of a weight. And then, "Thank God you are still safe!" she added; "I knew, if you were, you would be here." (Was not this strange? So swiftly and wisely does Nature prepare our hearts for these great lifelong intimacies, that both my wife and I had been given a presentiment on this the second day of our acquaintance. I had even then hoped that she would seek me; she had felt sure that she would find me.) "Do not," she went on swiftly, "do not stay in this place. Promise me that you will sleep no longer in that wood. You do not know how I suffer; all last night I could not sleep for thinking of your peril."

"Peril?" I repeated. "Peril from whom? From Northmour?"

"Not so," she said. "Did you think I would tell him after what you said?"

"Not from Northmour?" I repeated. "Then how? From whom? I see none to be afraid of."

"You must not ask me," was her reply, "for I am not free to tell you. Only believe me, and go hence – believe me, and go away quickly, quickly, for your life!"

An appeal to his alarm is never a good plan to rid oneself of a spirited young man. My obstinacy was but increased by what she said, and I made it a point of honour to remain. And her solicitude for my safety still more confirmed me in the resolve.

"You must not think me inquisitive, madam," I replied; "but, if Graden is so dangerous a place, you yourself perhaps remain here at some risk."

She only looked at me reproachfully.

"You and your father –" I resumed; but she interrupted me almost with a gasp.

"My father! How do you know that?" she cried.

"I saw you together when you landed," was my answer; and I do not know why, but it seemed satisfactory to both of us, as indeed it was the truth. "But," I continued, "you need have no fear from me. I see you have some reason to be secret, and, you may believe me, your secret is as safe with me as if I were in Graden Floe. I have scarce spoken to anyone for years; my horse is my only companion and even he, poor beast, is not beside me. You see, then, you may count on me for silence. So tell me the truth, my dear young lady, are you not in danger?"

"Mr. Northmour says you are an honourable man," she returned, "and I believe it when I see you. I will tell you so much; you are right; we are in dreadful, dreadful danger, and you share it by remaining where you are."

"Ah!" said I; "you have heard of me from Northmour? And he gives me a good character?"

"I asked him about you last night," was her reply. "I pretended," she hesitated, "pretended to have met you long ago, and spoke to you of him. It was not true; but I could not help myself without betraying you, and you had put me in a difficulty. He praised you highly."

"And – you may permit me one question – does this danger come from Northmour?" I asked.

"From Mr. Northmour?" she cried. "Oh no; he stays with us to share it."

"While you propose that I should run away?" I said. "You do not rate me very high."

"Why should you stay?" she asked. "You are no friend of ours."

I know not what came over me, for I had not been conscious of a similar weakness since I was a child, but I was so mortified by this retort that my eyes pricked and filled wth tears, as I continued to gaze upon her face.

"No, no," she said, in a changed voice; "I did not mean the words unkindly."

"It was I who offended," I said; and I held out my hand with a look of appeal that somehow touched her, for she gave me hers at once, and even eagerly. I held it for awhile in mine, and gazed into her eyes. It was she who first tore her hand away and, forgetting all about her request and the promise she had sought to extort, ran at the top of her speed, and without turning, till she was out of sight. And then I knew that I loved her, and thought in my glad heart that she – she herself – was not indifferent to my suit. Many a time she has denied it in after days, but it was with a smiling and not a serious denial. For my part, I am sure our hands would not have lain so closely in each other if she had not begun to melt to me already. And, when all is said, it is no great contention, since by her own avowal, she began to love me on the morrow.

And yet on the morrow very little took place. She came and called me down as on the day before, upbraided me for lingering at Graden, and, when she found I was still obdurate, began to ask me more particularly as to my arrival. I told her by what series of accidents I had come to witness their disembarkation, and how I had determined to remain, partly from the interest which had been wakened in me by Northmour's guests, and partly because of his own murderous attack. As to the former, I fear I was disingenuous and led her to regard herself as having been an attraction to me from the first moment I saw her on the links. It relieves my heart to make this confession even now, when my wife is with God, and already knows all things, and the honesty of my purpose even in this; for while she lived, although it often pricked my conscience, I had never the hardihood to undeceive her. Even a little secret, in such a married life as ours, is like the rose-leaf which kept the Princess from her sleep.

From this the talk branched into other subjects, and I told her much about my lonely and wandering existence; she, for her part, giving ear, and saying little. Although we spoke very naturally, and latterly on topics that might seem indifferent, we were both sweetly agitated. Too soon it was time for her to go; and we separated, as if by mutual consent, without shaking hands, for both knew that, between us, it was no idle ceremony.

The next, and that was the fourth day of our acquaintance, we met in the same spot, but early in the morning, with much familiarity and yet much timidity on either side. When she had once more spoken about my danger – and that, I understood, was her excuse for coming – I, who had prepared a great deal of talk during the night, began to tell her how highly I valued her kind interest, and how no one had ever cared to hear about my life, nor had I ever cared to relate it, before yesterday. Suddenly she interrupted me, saying with vehemence –

"And yet, if you knew who I was, you would not so much as speak to me!"

I told her such a thought was madness, and little as we had met, I counted her already a dear friend; but my protestations seemed only to make her more desperate.

"My father is in hiding!" she cried.

"My dear," I said, forgetting for the first time to add "young lady", "what do I care? If he were in hiding twenty times over, would it make one thought of change in you?"

"Ah, but the cause!" she cried, "the cause! It is –" she faltered for a second – "it is disgraceful to us!"

CHAPTER IV

Tells in what a startling manner I learned that
I was not alone in Graden Sea-Wood

This was my wife's story, as I drew it from her among tears and sobs. Her name was Clara Huddlestone: it sounded very beautiful in my ears; but not so beautiful as that other name of Clara Cassilis, which she wore during the longer and, I thank God, the happier portion of her life. Her father, Bernard Huddlestone, had been a private banker in a very large way of business. Many years before, his affairs becoming disordered, he had been led to try dangerous, and at last criminal, expedients to retrieve himself from ruin. All was in vain; he became more and more cruelly involved, and found his honour lost at the same moment with his fortune. About this period, Northmour had been courting his daughter with great assiduity, though with small encouragement; and to him, knowing him thus disposed in his favour, Bernard Huddlestone turned for help in his extremity. It was not merely ruin and dishonour, nor merely a legal condemnation, that the unhappy man had brought upon his head. It seems he could have gone to prison with a light heart. What he feared, what kept him awake at night or recalled him from slumber into frenzy, was some secret, sudden, and unlawful attempt upon his life. Hence, he desired to bury his existence and escape to one of the islands in the South Pacific, and it was in Northmour's yacht, the *Red Earl*, that he designed to go. The yacht picked them up clandestinely upon the coast of Wales, and had once more deposited them at Graden, till she could be refitted and provisioned for the longer voyage. Nor could Clara doubt that her hand had been stipulated as the price of passage. For, although Northmour was neither unkind nor even discourteous, he had shown himself in several instances somewhat overbold in speech and manner.

I listened, I need not say, with fixed attention, and put many questions as to the more mysterious part. It was in vain. She had no clear idea of what the blow was, nor of how it was expected to fall. Her father's alarm was unfeigned and physically prostrating, and he had thought more than once of making an unconditional surrender to the police. But the scheme was finally abandoned, for he was convinced that not even the strength of our English prisons could shelter him from his pursuers. He had had many affairs with Italy, and with Italians resident in London, in the later years of his business; and these last, as Clara fancied, were somewhat connected with the doom that threatened him. He had shown great terror at the presence of an Italian seaman on board the *Red Earl*, and had bitterly and repeatedly accused Northmour in consequence. The latter had protested that Beppo (that was the seaman's name) was a capital fellow, and could be trusted to the death; but Mr. Huddlestone had continued ever since to declare that all was lost, that it was only a question of days, and that Beppo would be the ruin of him yet.

I regarded the whole story as the hallucination of a mind shaken by calamity. He had suffered heavy loss by his Italian transactions; and hence the sight of an Italian was hateful to him, and the principal part in his nightmare would naturally enough be played by one of that nation.

"What your father wants," I said, "is a good doctor and some calming medicine."

"But Mr. Northmour?" objected your mother. "He is untroubled by losses, and yet he shares in this terror."

I could not help laughing at what I considered her simplicity.

"My dear," said I, "you have told me yourself what reward he has to look for. All is fair in love, you must remember; and if Northmour foments your father's terrors, it is not at all because he is afraid of any Italian man, but simply because he is infatuated with a charming English woman."

She reminded me of his attack upon myself on the night of the disembarkation, and this I was unable to explain. In short, and from one thing to another, it was agreed between us, that I should set out at once for the fisher village, Graden Wester, as it was called, look up all the newspapers I could find, and see for myself if there seemed any basis of fact for these continued alarms. The next morning, at the same hour and place, I was to make my report to Clara. She said no more on that occasion about my departure; nor, indeed, did she make it a secret that she clung to the thought of my proximity as something helpful and pleasant; and, for my part, I could not have left her, if she had gone upon her knees to ask it.

I reached Graden Wester before ten in the forenoon; for in those days I was an excellent pedestrian, and the distance, as I think I have said, was little over seven miles; fine walking all the way upon the springy turf. The village is one of the bleakest on that coast, which is saying much: there is a church in a hollow; a miserable haven in the rocks, where many boats have been lost as they returned from fishing; two or three score of stone houses arranged along the beach and in two streets, one leading from the harbour, and another striking out from it at right angles; and, at the corner of these two, a very dark and cheerless tavern, by way of principal hotel.

I had dressed myself somewhat more suitably to my station in life, and at once called upon the minister in his little manse beside the graveyard. He knew me, although it was more than nine years since we had met; and when I told him that I had been long upon a walking tour, and was behind with the news, readily lent me an armful of newspapers, dating from a month back to the day before. With these I sought the tavern, and, ordering some breakfast, sat down to study the "Huddlestone Failure."

It had been, it appeared, a very flagrant case. Thousands of persons were reduced to poverty; and one in particular had blown out his brains as soon as payment was suspended. It was strange to myself that, while I read these details, I continued rather to sympathise with Mr. Huddlestone than with his victims; so complete already was the empire of my love for my wife. A price was naturally set upon the banker's head; and, as the case was inexcusable and the public indignation thoroughly aroused, the unusual figure of £750 was offered for his capture. He was reported to have large sums of money in his possession. One day, he had been heard of in Spain; the next, there was sure intelligence that he was still lurking between Manchester and Liverpool, or along the border of Wales; and the day after, a telegram would announce his arrival in Cuba or Yucatan. But in all this there was no word of an Italian, nor any sign of mystery.

In the very last paper, however, there was one item not so clear. The accountants who were charged to verify the failure had, it seemed, come upon the traces of a very large number of thousands, which figured for some time in the transactions of the house of Huddlestone; but which came from nowhere, and disappeared in the same mysterious fashion. It was only once referred to by name, and then under the initials "X.X."; but it had plainly been floated for the first time into the business at a period of great depression some six years ago. The name of a distinguished Royal personage had been mentioned by rumour in connection with this sum. "The cowardly desperado" – such, I remember, was the editorial expression – was supposed to have escaped with a large part of this mysterious fund still in his possession.

I was still brooding over the fact, and trying to torture it into some connection with Mr. Huddlestone's danger, when a man entered the tavern and asked for some bread and cheese with a decided foreign accent.

"*Siete Italiano?*" said I.

"*Sì, signor,*" was his reply.

I said it was unusually far north to find one of his compatriots; at which he shrugged his shoulders, and replied that a man would go anywhere to find work. What work he could hope to find at Graden Wester, I was totally unable to conceive; and the incident struck so unpleasantly upon my mind, that I asked the landlord, while he was counting me some change, whether he had ever before seen an Italian in the village. He said he had once seen some Norwegians, who had been shipwrecked on the other side of Graden Ness and rescued by the lifeboat from Cauldhaven.

"No!" said I; "but an Italian like the man who has just had bread and cheese."

"What?" cried he, "yon black-avised fellow wi' the teeth? Was he an I-talian? Weel, yon's the first that ever I saw, an' I dare say he's like to be the last."[4]

Even as he was speaking, I raised my eyes, and, casting a glance into the street, beheld three men in earnest conversation together, and not thirty yards away. One of them was my recent companion in the tavern parlour; the other two, by their handsome, sallow features and soft hats, should evidently belong to the same race. A crowd of village children stood around them, gesticulating and talking gibberish in imitation. The trio looked singularly foreign to the bleak dirty street in which they were standing, and the dark grey heaven that overspread them; and I confess my incredulity received at that moment a shock from which it never recovered. I might reason with myself as I pleased, but I could not argue down the effect of what I had seen, and I began to share in the Italian terror.

It was already drawing towards the close of the day before I had returned the newspapers at the manse, and got well forward on to the links on my way home. I shall never forget that walk. It grew very cold and boisterous; the wind sang in the short grass about my feet; thin rain showers came running on the gusts; and an immense mountain range of clouds began to arise out of the bosom of the sea. It would be hard to imagine a more dismal evening; and whether it was from these external influences, or because my nerves were already affected by what I had heard and seen, my thoughts were as gloomy as the weather.

The upper windows of the pavilion commanded a considerable spread of links in the direction of Graden Wester. To avoid observation it was necessary to hug the beach until I had gained cover from the higher sand-hills on the little headland, when I might strike across, through the hollows, for the margin of the wood. The sun was about setting; the tide was low, and all the quicksands uncovered; and I was moving along, lost in unpleasant thought, when I was suddenly thunderstruck to perceive the prints of human feet. They ran parallel to my own course, but low down upon the beach instead of along the border of the turf; and, when I examined them, I saw at once, by the size and coarseness of the impression, that it was a stranger to me and to those in the pavilion who had recently passed that way. Not only so; but from the recklessness of the course which he had followed, steering near to the most formidable portions of the sand, he was as evidently a stranger to the country and to the ill-repute of Graden beach.

Step by step I followed the prints; until, a quarter of a mile farther, I beheld them die away into the south-eastern boundary of Graden Floe. There, whoever he was, the miserable man had perished. One or two gulls, who had, perhaps, seen him disappear, wheeled over his sepulchre with their usual melancholy piping. The sun had broken through the clouds by a last effort, and coloured the wide level of quicksands with a dusky purple. I stood for some time gazing at the spot, chilled and disheartened by my own reflections, and with a strong and commanding consciousness of death. I remember wondering how long the tragedy had taken, and whether his screams had been audible at the pavilion. And then, making a strong resolution, I was about to tear myself away, when a gust fiercer than usual fell upon this quarter of the beach, and I saw now, whirling high in air, now skimming lightly across the surface of the sands, a soft, black, felt hat, somewhat conical in shape, such as I had remarked already on the heads of the Italians.

I believe, but I am not sure, that I uttered a cry. The wind was driving the hat shoreward, and I ran round the border of the floe to be ready against its arrival. The gust fell, dropping the hat for a while upon the quicksand, and then, once more freshening, landed it a few yards from where I stood. I seized it with the interest you may imagine. It had seen some service; indeed, it was rustier than either of those I had seen that day upon the street. The lining was red, stamped with the name of the maker, which I have forgotten, and that of the place of manufacture, *Venedig*. This (it is not yet forgotten) was the name given by the Austrians to the beautiful city of Venice, then, and for long after, a part of their dominions.

The shock was complete. I saw imaginary Italians upon every side; and for the first, and, I may say, for the last time in my experience, became overpowered by what is called a panic terror. I knew nothing, that is, to be afraid of, and yet I admit that I was heartily afraid; and it was with a sensible reluctance that I returned to my exposed and solitary camp in the Sea-Wood.[5]

There I ate some cold porridge which had been left over from the night before, for I was disinclined to make a fire; and, feeling strengthened and reassured, dismissed all these fanciful terrors from my mind, and lay down to sleep with composure.

How long I may have slept it is impossible for me to guess; but I was awakened at last by a sudden, blinding flash of light into my face. It woke me like a blow. In an instant I was upon my knees. But the light had gone as suddenly as it came. The darkness was intense. And, as it was blowing great guns from the sea and pouring with rain, the noises of the storm effectually concealed all others.

It was, I dare say, half a minute before I regained my self-possession. But for two circumstances, I should have thought I had been awakened by some new and vivid form of nightmare. First, the flap of my tent which I had shut carefully when I retired, was now unfastened; and, second, I could still perceive, with a sharpness that excluded any theory of hallucination, the smell of hot metal and of burning oil. The conclusion was obvious. I had been wakened by someone flashing a bull's-eye lantern in my face. It had been but a flash, and away. He had seen my face, and then gone. I asked myself the object of so strange a proceeding, and the answer came pat. The man, whoever he was, had thought to recognise me, and he had not. There was yet another question unresolved; and to this, I may say, I feared to give an answer; if he had recognised me, what would he have done?

My fears were immediately diverted from myself, for I saw

that I had been visited in a mistake; and I became persuaded that some dreadful danger threatened the pavilion. It required some nerve to issue forth into the black and intricate thicket which surrounded and overhung the den; but I groped my way to the links, drenched with rain, beaten upon and deafened by the gusts, and fearing at every step to lay my hand upon some lurking adversary. The darkness was so complete that I might have been surrounded by an army and yet none the wiser, and the uproar of the gale so loud that my hearing was as useless as my sight.

For the rest of that night, which seemed interminably long, I patrolled the vicinity of the pavilion, without seeing a living creature or hearing any noise but the concert of the wind, the sea, and the rain. A light in the upper storey filtered through a cranny of the shutter, and kept me company till the approach of dawn.

CHAPTER V

Tells of an interview between Northmour, Clara, and myself

With the first peep of day, I retired from the open to my old lair among the sand-hills, there to wait the coming of my wife. The morning was grey, wild, and melancholy; the wind moderated before sunrise, and then went about, and blew in puffs from the shore; the sea began to go down, but the rain still fell without mercy. Over all the wilderness of links there was not a creature to be seen. Yet I felt sure the neighbourhood was alive with skulking foes. The light that had been so suddenly and surprisingly flashed upon my face as I lay sleeping, and the hat that had been blown ashore by the wind from over Graden Floe, were two speaking signals of the peril that environed Clara and the party in the pavilion.

It was, perhaps, half-past seven, or nearer eight, before I saw the door open, and that dear figure come towards me in the rain. I was waiting for her on the beach before she had crossed the sand-hills.

"I have had such trouble to come!" she cried. "They did not wish me to go walking in the rain."

"Clara," I said, "you are not frightened!"

"No," said she, with a simplicity that filled my heart with confidence. For my wife was the bravest as well as the best of women; in my experience, I have not found the two go always together, but with her they did; and she combined the extreme of fortitude with the most endearing and beautiful virtues.

I told her what had happened; and, though her cheek grew visibly paler, she retained perfect control over her senses.

"You see now that I am safe," said I, in conclusion. "They do not mean to harm me; for, had they chosen, I was a dead man last night."

She laid her hand upon my arm.

"And I had no presentiment!" she cried.

Her accent thrilled me with delight. I put my arm about her, and strained her to my side; and, before either of us was aware, her hands were on my shoulders and my lips upon her mouth. Yet up to that moment no word of love had passed between us. To this day I remember the touch of her cheek, which was wet and cold with the rain; and many a time since, when she has been washing her face, I have kissed it again for the sake of that morning on the beach. Now that she is taken from me, and I finish my pilgrimage alone, I recall our old loving-kindnesses and the deep honesty and affection which united us, and my present loss seems but a trifle in comparison.

We may have thus stood for some seconds – for time passes quickly with lovers – before we were startled by a peal of laughter close at hand. It was not natural mirth, but seemed to be affected in order to conceal an angrier feeling. We both turned, though I still kept my left arm about Clara's waist; nor did she seek to withdraw herself; and there, a few paces off upon the beach, stood Northmour, his head lowered, his hands behind his back, his nostrils white with passion.

"Ah! Cassilis!" he said, as I disclosed my face.

"That same," said I; for I was not at all put about.

"And so, Miss Huddlestone," he continued slowly but savagely, "this is how you keep your faith to your father and to me? This is the value you set upon your father's life? And you are so infatuated with this young gentleman that you must brave ruin, and decency, and common human caution –"

"Miss Huddlestone –" I was beginning to interrupt him, when he, in his turn, cut in brutally –

"You hold your tongue," said he; "I am speaking to that girl."

"That girl, as you call her, is my wife," said I; and my wife only leaned a little nearer, so that I knew she had affirmed my words.

"Your what?" he cried. "You lie!"

"Northmour," I said, "we all know you have a bad temper, and I am the last man to be irritated by words. For all that, I propose that you speak lower for I am convinced that we are not alone."

He looked round him, and it was plain my remark had in some degree sobered his passion. "What do you mean?" he asked.

I only said one word: "Italians."

He swore a round oath, and looked at us, from one to the other.

"Mr. Cassilis knows all that I know," said my wife.

"What I want to know," he broke out, "is where the devil Mr. Cassilis comes from, and what the devil Mr. Cassilis is doing here. You say that you are married; that I do not believe. If you were, Graden Floe would soon divorce you; four minutes and a half, Cassilis. I keep my private cemetery for my friends."

"It took somewhat longer," said I, "for that Italian."

He looked at me for a moment half daunted, and then, almost civilly, asked me to tell my story. "You have too much the advantage of me, Cassilis," he added. I complied of course; and he listened, with several ejaculations, while I told him how I had come to Graden: that it was I whom he had tried to murder on the night of landing; and what I had subsequently seen and heard of the Italians.

"Well," said he, when I had done, "it is here at last; there is no mistake about that. And what, may I ask, do you propose to do?"

"I propose to stay with you and lend a hand," said I.

"You are a brave man," he returned, with a peculiar intonation.

"I am not afraid," said I.

"And so," he continued, "I am to understand that you two are married? And you stand up to it before my face, Miss Huddlestone?"

"We are not yet married," said Clara; "but we shall be as soon as we can."

"Bravo!" cried Northmour. "And the bargain? D—n it, you're not a fool, young woman; I may call a spade a spade with you. How about the bargain? You know as well as I do what your father's life depends upon. I have only to put my hands under my coat-tails and walk away, and his throat would be cut before the evening."

"Yes, Mr. Northmour," returned Clara, with great spirit; "but that is what you will never do. You made a bargain that was unworthy of a gentleman; but you are a gentleman for all that, and you will never desert a man whom you have begun to help."

"Aha!" said he. "You think I will give my yacht for nothing? You think I will risk my life and liberty for love of the old gentleman; and then, I suppose, be best man at the wedding, to wind up? Well," he added, with an odd smile, "perhaps you are not altogether wrong. But ask Cassilis here. *He* knows me. Am I a man to trust? Am I safe and scrupulous? Am I kind?"

"I know you talk a great deal, and sometimes, I think very foolishly," replied Clara, "but I know you are a gentleman, and I am not the least afraid."

He looked at her with a peculiar approval and admiration; then, turning to me, "Do you think I would give her up without a struggle, Frank?" said he, "I tell you plainly, you look out. The next time we come to blows –"

"Will make the third," I interrupted, smiling.

"Aye, true; so it will," he said. "I had forgotten. Well, the third time's lucky."

"The third time, you mean, you will have the crew of the *Red Earl* to help," I said.

"Do you hear him?" he asked, turning to my wife.

"I hear two men speaking like cowards," said she. "I should despise myself either to think or speak like that. And neither of you believe one word that you are saying, which makes it the more wicked and silly."

"She's a trump!" cried Northmour. "But she's not yet Mrs. Cassilis. I say no more. The present is not for me."

Then my wife surprised me.

"I leave you here," she said suddenly. "My father has been too long alone. But remember this: you are to be friends, for you are both good friends to me."

She has since told me her reason for this step. As long as she remained, she declares that we two would have continued to quarrel; and I suppose that she was right, for when she was gone we fell at once into a sort of confidentiality.

Northmour stared after her as she went away over the sand-hill.

"She is the only woman in the world!" he exclaimed with an oath. "Look at her action."

I, for my part, leaped at this opportunity for a little further light. "See here, Northmour," said I; "we are all in a tight place, are we not?"

"I believe you, my boy," he answered, looking me in the eyes, and with great emphasis. "We have all hell upon us, that's the truth. You may believe me or not, but I'm afraid of my life."

"Tell me one thing," said I, "What are they after, these Italians? What do they want with Mr. Huddlestone?"

"Don't you know?" he cried. "The black old scamp had *carbonaro* funds on a deposit – two hundred and eighty thousand; and of course he gambled it away on stocks. There was to have been a revolution in the Tridentino, or Parma; but the revolution is off, and the whole wasp's nest is after Huddlestone. We shall all be lucky if we can save our skins."

"The *carbonari!*"[6] I exclaimed: "God help him indeed!"

"Amen!" said Northmour. "And now, look here: I have said that we are in a fix; and, frankly, I shall be glad of your help. If I can't save Huddlestone, I want at least to save the girl. Come and stay in the pavilion; and, there's my hand on it, I shall act as your friend until the old man is either clear or dead. But," he added, "once that is settled, you become my rival once again and I warn you – mind yourself."

"Done!" said I; and we shook hands.

"And now let us go directly to the fort," said Northmour; and he began to lead the way through the rain.

CHAPTER VI

Tells of my introduction to the tall man

We were admitted to the pavilion by Clara, and I was surprised by the completeness and security of the defences. A barricade of great strength, and yet easy to displace, supported the door against any violence from without; and the shutters of the dining-room, into which I was led directly, and which was feebly illuminated by a lamp, were even more elaborately fortified. The panels were strengthened by bars and cross-bars; and these, in their turn, were kept in position by a system of braces and struts, some abutting on the floor, some on the roof, and others, in fine, against the opposite wall of the apartment. It was at once a solid and well-designed piece of carpentry; and I did not seek to conceal my admiration.

"I am the engineer," said Northmour. "You remember the planks in the garden? Behold them!"

"I did not know you had so many talents," said I.

"Are you armed?" he continued, pointing to an array of guns and pistols, all in admirable order, which stood in line against the wall or were displayed upon the sideboard.

"Thank you," I returned; "I have gone armed since our last encounter. But, to tell you the truth, I have had nothing to eat since early yesterday evening."

Northmour produced some cold meat, to which I eagerly set myself, and a bottle of good Burgundy, by which, wet as I was, I did not scruple to profit. I have always been an extreme temperance man on principle; but it is useless to push principle to excess, and on this occasion I believe that I finished three-quarters of the bottle. As I ate, I still continued to admire the preparations for defence.

"We could stand a siege," I said at length.

"Ye—es," drawled Northmour; "a very little one, per—haps. It is not so much the strength of the pavilion I misdoubt; it is the double danger that kills me. If we get to shooting, wild as the country is some one is sure to hear it, and then – why then it's the same thing, only different, as they say: caged by law, or killed by *carbonari*. There's the choice. It is a devilish bad thing to have the law against you in the world, and so I tell the old gentleman upstairs. He is quite of my way of thinking."

"Speaking of that," said I, "what kind of person is he?"

"Oh, he!" cried the other; "he's a rancid fellow, as far as he goes. I should like to have his neck wrung tomorrow by all the devils in Italy. I am not in this affair for him. You take me? I made a bargain for Missy's hand, and I mean to have it too."

"That by the way," said I. "I understand. But how will Mr. Huddlestone take my intrusion?"

"Leave that to Clara," returned Northmour.

I could have struck him in the face for this coarse familiarity; but I respected the truce, as, I am bound to say, did Northmour, and so long as the danger continued not a cloud arose in our relation. I bear him this testimony with the most unfeigned satis-faction; nor am I without pride when I look back upon my own behaviour. For surely no two men were ever left in a position so invidious and irritating.

As soon as I had done eating, we proceeded to inspect the lower floor. Window by window we tried the different supports, now and then making an inconsiderable change; and the strokes of the hammer sounded with startling loudness through the house. I proposed, I remember, to make loopholes; but he told me they were already made in the windows of the upper storey. It was an anxious business this inspection, and left me down-hearted. There were two doors and five windows to protect, and, counting Clara, only four of us to defend them against an unknown number of foes. I communicated my doubts to Northmour, who assured me, with unmoved composure, that he entirely shared them.

"Before morning," said he, "we shall all be butchered and buried in Graden Floe. For me, that is written."

I could not help shuddering at the mention of the quick-sand, but reminded Northmour that our enemies had spared me in the wood.

"Do not flatter yourself," said he. "Then you were not in the same boat with the old gentleman; now you are. It's the floe for all of us, mark my words."

I trembled for Clara; and just then her dear voice was heard calling us to come upstairs. Northmour showed me the way, and, when he had reached the landing, knocked at the door of what used to be called *My Uncle's Bedroom,* as the founder of the pavilion had designed it especially for himself.

"Come in, Northmour; come in, dear Mr. Cassilis," said a voice from within.

Pushing open the door, Northmour admitted me before him into the apartment. As I came in I could see the daughter slipping out by the side door into the study, which had been prepared as her bedroom. In the bed, which was drawn back against the wall, instead of standing, as I had last seen it, boldly across the window, sat Bernard Huddlestone, the defaulting banker. Little as I had seen of him by the shifting of the lantern on the links, I had no difficulty in recognising him for the same. He had a long and sallow countenance, surrounded by a long red beard and side whis-kers. His broken nose and high cheekbones gave him somewhat the air of a Kalmuck, and his light eyes shone with the excitement of a high fever. He wore a skull-cap of black silk; a huge Bible lay open before him on the bed, with a pair of gold spectacles in the place, and a pile of other books lay in the stand by his side. The green curtains lent a cadaverous shade to his cheek; and, as he sat propped on pillows, his great stature was plainly hunched, and his head protruded till it overhung his knees. I believe if he had not died otherwise, he must have fallen a victim to consumption in the course of but a very few weeks.

He held out to me a hand, long, thin, and disagreeably hairy.

"Come in, come in, Mr. Cassilis," said he. "Another protector – ahem! – another protector. Always welcome as a friend of my daughter's, Mr. Cassilis. How they have rallied about me, my daughter's friends! May God in heaven bless and reward them for it!"

I gave him my hand, of course, because I could not help it; but the sympathy I had been prepared to feel for Clara's father was immediately soured by his appearance, and the wheedling, unreal tones in which he spoke.

"Cassilis is a good man," said Northmour; "worth ten."

"So I hear," cried Mr. Huddlestone eagerly, "so my girl tells me. Ah, Mr. Cassilis, my sin has found me out, you see! I am very low, very low; but I hope equally penitent. We must all come to the throne of grace at last, Mr. Cassilis. For my part, I come late indeed; but with unfeigned humility, I trust."

"Fiddle-de-dee!" said Northmour roughly.

"No, no, dear Northmour!" cried the banker. "You must not say that; you must not try to shake me. You forget, my dear, good boy, you forget I may be called this very night before my Maker."

His excitement was pitiful to behold; and I felt myself grow indignant with Northmour, whose infidel opinions I well knew, and heartily derided, as he continued to taunt the poor sinner out of his humour of repentance.

"Pooh, my dear Huddlestone!" said he. "You do yourself injustice. You are a man of the world inside and out, and were up to all kinds of mischief before I was born. Your conscience is tanned like South American leather – only you forgot to tan your liver, and that, if you will believe me, is the seat of the annoyance."

"Rogue, rogue! bad boy!" said Mr. Huddlestone, shaking his finger. "I am no precisian, if you come to that; I always hated a precisian; but I never lost hold of something better through it all. I have been a bad boy, Mr. Cassilis; I do not seek to deny that;

but it was after my wife's death, and you know, with a widower, it's a different thing: sinful – I won't say no; but there is a gradation, we shall hope. And talking of that – Hark!" he broke out suddenly, his hand raised, his fingers spread, his face racked with interest and terror. "Only the rain, bless God!" he added, after a pause, and with indescribable relief.

For some seconds he lay back among the pillows like a man near to fainting; then he gathered himself together, and, in somewhat tremulous tones, began once more to thank me for the share I was prepared to take in his defence.

"One question, sir," said I, when he had paused. "Is it true that you have money with you?"

He seemed annoyed by the question, but admitted with reluctance that he had a little.

"Well," I continued, "it is their money they are after, is it not? Why not give it to them?"

"Ah!" replied he, shaking his head, "I have tried that already, Mr. Cassilis; and alas that it should be so! but it is blood they want."

"Huddlestone, that's a little less than fair," said Northmour. "You should mention that what you offered them was upwards of two hundred thousand short. The deficit is worth a reference; it is for what they call a cool sum, Frank. Then, you see, the fellows reason in their clear Italian way; and it seems to them, as indeed it seems to me, that they may just as well have both while they're about it – money and blood together, by George, and no more trouble for the extra pleasure."

"Is it in the pavilion?" I asked.

"It is; and I wish it were in the bottom of the sea instead," said Northmour; and then suddenly – "What are you making faces at me for?" he cried to Mr. Huddlestone, on whom I had unconsciously turned my back. "Do you think Cassilis would sell you?"

Mr. Huddlestone protested that nothing had been further from his mind.

"It is a good thing," retorted Northmour in his ugliest manner. "You might end by wearying us. What were you going to say?" he added, turning to me.

"I was going to propose an occupation for the afternoon," said I. "Let us carry that money out, piece by piece, and lay it down before the pavilion door. If the *carbonari* come, why, it's theirs at any rate."

"No, no," cried Mr. Huddlestone; "it does not, it cannot

belong to them! It should be distributed *pro rata* among all my creditors."

"Come now, Huddlestone," said Northmour, "none of that."

"Well, but my daughter," moaned the wretched man.

"Your daughter will do well enough. Here are two suitors, Cassilis and I, neither of us beggars, between whom she has to choose. And as for yourself, to make an end of arguments, you have no right to a farthing, and, unless I'm much mistaken, you are going to die."

It was certainly very cruelly said; but Mr. Huddlestone was a man who attracted little sympathy; and, although I saw him wince and shudder, I mentally endorsed the rebuke; nay, I added a contribution of my own.

"Northmour and I," I said, "are willing enough to help you to save your life, but not to escape with stolen property."

He struggled for awhile with himself, as though he were on the point of giving way to anger, but prudence had the best of the controversy.

"My dear boys," he said, "do with me or my money what you will. I leave all in your hands. Let me compose myself."

And so we left him, gladly enough I am sure. The last that I saw, he had once more taken up his great Bible, and with tremulous hands was adjusting his spectacles to read.

CHAPTER VII

Tells how a word was cried through the pavilion window

The recollection of that afternoon will always be graven on my mind. Northmour and I were persuaded that an attack was imminent; and if it had been in our power to alter in any way the order of events, that power would have been used to precipitate rather than delay the critical moment. The worst was to be anticipated; yet we could conceive no extremity so miserable as the suspense we were now suffering. I have never been an eager, though always a great, reader; but I never knew books so insipid as those which I took up and cast aside that afternoon in the pavilion. Even talk became impossible, as the hours went on. One or other was always listening for some sound, or peering from an upstairs window over the links. And yet not a sign indicated the presence of our foes.

We debated over and again my proposal with regard to the money; and had we been in complete possession of our faculties, I am sure we should have condemned it as unwise; but we were flustered with alarm, grasped at a straw, and determined, although it was as much as advertising Mr. Huddlestone's presence in the pavilion, to carry my proposal into effect.

The sum was part in specie, part in bank paper, and part in circular notes payable to the name of James Gregory. We took it out, counted it, enclosed it once more in a despatch-box belonging to Northmour, and prepared a letter in Italian which he tied to handle. It was signed by both of us under oath, and declared that this was all the money which had escaped the failure of the house of Huddlestone. This was, perhaps, the maddest action ever perpetrated by two persons professing to be sane. Had the despatch-box fallen into other hands than those for which it was intended, we stood criminally convicted on our own written testimony; but, as I have said, we were neither of us in a condition to judge soberly, and had a thirst for action that drove us to do something, right or wrong, rather than endure the agony of waiting. Moreover, as we were both convinced that the hollows of the links were alive with hidden spies upon our movements, we hoped that our appearance with the box might lead to a parley, and, perhaps, a compromise.

It was nearly three when we issued from the pavilion. The rain had taken off; the sun shone quite cheerfully. I have never seen the gulls fly so close about the house or approach so fearlessly to human beings. On the very doorstep one flapped heavily past our heads, and uttered its wild cry in my very ear.

"There is an omen for you," said Northmour, who like all freethinkers was much under the influence of superstition. "They think we are already dead."

I made some light rejoinder, but it was with half my heart; for the circumstance had impressed me.

A yard or two before the gate, on a patch of smooth turf, we set down the despatch-box; and Northmour waved a white handkerchief over his head. Nothing replied. We raised our voices, and cried aloud in Italian that we were there as ambassadors to arrange the quarrel; but the stillness remained unbroken save by the sea-gulls and the surf. I had a weight at my heart when we desisted; and I saw that even Northmour was unusually pale. He looked over his shoulder nervously, as though he feared that some one had crept between him and the pavilion door.

"By God," he said in a whisper, "this is too much for me!"

I replied in the same key: "Suppose there should be none, after all!"

"Look there," he returned, nodding with his head, as though he had been afraid to point.

I glanced in the direction indicated; and there, from the northern quarter of the Sea-Wood, beheld a thin column of smoke rising steadily against the now cloudless sky.

"Northmour", I said (we still continued to talk in whispers), "it is not possible to endure this suspense. I prefer death fifty times over. Stay you here to watch the pavilion; I will go forward and make sure, if I have to walk right into their camp."

He looked once again all round him with puckered eyes, and then nodded assentingly to my proposal.

My heart beat like a sledge-hammer as I set out walking rapidly in the direction of the smoke; and, though up to that moment I had felt chill and shivering, I was suddenly conscious of a glow of heat over all my body. The ground in this direction was very uneven; a hundred men might have lain hidden in as many square yards about my path. But I had not practised the business in vain, chose such routes as cut at the very root of concealment, and, by keeping along the most convenient ridges, commanded several hollows at a time. It was not long before I was rewarded for my caution. Coming suddenly on to a mound somewhat more elevated than the surrounding hummocks, I saw, not thirty yards away, a man bent almost double, and running as fast as his attitude permitted, along the bottom of a gully. I had dislodged one of the spies from his ambush. As soon as I sighted him, I called loudly both in English and Italian; and he, seeing concealment was no longer possible, straightened himself out, leaped from the gully, and made off as straight as an arrow for the borders of the wood.

It was none of my business to pursue; I had learned what I wanted – that we were beleaguered and watched in the pavilion; and I returned at once, and walking as nearly as possible in my old footsteps, to where Northmour awaited me beside the despatch-box. He was even paler than when I had left him, and his voice shook a little.

"Could you see what he was like?" he asked.

"He kept his back turned," I replied.

"Let us get into the house, Frank. I don't think I'm a coward, but I can stand no more of this," he whispered.

All was still and sunshiny about the pavilion as we turned to re-enter it; even the gulls had flown in a wider circuit, and were seen flickering along the beach and sand-hills; and this loneliness terrified me more than a regiment under arms. It was not until the door was barricaded that I could draw a full inspiration and relieve the weight that lay upon my bosom. Northmour and I exchanged a steady glance; and I suppose each made his own reflections on the white and startled aspect of the other.

"You were right," I said. "All is over. Shake hands, old man, for the last time."

"Yes," replied he, "I will shake hands; for, as sure as I am here, I bear no malice. But, remember, if, by some impossible accident, we should give the slip to these blackguards, I'll take the upper hand of you by fair or foul."

"Oh," said I, "you weary me!"

He seemed hurt, and walked away in silence to the foot of the stairs, where he paused.

"You do not understand," said he. "I am not a swindler, and I guard myself; that is all. It may weary you or not, Mr. Cassilis, I do not care a rush; I speak for my own satisfaction, and not for your amusement. You had better go upstairs and court the girl; for my part, I stay here."

"And I stay with you," I returned. "Do you think I would steal a march, even with your permission?"

"Frank," he said, smiling, "it's a pity you are an ass, for you have the makings of a man. I think I must be *fey* to-day; you cannot irritate me even when you try. Do you know," he continued softly, "I think we are the two most miserable men in England, you and I? we have got on to thirty without wife or child, or so much as a shop to look after – poor, pitiful, lost devils, both! And now we clash about a girl! As if there were not several millions in the United Kingdom! Ah, Frank, Frank, the one who loses this throw, be it you or me, he has my pity! It were better for him – how does the Bible say? – that a millstone were hanged about his neck and he were cast into the depth of the sea. Let us take a drink," he concluded suddenly, but without any levity of tone.

I was touched by his words, and consented. He sat down on the table in the dining-room, and held up the glass of sherry to his eye.

"If you beat me, Frank," he said, "I shall take to drink. What will you do, if it goes the other way?"

"God knows," I returned.

"Well," said he, "here is a toast in the meantime: '*Italia irredenta!*'"

The remainder of the day was passed in the same dreadful tedium and suspense. I laid the table for dinner, while Northmour and Clara prepared the meal together in the kitchen. I could hear their talk as I went to and fro, and was surprised to find it ran all the time upon myself. Northmour again bracketed us together, and rallied Clara on a choice of husbands; but he continued to speak of me with some feeling, and uttered nothing to my prejudice unless he included himself in the condemnation. This awakened a sense of gratitude in my heart, which combined with the immediateness of our peril to fill my eyes with tears. After all, I thought – and perhaps the thought was laughably vain – we were here three very noble human beings to perish in defence of a thieving banker.

Before we sat down to table, I looked forth from an upstairs window. The day was beginning to decline; the links were utterly deserted; the despatch-box still lay untouched where we had left it hours before.

Mr. Huddlestone, in a long yellow dressing-gown, took one end of the table, Clara the other; while Northmour and I faced each other from the sides. The lamp was brightly trimmed; the wine was good; the viands, although mostly cold, excellent of their sort. We seemed to have agreed tacitly; all reference to the impending catastrophe was carefully avoided; and, considering our tragic circumstances, we made a merrier party than could have been expected. From time to time, it is true, Northmour or I would rise from table and make a round of the defences; and, on each of these occasions, Mr. Huddlestone was recalled to a sense of his tragic predicament, glanced up with ghastly eyes, and bore for an instant on his countenance the stamp of terror. But he hastened to empty his glass, wiped his forehead with his handkerchief, and joined again in the conversation.

I was astonished at the wit and information he displayed. Mr. Huddlestone's was certainly no ordinary character; he had read and observed for himself; his gifts were sound; and, though I could never have learned to love the man, I began to understand his success in business, and the great respect in which he had been held before his failure. He had, above all, the talent of society; and though I never heard him speak but on this one and most unfavourable occasion, I set him down among the most brilliant conversationalists I ever met.

He was relating with great gusto, and seemingly no feeling of shame, the manoeuvres of a scoundrelly commission merchant whom he had known and studied in his youth, and we were all listening with an odd mixture of mirth and embarrassment, when our little party was brought abruptly to an end in the most startling manner.

A noise like that of a wet finger on the window-pane interrupted Mr. Huddlestone's tale; and in an instant we were all four as white as paper, and sat tongue-tied and motionless round the table.

"A snail," I said at last; for I had heard that these animals make a noise somewhat similar in character.

"Snail be d—d!" said Northmour. "Hush!"

The same sound was repeated twice at regular intervals; and then a formidable voice shouted through the shutters the Italian word "*Traditore!*"

Mr. Huddlestone threw his head in the air; his eyelids quivered; next moment he fell insensible below the table. Northmour and I had each run to the armoury and seized a gun. Clara was on her feet with her hand at her throat.

So we stood waiting, for we thought the hour of attack was certainly come; but second passed after second, and all but the surf remained silent in the neighbourhood of the pavilion.

"Quick," said Northmour; "upstairs with him before they come."

CHAPTER VIII

Tells the last of the tall man

Somehow or other, by hook and crook, and between the three of us, we got Bernard Huddlestone bundled upstairs and laid upon the bed in *My Uncle's Room*. During the whole process, which was rough enough, he gave no sign of consciousness, and he remained, as we had thrown him, without changing the position of a finger. His daughter opened his shirt and began to wet his head and bosom; while Northmour and I ran to the window. The weather continued clear; the moon, which was now about full, had risen and shed a very clear light upon the links; yet, strain our eyes as we might, we could distinguish nothing moving. A few dark spots, more or less, on the uneven expanse were not to be identified; they might be crouching men, they might be shadows; it was impossible to be sure.

"Thank God," said Northmour, "Aggie is not coming to-night."

Aggie was the name of the old nurse; he had not thought of her till now; but that he should think of her at all, was a trait that surprised me in the man.

We were again reduced to waiting. Northmour went to the fireplace and spread his hands before the red embers, as if he were cold. I followed him mechanically with my eyes, and in so doing turned my back upon the window. At that moment a very faint report was audible from without, and a ball shivered a pane of glass, and buried itself in the shutter two inches from my head. I heard Clara scream; and though I whipped instantly out of range and into a corner, she was there, so to speak, before me, beseeching to know if I were hurt. I felt that I could stand to be shot at every day and all day long, with such marks of solicitude for a reward; and I continued to reassure her, with the tenderest caresses and in complete forgetfulness of our situation, till the voice of Northmour recalled me to myself.

"An air-gun," he said. "They wish to make no noise."

I put Clara aside, and looked at him. He was standing with his back to the fire and his hands clasped behind him; and I knew by the black look on his face, that passion was boiling within. I had seen just such a look before he attacked me, that March night, in the adjoining chamber; and, though I could make ever allowance for his anger, I confess I trembled for the consequences. He gazed straight before him; but he could see us with the tail of his eye, and his temper kept rising like a gale of wind. With regular battle awaiting us outside, this prospect of an internecine strife within the walls began to daunt me.

Suddenly, as I was thus closely watching his expression and prepared against the worst, I saw a change, a flash, a look of relief upon his face. He took up the lamp which stood beside him on the table, and turned to us with an air of some excitement.

"There is one point that we must know," said he. "Are they going to butcher the lot of us, or only Huddlestone? Did they take you for him, or fire at you for your own *beaux yeux?*"

"They took me for him, for certain," I replied. "I am near as tall, and my head is fair."

"I am going to make sure," returned Northmour; and he stepped up to the window, holding the lamp above his head, and stood there, quietly affronting death, for half a minute.

Clara sought to rush forward and pull him from the place of danger; but I had the pardonable selfishness to hold her back by force.

"Yes," said Northmour, turning coolly from the window; "it's only Huddlestone they want."

"Oh, Mr. Northmour!" cried Clara; but found no more to add; the temerity she had just witnessed seeming beyond the reach of words.

He, on his part, looked at me, cocking his head, with a fire of triumph in his eyes; and I understood at once that he had thus hazarded his life, merely to attract Clara's notice, and depose me from my position as the hero of the hour. He snapped his fingers.

"The fire is only beginning," said he. "When they warm up to their work, they won't be so particular."

A voice was now heard hailing us from the entrance. From the window we could see the figure of a man in the moonlight; he stood motionless, his face uplifted to ours, and a rag of something white on his extended arm; and as we looked right down upon him, though he was a good many yards distant on the links, we could see the moonlight glitter on his eyes.

He opened his lips again, and spoke for some minutes on end, in a key so loud that he might have been heard in every corner of the pavilion, and as far away as the borders of the wood. It was the same voice that had already shouted "*Traditore!*" through the shutters of the dining-room; this time it made a complete and clear statement. If the traitor "Oddlestone" were given up, all others should be spared; if not, no one should escape to tell the tale.

"Well, Huddlestone, what do you say to that?" asked Northmour, turning to the bed.

Up to that moment the banker had given no sign of life, and I, at least, had supposed him to be still lying in a faint; but he replied at once, and in such tones as I have never heard elsewhere, save from a delirious patient, adjured and besought us not to desert him. It was the most hideous and abject performance that my imagination can conceive.

"Enough," cried Northmour; and then he threw open the window, leaned out into the night, and in a tone of exultation, and with a total forgetfulness of what was due to the presence of a lady, poured out upon the ambassador a string of the most abominable raillery both in English and Italian, and bade him be gone where he had come from. I believe that nothing so delighted Northmour at that moment as the thought that we must all infallibly perish before the night was out.

Meantime the Italian put his flag of truce into his pocket, and disappeared, at a leisurely pace, among the sand-hills.

"They make honourable war," said Northmour. "They are all gentlemen and soldiers. For the credit of the thing, I wish we could change sides – you and I, Frank, and you too, Missy, my darling – and leave that being on the bed to some one else. Tut! Don't look shocked! We are all going post to what they call eternity, and may as well be above-board while there's time. As far as I'm concerned, if I could first strangle Huddlestone and then get Clara in my arms, I could die with some pride and satisfaction. And as it is, by God, I'll have a kiss!"

Before I could do anything to interfere, he had rudely embraced and repeatedly kissed the resisting girl. Next moment I had pulled him away with a fury, and flung him heavily against the wall. He laughed long and loud, and I feared his wits had given way under the strain; for even in the best of days he had been a sparing and a quiet laugher.

"Now, Frank," said he, when his mirth was somewhat appeased, "it's your turn. Here's my hand. Good-bye; farewell!" Then seeing me stand rigid and indignant and holding Clara to my side – "Man!" he broke out, "are you angry? Did you think we were going to die with all airs and graces of society? I took a kiss; I'm glad I had it; and now you can take another if you like, and square accounts."

I turned from him with a feeling of contempt which I did not seek to dissemble.

"As you please," said he. "You've been a prig in life; a prig you'll die."

And with that he sat down in a chair, a rifle over his knee, and amused himself with snapping the lock; but I could see that his ebullition of light spirits (the only one I ever knew him to display) had already come to an end, and was succeeded by a sullen, scowling humour.

All this time our assailants might have been entering the house, and we been none the wiser; we had in truth almost forgotten the danger that so imminently overhung our days. But just then Mr. Huddlestone uttered a cry, and leaped from the bed.

I asked him what was wrong.

"Fire!" he cried. "They have set the house on fire!"

Northmour was on his feet in an instant, and he and I ran through the door of communication with the study. The room was illuminated by a red and angry light. Almost at the moment of our entrance, a tower of flame arose in front of the window, and, with a tingling report, a pane fell inwards on the carpet. They had set fire to the lean-to outhouse, where Northmour used to nurse his negatives.

"Hot work," said Northmour. "Let us try in your old room."

We ran thither in a breath, threw up the casement, and looked forth. Along the whole back wall of the pavilion piles of fuel had been arranged and kindled; and it is probable they had been drenched with mineral oil, for, in spite of the morning's rain, they all burned bravely. The fire had taken a firm hold already on the outhouse, which blazed higher and higher every moment; the back door was in the centre of a red-hot bonfire; the eaves we could see, as we looked upward, were already smouldering, for the roof overhung, and was supported by considerable beams of wood. At the same time, hot, pungent, and choking volumes of smoke began to fill the house. There was not a human being to be seen to right or left.

"Ah, well!" said Northmour, "here's the end, thank God."

And we returned to *My Uncle's Room*. Mr Huddlestone was putting on his boots, still violently trembling, but with an air of determination such as I had not hitherto observed. Clara stood close by him, with her cloak in both hands ready to throw about her shoulders, and a strange look in her eyes, as if she were half hopeful, half doubtful of her father.

"Well, boys and girls," said Northmour, "how about a sally? The oven is heating; it is not good to stay here and be baked; and, for my part, I want to come to my hands with them, and be done."

"There is nothing else left," I replied.

And both Clara and Mr. Huddlestone, though with a very different intonation, added, "Nothing."

As we went downstairs the heat was excessive, and the roaring of the fire filled our ears; and we had scarce reached the passage before the stairs window fell in, a branch of flame shot brandishing through the aperture, and the interior of the pavilion became lit up with that dreadful and fluctuating glare. At the same moment we heard the fall of something heavy and inelastic in the upper storey. The whole pavilion, it was plain, had gone alight like a box of matches, and now not only flamed sky-high to land and sea, but threatened with every moment to crumble and fall in about our ears.

Northmour and I cocked our revolvers. Mr. Huddlestone, who had already refused a firearm, put us behind him with a manner of command.

"Let Clara open the door," said he. "So, if they fire a volley, she will be protected. And in the meantime stand behind me. I am the scapegoat; my sins have found me out."

I heard him, as I stood breathless by his shoulder, with my pistol ready, pattering off prayers in a tremulous, rapid whisper; and I confess, horrid as the thought may seem, I despised him for thinking of supplications in a moment so critical and thrilling. In the meantime, Clara, who was dead white but still possessed her faculties, had displaced the barricade from the front door. Another moment, and she had pulled it open. Firelight and moonlight illuminated the links with confused and changeful lustre, and far away against the sky we could see a long trail of glowing smoke.

Mr. Huddlestone, filled for the moment with a strength greater than his own, struck Northmour and myself a back-hander in the chest; and while we were thus for the moment incapacitated from action, lifting his arms above his head like one about to dive, he ran straight forward out of the pavilion.

"Here am I!" he cried – "Huddlestone! Kill me, and spare the others!"

His sudden appearance daunted, I suppose, our hidden enemies; for Northmour and I had time to recover, to seize Clara between us, one by each arm, and to rush forth to his assistance, ere anything further had taken place. But scarce had we passed the threshold when there came near a dozen reports and flashes from every direction among the hollows of the links. Mr. Huddlestone staggered, uttered a weird and freezing cry, threw up his arms over his head, and fell backward on the turf.

"*Traditore! Traditore!*" cried the invisible avengers.

And just then, a part of the roof of the pavilion fell in, so rapid was the progress of the fire. A loud, vague, and horrible noise accompanied the collapse, and a vast volume of flame went soaring up to heaven. It must have been visible at that moment from twenty miles out at sea, from the shore at Graden Wester, and far inland from the peak of Graystiel, the most eastern summit of the Caulder Hills. Bernard Huddlestone, although God knows what were his obsequies, had a fine pyre at the moment of his death.

CHAPTER IX

Tells how Northmour carried out his threat

I should have the greatest difficulty to tell you what followed next after this tragic circumstance. It is all to me, as I look back upon it, mixed, strenuous, and ineffectual, like the struggles of a sleeper in a nightmare. Clara, I remember, uttered a broken sigh and would have fallen forward to earth, had not Northmour and I supported her insensible body. I do not think we were attacked; I do not remember even to have seen an assailant; and I believe we deserted Mr. Huddlestone without a glance. I only remember running like a man in a panic, now carrying Clara altogether in my own arms, now sharing her weight with Northmour, now scuffling confusedly for the possession of that dear burden. Why we should have made for my camp in the Hemlock Den, or how we reached it, are points lost for ever to my recollection. The first moment at which I became definitely sure, Clara had been suffered to fall against the outside of my little tent, Northmour and I were tumbling together on the ground, and he, with contained ferocity, was striking for my head with the butt of his revolver. He had already twice wounded me on the scalp; and it is to the consequent loss of blood that I am tempted to attribute the sudden clearness of my mind.

I caught him by the wrist.

"Northmour," I remember saying, "you can kill me afterwards. Let us first attend to Clara."

He was at that moment uppermost. Scarcely had the words passed my lips, when he had leaped to his feet and ran towards the tent; and the next moment, he was straining Clara to his heart and covering her unconscious hands and face with his caresses.

"Shame!" I cried. "Shame to you, Northmour!"

And, giddy though I still was, I struck him repeatedly upon the head and shoulders.

He relinquished his grasp, and faced me in the broken moonlight.

"I had you under, and I let you go," said he; "and now you strike me! Coward!"

"You are the coward," I retorted. "Did she wish your kisses while she was still sensible of what she wanted? Not she! And now she may be dying; and you waste this precious time, and abuse her helplessness. Stand aside, and let me help her."

He confronted me for a moment, white and menacing; then suddenly he stepped aside.

"Help her then," said he.

I threw myself on my knees beside her, and loosened, as well as I was able, her dress and corset; but while I was thus engaged, a grasp descended on my shoulder.

"Keep your hands off her," said Northmour fiercely. "Do you think I have no blood in my veins?"

"Northmour," I cried, "if you will neither help her yourself nor let me do so, do you know that I shall have to kill you?"

"That is better!" he cried. "Let her die also, where's the harm? Step aside from that girl! and stand up to fight."

"You will observe," said I, half rising, "that I have not kissed her yet."

"I dare you to," he cried.

I do not know what possessed me; it was one of the things I am most ashamed of in my life, though, as my wife used to say, I knew that my kisses would be always welcome were she dead or living; down I fell again upon my knees, parted the hair from her forehead, and, with the dearest respect, laid my lips for a moment on that cold brow. It was such a caress as a father might have given; it was such a one as was not unbecoming from a man soon to die to a woman already dead.

"And now," said I, "I am at your service, Mr. Northmour."

But I saw, to my surprise, that he had turned his back upon me.

"Do you hear?" I asked.

"Yes", said he, "I do. If you wish to fight, I am ready. If not, go on and save Clara. All is one to me."

I did not wait to be twice bidden; but, stooping again over

Clara, continued my efforts to revive her. She still lay white and lifeless; I began to fear that her sweet spirit had indeed fled beyond recall, and horror and a sense of utter desolation seized upon my heart. I called her by name with the most endearing inflections; I chafed and beat her hands; now I laid her head low, now supported it against my knee; but all seemed to be in vain, and the lids still lay heavy on her eyes.

"Northmour," I said, "there is my hat. For God's sake bring some water from the spring."

Almost in a moment he was by my side with the water.

"I have brought it in my own," he said. "You do not grudge me the privilege?"

"Northmour," I was beginning to say as I laved her head and breast; but he interrupted me savagely.

"Oh, you hush up!" he said. "The best thing you can do is to say nothing."

I had certainly no desire to talk, my mind being swallowed up in concern for my dear love and her condition; so I continued in silence to do my best towards her recovery, and, when the hat was empty, returned it to him, with one word – "More." He had, perhaps, gone several times upon this errand, when Clara reopened her eyes.

"Now," said he, "since she is better, you can spare me, can you not? I wish you a good night, Mr. Cassilis."

And with that he was gone among the thicket. I made a fire, for I had now no fear of the Italians, who had even spared all the little posssessions left in my encampment; and, broken as she was by the excitement and the hideous catastrophe of the evening, I managed, in one way or another – by persuasion, encouragement, warmth, and such simple remedies as I could lay my hand on – to bring her back to some composure of mind and strength of body.

Day had already come, when a sharp "Hist!" sounded from the thicket. I started from the ground; but the voice of Northmour was heard adding, in the most tranquil tones: "Come here, Cassilis, and alone; I want to show you something."

I consulted Clara with my eyes, and, receiving her tacit permission, left her alone, and clambered out of the den. At some distance off I saw Northmour leaning against an elder; and, as soon as he perceived me, he began walking seaward. I had almost overtaken him as he reached the outskirts of the wood.

"Look," said he, pausing.

A couple of steps more brought me out of the foliage. The light of the morning lay cold and clear over that well-known scene. The pavilion was but a blackened wreck; the roof had fallen in, one of the gables had fallen out; and, far and near, the face of the links was cicatrised with little patches of burnt furze. Thick smoke still went straight upwards in the windless air of the morning, and a great pile of ardent cinders filled the bare walls of the house, like coals in a open grate. Close by the islet a schooner yacht lay to, and a well-manned boat was pulling vigorously for the shore.

"The *Red Earl!*" I cried. "The *Red Earl* twelve hours too late!"

"Feel in your pocket, Frank. Are you armed?" asked Northmour.

I obeyed him, and I think I must have become deadly pale. My revolver had been taken from me.

"You see I have you in my power," he continued. "I disarmed you last night while you were nursing Clara; but this morning – here – take your pistol. No thanks!" he cried, holding up his hand. "I do not like them; that is the only way you can annoy me now."

He began to walk forward across the links to meet the boat, and I followed a step or two behind. In front of the pavilion I paused to see where Mr. Huddlestone had fallen; but there was no sign of him, nor so much as a trace of blood.

"Graden Floe," said Northmour.

He continued to advance till we had come to the head of the beach.

"No farther, please," said he. "Would you like to take her to Graden House?"

"Thank you," replied I; "I shall try to get her to the minister's at Graden Wester."

The prow of the boat here grated on the beach, and a sailor jumped ashore with a line in his hand.

"Wait a minute, lads!" cried Northmour; and then lower and to my private ear: "You had better say nothing of all this to her," he added.

"On the contrary!" I broke out, "she shall know everything that I can tell."

"You do not understand," he returned, with an air of great dignity. "It will be nothing to her; she expects it of me. Good-bye!" he added, with a nod.

I offered him my hand.

"Excuse me," said he. "It's small, I know; but I can't push

things quite so far as that. I don't wish any sentimental business, to sit by your hearth a white-haired wanderer, and all that. Quite the contrary: I hope to God I shall never again clap eyes on either one of you."

"Well, God bless you, Northmour!" I said heartily.

"Oh, yes," he returned.

He walked down the beach; and the man who was ashore gave him an arm on board, and then shoved off and leaped into the bows himself. Northmour took the tiller; the boat rose to the waves, and the oars between the thole-pins sounded crisp and measured in the morning air.

They were not yet half-way to the *Red Earl,* and I was still watching their progress, when the sun rose out of the sea.

One word more, and my story is done. Years after, Northmour was killed fighting under the colours of Garibaldi for the liberation of the Tyrol.[7]

Thrawn Janet[1]

✳

The Reverend Murdoch Soulis was long minister of the moorland parish of Balweary, in the vale of Dule.[2] A severe, bleak- faced old man, dreadful to his hearers, he dwelt in the last years of his life, without relative or servant or any human company, in the small and lonely manse under the Hanging Shaw. In spite of the iron composure of his features, his eye was wild, scared, and uncertain; and when he dwelt, in private admonition, on the future of the impenitent, it seemed as if his eye pierced through the storms of time to the terrors of eternity. Many young persons, coming to prepare themselves against the season of the Holy Communion, were dreadfully affected by his talk. He had a sermon on 1st Peter, v. and 8th, "The devil as a roaring lion,"[3] on the Sunday after every seventeenth of August, and he was accustomed to surpass himself upon that text both by the appalling nature of the matter and the terror of his bearing in the pulpit. The children were frightened into fits, and the old looked more than usually oracular, and were, all that day, full of those hints that Hamlet deprecated. The manse itself, where it stood by the water of Dule among some thick trees, with the Shaw overhanging it on the one side, and on the other many cold, moorish hill-tops rising toward the sky, had begun, at a very early period of Mr. Soulis's ministry, to be avoided in the dusk hours by all who valued themselves upon their prudence; and guidmen sitting at the clachan alehouse shook their heads together at the thought of passing late by that uncanny neighbourhood. There was one spot, to be more particular, which was regarded with especial awe. The manse stood between the highroad and the water of Dule, with a gable to each; its back was towards the kirktown of Balweary, nearly half a mile away; in front of it, a bare garden, hedged with thorn, occupied that land between the river and the road. The house was two stories high, with two large rooms on each. It opened not directly on the garden, but on a causewayed path, or passage, giving on the road on the one hand, and closed on the other by the tall willows and elders that bordered on the stream. And it was this strip of causeway that enjoyed among the young parishioners of Balweary so infamous a reputation. The minister walked there often after dark, sometimes groaning aloud in the instancy of his unspoken prayers; and when he was from home, and the manse door was locked, the more daring schoolboys ventured, with beating hearts, to "follow my leader" across that legendary spot.

This atmosphere of terror, surrounding as it did, a man of God of spotless character and orthodoxy, was a common cause of wonder and subject of inquiry among the few strangers who were led by chance or business to that unknown, outlying country. But many even of the people of the parish were ignorant of the strange events which had marked the first year of Mr. Soulis's ministrations; and among those who were better informed, some were naturally reticent, and others shy of that particular topic. Now and again, only, one of the older folk would warm into courage over his third tumbler, and recount the cause of the minister's strange looks and solitary life.

Fifty years syne, when Mr. Soulis cam' first into Ba'weary, he was still a young man – a callant, the folk said – fu' o' book-learnin' an' grand at the exposition, but, as was natural in sae young a man, wi' nae leevin' experience in religion. The younger sort were greatly taken wi' his gifts and his gab; but auld, concerned, serious men and women were moved even to prayer for the young man, whom they took to be a self-deceiver, and the parish that was like to be sae ill-supplied. It was before the days o' the moderates – weary fa' them; but ill things are like guid – they baith come bit by bit, a pickle at a time; and there were folk even then that said the Lord had left the college professors to their ain devices, an' the lads that went to study wi' them wad hae done mair an' better sittin' in a peat-bog, like their forbears of the persecution, wi' a Bible under their oxter an' a speerit o' prayer in their heart. There was nae doubt onyway, but that Mr. Soulis had been ower lang at the college. He was careful and troubled for mony things besides the ae thing needful. He had a feck o' books wi' him – mair than had ever been seen before in a' that presbytery; and a sair wark the carrier had wi' them, for they were a' like to have smoored in the De'il's Hag between this and Kilmackerlie. They were books o' divinity, to be sure, or so they ca'd them; but the serious were o' opinion there was little service for sae mony, when the hail o'

God's Word would gang in the neuk o' a plaid. Then he wad sit half the day and half the nicht forbye, which was scant decent – writin', nae less; an' first they were feared he wad read his sermons; an' syne it proved he was writin' a book himsel', which was surely no' fittin' for ane o' his years an' sma' experience.

Onyway it behoved him to get an auld, decent wife to keep the manse for him an' see to his bit denners; an' he was recommended to an auld limmer – Janet M'Clour, they ca'd her – an' sae far left to himsel' as to be ower persuaded.[4] There was mony advised him to the contrar, for Janet was mair than suspeckit by the best folk in Ba'weary. Lang or that, she had had a wean to a dragoon; she hadna come forrit[*] for maybe thretty year; and bairns had seen her mumblin' to hersel' up on Key's Loan in the gloamin', whilk was an unco time an' place for a God-fearin' woman. Howsoever, it was the laird himsel' that had first tauld the minister o' Janet; an' in thae days he wad hae gane a far gate to pleesure the laird. When folk tauld him that Janet was sib to the de'il, it was a' superstition by his way o' it; an' when they cast up the Bible to him an' the witch of Endor,[5] he wad threep it doun their thrapples that thir days were a' gane by, an' the de'il was mercifully restrained.

Weel, when it got about the clachan that Janet M'Clour was to be servant at the manse, the folk were fair mad wi' her an' him thegither; an' some o' the guidwives had nae better to dae than get round her door-cheeks and chairge her wi' a' that was ken't again' her, frae the sodger's bairn to John Tamson's twa kye. She was nae great speaker; folk usually let her gang her ain gate, an' she let them gang theirs, wi' neither Fair-guid-een nor Fair-guid-day; but when she buckled to, she had a tongue to deave the miller. Up she got, an' there wasna an auld story in Ba'weary but she gart somebody lowp for it that day; they couldna say ae thing but she could say twa to it; till, at the hinder end, the guidwives up an' claught haud of her, an' clawed the coats aff her back, and pu'd her doun the clachan to the water o' Dule, to see if she were a witch or no, soom or droun. The carline skirled till ye could hear her at the Hangin' Shaw, an' she focht like ten; there was mony a guidwife bure the mark o' her neist day an' mony a lang day after; an' just in the hettest o' the collieshangie, wha suld come up (for his sins) but the new minister!

"Women," said he (an' he had a grand voice), "I charge you

---

[*] "To come forrit" – to offer oneself as a communicant [R.L.S.].

in the Lord's name to let her go."

Janet ran to him – she was fair wud wi' terror – an' clang to him, an' prayed him, for Christ's sake, save her frae the cummers; an' they, for their pairt, tauld him a' that was ken't, an' maybe mair.

"Woman," says he to Janet, "is this true?"

"As the Lord sees me," says she, "as the Lord made me, no' a word o't. Forbye the bairn," says she, "I've been a decent woman a' my days."

"Will you," says Mr. Soulis, "in the name of God, and before me, His unworthy minister, renounce the devil and his works?"

Weel, it wad appear that when he askit that, she gave a girn that fairly frichit them that saw her, an' they could hear her teeth play dirl thegither in her chafts; but there was naething for it but the ae way or the ither; an' Janet lifted up her hand an' renounced the de'il before them a'.

"And now," says Mr. Soulis to the guidwives, "home with ye, one and all, and pray to God for His forgiveness."

An' he gied Janet his arm, though she had little on her but a sark, and took her up the clachan to her ain door like a leddy o' the land; an' her screighin' an' laughin' as was a scandal to be heard.

There were mony grave folk lang ower their prayers that nicht; but when the morn cam' there was sic a fear fell upon a' Ba'weary that the bairns hid theirsels, an' even the men-folk stood an' keekit frae their doors. For there was Janet comin' doun the clachan – her or her likeness, nane could tell – wi' her neck thrawn, an' her heid on ae side, like a body that has been hangit, an' a girn on her face like an unstreakit corp. By an' by they got used wi' it, an' even speered at her to ken what was wrang; but frae that day forth she couldna speak like a Christian woman, but slavered an' played click wi' her teeth like a pair o' shears; an' frae that day forth the name o' God cam' never on her lips. Whiles she wad try to say it, but it michtna be. Them that kenned best said least; but they never gied that Thing the name o' Janet M'Clour; for the auld Janet, by their way o't, was in muckle hell that day. But the minister was neither to haud nor to bind; he preached about naething but the folk's cruelty that had gi'en her a stroke of the palsy; he skelpit the bairns that meddled her; an' he had her up to the manse that same nicht, an' dwalled there a' his lane wi' her under the Hangin' Shaw.

Weel, time gaed by: and the idler sort commenced to think

mair lichtly o' that black business. The minister was weel thocht o'; he was aye late at the writing, folk wad see his can'le doon by the Dule water after twal' at e'en; and he seemed pleased wi' himsel' an' upsitten as at first, though a' body could see that he was dwin-ing. As for Janet she cam' an' she gaed; if she didna speak muckle afore, it was reason she should speak less then; she meddled nae-body; but she was an eldritch thing to see, an' nane wad hae mistrysted wi' her for Ba'weary glebe.

About the end o' July there cam' a spell o' weather, the like o't never was in that country-side; it was lown an' het an' heartless; the herds couldna win up the Black Hill, the bairns were ower weariet to play; an' yet it was gousty too, wi' claps o' het wund that rumm'led in the glens, and bits o' shouers that slockened naething. We aye thocht it büt to thun'er on the morn; but the morn cam', an' the morn's morning, an' it was aye the same uncanny weather, sair on folks and bestial. O' a' that were the waur, nane suffered like Mr. Soulis; he could neither sleep nor eat, he tauld his elders; an' when he wasna writin' at his weary book, he wad be stravaguin' ower a' the country-side like a man possessed, when a' body else was blithe to keep caller ben the house.

Abune Hangin' Shaw, in the bield o' the Black Hill, there's a bit enclosed grund wi' an iron yett; an' it seems, in the auld days, that was the kirkyaird o' Ba'weary, an' consecrated by the Papists before the blessed licht shone upon the kingdom.[6] It was a great howff, o' Mr. Soulis's onyway; there he wad sit an' consider his sermons; an' indeed it's a bieldy bit. Weel, as he cam' ower the wast end o' the Black Hill, ae day, he saw first twa, an' syne fower, an' syne seeven corbie craws fleein' round an' round abune the auld kirkyaird. They flew laigh an' heavy, an' squawked to ither as they gaed; an' it was clear to Mr. Soulis that something had put them frae their ordinar. He wasna easy fleyed, an' gaed straucht up to the wa's; an' what suld he find there but a man, or the appearance o' a man, sittin' in the inside upon a grave. He was of a great stature, an' black as hell, and his e'en were singular to see.[*] Mr. Soulis had heard tell o' black men, mony's the time; but there was something unco about this black man that daunted him. Het as he was, he took a kind o' cauld grue in the marrow

---

It was a common belief in Scotland that the devil appeared as a black man. This appears in several witch trials and I think in Law's *Memorials*, that delightful storehouse of the quaint and grisly [R.L.S.].[7]

o' his banes; but up he spak for a' that; an' says he: "My friend, are you a stranger in this place?" The black man answered never a word; he got upon his feet, an' begoud on to hirsle to the wa' on the far side; but he aye lookit at the minister; an' the minister stood an' lookit back; till a' in a meenit the black man was ower the wa' an' rinnin' for the bield o' the trees. Mr. Soulis, he hardly kenned why, ran after him; but he was fair forjeskit wi' his walk an' the het, unhalesome weather; an' rin as he likit, he got nae mair than a glisk o' the black man amang the birks, till he won doun to the foot o' the hillside, an' there he saw him ance mair, gaun, hap-step-an'-lawp, ower Dule water to the manse.

Mr. Soulis wasna weel pleased that this fearsome gangrel suld mak' sae free wi' Ba'weary manse; an' he ran the harder, an', wet shoon, ower the burn, an' up the walk; but the de'il a black man was there to see. He stepped out upon the road, but there was naebody there; he gaed a' ower the gairden, but na, nae black man. At the hinder end, an' a bit feared as was but natural, he lifted the hasp an' into the manse; and there was Janet M'Clour before his e'en, wi' her thrawn craig, an' nane sae pleased to see him. An' he aye minded sinsyne, when first he set his e'en upon her, he had the same cauld and deidly grue.

"Janet", says he, "have you seen a black man?"

"A black man!" quo' she. "Save us a'! Ye're no wise, minister. There's a nae black man in a' Ba'weary."

But she didna speak plain, ye maun understand; but yam-yammered, like a powney wi' the bit in its moo.

"Weel," says he, "Janet, if there was nae black man, I have spoken with the Accuser of the Brethren."

An' he sat doun like ane wi' a fever, an' his teeth chittered in his heid.

"Hoots," says she, "think shame to yoursel', minister"; an' gied him a drap brandy that she keept aye by her.

Syne Mr. Soulis gaed into his study amang a' his books. It's a lang, laigh, mirk chalmer, perishin' cauld in winter, an' no' very dry even in the top o' the simmer, for the manse stands near the burn. Sae doun he sat, and thocht of a' that had come an' gane since he was in Ba'weary, an' his hame, an' the days when he was a bairn an' ran daffin' on the braes; an' that black man aye ran in his heid like the owercome of a sang. Aye the mair he thocht, the mair he thocht o' the black man. He tried the prayer, an' the words wouldna come to him; an' he tried, they say, to write at his book, but he couldna mak' nar mair o' that. There was whiles he thocht the black man was at his oxter, an' the swat stood upon him cauld as well-water; and there was ither whiles, when he cam' to himsel' like a christened bairn an' minded naething.

The upshot was that he gaed to the window an' stood glowrin' at Dule water. The trees are unco thick, an' the water lies deep an' black under the manse; an' there was Janet washin' the cla'es wi' her coats kilted. She had her back to the minister, an' he, for his pairt, hardly kenned what he was lookin' at. Syne she turned round, an' shawed her face; Mr. Soulis had the same cauld grue as twice that day afore, an' it was borne in upon him what folk said, that Janet was deid lang syne, an' this was a bogle in her clay-cauld flesh. He drew back a pickle and he scanned her narrowly. She was tramp-trampin' in the cla'es croonin' to hersel'; and eh! Gude guide us, but it was a fearsome face. Whiles she sang louder, but there was nae man born o' woman that could tell the words o' her sang; an' whiles she lookit side-lang doun, but there was naething there for her to look at. There gaed a scunner through the flesh upon his banes; an' that was Heeven's advertisement. But Mr. Soulis just blamed himsel', he said, to think sae ill o' a puir, auld afflicted wife that hadna a freend forbye himsel'; an' he put up a bit prayer for him an' her, an' drank a little caller water – for his heart rose again' the meat – an' gaed up to his naked bed in the gloamin'.

That was a nicht that has never been forgotten in Ba'weary, the nicht o' the seeventeenth o' August, seeventeen hun'er an' twal'. It had been het afore, as I hae said, but that nicht it was hetter than ever. The sun gaed doun amang unco-lookin' clouds; it fell as mirk as the pit; no' a star, no' a breath o' wund; ye couldna see your han' afore your face, an' even the auld folk cuist the covers frae their beds an' lay pechin' for their breath. Wi' a' that he had upon his mind, it was gey an' unlikely Mr. Soulis wad get muckle sleep. He lay an' he tummled; the gude, caller bed that he got into brunt his very banes; whiles he slept, an' whiles he waukened; whiles he heard the time o' nicht, an' whiles a tyke yowlin' up the muir, as if somebody was deid; whiles he thocht he heard bogles claverin' in his lug, an' whiles he saw spunkies in the room. He behoved, he judged, to be sick; an' sick he was – little he jaloosed the sickness.

At the hinder end, he got a clearness in his mind, sat up in his sark on the bed-side, an' fell thinkin' ance mair o' the black man an' Janet. He couldna weel tell how – maybe it was the cauld to his feet – but it cam' in upon him wi' a spate that there was some connection between thir twa, an' that either or baith o' them were bogles. An' just at that moment, in Janet's room, which was neist to his, there cam' a stramp o' feet as if men were wars'lin', an' then a loud bang; an' then a wund gaed reishling round the fower quarters o' the house; an' then a' was ance mair as seelent as the grave.

Mr. Soulis was feared for neither man nor de'il. He got his tinder-box, an' lit a can'le, an' made three steps o't ower to Janet's door. It was on the hasp, an' he pushed it open, an' keeked bauldly in. It was a big room, as big as the minister's ain, an' plenished wi' grand, auld solid gear, for he had naething else. There was a fower-posted bed wi' auld tapestry; an' a braw cabinet o' aik, that was fu' o' the minister's divinity books, an' put there to be out o' the gate; an' a wheen duds o' Janet's lying here an' there about the floor. But nae Janet could Mr. Soulis see; nor ony sign o' a contention. In he gaed (an' there's few that wad hae followed him) an' lookit a' round, an' listened. But there was naething to be heard, neither inside the manse nor in a' Ba'weary parish, an' naething to be seen but the muckle shadows turnin' round the can'le. An' then, a' at aince, the minister's heart played dunt an' stood stock-still; an' a cauld wund blew amang the hairs o' his heid. Whaten a weary sicht was that for the puir man's e'en! For there was Janet hangin' frae a nail beside the auld aik cabinet: her heid aye lay on her shouther, her e'en were steekit, the tongue projected frae her mouth, an' her heels were twa feet clear abune the floor.

"God forgive us all!" thocht Mr. Soulis, "poor Janet's dead."

He cam' a step nearer to the corp; an' then his heart fair whammled in his inside. For by what cantrip it wad ill beseem a man to judge, she was hangin' frae a single nail an' by a single wursted thread for darnin' hose.

It's a awfu' thing to be your lane at nicht wi' siccan prodigies o' darkness; but Mr. Soulis was strong in the Lord. He turned an' gaed his ways oot o' that room, an' lockit the door ahint him; an' step by step, doun the stairs, as heavy as leed; and set doun the can'le on the table at the stairfoot. He couldna pray, he couldna think, he was dreepin' wi' caul' swat, an' naething could he hear but the dunt-dunt-duntin' o' his ain heart. He micht maybe hae stood there an hour, or maybe twa, he minded sae little; when a' o' a sudden, he heard a laigh, uncanny steer up-stairs; a foot gaed to an' fro in the chalmer whaur the corp was hangin'; syne the door was opened, though he minded weel that he had lockit it; an' syne there was a step upon the landin', an' it seemed to him as if the corp was lookin' ower the rail and doun upon him whaur he stood.

He took up the can'le again (for he couldna want the licht), an' as saftly as ever he could, gaed straucht out o' the manse an' to the far end o' the causeway. It was aye pit-mirk; the flame o' the can'le, when he set it on the grund, brunt steedy and clear as in a room; naething moved, but the Dule water seepin' and sabbin' doun the glen, an' yon unhaly footstep that cam' ploddin' doun the stairs inside the manse. He kenned the foot ower weel, for it was Janet's; an' at ilka step that cam' a wee thing nearer, the cauld got deeper in his vitals. He commended his soul to Him that made an' keepit him; "and, O Lord," said he, "give me strength this night to war against the powers of evil."

By this time the foot was comin' through the passage for the door; he could hear a hand skirt alang the wa', as if the fearsome thing was feelin' for its way. The saughs tossed an' maned thegither, a long sigh cam' ower the hills, the flame o' the can'le was blawn aboot; an' there stood the corp of Thrawn Janet, wi' her grogram goun an' her black mutch, wi' the heid aye upon the shouther, an' the girn still upon the face o't – leevin', ye wad hae said – deid, as Mr. Soulis weel kenned – upon the threshold o' the manse.

It's a strange thing that the soul of man should be that thirled into his perishable body; but the minister saw that, an' his heart didna break.

She didna stand there lang; she began to move again an' cam' slowly towards Mr. Soulis whaur he stood under the saughs. A' the life o' his body, a' the strength o' his speerit, were glowerin' frae his e'en. It seemed she was gaun to speak, but wanted words, an' made a sign wi' the left hand. There cam' a clap o' wund, like a cat's fuff; oot gaed the can'le, the saughs skreighed like folk; an' Mr. Soulis kenned that, live or die, this was the end o't.

"Witch, beldame, devil!" he cried, "I charge you, by the power of God, begone – if you be dead, to the grave – if you be damned, to hell."

An' at that moment the Lord's ain hand out o' the Heevens struck the Horror whaur it stood; the auld, deid, desecrated corp o' the witch-wife, sae lang keepit frae the grave and hirsled round by de'ils, lowed up like a brunstane spunk an' fell in ashes to the grund; the thunder followed, peal on dirlin' peal, the rairin' rain upon the back o' that; and Mr. Soulis lowped through the garden hedge, an' ran, wi' skelloch upon skelloch, for the clachan.

That same mornin', John Christie saw the Black Man pass the Muckle Cairn as it was chappin' six; before eicht, he gaed by the change-house at Knockdow; an' no' lang after, Sandy M'Lellan saw him gaun linkin' doun the braes frae Kilmackerlie. There's little doubt but it was him that dwalled sae lang in Janet's body; but he was awa' at last; an' sinsyne the de'il has never fashed us in Ba'weary.

But it was a sair dispensation for the minister; lang, lang he lay ravin' in his bed; an' frae that hour to this, he was the man ye ken the day.

The Body Snatcher[1]

✻

Every night in the year, four of us sat in the small parlour of the George at Debenham – the undertaker, and the landlord, and Fettes, and myself. Sometimes there would be more; but blow high, blow low, come rain or snow or frost, we four would be each planted in his own particular arm-chair. Fettes was an old drunken Scotsman, a man of education obviously, and a man of some property, since he lived in idleness. He had come to Debenham years ago, while still young, and by a mere continuance of living had grown to be an adopted townsman. His blue camlet cloak was a local antiquity, like the church-spire. His place in the parlour at the George, his absence from church, his old, crapulous, disreputable vices, were all things of course in Debenham. He had some vague Radical opinions and some fleeting infidelities, which he would now and again set forth and emphasise with tottering slaps upon the table. He drank rum – five glasses regularly every evening; and for the greater portion of his nightly visit to the George sat, with his glass in his right hand, in a state of melancholy alcoholic saturation. We called him the Doctor, for he was supposed to have some special knowledge of medicine, and had been known, upon a pinch, to set a fracture or reduce a dislocation; but, beyond these slight particulars, we had no knowledge of his character and antecedents.

One dark winter night – it had struck nine some time before the landlord joined us – there was a sick man in the George, a great neighbouring proprietor suddenly struck down with apoplexy on his way to Parliament; and the great man's still greater London doctor had been telegraphed to his bedside. It was the first time that such a thing had happened in Debenham, for the railway was but newly open, and we were all proportionately moved by the occurrence.

"He's come," said the landlord, after he had filled and lighted his pipe.

"He?" said I. "Who? – not the doctor?"

"Himself," replied our host.

"What is his name?"

"Dr. Macfarlane," said the landlord.

Fettes was far through his third tumbler, stupidly fuddled, now nodding over, now staring mazily around him; but at the last word he seemed to awaken, and repeated the name "Macfarlane" twice, quietly enough the first time, but with sudden emotion at the second.

"Yes," said the landlord, "that's his name, Doctor Wolfe Macfarlane."

Fettes became instantly sober; his eyes awoke, his voice became clear, loud, and steady, his language forcible and earnest. We were all startled by the transformation, as if a man had risen from the dead.

"I beg your pardon," he said, "I am afraid I have not been paying much attention to your talk. Who is this Wolfe Macfarlane?" And then, when he had heard the landlord out, "It cannot be, it cannot be," he added; "and yet I would like well to see him face to face."

"Do you know him, Doctor?" asked the undertaker, with a gasp.

"God forbid!" was the reply. "And yet the name is a strange one; it were too much to fancy two. Tell me, landlord, is he old?"

"Well," said the host, "he's not a young man, to be sure, and his hair is white; but he looks younger than you."

"He is older, though; years older. But," with a slap upon the table, "it's the rum you see in my face – rum and sin. This man, perhaps, may have an easy conscience and a good digestion. Conscience! Hear me speak. You would think I was some good, old, decent Christian, would you not? But no, not I; I never canted. Voltaire might have canted if he'd stood in my shoes; but the brains" – with a rattling fillip on his bald head – "the brains were clear and active, and I saw and made no deductions."

"If you know this doctor," I ventured to remark, after a somewhat awful pause, "I should gather that you do not share the landlord's good opinion."

Fettes paid no regard to me.

"Yes," he said, with sudden decision, "I must see him face to face."

There was another pause, and then a door was closed rather sharply on the first floor, and a step was heard upon the stair.

"That's the doctor," cried the landlord. "Look sharp, and you can catch him."

It was but two steps from the small parlour to the door of the old George Inn; the wide oak staircase landed almost in the street; there was room for a Turkey rug and nothing more between the threshold and the last round of the descent; but this little space was every evening brilliantly lit up, not only by the light upon the stair and the great signal-lamp below the sign, but by the warm radiance of the bar-room window. The George thus brightly advertised itself to passers-by in the cold street. Fettes walked steadily to the spot, and we, who were hanging behind, beheld the two men meet, as one of them had phrased it, face to face. Dr. Macfarlane was alert and vigorous. His white hair set off his pale and placid, although energetic, countenance. He was richly dressed in the finest of broadcloth and the whitest of linen, with a great gold watchchain, and studs and spectacles of the same precious material. He wore a broad-folded tie, white and speckled with lilac, and he carried on his arm a comfortable driving-coat of fur. There was no doubt but he became his years, breathing, as he did, of wealth and consideration; and it was a surprising contrast to see our parlour sot – bald, dirty, pimpled, and robed in his old camlet cloak – confront him at the bottom of the stairs.

"Macfarlane!" he said somewhat loudly, more like a herald than a friend.

The great doctor pulled up short on the fourth step, as though the familiarity of the address surprised and somewhat shocked his dignity.

"Toddy Macfarlane!" repeated Fettes.

The London man almost staggered. He stared for the swiftest of seconds at the man before him, glanced behind him with a sort of scare, and then in a startled whisper, "Fettes!" he said, "you!"

"Ay," said the other, "me! Did you think I was dead too? We are not so easy shut of our acquaintance."

"Hush, hush!" exclaimed the doctor. "Hush, hush! this meeting is so unexpected – I can see you are unmanned. I hardly knew you, I confess, at first; but I am overjoyed – overjoyed to have this opportunity. For the present it must be how-d'ye-do and good-bye in one, for my fly is waiting, and I must not fail the train; but you shall – let me see – yes – you shall give me your address, and you can count on early news of me. We must do something for you, Fettes. I fear you are out at elbows; but we must see to that for auld lang syne, as once we sang at suppers."

"Money!" cried Fettes; "money from you! The money that I had from you is lying where I cast it in the rain."

Dr. Macfarlane had talked himself into some measure of superiority and confidence, but the uncommon energy of this refusal cast him back into his first confusion.

A horrible, ugly look came and went across his almost venerable countenance. "My dear fellow," he said, "be it as you please; my last thought is to offend you. I would intrude on none. I will leave you my address, however – "

"I do not wish it – I do not wish to know the roof that shelters you," interrupted the other. "I heard your name; I feared it might be you; I wished to know if, after all, there were a God; I know now that there is none. Begone!"

He still stood in the middle of the rug, between the stair and the doorway; and the great London physician, in order to escape, would be forced to step to one side. It was plain that he hesitated before the thought of this humiliation. White as he was, there was a dangerous glitter in his spectacles; but while he still paused uncertain, he became aware that the driver of his fly was peering in from the street at this unusual scene and caught a glimpse at the same time of our little body from the parlour, huddled by the corner of the bar. The presence of so many witnesses decided him at once to flee. He crouched together, brushing on the wainscot, and made a dart like a serpent, striking for the door. But his tribulation was not yet entirely at an end, for even as he was passing Fettes clutched him by the arm and these words came in a whisper, and yet painfully distinct, "Have you seen it again?"

The great rich London doctor cried out aloud with a sharp, throttling cry; he dashed his questioner across the open space, and, with his hands over his head, fled out of the door like a detected thief. Before it had occurred to one of us to make a movement, the fly was already rattling toward the station. The scene was over like a dream, but the dream had left proofs and traces of its passage. Next day the servant found the fine gold spectacles broken on the threshold, and that very night we were all standing breathless by the bar-room window, and Fettes at our side, sober, pale, and resolute in look.

"God protect us, Mr. Fettes!" said the landlord, coming first into possession of his customary senses. "What in the universe is all this? These are strange things you have been saying."

Fettes turned toward us; he looked us each in succession in the face. "See if you can hold your tongues," said he. "That man Macfarlane is not safe to cross; those that have done so already have repented it too late."

And then, without so much as finishing his third glass, far less waiting for the other two, he bade us good-bye and went forth, under the lamp of the hotel, into the black night.

We three turned to our places in the parlour, with the big red fire and four clear candles; and as we recapitulated what had passed the first chill of our surprise soon changed into a glow of curiosity. We sat late; it was the latest session I have known in the old George. Each man, before we parted, had his theory that he was bound to prove; and none of us had any nearer business in this world than to track out the past of our condemned companion, and surprise the secret that he shared with the great London doctor. It is no great boast, but I believe I was a better hand at worming out a story than either of my fellows at the George; and perhaps there is now no other man alive who could narrate to you the following foul and unnatural events.

In his young days Fettes studied medicine in the schools of Edinburgh. He had talent of a kind, the talent that picks up swiftly what it hears and readily retails it for its own. He worked little at home; but he was civil, attentive, and intelligent in the presence of his masters. They soon picked him out as a lad who listened closely and remembered well; nay, strange as it seemed to me when I first heard it, he was in those days well favoured, and pleased by his exterior. There was, at that period, a certain extramural teacher of anatomy, whom I shall here designate by the letter K.[2] His name was subsequently too well known. The man who bore it skulked through the streets of Edinburgh in disguise, while the mob that applauded at the execution of Burke[3] called loudly for the blood of his employer. But Mr. K— was then at the top of his vogue; he enjoyed a popularity due partly to his own talent and address, partly to the incapacity of his rival, the university professsor. The students, at least, swore by his name, and Fettes believed himself, and was believed by others, to have laid the foundations of success when he had acquired the favour of this meteorically famous man. Mr. K— was a *bon vivant* as well as an accomplished teacher; he liked a sly allusion no less than a careful preparation. In both capacities Fettes enjoyed and deserved his notice, and by the second year of his attendance he held the half-regular position of second demonstrator or sub-assistant in his class.

In this capacity, the charge of the theatre and lecture room devolved in particular upon his shoulders. He had to answer for the cleanliness of the premises and the conduct of the other students, and it was a part of his duty to supply, receive, and divide the various subjects. It was with a view to this last – at that time very delicate – affair that he was lodged by Mr. K— in the same wynd, and at last in the same building, with the dissecting-rooms. Here, after a night of turbulent pleasures, his hand still tottering, his sight still misty and confused, he would be called out of bed in the black hours before the winter dawn by the unclean and desperate interlopers who supplied the table. He would open the door to these men, since infamous throughout the land. He would help them with their tragic burthen, pay them their sordid price, and remain alone, when they were gone, with the unfriendly relics of humanity. From such a scene he would return to snatch another hour or two of slumber, to repair the abuses of the night, and refresh himself for the labours of the day.

Few lads could have been more insensible to the impressions of a life thus passed among the ensigns of mortality. His mind was closed against all general considerations. He was incapable of interest in the fate and fortunes of another, the slave of his own desires and low ambitions. Cold, light, and selfish in the last resort, he had that modicum of prudence, miscalled morality, which keeps a man from inconvenient drunkenness or punishable theft. He coveted, besides, a measure of consideration from his masters and his fellow-pupils, and he had no desire to fail conspicuously in the external parts of life. Thus he made it his pleasure to gain some distinction in his studies, and day after day rendered unimpeachable eye-service to his employer, Mr. K—. For his day of work he indemnified himself by nights of roaring, blackguardly enjoyment; and when that balance had been struck, the organ that he called his conscience declared itself content.

The supply of subjects was a continual trouble to him as well as to his master. In that large and busy class, the raw material of the anatomists kept perpetually running out; and the business thus rendered necessary was not only unpleasant in itself, but threatened dangerous consequences to all who were concerned. It was the policy of Mr. K— to ask no questions in his dealings with the trade. "They bring the body, and we pay the price," he used to say, dwelling on the alliteration – "*quid pro quo.*" And, again, and somewhat profanely, "Ask no questions," he would tell his assistants, "for conscience' sake." There was no understanding that the subjects were provided by the crime of murder. Had that idea been broached to him in words, he would have recoiled in horror; but the lightness of his speech upon so grave a matter was, in itself, an offence against good manners, and a temptation to the men with whom he dealt. Fettes, for instance, had often remarked to himself upon the singular freshness of the bodies. He had been struck again and again by the hangdog, abominable looks of the ruffians who came to him before the dawn; and, putting things together clearly in his private thoughts, he perhaps attributed a meaning too immoral and too categorical to the unguarded counsels of his master. He understood his duty, in short, to have three branches: to take what was brought, to pay the price, and to avert the eye from any evidence of crime.

One November morning this policy of silence was put sharply to the test. He had been awake all night with a racking toothache – pacing his room like a caged beast or throwing himself in fury on his bed – and had fallen at last into that profound, uneasy slumber that so often follows on a night of pain, when he was awakened by the third or fourth angry repetition of the concerted signal. There was a thin, bright moonshine: it was bitter cold, windy, and frosty; the town had not yet awakened, but an indefinable stir already preluded the noise and business of the day. The ghouls had come later than usual, and they seemed more than usually eager to be gone. Fettes, sick with sleep, lighted them upstairs. He heard their grumbling Irish voices[4] through a dream; and as they stripped the sack from their sad merchandise he leaned dozing, with his shoulder propped against the wall; he had to shake himself to find the men their money. As he did so his eyes lighted on the dead face. He started; he took two steps nearer, with the candle raised.

"God Almighty!" he cried. "That is Jane Galbraith!"

The men answered nothing, but they shuffled nearer the door.

"I know her, I tell you," he continued. "She was alive and hearty yesterday. It's impossible she can be dead; it's impossible you should have got this body fairly."

"Sure, sir, you're mistaken entirely," said one of the men.

But the other looked at Fettes darkly in the eyes, and demanded the money on the spot.

It was impossible to misconceive the threat or to exaggerate the danger. The lad's heart failed him. He stammered some excuses, counted out the sum, and saw his hateful visitors depart. No sooner were they gone than he hastened to confirm his doubts. By a dozen unquestionable marks he identified the girl he had jested with the day before. He saw, with horror, marks upon her body that might well betoken violence. A panic seized him, and he took refuge in his room. There he reflected at length over the discovery that he had made; considered soberly the bearing of Mr. K—'s instructions and the danger to himself of interference in so serious a business, and at last, in sore perplexity, determined to wait for the advice of his immediate superior, the class assistant.[5]

This was a young doctor, Wolfe Macfarlane, a high favourite among all the reckless students, clever, dissipated, and unscrupulous to the last degree. He had travelled and studied abroad. His manners were agreeable and a little forward. He was an authority on the stage, skilful on the ice or the links with skate or golf-club; he dressed with nice audacity, and, to put the finishing touch upon his glory, he kept a gig and a strong trotting-horse. With Fettes he was on terms of intimacy; indeed, their relative positions called for some community of life; and when subjects were scarce the pair would drive far into the country in Macfarlane's gig, visit and desecrate some lonely graveyard, and return before dawn with their booty to the door of the dissecting room.

On that particular morning Macfarlane arrived somewhat earlier than his wont. Fettes heard him, and met him on the stairs, told him his story, and showed him the cause of his alarm. Macfarlane examined the marks on her body.

"Yes," he said with a nod, "it looks fishy."

"Well, what should I do?" asked Fettes.

"Do?" repeated the other. "Do you want to do anything? Least said soonest mended, I should say."

"Someone else might recognise her," objected Fettes. "She was as well known as the Castle Rock."

"We'll hope not," said Macfarlane, "and if anybody does – well, you didn't, don't you see, and there's an end. The fact is, this has been going on too long. Stir up the mud, and you'll get K— into the most unholy trouble; you'll be in a shocking box yourself. So will I, if you come to that. I should like to know how any one of us would look, or what the devil we should have to say for ourselves, in any Christian witness-box. For me, you know there's one thing certain – that, practically speaking, all our subjects have been murdered."

"Macfarlane!" cried Fettes.

"Come now!" sneered the other. "As if you hadn't suspected it yourself!"

"Suspecting is one thing – "

"And proof another. Yes, I know; and I'm as sorry as you are this should have come here," tapping the body with his cane. "The next best thing for me is not to recognise it; and," he added coolly, "I don't. You may, if you please. I don't dictate, but I think a man of the world would do as I do; and I may add, I fancy that is what K— would look for at our hands. The question is, Why did he choose us two for his assistants? And I answer, because he didn't want old wives."

This was the tone of all others to affect the mind of a lad like Fettes. He agreed to imitate Macfarlane. The body of the unfortunate girl was duly dissected, and no one remarked or appeared to recognise her.

One afternoon, when his day's work was over, Fettes dropped into a popular tavern and found Macfarlane sitting with a stranger. This was a small man, very pale and dark, with coal-black eyes. The cut of his features gave a promise of intellect and refinement which was but feebly realised in his manners, for he proved, upon a nearer acquaintance, coarse, vulgar, and stupid. He exercised, however, a very remarkable control over Macfarlane; issued orders like the Great Bashaw; became inflamed at the least discussion or delay, and commented rudely on the servility with which he was obeyed. This most offensive person took a fancy to Fettes on the spot, plied him with drinks, and honoured him with unusual confidences on his past career. If a tenth part of what he confessed were true, he was a very loathsome rogue; and the lad's vanity was tickled by the attention of so experienced a man.

"I'm a pretty bad fellow myself," the stranger remarked, "but Macfarlane is the boy – Toddy Macfarlane I call him. Toddy, order your friend another glass." Or it might be, "Toddy, you jump up and shut the door." "Toddy hates me," he said again. "Oh, yes, Toddy, you do!"

"Don't you call me that confounded name," growled Macfarlane.

"Hear him! Did you ever see the lads play knife? He would like to do that all over my body," remarked the stranger.

"We medicals have a better way than that," said Fettes. "When we dislike a dead friend of ours, we dissect him."

Macfarlane looked up sharply, as though this jest was scarcely to his mind.

The afternoon passed. Gray, for that was the stranger's name, invited Fettes to join them at dinner, ordered a feast so sumptuous that the tavern was thrown in commotion, and when all was done commanded Macfarlane to settle the bill. It was late before they separated; the man Gray was incapably drunk. Macfarlane, sobered by his fury, chewed the cud of the money he had been forced to squander and the slights he had been obliged to swallow. Fettes, with various liquors singing in his head, returned home with devious footsteps and a mind entirely in abeyance. Next day Macfarlane was absent from the class, and Fettes smiled to himself as he imagined him still squiring the intolerable Gray from tavern to tavern. As soon as the hour of liberty had struck he posted from place to place in quest of his last night's companions. He could find them, however, nowhere; so returned early to his rooms, went early to bed, and slept the sleep of the just.

At four in the morning he was awakened by the well-known signal. Descending to the door, he was filled with astonishment to find Macfarlane with his gig, and in the gig one of those long and ghastly packages with which he was so well acquainted.

"What?" he cried. "Have you been out alone? How did you manage?"

But Macfarlane silenced him roughly, bidding him turn to business. When they had got the body upstairs and laid it on the table, Macfarlane made at first as if he were going away. Then he paused and seemed to hesitate; and then, "You had better look at the face," said he, in tones of some constraint. "You had better," he repeated, as Fettes only stared at him in wonder.

"But where, and how, and when did you come by it?" cried the other.

"Look at the face," was the only answer.

Fettes was staggered; strange doubts assailed him. He looked from the young doctor to the body, and then back again. At last, with a start, he did as he was bidden. He had almost expected the sight that met his eyes, and yet the shock was cruel. To see, fixed in the rigidity of death and naked on that coarse layer of sack-cloth, the man whom he had left well-clad and full of meat and sin upon the threshold of a tavern, awoke, even in the thoughtless Fettes, some of the terrors of the conscience. It was a *cras tibi* which re-echoed in his soul, that two whom he had known should have come to lie upon these icy tables. Yet these were only secondary thoughts. His first concern regarded Wolfe. Unprepared for a challenge so momentous, he knew not how to look his comrade in the face. He durst not meet his eye, and he had neither words nor voice at his command.

It was Macfarlane himself who made the first advance. He came up quietly behind and laid his hand gently but firmly on the other's shoulder.

"Richardson," said he, "may have the head."

Now Richardson was a student who had long been anxious for that portion of the human subject to dissect. There was no answer, and the murderer resumed: "Talking of business, you must pay me; your accounts, you see, must tally."

Fettes found a voice, the ghost of his own: "Pay you!" he cried. "Pay you for that?"

"Why, yes, of course you must. By all means and on every possible account, you must," returned the other. "I dare not give it for nothing, you dare not take it for nothing; it would compromise us both. This is another case like Jane Galbraith's. The more things are wrong the more we must act as if all were right. Where does old K— keep his money?"

"There," answered Fettes hoarsely, pointing to a cupboard in the corner.

"Give me the key, then," said the other, calmly, holding out his hand.

There was an instant's hesitation, and the die was cast. Macfarlane could not suppress a nervous twitch, the infinitesimal mark of an immense relief, as he felt the key between his fingers. He opened the cupboard, brought out pen and ink and a paper-book that stood in one compartment, and separated from the funds in a drawer a sum suitable to the occasion.

"Now, look here," he said, "there is the payment made – first proof of your good faith: first step to your security. You have now to clinch it by a second. Enter the payment in your book, and then you for your part may defy the devil."

The next few seconds were for Fettes an agony of thought; but in balancing his terrors it was the most immediate that triumphed. Any future difficulty seemed almost welcome if he could avoid a present quarrel with Macfarlane. He set down the candle which he had been carrying all the time, and with a steady hand entered the date, the nature, and the amount of the transaction.

"And now," said Macfarlane, "it's only fair that you should pocket the lucre. I've had my share already. By-the-by, when a man of the world falls into a bit of luck, has a few shillings extra in his pocket – I'm ashamed to speak of it, but there's a rule of conduct in the case. No treating, no purchase of expensive class-books, no squaring of old debts; borrow, don't lend."

"Macfarlane," began Fettes, still somewhat hoarsely, "I have put my neck in a halter to oblige you."

"To oblige me?" cried Wolfe. "Oh, come! You did, as near as I can see the matter, what you downright had to do in self-defence. Suppose I got into trouble, where would you be? This second little matter flows clearly from the first. Mr. Gray is the continuation of Miss Galbraith. You can't begin and then stop. If you begin, you must keep on beginning; that's the truth. No rest for the wicked."

A horrible sense of blackness and the treachery of fate seized hold upon the soul of the unhappy student.

"My God!" he cried, "but what have I done? and when did I begin? To be made a class assistant – in the name of reason, where's the harm in that? Service wanted the position; Service might have got it. Would he have been where I am now?"

"My dear fellow," said Macfarlane, "what a boy you are! What harm has come to you? What harm can come to you if you hold your tongue? Why, man, do you know what this life is? There are two squads of us – the lions and the lambs. If you're a lamb, you'll come to lie upon these tables like Gray or Jane Galbraith; if you're a lion, you'll live and drive a horse like me, like K——, like all the world with any wit or courage. You're staggered at the first. But look at K——! My dear fellow, you're clever, you have pluck. I like you, and K—— likes you. You were born to lead the hunt; and I tell you, on my honour and my experience of life, three days from now you'll laugh at all these scarecrows like a high-school boy at a farce."

And with that Macfarlane took his departure and drove off up the wynd in his gig to get under cover before daylight. Fettes was thus left alone with his regrets. He saw the miserable peril in which he stood involved. He saw, with inexpressible dismay, that there was no limit to his weakness, and that, from concession to concession, he had fallen from the arbiter of Macfarlane's destiny to his paid and helpless accomplice. He would have given the world to have been a little braver at the time, but it did not occur to him that he might still be brave. The secret of Jane Galbraith and the cursed entry in the day-book closed his mouth.

Hours passed; the class began to arrive; the members of the unhappy Gray were dealt out to one and to another, and received without remark. Richardson was made happy with the head; and before the hour of freedom rang Fettes trembled with exultation to perceive how far they had already gone toward safety.

For two days he continued to watch, with increasing joy, the dreadful process of disguise.

On the third day Macfarlane made his appearance. He had been ill, he said; but he made up for lost time by the energy with which he directed the students. To Richardson in particular he extended the most valuable assistance and advice, and that student, encouraged by the praise of the demonstrator, burned high with ambitious hopes, and saw the medal already in his grasp.

Before the week was out Macfarlane's prophecy had been fulfilled. Fettes had outlived his terrors and had forgotten his baseness. He began to plume himself upon his courage, and had so arranged the story in his mind that he could look back on these events with an unhealthy pride. Of his accomplice he saw but little. They met, of course, in the business of the class; they received their orders together from Mr. K—. At times they had a word or two in private, and Macfarlane was from first to last particularly kind and jovial. But it was plain that he avoided any reference to their common secret; and even when Fettes whispered to him that he had cast in his lot with the lions and foresworn the lambs, he only signed to him smilingly to hold his peace.

At length an occasion arose which threw the pair once more into a closer union. Mr. K— was again short of subjects; pupils were eager, and it was a part of this teacher's pretensions to be always well supplied. At the same time there came the news of a burial in the rustic graveyard of Glencorse. Time has little changed the place in question. It stood then, as now, upon a cross-road, out of call of human habitations, and buried fathom deep in the foliage of six cedar trees. The cries of the sheep upon the neighbouring hills, the streamlets upon either hand, one loudly singing among pebbles, the other dripping furtively from pond to pond, the stir of the wind in mountainous old flowering chestnuts, and once in seven days the voice of the bell and the old tunes of the precentor, were the only sounds that disturbed the silence around the rural church. The Resurrection Man – to use a by-name of the period – was not to be deterred by any of the sanctities of customary piety. It was part of his trade to despise and desecrate the scrolls and trumpets of old tombs, the paths worn by the feet of worshippers and mourners, and the offerings and the inscriptions of bereaved affection. To rustic neighbourhoods, where love is more than commonly tenacious, and where some bonds of blood or fellowship unite the entire society of a parish, the body-snatcher, far from being repelled by natural respect, was attracted by the ease and safety of the task. To bodies that had been laid in earth, in joyful expectation of a far different awakening, there came that hasty, lamp-lit, terror-haunted resurrection of the spade and mattock. The coffin was forced, the cerements torn, and the melancholy relics, clad in sackcloth, after being rattled for hours on moonless by-ways, were at length exposed to uttermost indignities before a class of gaping boys.

Somewhat as two vultures may swoop upon a dying lamb, Fettes and Macfarlane were to be let loose upon a grave in that green and quiet resting-place. The wife of a farmer, a woman who had lived for sixty years, and been known for nothing but good butter and a godly conversation, was to be rooted from her grave at midnight and carried, dead and naked, to that far-away city that she had always honoured with her Sunday best; the place beside her family was to be empty till the crack of doom; her innocent and almost venerable members to be exposed to that last curiosity of the anatomist.

Late one afternoon the pair set forth, well wrapped in cloaks and furnished with a formidable bottle. It rained without remission – a cold, dense, lashing rain. Now and again there blew a puff of wind, but these sheets of falling water kept it down. Bottle and all, it was a sad and silent drive as far as Penicuik, where they were to spend the evening. They stopped once, to hide their implements in a thick bush not far from the churchyard, and once again at the Fisher's Tryst, to have a toast before the kitchen fire and vary their nips of whisky with a glass of ale. When they reached their journey's end the gig was housed, the horse was fed and comforted, and the two young doctors in a private room sat down to the best dinner and the best wine the house afforded. The lights, the fire, the beating rain upon the window, the cold, incongruous work that lay before them, added zest to their enjoyment of the meal. With every glass their cordiality increased. Soon Macfarlane handed a little pile of gold to his companion.

"A compliment," he said. "Between friends these little d—d accommodations ought to fly like pipe-lights."

Fettes pocketed the money, and applauded the sentiment to the echo. "You are a philosopher," he cried. "I was an ass till I knew you. You and K— between you, by the Lord Harry! but you'll make a man of me."

"Of course we shall," applauded Macfarlane. "A man? I tell you, it required a man to back me up the other morning. There are some big, brawling, forty-year-old cowards who would have turned sick at the look of the d—d thing; but not you – you kept your head. I watched you."

"Well, and why not?" Fettes thus vaunted himself. "It was no affair of mine. There was nothing to gain on the one side but disturbance, and on the other I could count on your gratitude, don't you see?" And he slapped his pocket till the gold pieces rang.

Macfarlane somehow felt a certain touch of alarm at these unpleasant words. He may have regretted that he had taught his young companion so successfully, but he had no time to interfere, for the other noisily continued in this boastful strain:

"The great thing is not to be afraid. Now, between you and me, I don't want to hang – that's practical; but for all cant, Macfarlane, I was born with a contempt. Hell, God, Devil, right, wrong, sin, crime, and all the old gallery of curiosities – they may frighten boys, but men of the world, like you and me, despise them. Here's to the memory of Gray!"

It was by this time growing somewhat late. The gig, according to order, was brought round to the door with both lamps brightly shining, and the young men had to pay their bill and take the road. They announced that they were bound for Peebles, and drove in that direction till they were clear of the last houses of the town; then, extinguishing the lamps, returned upon their course, and followed a by-road toward Glencorse. There was no sound but that of their own passage, and the incessant, strident pouring of the rain. It was pitch dark; here and there a white gate or a white stone in the wall guided them for a short space across the night; but for the most part it was at a foot pace, and almost groping, that they picked their way through that resonant blackness to their solemn and isolated destination. In the sunken woods that traverse the neighbourhood of the burying-ground the last glimmer failed them, and it became necessary to kindle a match and reillumine one of the lanterns of the gig. Thus, under the dripping trees, and environed by huge and moving shadows, they reached the scene of their unhallowed labours.

They were both experienced in such affairs, and powerful with the spade; and they had scarce been twenty minutes at their task before they were rewarded by a dull rattle on the coffin lid. At the same moment Macfarlane, having hurt his hand upon a stone, flung it carelessly above his head. The grave, in which they now stood almost to the shoulders, was close to the edge of the plateau of the graveyard; and the gig lamp had been propped, the better to illuminate their labours, against a tree, and on the immediate verge of the steep bank descending to the stream. Chance had taken a sure aim with the stone. Then came a clang of broken glass; night fell upon them; sounds alternatively dull and ringing announced the bounding of the lantern down the bank, and its occasional collision with the trees. A stone or two, which it had dislodged in its descent, rattled behind it into the profundities of the glen; and then silence, like night, resumed its sway; and they might bend their hearing to its utmost pitch, but naught was to be heard except the rain, now marching to the wind, now steadily falling over miles of open country.

They were so nearly at an end of their abhorred task that they judged it wisest to complete it in the dark. The coffin was exhumed and broken open; the body inserted in the dripping sack and carried between them to the gig; one mounted to keep it in its place, and the other, taking the horse by the mouth, groped along by wall and bush until they reached the wider road by the Fisher's Tryst. Here was a faint, diffused radiancy, which they hailed like daylight; by that they pushed the horse to a good pace and began to rattle along merrily in the direction of the town.

They had both been wetted to the skin during their operations, and now, as the gig jumped among the deep ruts, the thing that stood propped between them fell now upon one and now upon the other. At every repetition of the horrid contact each instinctively repelled it with greater haste; and the process, natural although it was, began to tell upon the nerves of the companions. Macfarlane made some ill-favoured jest about the farmer's wife, but it came hollowly from his lips, and was allowed to drop in silence. Still their unnatural burthen bumped from side to side; and now the head would be laid, as if in confidence, upon their shoulders, and now the drenching sackcloth would flap icily about their faces. A creeping chill began to possess the soul of Fettes. He peered at the bundle, and it seemed somehow larger than at first. All over the countryside, and from every degree of distance, the farm dogs accompanied their passage with tragic ululations; and it grew and grew upon his mind that some unnatural miracle had been accomplished, that some nameless change had befallen the dead body, and that it was in fear of their unholy burden that the dogs were howling.

"For God's sake," said he, making a great effort to arrive at speech, "for God's sake, let's have a light!"

Seemingly, Macfarlane was affected in the same direction; for though he made no reply, he stopped the horse, passed the reins to his companion, got down, and proceeded to kindle the remaining lamp. They had by that time got no farther than the cross-road down to Auchendinny. The rain still poured as though the deluge were returning, and it was no easy matter to make a light in such a world of wet and darkness. When at last the flickering blue flame had been transferred to the wick and began to expand and clarify, and shed a wide circle of misty brightness round the gig, it became possible for the two young men to see each other and the thing they had along with them. The rain had moulded the rough sacking to the outlines of the body underneath; the head was distinct from the trunk, the shoulders plainly modelled; something at once spectral and human riveted their eyes upon the ghastly comrade of their drive.

For some time Macfarlane stood motionless, holding up the lamp. A nameless dread was swathed, like a wet sheet, about the body, and tightened the white skin upon the face of Fettes; a fear that was meaningless, a horror of what could not be, kept mounting to his brain. Another beat of the watch, and he had spoken. But his comrade forestalled him.

"That is not a woman," said Macfarlane, in a hushed voice.

"It was a woman when we put her in," whispered Fettes.

"Hold that lamp," said the other. "I must see her face."

And as Fettes took the lamp his companion untied the fastenings of the sack and drew down the cover from the head. The light fell very clear upon the dark, well-moulded features and smooth-shaven cheeks of a too familiar countenance, often beheld in dreams of both of these young men. A wild yell rang up into the night; each leaped from his own side into the roadway; the

HIGHLAND PARK PUBLIC LIBRARY

lamp fell, broke, and was extinguished; and the horse, terrified by this unusual commotion, bounded and went off toward Edinburgh at a gallop, bearing along with it, sole occupant of the gig, the body of the dead and long-dissected Gray.[6]

The Merry Men[1]

✳

CHAPTER I

Eilean Aros[2]

It was a beautiful morning in the late July when I set forth on foot for the last time for Aros. A boat had put me ashore the night before at Grisapol; I had such breakfast as the little inn afforded, and, leaving all my baggage till I had an occasion to come round for it by sea, struck right across the promontory with a cheerful heart.

I was far from being a native of these parts, springing, as I did, from an unmixed Lowland stock. But an uncle of mine, Gordon Darnaway, after a poor, rough youth, and some years at sea, had married a young wife in the islands; Mary Maclean she was called, the last of her family; and when she died in giving birth to a daughter, Aros, the sea-girt farm, had remained in his possession. It brought him in nothing but the means of life, as I was well aware; but he was a man whom ill-fortune had pursued; he feared, cumbered as he was with the young child, to make a fresh adventure upon life; and remained in Aros, biting his nails at destiny. Years passed over his head in that isolation, and brought neither help nor contentment. Meantime our family was dying out in the Lowlands; there is little luck for any of that race; and perhaps my father was the luckiest of all, for not only was he one of the last to die, but he left a son to his name and a little money to support it. I was a student of Edinburgh University, living well enough at my own charges, but without kith or kin; when some news of me found its way to Uncle Gordon on the Ross of Grisapol; and he, as he was a man who held blood thicker than water, wrote to me the day he heard of my existence, and taught me to count Aros as my home. Thus it was that I came to spend my vacations in that part of the country, so far from all society and comfort, between the codfish and the moorcocks; and thus it was that now, when I had done with my classes, I was returning thither with so light a heart that July day.

The Ross, as we call it, is a promontory neither wide nor high, but as rough as God made it to this day; the deep sea on either hand of it, full of rugged isles and reefs most perilous to seamen – all overlooked from the eastward by some very high cliffs and the great peak of Ben Kyaw. *The Mountain of the Mist*, they say the words signify in the Gaelic tongue; and it is well named. For that hilltop, which is more than three thousand feet in height, catches all the clouds that come blowing from the seaward; and, indeed, I used often to think that it must make them for itself; since when all heaven was clear to the sea-level, there would ever be a streamer on Ben Kyaw. It brought water, too, and was mossy* to the top in consequence. I have seen us sittng in broad sunshine on the Ross, and the rain falling black like crape upon the mountain. But the wetness of it made it often appear more beautiful to my eyes; for when the sun struck upon the hillsides, there were many wet rocks and watercourses that shone like jewels even as far as Aros, fifteen miles away.

The road that I followed was a cattle-track. It twisted so as nearly to double the length of my journey; it went over rough boulders so that a man had to leap from one to another, and through soft bottoms where the moss came nearly to the knee. There was no cultivation anywhere and not one house in the ten miles from Grisapol to Aros. Houses of course there were – three at least; but they lay so far on the one side or the other that no stranger could have found them from the track. A large part of the Ross is covered with big granite rocks, some of them larger than a two-roomed house, one beside another, with fern and deep heather in between them where the vipers breed. Any way the wind was, it was always sea-air, as salt as on a ship; the gulls were as free as moorfowl over all the Ross; and whenever the way rose a little, your eye would kindle with the brightness of the sea. From the very midst of the land, on a day of wind and high spring, I have heard the Roost roaring like a battle where it runs by Aros, and the great and fearful voices of the breakers that we call the Merry Men.

Aros itself – Aros Jay, I have heard the natives call it, and they say it means *the House of God* – Aros itself was not properly a piece of the Ross, nor was it quite an islet. It formed the south-

* Boggy [R.L.S.]

west corner of the land, fitted close to it, and was in one place only separated from the coast by a little gut of the sea, not forty feet across the narrowest. When the tide was full, this was clear and still, like a pool on a land river; only there was a difference in the weeds and fishes and the water itself was green instead of brown; but when the tide went out, in the bottom of the ebb, there was a day or two in every month when you could pass dryshod from Aros to the mainland. There was some good pasture, where my uncle fed the sheep he lived on; perhaps the feed was better because the ground rose higher on the islet than the main level of the Ross, but this I am not skilled enough to settle. The house was a good one for that country, two stories high. It looked westward over a bay, with a pier hard by for a boat, and from the door you could watch the vapours blowing on Ben Kyaw.

On all this part of the coast, and especially near Aros, these great granite rocks that I have spoken of go down together in troops into the sea, like cattle on a summer's day. There they stand, for all the world like their neighbours ashore; only the salt water sobbing between them instead of the quiet earth, and clots of sea-pink blooming on their sides instead of heather; and the great sea-conger to wreathe about the base of them instead of the poisonous viper of the land. On calm days you can go wandering between them in a boat for hours, echoes following you about the labyrinth; but when the sea is up, Heaven help the man that hears that caldron boiling.

Off the south-west end of Aros these blocks are very many, and much greater in size. Indeed, they must grow monstrously bigger out to sea, for there must be ten sea-miles of open water sown with them as thick as a country place with houses, some standing thirty feet above the tides, some covered, but all perilous to ships; so that on a clear, westerly blowing day, I have counted, from the top of Aros, the great rollers breaking white and heavy over as many as six-and-forty buried reefs. But it is nearer in shore that the danger is worst; for the tide, here running like a mill-race, makes a long belt of broken water – a *Roost* we call it – at the tail of the land. I have often been out there in a dead calm at the slack of the tide; and a strange place it is, with the sea swirling and combing up and boiling like the caldrons of a linn, and now and again a little dancing mutter of sound as though the *Roost* were talking to itself. But when the tide begins to run again, and above all in heavy weather, there is no man could take a boat

within half a mile of it, nor a ship afloat that could either steer
or live in such a place. You can hear the roaring of it six miles
away. At the seaward end there comes the strongest of the bubble;
and it's here that these big breakers dance together – the dance
of death, it may be called – that have got the name, in these parts,
of the Merry Men.[3] I have heard it said that they run fifty feet
high; but that must be the green water only, for the spray runs
twice as high as that. Whether they got the name from their
movements, which are swift and antic, or from the shouting they
make about the turn of the tide, so that all Aros shakes with it,
is more than I can tell.

The truth is, that in a south-westerly wind, that part of our archi-
pelago is no better than a trap. If a ship got through the reefs, and
weathered the Merry Men, it would be to come ashore on the south
coast of Aros, in Sandag Bay, where so many dismal things befell our
family, as I propose to tell. The thought of all these dangers, in
the place I knew so long, makes me particularly welcome the works
now going forward to set lights upon the headlands and buoys
along the channels of our iron-bound, inhospitable islands.

The country people had many a story about Aros, as I used
to hear from my uncle's man, Rorie, an old servant of the Mac-
leans, who had transferred his services without afterthought on
the occasion of the marriage. There was some tale of an unlucky
creature, a sea-kelpie, that dwelt and did business in some fearful
manner of his own among the boiling breakers of the Roost. A
mermaid had once met a piper on Sandag beach, and there sang
to him a long, bright midsummer's night, so that in the morning
he was found stricken crazy, and from thenceforward, till the day
he died, said only one form of words; what they were in the original
Gaelic I cannot tell, but they were thus translated: "Ah, the sweet
singing out of the sea." Seals that haunted on that coast have
been known to speak to man in his own tongue, presaging great
disasters. It was here that a certain saint first landed on his voyage
out of Ireland to convert the Hebrideans.[4] And, indeed, I think
he had some claim to be called a saint; for, with the boats of that
past age, to make so rough a passage, and land on such a ticklish
coast, was surely not far short of the miraculous. It was to him,
or to some of his monkish underlings who had a cell there, that
the islet owes its holy and beautiful name, the House of God.

Among these old wives' stories there was one which I was
inclined to hear with more credulity. As I was told, in that tempest

which scattered the ships of the Invincible Armada over all the north and west of Scotland, one great vessel came ashore on Aros, and before the eyes of some solitary people on a hilltop, went down in a moment with all hands, her colours flying even as she sank. There was some likelihood in this tale; for another of that fleet lay sunk on the north side, twenty miles from Grisapol. It was told, I thought, with more detail and gravity than its companion stories, and there was one particularity which went far to convince me of its truth: the name, that is, of the ship was still remembered, and sounded, in my ears, Spanishly. The *Espirito Santo* they called it, a great ship of many decks of guns, laden with treasure and grandees of Spain, and fierce soldadoes, that now lay fathom deep to all eternity, done with her wars and voyages, in Sandag Bay, upon the west of Aros. No more salvos of ordnance for that tall ship, the "Holy Spirit," no more fair winds or happy ventures; only to rot there deep in the sea-tangle and hear the shoutings of the Merry Men as the tide ran high about the island. It was a strange thought to me first and last, and only grew stranger as I learned the more of the way in which she had set sail with so proud a company, and King Philip, the wealthy king, that sent her on that voyage.

And now I must tell you, as I walked from Grisapol that day, the *Espirito Santo* was very much in my reflections. I had been favourably remarked by our then Principal in Edinburgh College, the famous writer, Dr. Robertson,[5] and by him had been set to work on some papers of an ancient date to rearrange and sift of what was worthless; and in one of these, to my great wonder, I found a note of this very ship, the *Espirito Santo*, with her captain's name, and how she carried a great part of the Spaniard's treasure, and had been lost upon the Ross of Grisapol; but in what particular spot, the wild tribes of that place and period would give no information to the King's inquiries.[6] Putting one thing with another, and taking our island tradition together with this note of old King Jamie's perquisitions after wealth,[7] it had come strongly on my mind that the spot for which he sought in vain could be no other than the small bay of Sandag on my uncle's land; and being a fellow of a mechanical turn, I had ever since been plotting how to weigh that good ship up again with all her ingots, ounces, and doubloons, and bring back our house of Darnaway to its long-forgotten dignity and wealth.

This was a design of which I soon had reason to repent. My

mind was sharply turned on different reflections; and since I became the witness of a strange judgment of God's, the thought of dead men's treasures has been intolerable to my conscience. But even at that time I must acquit myself of sordid greed; for if I desired riches, it was not for their own sake, but for the sake of a person who was dear to my heart – my uncle's daughter, Mary Ellen. She had been educated well, and had been a time to school upon the mainland; which, poor girl, she would have been happier without. For Aros was no place for her with old Rorie the servant, and her father, who was one of the unhappiest men in Scotland, plainly bred up in a country place among Cameronians,[8] long a skipper sailing out of the Clyde about the islands, and now, with infinite discontent, managing his sheep and a little 'long-shore fishing for the necessary bread. If it was sometimes weariful to me, who was there but a month or two, you may fancy what it was to her who dwelt in that same desert all the year round, with the sheep and flying seagulls, and the Merry Men singing and dancing in the Roost!

CHAPTER II

What the wreck had brought to Aros

It was half-flood when I got the length of Aros; and there was nothing for it but to stand on the far shore and whistle for Rorie with the boat. I had no need to repeat the signal. At the first sound, Mary was at the door flying a handkerchief by way of answer, and the old long-legged serving-man was shambling down the gravel to the pier. For all his hurry, it took him a long while to pull across the bay; and I observed him several times to pause, go into the stern, and look over curiously into the wake. As he came nearer, he seemed to me aged and haggard, and I thought he avoided my eye. The coble had been repaired, with two new thwarts and several patches of some rare and beautiful foreign wood, the name of it unknown to me.

"Why, Rorie," said I, as we began the return voyage, "this is fine wood. How came you by that?"

"It will be hard to cheesel," Rorie opined reluctantly; and just then, dropping the oars, he made another of those dives into the stern which I had remarked as he came across to fetch me, and, leaning his hand on my shoulder, stared with an awful look into the waters of the bay.

"What is wrong?" I asked, a good deal startled.

"It will be a great feesh," said the old man, returning to his oars; and nothing more could I get out of him, but strange glances and an ominous nodding of the head. In spite of myself, I was infected with a measure of uneasiness; I turned also, and studied the wake. The water was still and transparent, but, out here in the middle of the bay, exceeding deep. For some time I could see naught; but at last it did seem to me as if something dark – a great fish, or perhaps only a shadow – followed studiously in the track of the moving coble. And then I remembered one of Rorie's superstitions: how in a ferry in Morven, in some great, exterminating feud among the clans, a fish, the like of it unknown in all our waters, followed for some years the passage of the ferry-boat, until no man dared to make the crossing.

"He will be waiting for the right man," said Rorie.

Mary met me on the beach, and led me up the brae and into the house of Aros. Outside and inside there were many changes. The garden was fenced with the same wood that I had noted in the boat; there were chairs in the kitchen covered with strange brocade; curtains of brocade hung from the window; a clock stood silent on the dresser; a lamp of brass was swinging from the roof; the table was set for dinner with the finest of linen and silver; and all these new riches were displayed in the plain old kitchen that I knew so well, with the highbacked settle, and the stools, and the closet-bed for Rorie; with the wide chimney the sun shone into, and the clear-smouldering peats; with the pipes on the mantelshelf and the three-cornered spittoons, filled with seashells instead of sand, on the floor; with the bare stone walls and the bare wooden floor, and the three patchwork rugs that were of yore its sole adornment – poor man's patchwork, the like of it unknown in cities, woven with homespun, and Sunday black, and seacloth polished on the bench of rowing. The room, like the house, had been a sort of wonder in that countryside, it was so neat and habitable; and to see it now, shamed by these incongruous additions, filled me with indignation and a kind of anger. In view of the errand I had come upon to Aros, the feeling was baseless and unjust; but it burned high, at the first moment, in my heart.

"Mary, girl", said I, "this is the place I had learned to call my home, and I do not know it."

"It is my home by nature, not by the learning," she replied; "the place I was born and the place I'm like to die in; and I neither like these changes, nor the way they came, nor that which came with them. I would have liked better, under God's pleasure, they had gone down into the sea, and the Merry Men were dancing on them now."

Mary was always serious; it was perhaps the only trait that she shared with her father; but the tone with which she uttered these words was even graver than of custom.

"Ay," said I, "I feared it came by wreck, and that's by death; yet when my father died, I took his goods without remorse."

"Your father died a clean-strae death, as the folk say," said Mary.

"True," I returned; "and a wreck is like a judgment. What was she called?"

"They ca'd her the *Christ-Anna*,"[9] said a voice behind me; and, turning round, I saw my uncle standing in the doorway.

He was a sour, small, bilious man, with a long face and very dark eyes; fifty-six years old, sound and active in body, and with an air somewhat between that of a shepherd and that of a man following the sea. He never laughed, that I heard; read long at the Bible; prayed much, like the Cameronians he had been brought up among; and indeed, in many ways, used to remind me of one of the hill-preachers in the killing times before the Revolution. But he never got much comfort, nor even, as I used to think, much guidance, by his piety. He had his black fits when he was afraid of hell; but he had led a rough life, to which he would look back with envy, and was still a rough, cold, gloomy man.

As he came in at the door out of the sunlight, with his bonnet on his head and a pipe hanging in his buttonhole, he seemed, like Rorie, to have grown older and paler, the lines were deeplier ploughed upon his face, and the whites of his eyes were yellow, like old stained ivory, or the bones of the dead.

"Ay," he repeated, dwelling upon the first part of the word, "the *Christ-Anna*. It's an awfu' name."

I made him my salutations, and complimented him upon his look of health; for I feared he had perhaps been ill.

"I'm in the body," he replied, ungraciously enough; "aye in the body and the sins of the body, like yoursel'. Denner," he said abruptly to Mary, and then ran on to me: "They're grand braws, thir that we hae gotten, are they no'? Yon's a bonny knock,* but it'll no gang; and the napery's by ordnar. Bonny, bairnly braws; it's for the like o' them folk sells the peace of God that passeth understanding; it's for the like o' them, an' maybe no' even sae muckle worth, folk daunton God to His face and burn in muckle hell; and it's for that reason the Scripture ca's them, as I read the passage, the accursed thing. Mary, ye girzie," he interrupted himself to cry with some asperity, "what for hae ye no' put out the twa candlesticks?"

"Why should we need them at high noon?" she asked. But my uncle was not to be turned from his idea. "We'll bruik† them while we may," he said; and so two massive candlesticks of wrought silver were added to the table equipage, already so unsuited to that rough seaside farm.

"She cam' ashore Februar' 10, about ten at nicht," he went on to me. "There was nae wind, and a sair run o' sea; and she was in the sook o' the Roost, as I jaloose. We had seen her a' day, Rorie and me, beating to the wind. She wasna a handy craft, I'm thinking, that *Christ-Anna*; for she would neither steer nor stey wi' them. A sair day they had of it; their hands was never aff the sheets, and it perishin' cauld – ower cauld to snaw; and aye they would get a bit nip o' wind, and awa' again, to pit the emp'y hope into them. Eh, man! but they had a sair day for the last o't! He would have had a prood, prood heart that won ashore upon the back o' that."

"And were all lost?" I cried. "God help them!"

"Wheesht!" he said sternly. "Nane shall pray for the deid on my hearth-stane."

I disclaimed a Popish sense for my ejaculation; and he seemed to accept my disclaimer with unusual facility, and ran on once more upon what had evidently become a favourite subject.

"We fand her in Sandag Bay, Rorie an' me, and a' thae braws in the inside of her. There's a kittle bit, ye see, about Sandag; whiles the sook rins strong for the Merry Men; an' whiles again, when the tide's makin' hard an' ye can hear the Roost blawin' at the far-end of Aros, there comes a back-spang of current straucht into Sandag Bay. Weel, there's the thing that got the grip on the *Christ-Anna*. She but to have come in ram-stam an' stern forrit; for the bows of her are aften under, and the back-side of her is clear at hie-water o' neaps. But, man! the dunt that she cam doon

* Clock [R.L.S.] † Enjoy [R.L.S.]

wi' when she struck! Lord save us a'! but it's an unco life to be a sailor – a cauld, wanchancy life. Mony's the gliff I got mysel' in the great deep; and why the Lord should hae made yon unco water is mair than ever I could win to understand. He made the vales and the pastures, the bonny green yaird, the halesome, canty land –

> And now they shout and sing to Thee,
> For Thou hast made them glad,

as the Psalms say in the metrical version.[10] No' that I would preen my faith to that clink neither; but it's bonny, and easier to mind. 'Who go to sea in ships,' they hae't again –

> and in
> Great waters trading be,
> Within the deep these men God's works
> And His great wonders see.[11]

Weel, it's easy sayin' sae. Maybe Dauvit wasna very weel acquaint wi' the sea. But troth, if it wasna prentit in the Bible, I wad whiles be temp'it to think it wasna the Lord, but the muckle, black deil that made the sea. There's naething good comes oot o't but the fish; an' the spentacle o' God riding on the tempest, to be shüre, whilk would be what Dauvit was likely ettling at. But, man, they were sair wonders that God showed to the *Christ-Anna* – wonders, do I ca' them? Judgments, rather: judgments in the mirk nicht among the draygons o' the deep. And their souls – to think o' that – their souls, man, maybe no prepared! The sea – a muckle yett to hell!"

I observed, as my uncle spoke, that his voice was unnaturally moved and his manner unwontedly demonstrative. He leaned forward at these last words, for example, and touched me on the knee with his spread fingers, looking up into my face with a certain pallor, and I could see that his eyes shone with a deep-seated fire, and that the lines about his mouth were drawn and tremulous.

Even the entrance of Rorie, and the beginning of our meal, did not detach him from his train of thought beyond a moment. He condescended, indeed, to ask me some questions as to my success at college, but I thought it was with half his mind; and even in his extempore grace, which was, as usual, long and wandering, I could find the trace of his preoccupation, praying, as he did, that God would "remember in mercy fower puir, feckless, fiddling sinful creatures here by their lee-lane beside the great and dowie waters."

Soon there came an interchange of speeches between him and Rorie.

"Was it there?" asked my uncle.

"Ou, ay!" said Rorie.

I observed that they both spoke in a manner of aside, and with some show of embarrassment, and that Mary herself appeared to colour, and looked down on her plate. Partly to show my knowledge, and so relieve the party from an awkward strain, partly because I was curious, I pursued the subject.

"You mean the fish?" I asked.

"Whatten fish?" cried my uncle. "Fish, quo' he! Fish! Your een are fu' o' fatness, man; your heid dozened wi' carnal leir. Fish! it's a bogle!"

He spoke with great vehemence, as though angry; and perhaps I was not very willing to be put down so shortly, for young men are disputatious. At least I remember I retorted hotly, crying out upon childish superstitions.

"And ye come frae the College!" sneered Uncle Gordon. "Gude kens what they learn folk there; it's no muckle service onyway. Do ye think, man, that there's naething in a' yon saut wilderness o' a world oot wast there, wi' the sea-grasses growin', an' the sea-beasts fechtin', an' the sun glintin' down into it, day by day? Na; the sea's like the land, but fearsomer. If there's folk ashore, there's folk in the sea – deid they may be, but they're folk whatever; and as for deils, there's nane that's like the sea-deils. There's no sae muckle harm in the land-deils, when a's said and done. Lang syne, when I was a callant in the south country, I mind there was an auld, bald bogle in the Peewie Moss. I got a glisk o' him mysel', sittin' on his hunkers in a hag, as grey 's a tombstane. An', troth, he was a fearsome-like taed. But he steered naebody. Nae doobt, if ane that was a reprobate, ane the Lord hated, had gane by there wi' his sin still upon his stamach, nae doobt the creature would hae lowped upo' the likes o' him. But there's deils in the deep sea would yoke on a communicant! Eh, sirs, if ye had gane doon wi' the puir lads in the *Christ-Anna*, ye would ken by now the mercy o' the seas. If ye had sailed it for as lang as me, ye would hate the thocht of it as I do. If ye had but used the een God gave ye, ye would hae learned the wickedness o' that fause, saut, cauld, bullering creature, and of a' that's in it by the Lord's permission: labsters an' partans, an' sic-like, howking in the deid; muckle, gutsy, blawing whales; an' fish – the hale clan o' them – cauld-wamed, blind-ee'd uncanny ferlies. Oh, sirs," he cried, "the horror – the horror o' the sea!"

We were all somewhat staggered by this outburst; and the speaker himself, after that last hoarse apostrophe, appeared to sink gloomily into his own thoughts. But Rorie, who was greedy of superstitious lore, recalled him to the subject by a question.

"You will not ever have seen a teevil of the sea?" he asked.

"No' clearly," replied the other, "I misdoobt if a mere man could see ane clearly and conteenue in the body. I hae sailed wi' a lad – they ca'd him Sandy Gabart; he saw ane, shüre eneuch, an' shüre eneuch it was the end of him. We were seeven days oot frae the Clyde – a sair wark we had had – gaun north wi' seeds an' braws an' things for Macleod. We had got in ower near under the Cutchull'ns, an' had just gane about by Soa, an' were off on a lang tack, we thocht would maybe hauld as far 's Copnahow. I mind the nicht weel; a mune smoored wi' mist; a fine gaun breeze upon the water, but no' steedy; an' – what nane o' us likit to hear – anither wund gurlin' owerheid, amang thae fearsome, auld stane craigs o' the Cutchull'ns. Weel, Sandy was forrit wi' the jib sheet; we couldna see him for the mains'l, that had just begude to draw, when a' at ance he gied a skirl. I luffed for my life, for I thocht we were ower near Soa; but na, it wasna that, it was puir Sandy Gabart's deid skreigh, or near-hand, for he was deid in half an hour. A 't he could tell was that a sea-deil, or sea-bogle, or sea-spenster, or sic-like, had clum up by the bowsprit, an' gi'en him ae cauld, uncanny look. An', or the life was oot o' Sandy's body, we kent weel what the thing betokened, and why the wund gurled in the taps o' the Cutchull'ns; for doon it cam' – a wund do I ca' it! it was the wund o' the Lord's anger – an' a' that nicht we foucht like men dementit, and the neist that we kenned we were ashore in Loch Uskevagh, an' the cocks were crawing in Benbecula."

"It will have been a merman," Rorie said.

"A merman!" screamed my uncle, with immeasurable scorn. "Auld wives' clavers! There's nae sic things as mermen."

"But what was the creature like?" I asked.

"What like was it? Gude forbid that we suld ken what like it was! It had a kind of a heid upon it – man could say nae mair."

Then Rorie, smarting under the affront, told several tales of mermen, mermaids, and sea-horses that had come ashore upon the islands and attacked the crews of boats upon the sea; and my uncle, in spite of incredulity, listened with uneasy interest.

"Aweel, aweel," he said, "it may be sae; I may be wrang; but I find nae word o' mermen in the Scriptures."

"And you will find nae word of Aros Roost, maybe," objected Rorie, and his argument appeared to carry weight.

When dinner was over, my uncle carried me forth with him to a bank behind the house. It was a very hot and quiet afternoon; scarce a ripple anywhere upon the sea, nor any voice but the familiar voice of sheep and gulls; and perhaps in consequence of this repose in nature, my kinsman showed himself more rational and tranquil than before. He spoke evenly and almost cheerfully of my career, with every now and then a reference to the lost ship or the treasures it had brought to Aros. For my part, I listened to him in a sort of trance, gazing with all my heart on that remembered scene, and drinking gladly the sea-air and the smoke of peats that had been lit by Mary.

Perhaps an hour had passed when my uncle, who had all the while been covertly gazing on the surface of the little bay, rose to his feet and bade me follow his example. Now I should say that the great run of tide at the south-west end of Aros exercises a perturbing influence round all the coast. In Sandag Bay, to the south, a strong current runs at certain periods of the flood and ebb respectively; but in this northern bay – Aros Bay, as it is called – where the house stands and on which my uncle was now gazing, the only sign of disturbance is towards the end of the ebb, and even then it is too slight to be remarkable. When there is any swell, nothing can be seen at all; but when it is calm, as it often is, there appear certain strange, undecipherable marks – sea runes, as we may name them – on the glassy surface of the bay. The like is common in a thousand places on the coast; and many a boy must have amused himself as I did, seeking to read in them some reference to himself or those he loved. It was to these marks that my uncle now directed my attention, struggling, as he did so, with an evident reluctance.

"Do ye see yon scart upo' the water?" he inquired; "yon ane wast the grey stane? Ay? Weel, it'll no' be like a letter, wull it?"

"Certainly it is," I replied. "I have often remarked it. It is like a C."

He heaved a sigh as if heavily disappointed with my answer, and then added below his breath: "Ay, for the *Christ-Anna*."

"I used to suppose, sir, it was for myself," said I; "for my name is Charles."

"And so ye saw 't afore?" he ran on, not heeding my remark. "Weel, weel, but that's unco strange. Maybe, it's been there waitin', as a man wad say, through a' the weary ages. Man, but that's awfu'." And then, breaking off: "Ye'll no' see anither, will ye?" he asked.

"Yes," said I. "I see another very plainly, near the Ross side, where the road comes down – an M."

"An M," he repeated very low; and then, again after another pause: "An' what wad ye make o' that?" he inquired.

"I had always thought it to mean Mary, sir," I answered, growing somewhat red, convinced as I was in my own mind that I was on the threshold of a decisive explanation.

But we were each following his own train of thought to the exclusion of the other's. My uncle once more paid no attention to my words: only hung his head and held his peace; and I might have been led to fancy that he had not heard me, if his next speech had not contained a kind of echo from my own.

"I would say naething o' thae clavers to Mary," he observed, and began to walk forward.

There is a belt of turf along the side of Aros Bay where walking is easy; and it was along this that I silently followed my silent kinsman. I was perhaps a little disappointed at having lost so good an opportunity to declare my love; but I was at the same time far more deeply exercised at the change that had befallen my uncle. He was never an ordinary, never, in the strict sense, an amiable, man; but there was nothing in even the worst that I had known of him before, to prepare me for so strange a transformation. It was impossible to close the eyes against one fact; that he had, as the saying goes, something on his mind; and as I mentally ran over the different words which might be represented by the letter M – misery, mercy, marriage, money, and the like – I was arrested with a sort of start by the word murder. I was still considering the ugly sound and fatal meaning of the word, when the direction of our walk brought us to a point from which a view was to be had to either side, back towards Aros Bay and homestead, and forward on the ocean, dotted to the north with isles, and lying to the southward blue and open to the sky. There my guide came to a halt, and stood staring for a while on that expanse. Then he turned to me and laid a hand on my arm.

"Ye think there's naething there?" he said, pointing with his pipe; and then cried out aloud, with a kind of exultation: "I'll tell ye, man! The deid are down there – thick like rattons!"

He turned at once, and, without another word, we retraced

our steps to the house of Aros.

I was eager to be alone with Mary; yet it was not till after supper, and then but for a short while, that I could have a word with her. I lost no time beating about the bush, but spoke out plainly what was on my mind.

"Mary," I said, "I have not come to Aros without a hope. If that should prove well founded, we may all leave and go somewhere else, secure of daily bread and comfort; secure, perhaps, of something far beyond that, which it would seem extravagant in me to promise. But there's a hope that lies nearer to my heart than money." And at that I paused. "You can guess fine what that is, Mary," I said. She looked away from me in silence, and that was small encouragement but I was not to be put off. "All my days I have thought the world of you," I continued; "the time goes on and I think always the more of you; I could not think to be happy or hearty in my life without you: you are the apple of my eye." Still she looked away, and said never a word; but I thought I saw that her hands shook. "Mary," I cried in fear, "do ye no' like me?"

"Oh, Charlie man," she said, "is this a time to speak of it? Let me be a while; let me be the way I am; it'll not be you that loses by the waiting!"

I made out by her voice that she was nearly weeping, and this put me out of any thought but to compose her. "Mary Ellen," I said, "say no more; I did not come to trouble you: your way shall be mine, and your time too; and you have told me all I wanted. Only just this one thing more: what ails you?"

She owned it was her father, but would enter into no particulars, only shook her head, and said he was not well and not like himself, and it was a great pity. She knew nothing of the wreck. "I havena been near it," said she. "What for would I go near it, Charlie lad? The poor souls are gone to their account long syne; and I would just have wished they had ta'en their gear with them – poor souls!"

This was scarcely any great encouragement for me to tell her of the *Espirito Santo*; yet I did so, and at the very first word she cried out in surprise. "There was a man at Grisapol," she said, "in the month of May – a little, yellow, black-avised body, they tell me, with gold rings upon his fingers, and a beard; and he was speiring high and low for that same ship."

It was towards the end of April that I had been given these papers to sort out by Dr. Robertson: and it came suddenly back upon my mind that they were thus prepared for a Spanish historian, or a man calling himself such, who had come with high recommendations to the Principal, on a mission of inquiry as to the dispersion of the great Armada. Putting one thing with another, I fancied that the visitor "with the gold rings upon his fingers" might be the same with Dr. Robertson's historian from Madrid. If that were so, he would be more likely after treasure for himself than information for a learned society. I made up my mind, I should lose no time over my undertaking; and if the ship lay sunk in Sandag Bay, as perhaps both he and I supposed, it should not be for the advantage of this ringed adventurer, but for Mary and myself, and for the good, old, honest, kindly family of the Darnaways.

CHAPTER III

Land and Sea in Sandag Bay

I was early afoot next morning; and as soon as I had a bite to eat, set forth upon a tour of exploration. Something in my heart distinctly told me that I should find the ship of the Armada; and although I did not give way entirely to such hopeful thoughts, I was still very light in spirits and walked upon air. Aros is a very rough islet, its surface strewn with great rocks and shaggy with fern and heather; and my way lay almost north and south across the highest knoll; and though the whole distance was inside of two miles, it took more time and exertion than four upon a level road. Upon the summit, I paused. Although not very high – not three hundred feet, as I think – it yet out-tops all the neighbouring lowlands of the Ross, and commands a great view of sea and islands. The sun, which had been up some time, was already hot upon my neck; the air was listless and thundery, although purely clear; away over the north-west, where the isles lie thickliest congregated, some half-a-dozen small and ragged clouds hung together in a covey; and the head of Ben Kyaw wore, not merely a few streamers, but a solid hood of vapour. There was a threat in the weather. The sea, it is true, was smooth like glass: even the Roost was but a seam in that wide mirror, and the Merry Men no more than caps of foam; but to my eye and ear, so long familiar with these places, the sea also seemed to lie uneasily; a sound of it, like a long sigh, mounted to me where I stood; and, quiet as it was, the Roost itself appeared to be revolving mischief. For I ought to say that all we dwellers in these parts attributed, if not prescience, at least a quality of warning, to that strange and dangerous creature of the tides.

I hurried on, then, with the greater speed, and had soon descended the slope of Aros to the part that we call Sandag Bay. It is a pretty large piece of water compared with the size of the isle; well sheltered from all but the prevailing wind; sandy and shoal and bounded by low sand-hills to the west, but to the east-ward lying several fathoms deep along a ledge of rocks. It is upon that side that, at a certain time each flood, the current mentioned by my uncle sets so strong into the bay; a little later, when the Roost begins to work higher, an undertow runs still more strongly in the reverse direction; and it is the action of this last, as I suppose, that has scoured that part so deep. Nothing is to be seen out of Sandag Bay but one small segment of the horizon and, in heavy weather, the breakers flying high over a deep sea-reef.

From half-way down the hill, I had perceived the wreck of February last, a brig of considerable tonnage, lying, with her back broken, high and dry on the east corner of the sands; and I was making directly towards it, and already almost on the margin of the turf, when my eyes were suddenly arrested by a spot, cleared of fern and heather, and marked by one of those long, low, and almost human-looking mounds that we see so commonly in grave-yards. I stopped like a man shot. Nothing had been said to me of any dead man or interment on the island; Rorie, Mary, and my uncle had all equally held their peace; of her at least, I was certain that she must be ignorant; and yet here, before my eyes, was proof indubitable of the fact. Here was a grave; and I had to ask myself, with a chill, what manner of man lay there in his last sleep, awaiting the signal of the Lord in that solitary, sea-beat resting-place? My mind supplied no answer but what I feared to entertain. Shipwrecked, at least, he must have been; perhaps, like the old Armada mariners, from some far and rich land over-sea; or perhaps one of my own race, perishing within eyesight of the smoke of home. I stood a while uncovered by his side, and I could have desired that it had lain in our religion to put up some prayer for that unhappy stranger or, in the old classic way, outwardly to honour his misfortune. I knew, although his bones lay there, a part of Aros, till the trumpet sounded, his imperishable soul was forth and far away, among the raptures of the everlasting Sabbath or the pangs of hell; and yet my mind misgave me even with a fear, that perhaps he was near me where I stood, guarding his sepulchre and lingering on the scene of his unhappy fate.

Certainly it was with a spirit somewhat overshadowed that I turned away from the grave to the hardly less melancholy spectacle of the wreck. Her stem was above the first arc of the flood; she was broken in two a little abaft the foremast – though indeed she had none, both masts having broken short in her disaster; and as the pitch of the beach was very sharp and sudden, and the bows lay many feet below the stern, the fracture gaped widely open, and you could see right through her poor hull upon the farther side. Her name was much defaced, and I could not make out clearly whether she was called *Christiania*, after the Norwegian city,[12] or *Christiana*, after the good woman, Christian's wife, in that old book the *Pilgrim's Progress*. By her build she was a foreign ship, but I was not certain of her nationality. She had been painted green, but the colour was faded and weathered, and the paint peeling off in strips. The wreck of the mainmast lay alongside, half-buried in sand. She was a forlorn sight, indeed, and I could not look without emotion at the bits of rope that still hung about her, so often handled of yore by shouting seamen; or the little scuttle where they had passed up and down to their affairs; or that poor noseless angel of a figure-head that had dipped into so many running billows.

I do not know whether it came most from the ship or from the grave, but I fell into some melancholy scruples, as I stood there, leaning with one hand against the battered timbers. The homelessness of men, and even of inanimate vessels, cast away upon strange shores, came strongly in upon my mind. To make a profit of such pitiful misadventures seemed an unmanly and a sordid act; and I began to think of my then quest as of something sacrilegious in its nature. But when I remembered Mary, I took heart again. My uncle would never consent to an imprudent marriage, nor would she, as I was persuaded, wed without his full approval. It behoved me, then, to be up and doing for my wife; and I thought with a laugh how long it was since that great sea-castle, the *Espirito Santo*, had left her bones in Sandag Bay, and how weak it would be to consider rights so long extinguished and misfortunes so long forgotten in the process of time.

I had my theory of where to seek for her remains. The set of the current and the soundings both pointed to the east side of the bay under the ledge of rocks. If she had been lost in Sandag Bay, and if, after these centuries, any portion of her held together, it was there that I should find it. The water deepens, as I have said, with great rapidity, and even close alongside the rocks several fathoms may be found. As I walked upon the edge I could see far and wide over the sandy bottom of the bay; the sun shone clear and green and steady in the deeps; the bay seemed rather like a great transparent crystal, as one sees them in a lapidary's shop; there was naught to show that it was water but an internal trembling, a hovering within of sun-glints and netted shadows, and now and then a faint lap and a dying bubble round the edge. The shadows of the rocks lay out for some distance at their feet, so that my own shadow, moving, pausing, and stopping on the top of that, reached sometimes half across the bay. It was above all in this belt of shadows that I hunted for the *Espirito Santo*; since it was there the undertow ran strongest, whether in or out. Cool as the whole water seemed this broiling day, it looked, in that part, yet cooler, and had a mysterious invitation for the eyes. Peer as I pleased, however, I could see nothing but a few fishes or a bush of sea-tangle, and here and there a lump of rock that had fallen from above and now lay separate on the sandy floor. Twice did I pass from one end to the other of the rocks, and in the whole distance I could see nothing of the wreck, nor any place but one where it was possible for it to be. This was a large terrace in five fathoms of water, raised off the surface of the sand to a considerable height, and looking from above like a mere outgrowth of the rocks on which I walked. It was one mass of great sea-tangles like a grove, which prevented me judging of its nature, but in shape and size it bore some likeness to a vessel's hull. At least it was my best chance. If the *Espirito Santo* lay not there under the tangles, it lay nowhere at all in Sandag Bay; and I prepared to put the question to the proof, once and for all, and either go back to Aros a rich man or cured for ever of my dreams of wealth.

I stripped to the skin, and stood on the extreme margin with my hands clasped, irresolute. The bay at that time was utterly quiet; there was no sound but from a school of porpoises somewhere out of sight behind the point; yet a certain fear withheld me on the threshold of my venture. Sad sea-feelings, scraps of my uncle's superstitions, thoughts of the dead, of the grave, of the old broken ships, drifted through my mind. But the strong sun upon my shoulders warmed me to the heart, and I stooped forward and plunged into the sea.

It was all that I could do to catch a trail of the sea-tangle that grew so thickly on the terrace; but once so far anchored I secured myself by grasping a whole armful of these thick and slimy stalks, and, planting my feet against the edge, I looked around me. On all sides the clear sand stretched forth unbroken; it came to the foot of the rocks, scoured into the likeness of an alley in a garden by the action of the tides; and before me, for as far as I could see, nothing was visible but the same many-folded sand upon the sun-bright bottom of the bay. Yet the terrace to which I was then holding was as thick with strong sea-growths as a tuft of heather, and the cliff from which it bulged hung draped below the water-line with brown lianas. In this complexity of forms, all swaying together in the current, things were hard to be distinguished; and I was still uncertain whether my feet were pressed upon the natural rock or upon the timbers of the Armada treasure-ship, when the whole tuft of tangle came away in my hand, and in an instant I was on the surface, and the shores of the bay and the bright water swam before my eyes in a glory of crimson.

I clambered back upon the rocks, and threw the plant of tangle at my feet. Something at the same moment rang sharply, like a falling coin. I stooped, and there, sure enough, crusted with the red rust, there lay an iron shoe-buckle. The sight of this poor human relic thrilled me to the heart, but not with hope nor fear, only with a desolate melancholy. I held it in my hand, and the thought of its owner appeared before me like the presence of an actual man. His weather-beaten face, his sailor's hands, his sea-voice hoarse with singing at the capstan, the very foot that had once worn that buckle and trod so much along the swerving decks – the whole human fact of him, as a creature like myself, with hair and blood and seeing eyes, haunted me in that sunny, solitary place, not like a spectre, but like some friend whom I had basely injured. Was the great treasure-ship indeed below there, with her guns and chain and treasure, as she had sailed from Spain; her decks a garden for the sea-weed, her cabin a breeding-place for fish, soundless but for the dredging water, motionless but for the waving of the tangle upon her battlements – that old, populous, sea-riding castle, now a reef in Sandag Bay? Or, as I thought it likelier, was this a waif from the disaster of the foreign brig – was this shoe-buckle bought but the other day and worn by a man of my own period in the world's history, hearing the same news from day to day, thinking the same thoughts, praying, perhaps, in the same temple with myself? However it was, I was assailed with dreary thoughts; my uncle's words, "the dead are down there," echoed in my ears; and though I determined to dive once more, it was with a strong repugnance that I stepped forward to the margin of the rocks.

A great change passed at that moment over the appearance of the bay. It was no more that clear, visible interior, like a house roofed with glass, where the green submarine sunshine slept so stilly. A breeze, I suppose, had flawed the surface, and a sort of trouble and blackness filled its bosom, where flashes of light and clouds of shadow tossed confusedly together. Even the terrace below obscurely rocked and quivered. It seemed a graver thing to venture on this place of ambushes; and when I leaped into the sea the second time it was with a quaking in my soul.

I secured myself as at first, and groped among the waving tangle. All that met my touch was cold and soft and gluey. The thicket was alive with crabs and lobsters, trundling to and fro lop-sidedly, and I had to harden my heart against the horror of their carrion neighbourhood. On all sides I could feel the grain and the clefts of hard, living stone; no planks, no iron, not a sign of any wreck; the *Espirito Santo* was not there. I remember I had almost a sense of relief in my disappointment, and I was about ready to leave go, when something happened that sent me to the surface with my heart in my mouth. I had already stayed somewhat late over my explorations; the current was freshening with the change of the tide, and Sandag Bay was no longer a safe place for a single swimmer. Well, just at the last moment there came a sudden flush of current, dredging through the tangles like a wave. I lost one hold, was flung sprawling on my side, and, instinctively grasping for a fresh support, my fingers closed on something hard and cold. I think I knew at that moment what it was. At least I instantly left hold of the tangle, leaped for the surface, and clambered out next moment on the friendly rocks with the bone of a man's leg in my grasp.

Mankind is a material creature, slow to think and dull to perceive connections. The grave, the wreck of the brig, and the rusty shoe-buckle were surely plain advertisements. A child might have read their dismal story, and yet it was not until I touched that actual piece of mankind that the full horror of the charnel ocean burst upon my spirit. I laid the bone beside the buckle, picked up my clothes, and ran as I was along the rocks towards the human shore. I could not be far enough from the spot; no fortune was vast enough to tempt me back again. The bones of the drowned dead should henceforth roll undisturbed by me, whether on tangle or minted gold. But as soon as I trod the good earth again and had covered my nakedness against the sun, I knelt down over against the ruins of the brig, and out of the fulness of my heart prayed long and passionately for all poor souls upon the sea. A generous prayer is never presented in vain; the petition may be refused, but the petitioner is always, I believe, rewarded by some gracious visitation. The horror, at least, was lifted from my mind; I could look with calm of spirit on that great bright creature, God's ocean; and as I set off homeward up the rough sides of Aros, nothing remained of any concern beyond a deep determination to meddle no more with the spoils of wrecked vessels or the treasures of the dead. [13]

I was already some way up the hill before I paused to breathe and look behind me. The sight that met my eyes was doubly strange.

For, first, the storm that I had foreseen was now advancing with almost tropical rapidity. The whole surface of the sea had been dulled from its conspicuous brightness to an ugly hue of corrugated lead; already in the distance the white waves, the "skipper's daughters," had begun to flee before a breeze that was still insensible on Aros; and already along the curve of Sandag Bay there was a splashing run of sea that I could hear from where I stood. The change upon the sky was even more remarkable. There had begun to arise out of the south-west a huge and solid continent of scowling cloud; here and there, through rents in its contexture, the sun still poured a sheaf of spreading rays; and here and there, from all its edges, vast inky streamers lay forth along the yet unclouded sky. The menace was express and imminent. Even as I gazed, the sun was blotted out. At any moment the tempest might fall upon Aros in its might.

The suddenness of this change of weather so fixed my eyes on heaven that it was some seconds before they alighted on the bay, mapped out below my feet, and robbed a moment later of the sun. The knoll which I had just surmounted overflanked a little amphitheatre of lower hillocks sloping towards the sea, and beyond that the yellow arc of beach and the whole extent of

Sandag Bay. It was a scene on which I had often looked down, but where I had never before beheld a human figure. I had but just turned my back upon it and left it empty, and my wonder may be fancied when I saw a boat and several men in that deserted spot. The boat was lying by the rocks. A pair of fellows, bareheaded, with their sleeves rolled up, and one with a boat-hook, kept her with difficulty to her moorings, for the current was growing brisker every moment. A little way off upon the ledge two men in black clothes, whom I judged to be superior in rank, laid their heads together over some task which at first I did not understand, but a second after I had made it out – they were taking bearings with the compass; and just then I saw one of them unroll a sheet of paper and lay his finger down, as though identifying features in a map. Meanwhile a third was walking to and fro, poking among the rocks and peering over the edge into the water. While I was still watching them with the stupefaction of surprise, my mind hardly yet able to work on what my eyes reported, this third person suddenly stooped and summoned his companions with a cry so loud that it reached my ears upon the hill. The others ran to him, even dropping the compass in their hurry, and I could see the bone and the shoe-buckle going from hand to hand, causing the most unusual gesticulations of surprise and interest. Just then I could hear the seamen crying from the boat, and saw them point westward to that cloud continent which was ever the more rapidly unfurling its blackness over heaven. The others seemed to consult; but the danger was too pressing to be braved, and they bundled into the boat carrying my relics with them, and set forth out of the bay with all speed of oars.

I made no more ado about the matter, but turned and ran for the house. Whoever these men were, it was fit my uncle should be instantly informed. It was not then altogether too late in the day for a descent of the Jacobites; and maybe Prince Charlie, whom I knew my uncle to detest, was one of the three superiors whom I had seen upon the rock. Yet as I ran, leaping from rock to rock, and turned the matter loosely in my mind, this theory grew ever the longer the less welcome to my reason. The compass, the map, the interest awakened by the buckle, and the conduct of that one among the strangers who had looked so often below him in the water, all seemed to point to a different explanation of their presence on that outlying, obscure islet of the western sea. The Madrid historian, the search instituted by Dr. Robertson, the bearded stranger with the rings, my own fruitless search that very morning in the deep water of Sandag Bay, ran together, piece by piece, in my memory, and I made sure that these strangers must be Spaniards in quest of ancient treasure and the lost ship of the Armada. But the people living in outlying islands, such as Aros, are answerable for their own security; there is none near by to protect or even to help them; and the presence in such a spot of a crew of foreign adventurers – poor, greedy, and most likely lawless – filled me with apprehensions for my uncle's money, and even for the safety of his daughter. I was still wondering how we were to get rid of them when I came, all breathless, to the top of Aros. The whole world was shadowed over; only in the extreme east, on a hill of the mainland, one last gleam of sunshine lingered like a jewel; rain had begun to fall, not heavily, but in great drops; the sea was rising with each moment, and already a band of white encircled Aros and the nearer coasts of Grisapol. The boat was still pulling seaward, but I now became aware of what had been hidden from me lower down – a large, heavily sparred, handsome schooner, lying-to at the south end of Aros. Since I had not seen her in the morning when I had looked around so closely at the signs of the weather, and upon these lone waters where a sail was rarely visible, it was clear she must have lain last night behind the uninhabited Eilean Gour, and this proved conclusively that she was manned by strangers to our coast, for that anchorage, though good enough to look at, is little better than a trap for ships. With such ignorant sailors upon so wild a coast, the coming gale was not unlikely to bring death upon its wings.

CHAPTER IV

The Gale

I found my uncle at the gable-end, watching the signs of the weather, with a pipe in his fingers.

"Uncle," said I, "there were men ashore at Sandag Bay – "

I had no time to go further; indeed, I not only forgot my words, but even my weariness, so strange was the effect on Uncle Gordon. He dropped his pipe and fell back against the end of the house with his jaw fallen, his eyes staring, and his long face as white as paper. We must have looked at one another silently for a quarter of a minute, before he made answer in this extraordinary fashion: "Had he a hair kep on?"

I knew as well as if I had been there that the man who now lay buried at Sandag had worn a hair cap, and that he had come ashore alive. For the first and only time I lost toleration for the man who was my benefactor and the father of the woman I hoped to call my wife.

"These were living men," said I, "perhaps Jacobites, perhaps the French, perhaps pirates, perhaps adventurers come here to seek the Spanish treasure-ship; but, whatever they may be, dangerous at least to your daughter and my cousin. As for your own guilty terrors, man, the dead sleeps well where you have laid him. I stood this morning by his grave; he will not wake before the trump of doom."

My kinsman looked upon me, blinking, while I spoke; then he fixed his eyes for a little on the ground and pulled his fingers foolishly; but it was plain that he was past the power of speech.

"Come," said I. "You must think for others. You must come up the hill with me, and see this ship."

He obeyed without a word or a look, following slowly after my impatient strides. The spring seemed to have gone out of his body, and he scrambled heavily up and down the rocks, instead of leaping, as he was wont, from one to another. Nor could I, for all my cries, induce him to make better haste. Only once he replied to me complainingly, and like one in bodily pain: "Ay, ay, man, I'm coming." Long before we had reached the top, I had no other thought for him but pity. If the crime had been monstrous, the punishment was in proportion.

At last we emerged above the sky-line of the hill, and could see around us. All was black and stormy to the eye; the last gleam of sun had vanished; a wind had sprung up, not yet high, but gusty and unsteady to the point; the rain, on the other hand, had ceased. Short as was the interval, the sea already ran vastly higher than when I had stood there last; already it had begun to break over some of the outward reefs, and already it moaned aloud in the sea-caves of Aros. I looked, at first in vain, for the schooner.

"There she is," I said at last. But her new position, and the course she was now lying, puzzled me. "They cannot mean to beat to sea," I cried.

"That's what they mean," said my uncle, with something like

joy; and just then the schooner went about and stood upon another tack which put the question beyond the reach of doubt. These strangers, seeing a gale on hand, had thought first of sea-room. With the wind that threatened, in these reef-sown waters and contending against so violent a stream of tide, their course was certain death.

"Good God!" said I, "they are all lost."

"Ay," returned my uncle, "a'—a' lost. They hadna a chance but to rin for Kyle Dona. The gate they're gaun the noo, they couldna win through an the muckle deil were there to pilot them. Eh, man," he continued, touching me on the sleeve, "it's a braw nicht for a shipwreck! Twa in ae twalmonth! Eh, but the Merry Men'll dance bonny!"

I looked at him, and it was then that I began to fancy him no longer in his right mind. He was peering up to me, as if for sympathy, a timid joy in his eyes. All that had passed between us was already forgotten in the prospect of this fresh disaster.

"If it were not too late," I cried with indignation, "I would take the coble and go out to warn them."

"Na, na," he protested, "ye maunna interfere; ye maunna meddle wi' the like o' that. It's His" – doffing his bonnet – "His wull. And, eh, man! but it's braw nicht for 't!"

Something like fear began to creep into my soul; and, reminding him that I had not yet dined, I proposed we should return to the house. But no; nothing would tear him from his place of outlook.

"I maun see the hail thing, man Charlie," he explained; and then as the schooner went about a second time, "Eh, but they han'le her bonny!" he cried. "The *Christ-Anna* was naething to this."

Already the men on board the schooner must have begun to realise some part, but not yet the twentieth, of the dangers that environed their doomed ship. At every lull of the capricious wind they must have seen how fast the current swept them back. Each tack was made shorter, as they saw how little it prevailed. Every moment the rising swell began to boom and foam upon another sunken reef; and ever and again a breaker would fall in sounding ruin under the very bows of her, and the brown reef and streaming tangle appear in the hollow of the wave. I tell you, they had to stand to their tackle; there was no idle man aboard that ship, God knows. It was upon the progress of a scene so horrible to any human-hearted man that my misguided uncle now pored and gloated like a connoisseur. As I turned to go down the hill, he was lying on his belly on the summit, with his hands stretched forth and clutching in the heather. He seemed rejuvenated, mind and body.

When I got back to the house already dismally affected, I was still more sadly downcast at the sight of Mary. She had her sleeves rolled up over her strong arms, and was quietly making bread. I got a bannock from the dresser and sat down to eat it in silence.

"Are ye wearied, lad?" she asked after a while.

"I am not so much wearied, Mary," I replied, getting on my feet, "as I am weary of delay, and perhaps of Aros too. You know me well enough to judge me fairly, say what I like. Well, Mary, you may be sure of this: you had better be anywhere but here."

"I'll be sure of one thing," she returned: "I'll be where my duty is."

"You forget, you have a duty to yourself," I said.

"Ay, man," she replied, pounding at the dough; "will you have found that in the Bible, now?"

"Mary," I said solemnly, "you must not laugh at me just now. God knows I am in no heart for laughing. If we could get your father with us, it would be best; but with him or without him, I want you far away from here, my girl; for your own sake, and for mine, ay, and for your father's too, I want you far – far away from here. I came with other thoughts; I came here as a man comes home; now it is all changed, and I have no desire nor hope but to flee – for that's the word – flee, like a bird out of the fowler's snare, from this accursed island."

She had stopped her work by this time.

"And do you think, now," said she, "do ye think, now, I have neither eyes nor ears? Do ye think I havena broken my heart to have these braws (as he calls them, God forgive him!) thrown into the sea? Do ye think I have lived with him, day in, day out, and not seen what you saw in an hour or two? No," she said, "I know there's wrong in it; what wrong, I neither know nor want to know. There was never an ill thing made better by meddling, that I could hear of. But, my lad, you must never ask me to leave my father. While the breath is in his body, I'll be with him. And he's not long for here, either: that I can tell you, Charlie – he's not long for here. The mark is on his brow; and better so – maybe better so."

I was a while silent, not knowing what to say; and when I roused my head at last to speak, she got before me.

"Charlie," she said, "what's right for me, needna be right for you. There's sin upon this house and trouble; you are a stranger; take your things upon your back and go your ways to better places and to better folk, and if you were ever minded to come back, though it were twenty years syne, you would find me aye waiting."

"Mary Ellen," I said, "I asked you to be my wife, and you said as good as yes. That's done for good. Wherever you are, I am; as I shall answer to my God."

As I said the words, the winds suddenly burst out raving, and then seemed to stand still and shudder round the house of Aros. It was the first squall, or prologue, of the coming tempest, and as we started and looked about us, we found that a gloom like the approach of evening, had settled round the house.

"God pity all poor folks at sea!" she said. "We'll see no more of my father till the morrow's morning."

And then she told me, as we sat by the fire and hearkened to the rising gusts, of how this change had fallen upon my uncle. All last winter he had been dark and fitful in his mind. Whenever the Roost ran high, or, as Mary said, whenever the Merry Men were dancing, he would lie out for hours together on the Head, if it were at night, or on the top of Aros by day, watching the tumult of the sea, and sweeping the horizon for a sail. After February the tenth, when the wealth-bringing wreck was cast ashore at Sandag, he had been at first unnaturally gay, and his excitement had never fallen in degree, but only changed in kind from dark to darker. He neglected his work, and kept Rorie idle. They two would speak together by the hour at the gable-end, in guarded tones and with an air of secrecy and almost of guilt; and if she questioned either, as at first she sometimes did, her inquiries were put aside with confusion. Since Rorie had first remarked the fish that hung about the ferry, his master had never set foot but once upon the mainland of the Ross. That once – it was in the height of the springs – he had passed dry-shod while the tide was out; but, having lingered over-long on the far side, found himself cut off from Aros by the returning waters. It was with a shriek of agony that he had leaped across the gut, and he had reached home thereafter in a fever-fit of fear. A fear of the sea, a constant haunting thought of the sea, appeared in his talk and devotions, and even in his looks when he was silent.

Rorie alone came in to supper; but a little later my uncle appeared, took a bottle under his arm, put some bread in his pocket, and set forth again to his outlook, followed this time by Rorie. I heard that the schooner was losing ground, but the crew were still fighting every inch with hopeless ingenuity and courage; and the news filled my mind with blackness.

A little after sundown the full fury of the gale broke forth, such a gale as I have never seen in summer, nor, seeing how swiftly it had come, even in winter. Mary and I sat in silence, the house quaking overhead, the tempest howling without, the fire between us sputtering with raindrops. Our thoughts were far away with the poor fellows on the schooner, or my not less unhappy uncle, house-less on the promontory; and yet ever and again we were startled back to ourselves, when the wind would rise and strike the gable like a solid body, or suddenly fall and draw away, so that the fire leaped into flame and our hearts bounded in our sides. Now the storm in its might would seize and shake the four corners of the roof, roaring like Leviathan in anger. Anon, in a lull, cold eddies of tempest moved shudderingly in the room, lifting the hair upon our heads and passing between us as we sat. And again the wind would break forth in a chorus of melancholy sounds, hooting low in the chimney, wailing with flutelike softness round the house.

It was perhaps eight o'clock when Rorie came in and pulled me mysteriously to the door. My uncle, it appeared, had frightened even his constant comrade; and Rorie, uneasy at his extravagance, prayed me to come out and share the watch. I hastened to do as I was asked; the more readily as, what with fear and horror, and the electrical tension of the night, I was myself restless and disposed for action. I told Mary to be under no alarm, for I should be a safeguard on her father; and wrapping myself warmly in a plaid, I followed Rorie into the open air.

The night, though we were so little past midsummer, was as dark as January. Intervals of a groping twilight alternated with spells of utter blackness; and it was impossible to trace the reason of these changes in the flying horror of the sky. The wind blew the breath out of a man's nostrils; all heaven seemed to thunder overhead like one huge sail; and when there fell a momentary lull on Aros, we could hear the gusts dismally sweeping in the distance. Over all the lowlands of the Ross, the wind must have blown as fierce as on the open sea; and God only knows the uproar that

was raging around the head of Ben Kyaw. Sheets of mingled spray
and rain were driven in our faces. All round the isle of Aros the
surf, with an incessant, hammering thunder, beat upon the reefs
and beaches. Now louder in one place, now lower in another, like
the combinations of orchestral music, the constant mass of sound
was hardly varied for a moment. And loud above all this hurly-burly
I could hear the changeful voices of the Roost and the intermittent
roaring of the Merry Men. At that hour, there flashed into my
mind the reason of the name that they were called. For the noise
of them seemed almost mirthful, as it out-topped the other noises
of the night; or if not mirthful, yet instinct with a portentous
joviality. Nay, and it seemed even human. As when savage men
have drunk away their reason, and, discarding speech, bawl
together in their madness by the hour; so, to my ears, these deadly
breakers shouted by Aros in the night.

Arm in arm, and staggering against the wind, Rorie and I
won every yard of ground with conscious effort. We slipped on
the wet sod, we fell together sprawling on the rocks. Bruised,
drenched, beaten, and breathless, it must have taken us near half
an hour to get from the house down to the Head that overlooks
the Roost. There, it seemed, was my uncle's favourite observatory.
Right in the face of it, where the cliff is highest and most sheer,
a hump of earth, like a parapet, makes a place of shelter from the
common winds, where a man may sit in quiet and see the tide
and the mad billows contending at his feet. As he might look
down from the window of a house upon some street disturbance,
so, from this post, he looks down upon the tumbling of the Merry
Men. On such a night, of course, he peers upon a world of blackness, where the waters wheel and boil, where the waves joust
together with the noise of an explosion, and the foam towers and
vanishes in the twinkling of an eye. Never before had I seen the
Merry Men thus violent. The fury, height, and transiency of their
spoutings was a thing to be seen and not recounted. High over
our heads on the cliff rose their white columns in the darkness;
and the same instant, like phantoms, they were gone. Sometimes
a gust took them, and the spray would fall about us, heavy as a
wave. And yet the spectacle was rather maddening in its levity
than impressive by its force. Thought was beaten down by the
confounding uproar; a gleeful vacancy possessed the brains of men,
a state akin to madness; and I found myself at times following the
dance of the Merry Men as it were a tune upon a jigging instrument.

I first caught sight of my uncle when we were still some yards away in one of the flying glimpses of twilight that chequered the pitch darkness of the night. He was standing up behind the parapet, his head thrown back and the bottle to his mouth. As he put it down, he saw and recognised us with a toss of one hand fleeringly above his head.

"Has he been drinking?" shouted I to Rorie.

"He will aye be drunk when the wind blaws," returned Rorie in the same high key, and it was all that I could do to hear him.

"Then – was he so – in February?" I inquired.

Rorie's "Ay" was a cause of joy to me. The murder, then, had not sprung in cold blood from calculation; it was an act of madness no more to be condemned than to be pardoned. My uncle was a dangerous madman, if you will, but he was not cruel and base as I had feared. Yet what a scene for a carouse, what an incredible vice was this that the poor man had chosen! I have always thought drunkenness a wild and almost fearful pleasure, rather demoniacal than human; but drunkenness, out here in the roaring blackness, on the edge of a cliff above that hell of waters, the man's head spinning like the Roost, his foot tottering on the edge of death, his ear watching for the signs of shipwreck, surely that, if it were credible in any one, was morally impossible in a man like my uncle, whose mind was set upon a damnatory creed and haunted by the darkest superstitions. Yet so it was; and, as we reached the bight of shelter and could breathe again, I saw the man's eye shining in the night with an unholy glimmer.

"Eh, Charlie man, it's grand!" he cried. "See to them!" he continued, dragging me to the edge of the abyss from whence arose that deafening clamour and those clouds of spray; "see to them dancin', man! Is that no' wicked?"

He pronounced the word with gusto, and I thought it suited the scene.

"They're yowlin' for thon schooner," he went on, his thin, insane voice clearly audible in the shelter of the bank, "an' she's comin' aye nearer, aye nearer, aye nearer an' nearer an' nearer; an' they ken't, the folk kens it, they ken weel it's by wi' them. Charlie, lad, they're a' drunk in yon schooner, a' dozened wi' drink. They were a' drunk in the *Christ-Anna*, at the hinder end. There's nane could droon at sea wantin' the brandy. Hoot awa, what do you ken?" with a sudden blast of anger. "I tell ye, it canna be; they daurna droon withoot it. Ha'e," holding out the bottle, "tak' a sowp."

I was about to refuse, but Rorie touched me as if in warning; and indeed I had already thought better of the movement. I took the bottle, therefore, and not only drank freely myself, but contrived to spill even more as I was doing so. It was pure spirit, and almost strangled me to swallow. My kinsman did not observe the loss, but, once more throwing back his head, drained the remainder to the dregs. Then, with a loud laugh, he cast the bottle forth among the Merry Men, who seemed to leap up, shouting, to receive it.

"Ha'e, bairns!" he cried, "there's your han'sel. Ye'll get bonnier nor that, or morning."

Suddenly, out in the black night before us, and not two hundred yards away, we heard, at a moment when the wind was silent, the clear note of a human voice. Instantly the wind swept howling down upon the Head, and the Roost bellowed, and churned, and danced with a new fury. But we had heard the sound, and we knew, with agony, that this was the doomed ship now close on ruin, and that what we had heard was the voice of her master issuing his last command. Crouching together on the edge, we waited, straining every sense, for the inevitable end. It was long, however, and to us it seemed like ages, ere the schooner suddenly appeared for one brief instant, relieved against a tower of glimmering foam. I still see her reefed mainsail flapping loose, as the boom fell heavily across the deck; I still see the black outline of the hull, and still think I can distinguish the figure of a man stretched upon the tiller. Yet the whole sight we had of her passed swifter than lightning; the very wave that disclosed her fell burying her for ever; the mingled cry of many voices at the point of death rose and was quenched in the roaring of the Merry Men. And with that the tragedy was at an end. The strong ship, with all her gear, and the lamp perhaps still burning in the cabin, the lives of so many men, precious surely to others, dear, at least, as heaven to themselves, had all, in that one moment, gone down into the surging waters. They were gone like a dream. And the wind still ran and shouted, and the senseless waters in the Roost still leaped and tumbled as before.

How long we lay there together, we three, speechless and motionless, is more than I can tell, but it must have been for long. At length, one by one, and almost mechanically, we crawled back into the shelter of the bank. As I lay against the parapet, wholly wretched and not entirely master of my mind, I could hear my kinsman maundering to himself in an altered and melancholy mood. Now he would repeat to himself with maudlin iteration, "Sic a fecht as they had – sic a sair fecht as they had, puir lads, puir lads!" and anon he would bewail that "a' the gear was as gude 's tint," because the ship had gone down among the Merry Men instead of stranding on the shore; and throughout, the name – the *Christ-Anna* – would come and go in his divagations, pronounced with shuddering awe. The storm all this time was rapidly abating. In half an hour the wind had fallen to a breeze, and the change was accompanied or caused by a heavy, cold, and plumping rain. I must then have fallen asleep, and when I came to myself, drenched, stiff, and unrefreshed, day had already broken, grey, wet, discomfortable day; the wind blew in faint and shifting capfuls, the tide was out, the Roost was at its lowest, and only the strong beating surf round all the coasts of Aros remained to witness of the furies of the night.

CHAPTER V

A man out of the sea

Rorie set out for the house in search of warmth and breakfast; but my uncle was bent upon examining the shores of Aros, and I felt it a part of duty to accompany him throughout. He was now docile and quiet, but tremulous and weak in mind and body; and it was with the eagerness of a child that he pursued his exploration. He climbed far down upon the rocks; on the beaches, he pursued the retreating breakers. The merest broken plank or rag of cordage was a treasure in his eyes to be secured at the peril of his life. To see him, with weak and stumbling footsteps, expose himself to the pursuit of the surf, or the snares and pitfalls of the weedy rock, kept me in a perpetual terror. My arm was ready to support him, my hand clutched him by the skirt, I helped him to draw his pitiful discoveries beyond the reach of the returning wave; a nurse accompanying a child of seven would have had no different experience.

Yet, weakened as he was by the reaction from his madness of the night before, the passions that smouldered in his nature were those of a strong man. His terror of the sea, although conquered for the moment, was still undiminished; had the sea been a lake of living flames, he could not have shrunk more panically from its touch; and once, when his foot slipped and he plunged to the mid-leg into a pool of water, the shriek that came up out of his soul was like the cry of death. He sat still for a while, panting like a dog, after that; but his desire for the spoils of shipwreck triumphed once more over his fears; once more he tottered among the curded foam; once more he crawled upon the rocks among the bursting bubbles; once more his whole heart seemed to be set on drift-wood, fit, if it was fit for anything, to throw upon the fire. Pleased as he was with what he found, he still incessantly grumbled at his ill-fortune.

"Aros," he said, "is no' a place for wrecks ava' – no' ava'. A' the years I've dwalt here, this ane maks the second; and the best o' the gear clean tint!"

"Uncle," said I, for we were now on a stretch of open sand, where there was nothing to divert his mind, "I saw you last night as I never thought to see you – you were drunk."

"Na, na," he said, "no' as bad as that. I had been drinking, though. And to tell ye the God's truth, it's a thing I canna mend. There's nae soberer man than me in my ordnar; but when I hear the wind blaw in my lug, it's my belief that I gang gyte."

"You are a religious man," I replied, "and this is sin."

"Ou," he returned, "if it wasna sin, I dinna ken that I would care for 't. Ye see, man, it's defiance. There's a sair spang o' the auld sin o' the warld in yon sea; it's an unchristian business at the best o't; an' whiles when it gets up, an' the wind skreighs – the wind an' her are a kind of sib, I'm thinking – an' thae Merry Men, the daft callants, blawin' and lauchin', and puir souls in the deid thraws warstlin' the leelang nicht wi' their bit ships – weel, it comes ower me like a glamour. I'm a deil, I ken 't. But I think naething o' the puir sailor lads; I'm wi' the sea, I'm just like ane o' her ain Merry Men."

I thought I should touch him in a joint of his harness. I turned me towards the sea; the surf was running gaily, wave after wave, with their manes blowing behind them, riding one after another up the beach, towering, curving, falling one upon another on the trampled sand. Without, the salt air, the scared gulls, the wide-spread army of the sea-chargers, neighing to each other, as they gathered together to the assault of Aros; and close before us, that line on the flat sands that, with all their number and their fury, they might never pass.

"Thus far shalt thou go," said I, "and no farther." And then I quoted as solemnly as I was able a verse that I had often before fitted to the chorus of the breakers:

"But yet the Lord that is on high,
Is more of might by far,
Than noise of many waters is,
Or great sea-billows are."[14]

"Ay," said my kinsman, "at the hinder end, the Lord will triumph; I dinna misdoobt that. But here on earth, even silly men-folk daur Him to His face. It is no' wise; I am no' sayin' that it's wise; but it's the pride of the eye, and it's the lust o' life, an' it's the wale o' pleesures."

I said no more, for we had now begun to cross a neck of land that lay between us and Sandag; and I withheld my last appeal to the man's better reason till we should stand upon the spot associated with his crime. Nor did he pursue the subject; but he walked beside me with a firmer step. The call that I had made upon his mind acted like a stimulant, and I could see that he had forgotten his search for worthless jetsam, in a profound, gloomy, and yet stirring train of thought. In three or four minutes we had topped the brae and begun to go down upon Sandag. The wreck had been roughly handled by the sea; the stem had been spun round and dragged a little lower down; and perhaps the stern had been forced a little higher, for the two parts now lay entirely separate on the beach. When we came to the grave I stopped, uncovered my head in the thick rain, and, looking my kinsman in the face, addressed him.

"A man," said I, "was in God's providence suffered to escape from mortal dangers; he was poor, he was naked, he was wet, he was weary, he was a stranger; he had every claim upon the bowels of your compassion; it may be that he was the salt of the earth, holy, helpful, and kind; it may be he was a man laden with iniquities to whom death was the beginning of torment. I ask you in the sight of Heaven: Gordon Darnaway, where is the man for whom Christ died?"

He started visibly at the last words; but there came no answer, and his face expressed no feeling but a vague alarm.

"You were my father's brother," I continued: "you have taught me to count your house as if it were my father's house; and we are both sinful men walking before the Lord among the sins and dangers of this life. It is by our evil that God leads us into good; we sin, I dare not say by His temptation, but I must say with His consent; and to any but the brutish man his sins are the beginning of wisdom. God has warned you by this crime; He warns you still by the bloody grave between our feet; and if there shall follow no repentance, no improvement, no return to Him, what can we look for but the following of some memorable judgment?"

Even as I spoke the words, the eyes of my uncle wandered from my face. A change fell upon his looks that cannot be described; his features seemed to dwindle in size, the colour faded from his cheeks, one hand rose waveringly and pointed over my shoulder into the distance, and the oft-repeated name fell once more from his lips: "The *Christ-Anna!*"

I turned; and if I was not appalled to the same degree, as I return thanks to Heaven that I had not the cause, I was still startled by the sight that met my eyes. The form of a man stood upright on the cabin-hutch of the wrecked ship; his back was towards us; he appeared to be scanning the offing with shaded eyes, and his figure was relieved to its full height, which was plainly very great, against the sea and sky. I have said a thousand times that I am not superstitious; but at that moment, with my mind running upon death and sin, the unexplained appearance of a stranger on that sea-girt, solitary island filled me with a surprise that bordered close on terror. It seemed scarce possible that any human soul should have come ashore alive in such a sea as had raged last night along the coasts of Aros; and the only vessel within miles had gone down before our eyes among the Merry Men. I was assailed with doubts that made suspense unbearable, and, to put the matter to the touch at once, stepped forward and hailed the figure like a ship.

He turned about, and I thought he started to behold us. At this my courage instantly revived and I called and signed to him to draw near, and he, on his part, dropped immediately to the sands and began slowly to approach, with many stops and hesitations. At each repeated mark of the man's uneasiness I grew the more confident myself; and I advanced another step, encouraging him as I did so with my head and hand. It was plain the castaway had heard indifferent accounts of our island hospitality; and indeed, about this time, the people farther north had a sorry reputation.

"Why," I said, "the man is black!"[15]

And just at that moment, in a voice that I could scarce have recognised, my kinsman began swearing and praying in a mingled stream. I looked at him; he had fallen on his knees, his face was agonised; at each step of the castaway's the pitch of his voice rose, the volubility of his utterance and the fervour of his language redoubled. I call it prayer, for it was addressed to God; but surely no such ranting incongruities were ever before addressed to the Creator by a creature: surely if prayer can be a sin, this mad harangue was sinful. I ran to my kinsman, I seized him by the shoulders, I dragged him to his feet.

"Silence, man," said I, "respect your God in words, if not in action. Here, on the very scene of your transgressions, He sends you an occasion of atonement. Forward and embrace it; welcome like a father yon creature who comes trembling to your mercy."

With that, I tried to force him towards the black; but he felled me to the ground, burst from my grasp, leaving the shoulder of his jacket, and fled up the hillside towards the top of Aros like a deer. I staggered to my feet again, bruised and somewhat stunned; the negro had paused in surprise, perhaps in terror, some half-way between me and the wreck; my uncle was already far away, bounding from rock to rock; and I thus found myself torn for a time between two duties. But I judged, and I pray Heaven that I judged rightly, in favour of the poor wretch upon the sands; his misfortune was at least not plainly of his own creation; it was one, besides, that I could certainly relieve; and I had begun by that time to regard my uncle as an incurable and dismal lunatic. I advanced accordingly towards the black, who now awaited my approach with folded arms, like one prepared for either destiny. As I came nearer, he reached forth his hand with a great gesture, such as I had seen from the pulpit, and spoke to me in something of a pulpit voice, but not a word was comprehensible. I tried him first in English, then in Gaelic, both in vain; so that it was clear we must rely upon the tongue of looks and gestures. Thereupon I signed to him to follow me, which he did readily and with a grave obeisance like a fallen king; all the while there had come no shade of alteration in his face, neither of anxiety while he was still waiting, nor of relief now that he was reassured; if he were a slave, as I supposed, I could not but judge he must have fallen from some high place in his own country, and fallen as he was, I could not but admire his bearing. As we passed the grave, I paused and raised my hands and eyes to heaven in token of respect and sorrow for the dead; and he, as if in answer, bowed low and spread his hands abroad; it was a strange motion, but done like a thing of common custom; and I supposed it was ceremonial in the land from which he came. At the same time he pointed to my uncle, whom he could just see perched upon a knoll, and touched his head to indicate that he was mad.

We took the long way round the shore, for I feared to excite my uncle if we struck across the island; and as we walked, I had time enough to mature the little dramatic exhibition by which I hoped to satisfy my doubts. Accordingly, pausing on a rock, I proceeded to imitate before the negro the action of the man whom I had seen the day before taking bearings with the compass at Sandag. He understood me at once, and, taking the imitation out of my hands, showed me where the boat was, pointed out seaward as if to indicate the position of the schooner, and then down along the edge of the rock with the words, "Espirito Santo," strangely pronounced, but clear enough for recognition. I had thus been right in my conjecture; the pretended historical inquiry had been but a cloak for treasure-hunting; the man who had played Dr. Robertson was the same as the foreigner who visited Grisapol in spring, and now, with many others, lay dead under the Roost of Aros; there had their greed brought them, there should their bones be tossed for evermore. In the meantime the black continued his imitation of the scene, now looking up skyward as though watching the approach of the storm; now, in the character of a seaman, waving the rest to come aboard; now as an officer, running along the rock and entering the boat; and anon bending over imaginary oars with the air of a hurried boatsman; but all with the same solemnity of manner, so that I was never even moved to smile. Lastly, he indicated to me, by a pantomime not to be described in words, how he himself had gone up to examine the stranded wreck, and, to his grief and indignation, had been deserted by his comrades; and thereupon folded his arms once more, and stooped his head, like one accepting fate.

The mystery of his presence being thus solved for me, I explained to him by means of a sketch the fate of the vessel and of all aboard her. He showed no surprise nor sorrow, and, with a sudden lifting of his open hand, seemed to dismiss his former friends or masters (whichever they had been) into God's pleasure. Respect came upon me and grew stronger, the more I observed him; I saw he had a powerful mind and a sober and severe character, such as I loved to commune with; and before we reached the house of Aros I had almost forgotten, and wholly forgiven him, his uncanny colour.

To Mary I told all that had passed without suppression, though I own my heart failed me; but I did wrong to doubt her sense of justice.

"You did the right," she said. "God's will be done." And she set out meat for us at once.

As soon as I was satisfied, I bade Rorie keep an eye upon the castaway, who was still eating, and set forth again myself to find my uncle. I had not gone far before I saw him sitting in the same place, upon the very topmost knoll, and seemingly in the same attitude as when I had last observed him. From that point, as I have said, the most of Aros and the neighbouring Ross would be spread below him like a map; and it was plain that he kept a bright look-out in all directions, for my head had scarcely risen above the summit of the first ascent before he had leaped to his feet and turned as if to face me. I hailed him at once, as well as I was able, in the same tones and words as I had often used before, when I had come to summon him to dinner. He made not so much as a movement in reply. I passed on a little farther, and again tried parley, with the same result. But when I began a second time to advance, his insane fears blazed up again, and still in dead silence, but with incredible speed, he began to flee from before me along the rocky summit of the hill. An hour before, he had been dead weary, and I had been comparatively active. But now his strength was recruited by the fervour of insanity, and it would have been vain for me to dream of pursuit. Nay, the very attempt, I thought, might have inflamed his terrors, and thus increased the miseries of our position. And I had nothing left but to turn homeward and make my sad report to Mary.

She heard it, as she had heard the first, with a concerned composure, and, bidding me lie down and take that rest of which I stood so much in need, set forth herself in quest of her misguided father. At that age it would have been a strange thing that put me from either meat or sleep; I slept long and deep; and it was already long past noon before I awoke and came down-stairs into the kitchen. Mary, Rorie, and the black castaway were seated about the fire in silence; and I could see that Mary had been weeping. There was cause enough, as I soon learned, for tears. First she, and then Rorie, had been forth to seek my uncle; each in turn had found him perched upon the hill-top, and from each in turn he had silently and swiftly fled. Rorie had tried to chase him, but in vain; madness lent a new vigour to his bounds; he sprang from rock to rock over the widest gullies; he scoured like the wind along the hill-tops; he doubled and twisted like a hare before the dogs; and Rorie at length gave in; and the last that he saw, my uncle was seated as before upon the crest of Aros. Even during the hottest excitement of the chase, even when the fleet-footed servant had come, for a moment, very near to capture him, the poor lunatic had uttered not a sound. He fled, and he was silent, like a beast; and this silence had terrified his pursuer.

There was something heart-breaking in the situation. How to capture the madman, how to feed him in the meanwhile, and what to do with him when he was captured, were the three difficulties that we had to solve.

"The black," said I, "is the cause of this attack. It may even be his presence in the house that keeps my uncle on the hill. We have done the fair thing; he has been fed and warmed under this roof; now I propose that Rorie put him across the bay in the coble, and take him through the Ross as far as Grisapol."

In this proposal Mary heartily concurred; and bidding the black follow us, we all three descended to the pier. Certainly, Heaven's will was declared against Gordon Darnaway; a thing had happened, never paralleled before in Aros; during the storm, the coble had broken loose, and striking on the rough splinters of the pier, now lay in four feet of water with one side stove in. Three days of work at least would be required to make her float. But I was not to be beaten. I led the whole party round to where the gut was narrowest, swam to the other side, and called to the black to follow me. He signed, with the same clearness and quiet as before, that he knew not the art; and there was truth apparent in his signals, it would have occurred to none of us to doubt his truth; and that hope being over, we must all go back even as we came to the house of Aros, the negro walking in our midst without embarrassment.

All we could do that day was to make one more attempt to communicate with the unhappy madman. Again he was visible on his perch; again he fled in silence. But food and a great cloak were at least left for his comfort; the rain, besides, had cleared away, and the night promised to be even warm. We might compose ourselves, we thought, until the morrow; rest was the chief requisite, that we might be strengthened for unusual exertions; and as none cared to talk, we separated at an early hour.

I lay long awake, planning a campaign for the morrow. I was to place the black on the side of Sandag, whence he should head my uncle towards the house; Rorie in the west, I on the east, were to complete the cordon, as best we might. It seemed to me, the more I recalled the configuration of the island, that it should be possible, though hard, to force him down upon the low ground along Aros Bay; and once there, even with the strength of his madness, ultimate escape was hardly to be feared. It was on his terror of the black that I relied; for I made sure, however he might run, it would not be in the direction of the man whom he supposed to have returned from the dead, and thus one point of the compass at least would be secure.

When at length I fell asleep, it was to be awakened shortly after by a dream of wrecks, black men, and submarine adventures; and I found myself so shaken and fevered that I arose, descended the stair, and stepped out before the house. Within, Rorie and the black were asleep together in the kitchen; outside was a wonderful clear night of stars, with here and there a cloud still hanging, last stragglers of the tempest. It was near the top of the flood, and the Merry Men were roaring in the windless quiet of the night. Never, not even in the height of the tempest, had I heard their song with greater awe. Now, when the winds were gathered home, when the deep was dandling itself back into its summer slumber, and when the stars rained their gentle light over land and sea, the voice of these tide-breakers was still raised for havoc. They seemed, indeed, to be a part of the world's evil and the tragic side of life. Nor were their meaningless vociferations the only sounds that broke the silence of the night. For I could hear, now shrill and thrilling and now almost drowned, the note of a human voice that accompanied the uproar of the Roost. I knew it for my kinsman's; and a great fear fell upon me of God's judgments, and the evil in the world. I went back again into the darkness of the house as into a place of shelter, and lay long upon my bed, pondering these mysteries.

It was late when I again awoke, and I leaped into my clothes and hurried to the kitchen. No one was there; Rorie and the black had both stealthily departed long before; and my heart stood still at the discovery. I could rely on Rorie's heart, but I placed no trust in his discretion. If he had thus set out without a word, he was plainly bent upon some service to my uncle. But what service

could he hope to render even alone, far less in the company of
the man in whom my uncle found his fears incarnated? Even if I
were not already too late to prevent some deadly mischief, it was
plain I must delay no longer. With the thought I was out of the
house; and often as I have run on the rough sides of Aros, I never
ran as I did that fatal morning. I do not believe I put twelve
minutes to the whole ascent.

My uncle was gone from his perch. The basket had indeed
been torn open and the meat scattered on the turf; but, as we
found afterwards, no mouthful had been tasted; and there was not
another trace of human existence in that wide field of view. Day
had already filled the clear heavens; the sun already lighted in a
rosy bloom upon the crest of Ben Kyaw; but all below me the rude
knolls of Aros and the shield of the sea lay steeped in the clear
darkling twilight of the dawn.

"Rorie!" I cried; and again "Rorie!" My voice died in the
silence, but there came no answer back. If there were indeed an
enterprise afoot to catch my uncle, it was plainly not in fleetness
of foot, but in dexterity of stalking, that the hunters placed their
trust. I ran on farther, keeping the higher spurs, and looking right
and left, nor did I pause again till I was on the mount above
Sandag. I could see the wreck, the uncovered belt of sand, the
waves idly beating the long ledge of rocks, and on either hand the
tumbled knolls, boulders, and gullies of the island. But still no
human thing.

At a stride the sunshine fell on Aros, and the shadows and
colours leaped into being. Not half a moment later, below me to
the west, sheep began to scatter as in a panic. There came a cry.
I saw my uncle running. I saw the black jump up in hot pursuit;
and before I had time to understand, Rorie also had appeared,
calling directions in Gaelic as to a dog herding sheep.

I took to my heels to interfere, and perhaps I had done better
to have waited where I was, for I was the means of cutting off the
madman's last escape. There was nothing before him from that
moment but the grave, the wreck, and the sea in Sandag Bay.
And yet Heaven knows that what I did was for the best.

My uncle Gordon saw in what direction, horrible to him,
the chase was driving him. He doubled, darting to the right and
left; but high as the fever ran in his veins, the black was still the
swifter. Turn where he would, he was still forestalled, still driven
toward the scene of his crime. Suddenly he began to shriek aloud,

so that the coast re-echoed; and now both I and Rorie were calling on the black to stop. But all was vain, for it was written otherwise. The pursuer still ran, the chase still sped before him screaming; they avoided the grave, and skimmed close past the timbers of the wreck; in a breath they had cleared the sand; and still my kinsman did not pause, but dashed straight into the surf; and the black, now almost within reach, still followed swiftly behind him. Rorie and I both stopped, for the thing was now beyond the hands of men, and these were the decrees of God that came to pass before our eyes. There was never a sharper ending. On that steep beach they were beyond their depth at a bound; neither could swim; the black rose once for a moment with a throttling cry; but the current had them, racing seaward; and if ever they came up again, which God alone can tell, it would be ten minutes after, at the far end of Aros Roost, where the sea-birds hover fishing.

The Misadventures of John Nicholson[1]

✳

CHAPTER I

In which John sows the wind

John Varey Nicholson was stupid; yet, stupider men than he are now sprawling in Parliament, and lauding themselves as the authors of their own distinction. He was of a fat habit, even from boyhood, and inclined to a cheerful and cursory reading of the face of life; and possibly this attitude of mind was the original cause of his misfortunes. Beyond this hint philosophy is silent on his career, and superstition steps in with the more ready explanation that he was detested of the gods.

His father – that iron gentleman – had long ago enthroned himself on the heights of the Disruption Principles.[2] What these are (and in spite of their grim name they are quite innocent) no array of terms would render thinkable to the merely English intelligence; but to the Scot they often prove unctuously nourishing, and Mr. Nicholson found in them the milk of lions. About the period when the Churches convene at Edinburgh in their annual assemblies, he was to be seen descending the Mound in the company of divers red-headed clergymen: these voluble, he only contributing oracular nods, brief negatives, and the austere spectacle of his stretched upper lip. The names of Candlish and Begg[3] were frequent in these interviews, and occasionally the talk ran on the Residuary Establishment[4] and the doings of one Lee.[5] A stranger to the tight little theological kingdom of Scotland might have listened and gathered literally nothing. And Mr. Nicholson (who was not a dull man) knew this, and raged at it. He knew there was a vast world outside, to whom Disruption Principles were as the chatter of tree-top apes; the paper brought him chill whiffs from it; he had met Englishmen who had asked lightly if he did not belong to the Church of Scotland, and then had failed to be much interested by his elucidation of that nice point; it was an evil, wild, rebellious world, lying sunk in *dozened ness*, for nothing short of a Scot's word will paint this Scotsman's feelings. And when he entered his own house in Randolph Crescent (south side), and shut the door behind him, his heart swelled with security. Here, at least, was a citadel unassailable by right-hand defections or left-hand extremes.[6] Here was a family where prayers came at the same hour, where the Sabbath literature was unimpeachably selected, where the guest who should have leaned to any false opinion was instantly set down, and over which there reigned all week, and grew denser on Sundays, a silence that was agreeable to his ear, and gloom that he found comfortable.[7]

Mrs. Nicholson had died about thirty, and left him with three children: a daughter two years and a son about eight years younger than John; and John himself, the unfortunate protagonist of the present history. The daughter, Maria, was a good girl – dutiful, pious, dull, but so easily startled that to speak to her was quite a perilous enterprise. "I don't think I care to talk about that, if you please," she would say, and strike the boldest speechless by her unmistakable pain; this upon all topics – dress, pleasure, morality, politics, in which the formula was changed to "my papa thinks otherwise," and even religion, unless it was approached with a particular whining tone of voice. Alexander, the younger brother, was sickly, clever, fond of books and drawing, and full of satirical remarks. In the midst of these, imagine that natural, clumsy, unintelligent, and mirthful animal, John; mighty well-behaved in comparison with other lads, although not up to the mark of the house in Randolph Crescent; full of a sort of blundering affection, full of caresses which were never very warmly received; full of sudden and loud laughter which rang out in that still house like curses. Mr. Nicholson himself had a great fund of humour, of the Scots order – intellectual, turning on the observation of men; his own character, for instance – if he could have seen it in another – would have been a rare feast to him; but his son's empty guffaws over a broken plate, and empty, almost light-hearted remarks, struck him with pain as the indices of a weak mind.

Outside the family John had early attached himself (much as a dog may follow a marquess) to the steps of Alan Houston, a lad about a year older than himself, idle, a trifle wild, the heir to a good estate which was still in the hands of a rigorous trustee, and so royally content with himself that he took John's devotion as a thing of course. The intimacy was gall to Mr. Nicholson; it took his son from the house, and he was a jealous parent; it kept him from the office, and he was a martinet; lastly, Mr. Nicholson was ambitious for his family (in which, and the Disruption Principles, he entirely lived), that he hated to see a son of his play second fiddle to an idler. After some hesitation, he ordered that the friendship should cease – an unfair command, though seemingly inspired by the spirit of prophecy; and John, saying nothing, continued to disobey the order under the rose.

John was nearly nineteen when he was one day dismissed rather earlier than usual from his father's office, where he was studying the practice of the law. It was Saturday; and except that he had a matter of four hundred pounds in his pocket which it was his duty to hand over to the British Linen Company's Bank, he had the whole afternoon at his disposal. He went by Princes Street, enjoying the mild sunshine, and the little thrill of easterly wind that tossed the flags along that terrace of palaces, and tumbled the green trees in the garden. The band was playing down in the valley under the castle; and when it came to the turn of the pipers, he heard their wild sounds with a stirring of the blood. Something distantly martial awoke in him; and he thought of Miss Mackenzie, whom he was to meet that day at dinner in his father's house.

Now, it is undeniable that he should have gone directly to the bank, but right in the way stood the billiard-room of the hotel where Alan was almost certain to be found; and the temptation proved too strong. He entered the billiard-room, and was instantly greeted by his friend, cue in hand.

"Nicholson," said he, "I want you to lend me a pound or two till Monday."

"You've come to the right shop, haven't you?" returned John. "I have twopence."

"Nonsense," said Alan. "You can get some. Go and borrow at your tailor's; they all do it. Or I'll tell you what: pop your watch."

"Oh, yes, I daresay," said John. "And how about my father?"

"How is he to know? He doesn't wind it up for you at night, does he?" inquired Alan, at which John guffawed. "No, seriously: I am in a fix," continued the tempter. "I have lost some money to a man here. I'll give it you to-night, and you can get the heirloom out again on Monday. Come; it's a small service, after all. I would do a good deal more for you."

Whereupon John went forth, and pawned his gold watch under the assumed name of John Froggs, 85 Pleasance. But the nervousness that assailed him at the door of that inglorious haunt – a pawnshop – and the effort necessary to invent the pseudonym (which somehow seemed to him a necessary part of the procedure), had taken more time that he imagined; and when he returned to the billiard-room with the spoils, the bank had already closed its doors.

This was a shrewd knock. "A piece of business had been neglected." He heard these words in his father's trenchant voice, and trembled, and then dodged the thought. After all, who was to know? He must carry four hundred pounds about with him till Monday, when the neglect could be surreptitiously repaired; and meanwhile, he was free to pass the afternoon on the encircling divan of the billiard-room, smoking his pipe, sipping a pint of ale, and enjoying to the mast-head the modest pleasures of admiration.

None can admire like a young man. Of all youth's passions and pleasures, this is the most common and least alloyed; and every flash of Alan's black eyes; every aspect of his curly head; every graceful reach, and easy, stand-off attitude of waiting, everything about him down even to his shirt-sleeves and wrist-links, were seen by John through a luxurious glory. He valued himself by the possession of that royal friend, hugged himself upon the thought, and swam in warm azure; his own defects, like vanquished difficulties, becoming things on which to plume himself. Only when he thought of Miss Mackenzie there fell upon his mind a shadow of regret; that young lady was worthy of better things than plain John Nicholson, still known among schoolmates by the derisive name of "Fatty"; and he felt that if he could chalk a cue or stand at ease, with such a careless grace as Alan, he could approach the object of his sentiments with a less crushing sense of inferiority.

Before they parted, Alan made a proposal that was startling in the extreme. He would be at Collette's that night about twelve, he said. Why should not John come there and get the money? To go to Collette's was to see life, indeed; it was wrong; it was against the laws; it partook, in a very dingy manner, of adventure. Were it known, it was the sort of exploit that disconsidered a young man for good with the more serious classes, but gave him a standing with the riotous. And yet Collette's was not a hell; it could not come, without vaulting hyperbole, under the rubric of a gilded saloon; and, if it was a sin to go there, the sin was merely local and municipal. Collette's (whose name I do not know how to spell, for I was never in epistolary communication with that hospitable outlaw) was simply an unlicensed publican, who gave suppers after eleven at night, the Edinburgh hour of closing. If you belonged to a club, you could get a much better supper at the same hour, and lose not a jot in public esteem. But if you lacked that qualification, and were an-hungered, or inclined towards conviviality at unlawful hours, Collette's was your only port. You were very ill-supplied. The company was not recruited from the Senate or the Church, though the Bar was very well represented on the only occasion on which I flew in the face of my country's laws, and, taking my reputation in my hand, penetrated into that grim supper-house. And Collette's frequenters, thrillingly conscious of wrong-doing and "that two-handed engine (the policeman) at the door," were perhaps inclined to somewhat feverish excess. But the place was in no sense a very bad one; and it is somewhat strange to me, at this distance of time, how it had acquired its dangerous repute.

In precisely the same spirit as a man may debate a project to ascend the Matterhorn or to cross Africa, John considered Alan's proposal, and, greatly daring, accepted it. As he walked home, the thoughts of this excursion out of the safe places of life into the wild and arduous, stirred and struggled in his imagination with the image of Flora Mackenzie – incongruous and yet kindred thoughts, for did not each imply unusual tightening of the pegs of resolution? did not each woo him forth and warn him back again into himself?

Between these two considerations, at least, he was more than usually moved; and when he got to Randolph Crescent, he quite forgot the four hundred pounds in the inner pocket of his greatcoat, hung up the coat, with its rich freight, upon his particular pin of the hat-stand; and in the very action sealed his doom.

CHAPTER II

In which John reaps the whirlwind

About half-past ten it was John's brave good fortune to offer his arm to Miss Mackenzie, and escort her home. The night was chill and starry; all the way east-ward the trees of the different gardens rustled and looked black. Up the stone gully of Leith Walk, when they came to cross it, the breeze made a rush and set the flames of the street-lamps quavering; and when at last they had mounted to the Royal Terrace, where Captain Mackenzie lived, a great salt freshness came in their faces from the sea. These phases of the walk remained written on John's memory, each emphasised by the touch of that light hand on his arm; and behind all these aspects of the nocturnal city he saw, in his mind's eye, a picture of the lighted drawing-room at home where he had sat talking with Flora; and his father, from the other end, had looked on with a kind and ironical smile. John had read the significance of that smile, which might have escaped a stranger. Mr. Nicholson had remarked his son's entanglement with satisfaction, tinged by humour; and his smile, if it still was a thought contemptuous, had implied consent.

At the captain's door the girl held out her hand, with a certain emphasis; and John took it and kept it a little longer, and said, "Good-night, Flora, dear," and was instantly thrown into much fear by his presumption. But she only laughed, ran up the steps, and rang the bell; and while she was waiting for the door to open, kept close in the porch, and talked to him from that point as out of a fortification. She had a knitted shawl over her head; her blue Highland eyes took the light from the neighbouring street-lamp and sparkled; and when the door opened and closed upon her, John felt cruelly alone.

He proceeded slowly back along the terrace in a tender glow; and when he came to Greenside Church, he halted in a doubtful mind. Over the crown of the Calton Hill, to his left, lay the way to Collette's, where Alan would soon be looking for his arrival, and where he would now have no more consented to go than he would have wilfully wallowed in a bog; the touch of the girl's hand on his sleeve, and the kindly light in his father's eyes, both loudly forbidding. But right before him was the way home, which pointed only to bed, a place of little ease for one whose fancy was strung to the lyrical pitch, and whose not very ardent heart was just then tumultuously moved. The hill-top, the cool air of the night, the company of the great monuments, the sight of the city under his feet, with its hills and valleys and crossing files of lamps, drew him by all he had of the poetic, and he turned that way; and by that quite innocent reflection, ripened the crop of his venial errors for the sickle of destiny.

On a seat on the hill above Greenside he sat for perhaps half an hour, looking down upon the lamps of Edinburgh, and up at the lamps of heaven. Wonderful were the resolves he formed; beautiful and kindly were the vistas of future life that sped before him. He uttered to himself the name of Flora in so many touching and dramatic keys, that he became at length fairly melted with tenderness, and could have sung aloud. At that juncture the sound of a certain creasing in his greatcoat caught his ear. He put his hand into his pocket, pulled for the envelope that held the money, and sat stupefied. The Calton Hill, about this period, had an ill name of nights; and to be sitting there with four hundred pounds that did not belong to him was hardly wise. He looked up. There was a man in a very bad hat a little on one side of him, apparently looking at the scenery; from a little on the other a second night-walker was drawing very quietly near. Up jumped John. The envelope fell from his hands; he stooped to get it, and at the same moment both men ran in and closed with him.

A little after, he got to his feet very sore and shaken, the poorer by a purse which contained exactly one penny postage-stamp, by a cambric handkerchief, and by the all-important envelope.

Here was a young man on whom, at the highest point of loverly exaltation, there had fallen a blow too sharp to be supported alone; and not many hundred yards away his greatest friend was sitting at supper – ay, and even expecting him. Was it not in the nature of man that he should run there? He went in quest of sympathy – in quest of that droll article that we all suppose ourselves to want when in a strait, and have agreed to call advice; and he went, besides, with vague but rather splendid expectations of relief. Alan was rich, or would be so when he came of age. By a stroke of the pen he might remedy this misfortune, and avert that dreaded interview with Mr. Nicholson, from which John now shrunk in imagination as the hand draws back from fire.

Close under the Calton Hill there runs a certain narrow avenue, part street, part by-road. The head of it faces the doors of the prison; its tail descends into the sunless slums of the Low Calton. On one hand it is overhung by the crags of the hill, on the other by an old grave-yard. Between these two the road-way runs in a trench, sparsely lighted at night, sparsely frequented by day, and bordered, when it has cleared the place of tombs, by dingy and ambiguous houses. One of these was the house of Collette; and at his door our ill-starred John was presently beating for admittance. In an evil hour he satisfied the jealous inquiries of the contraband hotelkeeper; in an evil hour he penetrated into the somewhat unsavoury interior. Alan, to be sure, was there, seated in a room lighted by noisy gas-jets, beside a dirty table-cloth, engaged on a coarse meal, and in the company of several tipsy members of the junior bar. But Alan was not sober; he had lost a thousand pounds upon a horse-race, had received the news at dinner-time, and was now, in default of any possible means of extrication, drowning the memory of his predicament. He to help John! The thing was impossible; he couldn't help himself.

"If you have a beast of a father," said he, "I can tell you I have a brute of a trustee."

"I'm not going to hear my father called a beast," said John, with a beating heart, feeling that he risked the last sound rivet of the chain that bound him for life.

But Alan was quite good-natured.

"All right, old fellow," said he. "Mos' respec'able man your father." And he introduced his friend to his companions as "old Nicholson the what-d'ye-call-um's son."

John sat in dumb agony. Collette's foul walls and maculate table-linen, and even down to Collette's villainous casters, seemed like objects in a nightmare. And just then there came a knock and a scurrying; the police, so lamentably absent from the Calton Hill, appeared upon the scene; and the party, taken *flagrante delicto*, with their glasses at their elbow, were seized, marched up to the police office, and all duly summoned to appear as witnesses in the consequent case against that arch-shebeener, Collette.

It was a sorrowful and a mightily sobered company that came forth again. The vague terror of public opinion weighed generally on them all; but there were private and particular horrors on the minds of individuals. Alan stood in dread of his trustee, already sorely tried. One of the group was the son of a country minister, another of a judge; John, the unhappiest of all, had David Nicholson to father, the idea of facing whom on such a scandalous subject was physically sickening. They stood a while consulting under the buttresses of Saint Giles; thence they adjourned to the lodgings of one of the number in North Castle Street, where (for that matter) they might have had quite as good a supper, and far better drink, than in the dangerous paradise from which they had been routed. There, over an almost tearful glass, they debated their position. Each explained he had the world to lose if the affair went on, and he appeared as a witness. It was remarkable what bright prospects were just then in the very act of opening before each of that little company of youths, and what pious consideration for the feelings of their families began now to well from them. Each, moreover, was in an odd state of destitution. Not one could bear his share of the fine; not one but evinced a wonderful twinkle of hope that each of the others (in succession) was the very man who could step in to make good the deficit. One took a high hand; he could not pay his share; if it went to a trial, he should bolt; he had always felt the English Bar to be his true sphere. Another branched out into touching details about his family, to which no one listened. John, in the midst of this disorderly competition of poverty and meanness, sat stunned, contemplating the mountain bulk of his misfortunes.

At last, upon a pledge that each should apply to his family with a common frankness, this convention of unhappy young asses broke up, went down the common stair, and in the grey of the spring morning, with the streets lying dead empty all about them, the lamps burning on into the daylight in indiminished lustre, and the birds beginning to sound premonitory notes from the groves of the town gardens, went each his own way with bowed head and echoing footfall.[8]

The rooks were awake in Randolph Crescent; but the windows looked down, discreetly blinded, on the return of the prodigal. John's pass-key was a recent privilege; this was the first time it had been used; and, oh! with what a sickening sense of his unworthiness he now inserted it into the well-oiled lock and entered that citadel of the proprieties! All slept; the gas in the hall had been left faintly burning to light his return; a dreadful stillness reigned, broken by the deep ticking of the eight-day clock. He put the gas out, and sat in a chair in the hall, waiting and counting the minutes, longing for any human countenance. But when at last he heard the alarm-clock spring its rattle in the lower story, and the servants begin to be about, he instantly lost heart, and fled to his own room, where he threw himself upon the bed.

CHAPTER III

In which John enjoys the harvest home

Shortly after breakfast, at which he assisted with a highly tragical countenance, John sought his father where he sat, presumably in religious meditation, on the Sabbath-mornings. The old gentleman looked up with that sour, inquisitive expression that came so near to smiling and was so different in effect.

"This is a time when I do not like to be disturbed," he said.

"I know that," returned John; "but I have – I want – I've made a dreadful mess of it," he broke out, and turned to the window.

Mr. Nicholson sat silent for an appreciable time, while his unhappy son surveyed the poles in the back green, and a certain yellow cat that was perched upon the wall. Despair sat upon John as he gazed; and he raged to think of the dreadful series of his misdeeds, and the essential innocence that lay behind them.

"Well," said his father, with an obvious effort, but in very quiet tones, "what is it?"

"Maclean gave me four hundred pounds to put in the bank, sir," began John; "and I'm sorry to say that I've been robbed of it!"

"Robbed of it?" cried Mr. Nicholson, with a strong rising inflection. "Robbed? Be careful what you say, John!"

"I can't say anything else, sir; I was just robbed of it," said John in desperation, sullenly.

"And where and when did this extraordinary event take place?" inquired the father.

"On the Calton Hill about twelve last night."

"The Calton Hill?" repeated Mr. Nicholson. "And what were you doing there at such a time of the night?"

"Nothing, sir," says John.

Mr. Nicholson drew in his breath.

"And how came the money in your hands at twelve last night?" he asked, sharply.

"I neglected that piece of business," said John, anticipating comment; and then in his own dialect: "I clean forgot all about it."

"Well," said his father, "it's a most extraordinary story. Have you communicated with the police?"

"I have," answered poor John, the blood leaping to his face.

"They think they know the men that did it. I daresay the money will be recovered, if that was all," said he, with a desperate indifference, which his father set down to levity; but which sprang from the consciousness of worse behind.

"Your mother's watch, too?" asked Mr. Nicholson.

"Oh, the watch is all right!" cried John. "At least, I mean I was coming to the watch – the fact is, I am ashamed to say, I – I had pawned the watch before. Here is the ticket; they didn't find that; the watch can be redeemed; they don't sell pledges." The lad panted out these phrases, one after another, like minute-guns; but at the last word, which rang in that stately chamber like an oath, his heart failed him utterly; and the dreaded silence settled on father and son.

It was broken by Mr. Nicholson picking up the pawn-ticket: "John Froggs, 85 Pleasance," he read; and then turning upon John, with a brief flash of passion and disgust, "Who is John Froggs?" he cried.

"Nobody," said John. "It was just a name."

"An *alias*," his father commented.

"Oh! I think scarcely quite that," said the culprit; "it's a form, they all do it, the man seemed to understand, we had a great deal of fun over the name – "

He paused at that, for he saw his father wince at the picture like a man physically struck; and again there was silence.

"I do not think," said Mr. Nicholson, at last, "that I am an ungenerous father. I have never grudged you money within reason, for any avowable purpose; you had just to come to me and speak. And now I find that you have forgotten all decency and all natural feeling, and actually pawned – pawned – your mother's watch. You must have had some temptation; I will do you the justice to suppose it was a strong one. What did you want with this money?"

"I would rather not tell you, sir," said John. "It will only make you angry."

"I will not be fenced with," cried his father. "There must be an end of disingenuous answers. What did you want with this money?"

"To lend it to Houston, sir," says John.

"I thought I had forbidden you to speak to that young man?" asked his father.

"Yes, sir," said John; "but I only met him."

"Where?" came the deadly question.

And "in a billiard-room" was the damning answer. Thus, had John's single departure from the truth brought instant punishment. For no other purpose but to see Alan would he have entered a billiard-room; but he had desired to palliate the fact of his disobedience, and now it appeared that he frequented these disreputable haunts upon his own account.

Once more Mr. Nicholson digested the vile tidings in silence; and when John stole a glance at his father's countenance, he was abashed to see the marks of suffering.

"Well," said the old gentleman, at last, "I cannot pretend not to be simply bowed down. I rose this morning what the world calls a happy man – happy, at least, in a son of whom I thought I could be reasonably proud – "

But it was beyond human nature to endure this longer, and John interrupted almost with a scream. "Oh, wheest!" he cried, "that's not all, that's not the worst of it – it's nothing! How could I tell you were proud of me? Oh! I wish, I wish that I had known; but you always said I was such a disgrace! And the dreadful thing is this: we were all taken up last night, and we have to pay Collette's fine among the six, or we'll be had up for evidence – shebeening it is. They made me swear to tell you; but for my part," he cried, bursting into tears, "I just wish that I was dead!" And he fell on his knees before a chair and hid his face.

Whether his father spoke, or whether he remained long in the room or at once departed, are points lost to history. A horrid turmoil of mind and body; bursting sobs; broken, vanishing thoughts, now of indignation, now of remorse; broken elementary whiffs of consciousness, of the smell of the horse-hair on the chair bottom, of the jangling of church bells that now began to make day horrible throughout the confines of the city, of the hard floor that bruised his knees, of the taste of tears that found their way into his mouth: for a period of time, the duration of which I cannot guess, while I refuse to dwell longer on its agony, these were the whole of God's world for John Nicholson.

When at last, as by the touching of a spring, he returned again to clearness of consciousness and even a measure of composure, the bells had but just done ringing, and the Sabbath silence was still marred by the patter of belated feet. By the clock above the fire, as well as by these more speaking signs, the service had not long begun; and the unhappy sinner, if his father had really gone to church, might count on near two hours of only comparative unhappiness. With his father, the superlative degree returned infallibly. He knew it by every shrinking fibre in his body, he knew it by the sudden dizzy whirling of his brain, at the mere thought of that calamity. An hour and a half, perhaps an hour and three quarters, if the doctor was long-winded, and then would begin again that active agony from which, even in the dull ache of the present, he shrunk as from the bite of fire. He saw, in a vision, the family pew, the somnolent cushions, the Bibles, the Psalm-books, Maria with her smelling-salts, his father sitting spectacled and critical; and at once he was struck with indignation, not unjustly. It was inhuman to go off to church, and leave a sinner in suspense, unpunished, unforgiven. And at the very touch of criticism, the paternal sanctity was lessened; yet the paternal terror only grew; and the two strands of feeling pushed him in the same direction.

And suddenly there came upon him a mad fear lest his father should have locked him in. The notion had no ground in sense; it was probably no more than a reminiscence of similar calamities in childhood, for his father's room had always been the chamber of inquisition and the scene of punishment; but it stuck so rigorously in his mind that he must instantly approach the door and prove its untruth. As he went, he struck upon a drawer left open in the business table. It was the money-drawer, a measure of his father's disarray: the money-drawer – perhaps a pointing providence! Who is to decide, when even divines differ between a providence and a temptation? or who, sitting calmly under his own vine, is to pass a judgment on the doings of a poor, hunted dog, slavishly afraid, slavishly rebellious, like John Nicholson on that particular Sunday? His hand was in the drawer, almost before his mind had conceived the hope; and rising to his new situation, he wrote, sitting in his father's chair and using his father's blotting-pad, his pitiful apology and farewell:

"My Dear Father, – I have taken the money, but I will pay it back as soon as I am able. You will never hear of me again. I did not mean any harm by anything, so I hope you will try and forgive me. I wish you would say good-bye to Alexander and Maria, but not if you don't want to. I could not wait to see you, really. Please try to forgive me. Your affectionate son.

John Nicholson."

The coins abstracted and the missive written, he could not

be gone too soon from the scene of these transgressions; and remembering how his father had once returned from church, on some slight illness, in the middle of the second psalm, he durst not even make a packet of a change of clothes. Attired as he was, he slipped from the paternal doors, and found himself in the cool spring air, the thin spring sunshine, and the great Sabbath quiet of the city, which was now only pointed by the cawing of the rooks. There was not a soul in Randolph Crescent, nor a soul in Queensferry Street; in this out-door privacy and the sense of escape, John took heart again; and with a pathetic sense of leave-taking, he even ventured up the lane and stood a while, a strange peri at the gates of a quaint paradise, by the west end of St. George's Church. They were singing within; and by a strange chance, the tune was "St. George's, Edinburgh," which bears the name, and was first sung in the choir of that church. "Who is this King of Glory?" went the voices from within; and to John this was like the end of all Christian observances, for he was now to be a wild man like Ishmael, and his life was to be cast in homeless places and with godless people.[9]

It was thus, with no rising sense of the adventurous, but in mere desolation and despair, that he turned his back on his native city, and set out on foot for California, with a more immediate eye to Glasgow.[10]

CHAPTER IV

The second sowing

It is no part of mine to narrate the adventures of John Nicholson, which were many, but simply his more momentous misadventures, which were more than he desired, and, by human standards, more than he deserved; how he reached California, how he was rooked, and robbed, and beaten, and starved; how he was at last taken up by charitable folk, restored to some degree of self-complacency, and installed as a clerk in a bank in San Francisco, it would take too long to tell; nor in these episodes were there any marks of the peculiar Nicholsonic destiny, for they were just such matters as befell some thousands of other young adventurers in the same days and places. But once posted in the bank, he fell for a time into a high degree of good fortune, which, as it was only a longer way about to fresh disaster, it behoves me to explain.

It was his luck to meet a young man in what is technically called a "dive," and thanks to his monthly wages, to extricate this new acquaintance from a position of present disgrace and possible danger in the future. This young man was the nephew of one of the Nob Hill magnates, who run the San Francisco Stock Exchange, much as more humble adventurers, in the corner of some public park at home, may be seen to perform the simple artifice of pea and thimble: for their own profit, that is to say, and the discouragement of public gambling. It was thus in his power – and, as he was of grateful temper, it was among the things that he desired – to put John in the way of growing rich; and thus, without thought or industry, or so much as even understanding the game at which he played, but by simply buying and selling what he was told to buy and sell, that plaything of fortune was presently at the head of between eleven and twelve thousand pounds, or, as he reckoned it, of upward of sixty thousand dollars.

How he had come to deserve this wealth, any more than how he had formerly earned disgrace at home, was a problem beyond the reach of his philosophy. It was true that he had been industrious at the bank, but no more so than the cashier, who had seven small children and was visibly sinking in decline. Nor was the step which had determined his advance – a visit to a dive with a month's wages in his pocket – an act of such transcendent virtue, or even wisdom, as to seem to merit the favour of the gods. From some sense of this, and of the dizzy see-saw – heaven-high, hell-deep – on which men sit clutching; or perhaps fearing that the sources of his fortune might be insidiously traced to some root in the field of petty cash; he stuck to his work, said not a word of his new circumstances, and kept his account with a bank in a different quarter of the town. The concealment, innocent as it seems, was the first step in the second tragi-comedy of John's existence.

Meanwhile, he had never written home. Whether from diffidence or shame, or a touch of anger, or mere procrastination, or because (as we have seen) he had no skill in literary arts, or because (as I am sometimes tempted to suppose) there is a law in human nature that prevents young men – not otherwise beasts – from the performance of this simple act of piety – months and years had gone by, and John had never written. The habit of not writing, indeed, was already fixed before he had begun to come into his fortune; and it was only the difficulty of breaking this long silence that withheld him from an instant restitution of the money he had stolen or (as he preferred to call it) borrowed. In vain he sat before paper, attending on inspiration; that heavenly nymph, beyond suggesting the words, "my dear father," remained obstinately silent; and presently John would crumple up the sheet and decide, as soon as he had "a good chance," to carry the money home in person. And this delay, which is indefensible, was his second step into the snares of fortune.

Ten years had passed, and John was drawing near to thirty. He had kept the promise of his boyhood, and was now of a lusty frame, verging toward corpulence; good features, good eyes, a genial manner, a ready laugh, a long pair of sandy whiskers, a dash of an American accent, a close familiarity with the great American joke, and a certain likeness to a R-y-l P-rs-n-ge, who shall remain nameless for me, made up the man's externals as he could be viewed in society. Inwardly, in spite of his gross body and highly masculine whiskers, he was more like a maiden lady than a man of twenty-nine.

It chanced one day, as he was strolling down Market Street on the eve of his fortnight's holiday, that his eye was caught by certain railway bills, and in very idleness of mind he calculated that he might be home for Christmas if he started on the morrow. The fancy thrilled him with desire, and in one moment he decided he would go.

There was much to be done: his portmanteau to be packed, a credit to be got from the bank where he was a wealthy customer, and certain offices to be transacted for that other bank in which he was an humble clerk; and it chanced, in conformity with human nature, that out of all this business it was the last that came to be neglected. Night found him, not only equipped with money of his own, but once more (as on that former occasion) saddled with a considerable sum of other people's.

Now it chanced there lived in the same boarding-house a fellow-clerk of his, an honest fellow, with what is called a weakness for drink – though it might, in this case, have been called a strength, for the victim had been drunk for weeks together without the briefest intermission. To this unfortunate John entrusted a letter with an inclosure of bonds, addressed to the bank manager. Even as he did so he thought he perceived a certain haziness of eye and speech in his trustee; but he was too hopeful to be stayed, silenced the voice of warning in his bosom, and with one and the same gesture committed the money to the clerk, and himself into the hands of destiny.

I dwell, even at the risk of tedium, on John's minutest errors, his case being so perplexing to the moralist; but we have done with them now, the roll is closed, the reader has the worst of our poor hero, and I leave him to judge for himself whether he or John has been the less deserving. Henceforth we have to follow the spectacle of a man who was a mere whip-top for calamity; on whose unmerited misadventures not even the humourist can look without pity, and not even the philosopher without alarm.

That same night the clerk entered upon a bout of drunkenness so consistent as to surprise even his intimate acquaintance. He was speedily ejected from the boarding-house; deposited his portmanteau with a perfect stranger, who did not even catch his name; wandered he knew not where, and was at last hove-to, all standing, in a hospital at Sacramento. There, under the impenetrable *alias* of the number of his bed, the crapulous being lay for some more days unconscious of all things, and of one thing in particular: that the police were after him. Two months had come and gone before the convalescent in the Sacramento hospital was identified with Kirkman, the absconding San Francisco clerk; even then, there must elapse nearly a fortnight more till the perfect stranger could be hunted up, the portmanteau recovered, and John's letter carried at length to its destination, the seal still unbroken, the enclosure still intact.

Meanwhile, John had gone upon his holidays without a word, which was irregular; and there had disappeared with him a certain sum of money, which was out of all bounds of palliation. But he was known to be careless, and believed to be honest; the manager besides had a regard for him; and little was said, although something was no doubt thought, until the fortnight was finally at an end, and the time had come for John to reappear. Then, indeed, the affair began to look black; and when inquiries were made, and the penniless clerk was found to have amassed thousands of dollars, and kept them secretly in a rival establishment, the stoutest of his friends abandoned him, the books were overhauled for traces of ancient and artful fraud, and though none were found, there still prevailed a general impression of loss. The telegraph was set in motion; and the correspondent of the bank in Edinburgh, for which place it was understood that John had armed himself with extensive credits, was warned to communicate with the police.

Now this correspondent was a friend of Mr. Nicholson's; he was well acquainted with the tale of John's calamitous disappearance from Edinburgh; and putting one thing with another, hasted with the first word of this scandal, not to the police, but to his friend. The old gentleman had long regarded his son as one dead; John's place had been taken, the memory of his faults had already fallen to be one of those old aches, which awaken again indeed upon occasion, but which we can always vanquish by an effort of the will; and to have the long lost resuscitated in a fresh disgrace was doubly bitter.

"MacEwen," said the old man, "this must be hushed up, if possible . If I give you a check for this sum, about which they are certain, could you take it on yourself to let the matter rest?"

"I will," said MacEwen. "I will take the risk of it."

"You understand," resumed Mr. Nicholson, speaking precisely, but with ashen lips, "I do this for my family, not for that unhappy young man. If it should turn out that these suspicions are correct, and he has embezzled large sums, he must lie in his bed as he has made it." And then looking up at MacEwen with a nod, and one of his strange smiles: "Good-bye," said he; and MacEwen, perceiving the case to be too grave for consolation, took himself off and blessed God on his way home that he was childless.

CHAPTER V

The prodigal's return

By a little after noon on the eve of Christmas, John had left his portmanteau in the cloak-room, and stepped forth into Princes Street with a wonderful expansion of the soul, such as men enjoy in the completion of long-nourished schemes. He was at home again, incognito and rich; presently he could enter his father's house by means of the pass-key, which he had piously preserved through all his wanderings; he would throw down the borrowed money; there would be a reconciliation, the details of which he frequently arranged; and he saw himself, during the next month, made welcome in many stately houses at many frigid dinner-parties, taking his share in the conversation with the freedom of the man and the traveller, and laying down the law upon finance with the authority of the successful investor. But this programme was not to be begun before evening – not till just before dinner, indeed, at which meal the reassembled family were to sit roseate, and the best wine (the modern fatted calf) should flow for the prodigal's return.

Meanwhile he walked familiar streets, merry reminiscences crowding round him, sadness also, both with the same surprising pathos. The keen frosty air; the low, rosy, wintery sun; the castle, hailing him like an old acquaintance; the names of friends on door-plates; the sight of friends whom he seemed to recognise, and whom he eagerly avoided, in the streets; the pleasant chant of the north country accent; the dome of St. George's reminding him of his last penitential moments in the lane, and of the King of Glory whose name had echoed ever since in the saddest corner of his memory; and the gutters where he had learned to slide, and the shop where he had bought his skates, and the stones on which he had trod, and the railings on which he had rattled his clachan as he went to school; and all those thousand and one nameless particulars, which the eye sees without noting, which the memory keeps indeed yet without knowing, and which, taken one with another, build up for us the aspect of the place that we call home: and all these besieged him, as he went, with both delight and sadness.

His first visit was Houston, who had a house on Regent's Terrace, kept for him in old days by an aunt. The door was opened (to his surprise) upon the chain, and a voice asked him from within what he wanted.

"I want Mr. Houston – Mr. Alan Houston," said he.

"And who are ye?" said the voice.

"This is most extraordinary," thought John; and then aloud he told his name.

"No, young Mr. John?" cried the voice, with a sudden increase of Scottish accent, testifying to a friendlier feeling.

"The very same," said John.

And the old butler removed his defences, remarking only, "I thocht ye were that man." But his master was not there; he was staying, it appeared, at the house in Murrayfield; and though the butler would have been glad enough to have taken his place and given all the news of the family, John, struck with a little chill, was eager to be gone. Only, the door was scarce closed again, before he regretted that he had not asked about "that man."

He was to pay no more visits till he had seen his father and made all well at home; Alan had been the only possible exception, and John had not time to go as far as Murrayfield. But here he was on Regent's Terrace; there was nothing to prevent him going round the end of the hill, and looking from without on the Mackenzies' house. As he went, he reflected that Flora must now be a woman of near his own age, and it was within the bounds of possibility that she was married; but this dishonourable doubt he damned down.

There was the house, sure enough; but the door was of another colour, and what was this – two door plates? He drew nearer; the top one bore, with dignified simplicity the words, "Mr. Proudfoot"; the lower one was more explicit, and informed the passer-by that here was likewise the abode of "Mr. J. A. Dunlop Proudfoot, Advocate." The Proudfoots must be rich, for no advocate could look to have much business in so remote a quarter; and John hated them for their wealth and for their name, and for the sake of the house they desecrated with their presence. He remembered a Proudfoot he had seen at school, not known: a little, whey-faced urchin, the despicable member of some lower class. Could it be this abortion that had climbed to be an advocate, and now lived in the birthplace of Flora and the home of John's tenderest memories? The chill that had first seized upon him when he heard of Houston's absence deepened and struck inward. For a moment, as he stood under the doors of that estranged house, and looked east and west along the solitary pavement of the Royal Terrace, where not a cat was stirring, the sense of solitude and desolation took him by the throat, and he wished himself in San Francisco.

And then the figure he made, with his decent portliness, his whiskers, the money in his purse, the excellent cigar that he now lighted, recurred to his mind in consolatory comparison with that of a certain maddened lad who, on a certain spring Sunday ten years before, and in the hour of church-time silence, had stolen from that city by the Glasgow road. In the face of these changes, it were impious to doubt fortune's kindness. All would be well yet; the Mackenzies would be found, Flora, younger and lovelier and kinder than before; Alan would be found, and would have so nicely discriminated his behaviour as to have grown, on the one hand, into a valued friend of Mr. Nicholson's, and to have remained, upon the other, of that exact shade of joviality which

John desired in his companions. And so, once more, John fell to work discounting the delightful future; his first appearance in the family pew; his first visit to his uncle Greig, who thought himself so great a financier, and on whose purblind Edinburgh eyes John was to let in the dazzling daylight of the West; and the details in general of that unrivalled transformation scene, in which he was to display to all Edinburgh a portly and successful gentleman in the shoes of the derided fugitive.

The time began to draw near when his father would have returned from the office, and it would be the prodigal's cue to enter. He strolled westward by Albany Street, facing the sunset embers, pleased, he knew not why, to move in that cold air and indigo twilight, starred with street-lamps. But there was one more disenchantment waiting him by the way.

At the corner of Pitt Street he paused to light a fresh cigar; the vesta threw, as he did so, a strong light upon his features, and a man of about his own age stopped at sight of it.

"I think your name must be Nicholson," said the stranger.

It was too late to avoid recognition; and besides, as John was now actually on the way home, it hardly mattered, and he gave way to the impulse of his nature.

"Great Scott!" he cried, "Beatson!" and shook his hands with warmth. It scarce seemed he was repaid in kind.

"So you're home again?" said Beatson. "Where have you been all this long time?"

"In the States," said John – "California. I've made my pile though; and it suddenly struck me it would be a noble scheme to come home for Christmas."

"I see," said Beatson. "Well, I hope we'll see something of you now you're here."

"Oh, I guess so," said John, a little frozen.

"Well, ta-ta," concluded Beatson, and he shook hands again and went.

This was a cruel first experience. It was idle to blink facts: here was John home again, and Beatson – Old Beatson – did not care a rush. He recalled Old Beatson in the past – that merry and affectionate lad – and their joint adventures and mishaps, the window they had broken with a catapult in India Place, the escalade of the Castle rock, and many another inestimable bond of friendship; and his hurt surprise grew deeper. Well, after all, it was only on a man's own family that he could count; blood was thicker than water, he remembered; and the net result of this encounter was to bring him to the doorstep of his father's house, with tenderer and softer feelings.

The night had come; the fanlight over the door shone bright; the two windows of the dining-room where the cloth was being laid, and the three windows of the drawing-room where Maria would be waiting dinner, glowed softlier through yellow blinds. It was like a vision of the past. All this time of his absence, life had gone forward with an equal foot, and the fires and the gas had been lighted, and the meals spread, at the accustomed hours. At the accustomed hour, too, the bell had sounded thrice to call the family worship. And at the thought a pang of regret for his demerit seized him; he remembered the things that were good and that he had neglected and the things that were evil and that he had loved; and it was with a prayer upon his lips that he mounted the steps and thrust the key into the key-hole.

He stepped into the lighted hall, shut the door softly behind him, and stood there fixed in wonder. No surprise of strangeness could equal the surprise of that complete familiarity. There was the bust of Chalmers near the stair railings, there was the clothes-brush in the accustomed place; and there, on the hat-stand, hung hats and coats that must surely be the same as he remembered. Ten years dropped from his life, as a pin may slip between the fingers; and the ocean and the mountains, and the mines, and crowded marts and mingled races of San Francisco, and his own fortune and his own disgrace, became, for that one moment, the figures of a dream that was over.

He took off his hat, and moved mechanically towards the stand; and there he found a small change that was a great one to him. The pin that had been his from boyhood, where he had flung his balmoral hat when he loitered home from the academy, and his first hat when he came briskly back from college or the office – his pin was occupied.

"They might have at least respected my pin!" he thought, and he was moved as by a slight, and began at once to recollect that he was here an interloper, in a strange house, which he had entered almost by a burglary, and where at any moment he might be scandalously challenged.

He moved at once, his hat still in his hand, to the door of his father's room, opened it, and entered. Mr. Nicholson sat in the same place and posture as on that last Sunday morning; only he was older, and greyer, and sterner; and as he now glanced up and caught the eye of his son, a strange commotion and a dark flush sprang into his face.

"Father," said John, steadily, and even cheerfully, for this was a moment against which he was long ago prepared, "father, here I am, and here is the money that I took from you. I have come back to ask your forgiveness, and to stay Christmas with you and the children."

"Keep your money," said the father, "and go!"

"Father!" cried John; "For God's sake don't receive me this way. I've come for –"

"Understand me," interrupted Mr. Nicholson; "you are no son of mine; and in the sight of God, I wash my hands of you.[11] One last thing will I tell you; one warning I will give you; all is discovered, and you are being hunted for your crimes; if you are still at large it is thanks to me; but I have done all that I mean to do; and from this time forth I would not raise one finger – not one finger – to save you from the gallows! And now," with a low voice of absolute authority, and a single weighty gesture of the finger, "and now – go!"

CHAPTER VI

The house at Murrayfield[12]

How John passed the evening, in what windy confusion of mind, in what squalls of anger and lulls of sick collapse, in what pacing of streets and plunging into public-houses, it would profit little to relate. His misery, if it were not progressive, yet tended in no way to diminish; for in proportion as grief and indignation abated, fear began to take their place. At first, his father's menacing words lay by in some safe drawer of memory, biding their hour. At first, John was all thwarted affection and blighted hope; next bludgeoned vanity raised its head again, with twenty mortal gashes: and the father was disowned even as he had disowned the son. What was this regular course of life, that John should have admired it? what were these clockwork virtues, from which love was absent? Kindness was the test, kindness the aim and soul; and judged by such a standard, the discarded prodigal – now rapidly drowning his sorrows and his reason in successive drams – was a creature of a lovelier morality than his self-righteous father. Yes, he was the better man; he felt it, glowed with the consciousness, and entering a public-house at the corner of Howard Place (whither he had somehow wandered)[13] he pledged his own virtues in a glass – perhaps the fourth since his dismissal. Of that he knew nothing, keeping no account of what he did or where he went; and in the general crashing hurry of his nerves, unconscious of the approach of intoxication. Indeed, it is a question whether he were really growing intoxicated, or whether at first the spirits did not even sober him. For it was even as he drained this last glass that his father's ambiguous and menacing words – popping from their hiding-place in memory – startled him like a hand laid upon his shoulder. "Crimes, hunted, the gallows." They were ugly words; in the ears of an innocent man, perhaps all the uglier; for if some judicial error were in act against him, who should set a limit to its grossness or to how far it might be pushed? Not John, indeed; he was no believer in the powers of innocence, his cursed experience pointing in quite other ways; and his fears, once awakened, grew with every hour and hunted him about the city streets.

It was perhaps nearly nine at night; he had eaten nothing since lunch, he had drunk a good deal, and he was exhausted by emotion, when the thought of Houston came into his head. He turned, not merely to the man as a friend, but to his house as a place of refuge. The danger that threatened him was still so vague that he knew neither what to fear nor where he might expect it; but this much at least seemed undeniable, that a private house was safer than a public inn. Moved by these counsels, he turned at once to the Caledonian Station, passed (not without alarm) into the bright lights of the approach, redeemed his portmanteau from the cloak-room, and was soon whirling in a cab along the Glasgow road. The change of movement and position, the sight of the lamps twinkling to the rear, and the smell of damp and mould and rotten straw which clung about the vehicle, wrought in him strange alternations of lucidity and mortal giddiness.

"I have been drinking," he discovered; "I must go straight to bed, and sleep." And he thanked Heaven for the drowsiness that came upon his mind in waves.

From one of these spells he was wakened by the stoppage of the cab; and, getting down, found himself in quite a country road, the last lamp of the suburb shining some way below, and the high walls of a garden rising before him in the dark. The Lodge (as the place was named), stood, indeed, very solitary. To the south it adjoined another house, but standing in so large a garden as to be well out of cry; on all other sides, open fields stretched upward to the woods of Corstorphine Hill, or backward to the dells of Ravelston, or downward toward the valley of the Leith. The effect of seclusion was aided by the great height of the garden walls, which were, indeed, conventual, and, as John had tested in former days, defied the climbing schoolboy. The lamp of the cab threw a gleam upon the door and the not brilliant handle of the bell.

"Shall I ring for ye?" said the cabman, who had descended from his perch and was slapping his chest, for the night was bitter.

"I wish you would," said John, putting his hand to his brow in one of his accesses of giddiness.

The man pulled at the handle, and the clanking of the bell replied from farther in the garden; twice and thrice he did it, with sufficient intervals; in the great, frosty silence of the night, the sounds fell sharp and small.

"Does he expect ye?" asked the driver, with that manner of familiar interest that well became his port-wine face; and when John had told him no, "Well, then," said the cabman, "if ye'll tak' my advice of it, we'll just gang back. And that's disinterested, mind ye, for my stables are in the Glesgie road."

"The servants must hear," said John.

"Hout!" said the driver. "He keeps no servants here, man. They're a' in the town house; I drive him often; it's just a kind of hermitage, this."

"Give me the bell," said John; and he plucked at it like a man desperate.

The clamour had not yet subsided before they heard steps upon the gravel, and a voice of singular nervous irritability cried to them through the door, "Who are you, and what do you want?"

"Alan," said John, "it's me – it's Fatty – John, you know. I'm just come home, and I've come to stay with you."

There was no reply for a moment, and then the door was opened.

"Get the portmanteau down," said John to the driver.

"Do nothing of the kind," said Alan; and then to John, "Come in here a moment. I want to speak to you."

John entered the garden, and the door was closed behind him. A candle stood on the gravel walk, winking a little in the draughts; it threw inconstant sparkles on the clumped holly, struck the light and darkness to and fro like a veil on Alan's features, and set his shadow hovering behind him. All beyond was inscrutable; and John's dizzy brain rocked with the shadow. Yet even so, it struck him that Alan was pale, and his voice, when he spoke, unnatural.

"What brings you here to-night?" he began. "I don't want, God knows, to seem unfriendly; but I cannot take you in, Nicholson; I cannot do it."

"Alan," said John, "you've just got to! You don't know the mess I'm in; the governor's turned me out, and I daren't show my face in an inn, because they're down on me for murder or something!"

"For what?" cried Alan, starting.

"Murder, I believe," says John.

"Murder!" repeated Alan, and passed his hand over his eyes. "What was that you were saying?" he asked again.

"That they were down on me," said John. "I'm accused of murder, by what I can make out; and I've really had a dreadful day of it, Alan, and I can't sleep on the road-side on a night like this – at least, not with a portmanteau," he pleaded.

"Hush," said Alan, with his head on one side; and then, "did you hear nothing?" he asked.

"No," said John, thrilling, he knew not why, with communicated terror. "No, I heard nothing; why?" And then, as there was no answer, he reverted to his pleading: "But I say, Alan, you've just got to take me in. I'll go right away to bed if you have anything to do. I seem to have been drinking; I was that knocked over. I wouldn't turn you away, Alan, if you were down on your luck."

"No?" returned Alan. "Neither will I you, then. Come and let's get your portmanteau."

The cabman was paid, and drove off down the long, lamp-lit hill, and the two friends stood on the side-walk beside the portmanteau till the last rumble of the wheels had died in silence. It seemed to John as though Alan attached importance to this departure of the cab; and John, who was in no state to criticise, shared profoundly in the feeling.

When the stillness was once more perfect, Alan shouldered the portmanteau, carried it in, and shut and locked the garden door; and then, once more, abstraction seemed to fall upon him, and he stood with his hand on the key, until the cold began to nibble at John's fingers.

"Why are we standing here?" asked John.

"Eh?" said Alan blankly.

"Why, man, you don't seem yourself," said the other.

"No, I'm not myself," said Alan; and he sat down on the portmanteau and put his face in his hands.

John stood beside him swaying a little, and looking about him at the swaying shadows, the flitting sparkles, and the steady stars overhead, until the windless cold began to touch him through his clothes on the bare skin. Even in his bemused intelligence, wonder began to awake.

"I say, let's come on to the house," he said at last.

"Yes, let's come on to the house," repeated Alan.

And he rose at once, re-shouldered the portmanteau, and taking the candle in his other hand, moved forward to the Lodge. This was a long, low building, smothered in creepers; and now, except for some chinks of light between the dining-room shutters, it was plunged in darkness and silence.

In the hall Alan lighted another candle, gave it to John, and opened the door of a bedroom.

"Here," said he; "go to bed. Don't mind me, John. You'll be sorry for me when you know."

"Wait a bit," returned John; "I've got so cold with all that standing about. Let's go into the dining-room a minute. Just one glass to warm me, Alan."

On the table in the hall stood a glass, and a bottle with a whisky label on a tray. It was plain that the bottle had just been opened, for the cork and corkscrew lay beside it.

"Take that," said Alan, passing John the whisky, and then with a certain roughness pushed his friend into the bedroom, and closed the door behind him.

John stood amazed; then he shook the bottle, and, to his further wonder, found it partly empty. Three or four glasses were gone. Alan must have uncorked a bottle of whisky and drank three or four glasses one after the other, without sitting down, for there was no chair, and that in his own cold lobby on this freezing night! It fully explained his eccentricities, John reflected sagely, as he mixed himself a grog. Poor Alan! He was drunk; and what a dreadful thing was drink, and what a slave to it poor Alan was, to drink in this unsociable, uncomfortable fashion! The man who would drink alone, except for health's sake – as John was now doing –

was a man utterly lost. He took the grog out, and felt hazier, but warmer. It was hard work opening the portmanteau and finding his night things; and before he was undressed, the cold had struck home to him once more. "Well," said he; "just a drop more. There's no sense in getting ill with all this other trouble." And presently dreamless slumber buried him.

When John awoke it was day. The low winter sun was already in the heavens, but his watch had stopped, and it was impossible to tell the hour exactly. Ten, he guessed it, and made haste to dress, dismal reflections crowding on his mind. But it was less from terror than from regret that he now suffered; and with his regret there were mingled cutting pangs of penitence. There had fallen upon him a blow, cruel, indeed, but yet only the punishment of old misdoing; and he had rebelled and plunged into fresh sin. The rod had been used to chasten, and he had bit the chastening fingers. His father was right; John had justified him; John was no guest for decent people's houses, and no fit associate for decent people's children. And had a broader hint been needed, there was the case of his old friend. John was no drunkard, though he could at times exceed; and the picture of Houston drinking neat spirits at his hall-table struck him with something like disgust. He hung from meeting his old friend. He could have wished he had not come to him; and yet, even now, where else was he to turn?

These musings occupied him while he dressed and accompanied him into the lobby of the house. The door stood open on the garden; doubtless, Alan had stepped forth; and John did as he supposed his friend had done. The ground was hard as iron, the frost still rigorous as he brushed among the hollies, icicles jingled and glittered in their fall; and wherever he went, a volley of eager sparrows followed him. Here were Christmas weather and Christmas morning duly met, to the delight of children. This was the day of reunited families, the day to which he had so long looked forward, thinking to awake in his own bed in Randolph Crescent, reconciled with all men and repeating the foot-prints of his youth; and here he was alone, pacing the alleys of a wintry garden and filled with penitential thoughts.

And that reminded him: why was he left alone? and where was Alan? The thought of the festal morning and the due salutations reawakened his desire for his friend, and he began to call for him by name. As the sound of his voice died away, he was aware of the greatness of the silence that environed him. But for the twittering of the sparrows and the crunching of his own feet upon the frozen snow, the whole windless world of air hung over him entranced, and the stillness weighed upon his mind with a horror of solitude.

Still calling at intervals, but now with a moderated voice, he made the hasty circuit of the garden, and finding neither man nor trace of man in all its evergreen coverts, turned at last to the house. About the house the silence seemed to deepen strangely. The door, indeed, stood open as before; but the windows were still shuttered, the chimneys breathed no stain into the bright air, there sounded abroad none of the low stir (perhaps audible rather to the ear of the spirit than to the ear of the flesh) by which a house announces and betrays its human lodgers. And yet Alan must be there – Alan locked in drunken slumbers, forgetful of the return of day, of the holy season, and of the friend whom he had so coldly received and was now so churlishly neglecting. John's disgust redoubled at the thought; but hunger was beginning to grow stronger than repulsion, and as a step to breakfast, if nothing else, he must find and arouse the sleeper.

He made the circuit of the bedroom quarters. All, until he came to Alan's chamber, were locked from without, and bore the marks of a prolonged disuse. But Alan's was a room in commission, filled with clothes, knick-knacks, letters, books, and the conveniences of a solitary man. The fire had been lighted; but it had long ago burned out, and the ashes were stone cold. The bed had been made, but it had not been slept in.

Worse and worse, then; Alan must have fallen where he sat, and now sprawled brutishly, no doubt, upon the dining-room floor.

The dining-room was a very long apartment, and was reached through a passage; so that John, upon his entrance, brought but little light with him, and must move toward the windows with spread arms, groping and knocking on the furniture. Suddenly he tripped and fell his length over a prostrate body. It was what he had looked for, yet it shocked him; and he marvelled that so rough an impact should not have kicked a groan out of the drunkard. Men had killed themselves ere now in such excesses, a dreary and degraded end had made John shudder. What if Alan were dead? There would be a Christmas Day!

By this, John had his hand upon the shutters, and flinging them back, beheld once again the blessed face of the day. Even by that light the room had a discomfortable air. The chairs were scattered, and one had been overthrown; the table-cloth, laid as if for dinner, was twitched upon one side, and some of the dishes had fallen to the floor. Behind the table lay the drunkard, still unaroused, only one foot visible to John.

But now that light was in the room, the worst seemed over; it was a disgusting business, but not more than disgusting; and it was with no great apprehension that John proceeded to make the circuit of the table: his last comparatively tranquil moment for that day. No sooner had he turned the corner, no sooner had his eye alighted on the body, than he gave a smothered, breathless cry, and fled out of the room and out of the house.

It was not Alan who lay there, but a man well up in years, of stern countenance and iron-grey locks; and it was no drunkard, for the body lay in a black pool of blood, and the open eyes stared upon the ceiling.

To and fro walked John before the door. The extreme sharpness of the air acted on his nerves like an astringent, and braced them swiftly. Presently, he not relaxing in his disordered walk, the images began to come clearer and stay longer in his fancy; and next the power of thought came back to him, and the horror and danger of his situation rooted him to the ground.

He grasped his forehead, and staring on one spot of gravel, pieced together what he knew and what he suspected. Alan had murdered some one: possibly "that man" against whom the butler chained the door in Regent's Terrace; possibly another; some one at least: a human soul, whom it was death to slay and whose blood lay spilled upon the floor. This was the reason of the whisky drinking in the passage, of his unwillingness to welcome John, of his strange behaviour and bewildered words; this was why he had started at and harped upon the name of murder; this was why he had stood and hearkened, or sat and covered his eyes, in the black night. And now he was gone, now he had basely fled; and to all his perplexities and dangers John stood heir.

"Let me think – let me think," he said, aloud, impatiently, even pleadingly, as if to some merciless interrupter. In the turmoil of his wits, a thousand hints and hopes and threats and terrors dinning continuously in his ears, he was like one plunged in the hubbub of a crowd. How was he to remember – he, who had not a thought to spare – that he was himself the author, as well as the theatre, of so much confusion? But in hours of trial the junto of man's nature is dissolved, and anarchy succeeds.

It was plain he must stay no longer where he was, for here was a new Judicial Error in the very making. It was not so plain where he must go, for the old Judicial Error, vague as a cloud, appeared to fill the habitable world; whatever it might be, it watched for him, full-grown in Edinburgh; it must have had its birth in San Francisco; it stood guard no doubt, like a dragon, at the bank where he should cash his credit; and though there were doubtless many other places, who should say in which of them it was not ambushed? No, he could not tell where he was to go; he must not lose time on these insolubilities. Let him go back to the beginning. It was plain he must stay no longer where he was. It was plain, too, that he must not flee as he was, for he could not carry his portmanteau, and to flee and leave it, was to plunge deeper in the mire. He must go, leave the house unguarded, find a cab, and return – return after an absence? Had he courage for that?

And just then he spied a stain about a hand's breadth on his trouser-leg, and reached his finger down to touch it. The finger was stained red; it was blood; he stared upon it with disgust, and awe, and terror, and in the sharpness of the new sensation, fell instantly to act.

He cleansed his finger in the snow, returned into the house, drew near with hushed footsteps to the dining-room door, and shut and locked it. Then he breathed a little freer, for here at least was an oaken barrier between himself and what he feared. Next, he hastened to his room, tore off the spotted trousers which seemed in his eyes a link to bind him to the gallows, flung them in a corner, donned another pair, breathlessly crammed his night things into his portmanteau, locked it, swung it with an effort from the ground, and with a rush of relief, came forth again under the open heavens.

The portmanteau, being of Occidental build, was no feather-weight; it had distressed the powerful Alan; and as for John, he was crushed under its bulk, and the sweat broke upon him thickly. Twice he must set it down to rest before he reached the gate; and when he had come so far, he must do as Alan did, and take his seat upon one corner. Here, then, he sat a while and panted; but now his thoughts were sensibly lightened; now, with the trunk standing just inside the door, some part of his dissociation from the house of crime had been effected, and the cabman need not pass the garden wall. It was wonderful how that relieved him; for the house, in his eyes, was a place to strike the most cursory beholder with suspicion, as though the very windows had cried murder.

But there was to be no remission of the strokes of fate. As he thus sat, taking breath in the shadow of the wall and hopped about by sparrows, it chanced that his eye roved to the fastening of the door; and what he saw plucked him to his feet. The thing locked with a spring; once the door was closed, the bolt shut of itself; and without a key, there was no means of entering from without.

He saw himself obliged to one of two distasteful and perilous alternatives; either to shut the door altogether and set his portmanteau out upon the way-side, a wonder to all beholders; or to leave the door ajar, so that any thievish tramp or holiday school-boy might stray in and stumble on the grisly secret. To the last, as the least desperate, his mind inclined; but he must first insure himself that he was unobserved. He peered out, and down the long road: it lay dead empty. He went to the corner of the by-road that comes by way of Dean; there also not a passenger was stirring. Plainly it was, now or never, the high tide of his affairs; and he drew the door as close as he durst, slipped a pebble in the chink, and made off down hill to find a cab.

Half-way down a gate opened, and a troop of Christmas children sallied forth in the most cheerful humour, followed more soberly by a smiling mother.

"And this is Christmas Day!" thought John; and could have laughed aloud in tragic bitterness of heart.

CHAPTER VII

A tragi-comedy in a cab

In front of Donaldson's Hospital, John counted it good fortune to perceive a cab a great way off, and by much shouting and waving of his arm to catch the notice of the driver. He counted it good fortune, for the time was long to him till he should have done for ever with the Lodge; and the farther he must go to find a cab, the greater the chance that the inevitable discovery had taken place, and that he should return to find the garden full of angry

neighbours. Yet when the vehicle drew up he was sensibly chag-
rined to recognise the port-wine cabman of the night before.
"Here," he could not but reflect, "here is another link in the
Judicial Error."

The driver, on the other hand, was pleased to drop again
upon so liberal a fare; and as he was a man – the reader must
already have perceived – of easy, not to say familiar manners, he
dropped at once into a vein of friendly talk, commenting on the
weather, on the sacred season, which struck him chiefly in the
light of a day of liberal gratuities, on the chance which had reunited
him to a pleasing customer, and on the fact that John had been
(as he was pleased to call it) visibly "on the ran-dan" the night
before.

"And ye look dreidful bad the-day, sir, I must say that," he
continued. "There's nothing like a dram for ye – if ye'll take my
advice of it; and bein' as it's Christmas, I'm no' saying," he added,
with a fatherly smile, "but what I would join ye mysel'."

John had listened with a sick heart.

"I'll give you a dram when we've got through," said he, affecting a sprightliness which sat on him most unhandsomely, "and
not a drop till then. Business first, and pleasure afterward."

With this promise the jarvey was prevailed upon to clamber
to his place and drive, with hideous deliberation, to the door of
the Lodge. There were no signs as yet of any public emotion; only,
two men stood not far off in talk, and their presence, seen from
afar, set John's pulses buzzing. He might have spared himself his
fright, for the pair were lost in some dispute of a theological complexion, and with lengthened upper lip and enumerating fingers,
pursued the matter of their difference, and paid no heed to John.

But the cabman proved a thorn in the flesh. Nothing would
keep him on his perch; he must clamber down, comment upon
the pebble in the door (which he regarded as an ingenious but
unsafe device), help John with the portmanteau, and enliven
matters with a flow of speech, especially of questions, which I thus
condense:-

"He'll no' be here himsel', will he? No? Well, he's an eccentric
man – a fair oddity – if ye ken the expression. Great trouble with
his tenants, they tell me. I've driven the fam'ly for years. I drove
a cab at his father's waddin'. What'll your name be? – I should
ken your face. Baigrey, ye say? There were Baigreys about Gilmer-
ton; ye'll be one of that lot? Then this'll be a friend's portmantie,

like? Why? Because the name upon it's Nucholson! Oh, if ye're in a hurry, that's another job. Waverley Brig'? Are ye for away?"

So the friendly toper prated and questioned and kept John's heart in a flutter. But to this also, as to other evils under the sun, there came a period; and the victim of circumstances began at last to rumble towards the railway terminus at Waverley Bridge. During the transit, he sat with raised glasses in the frosty chill and mouldy fetor of his chariot, and glanced out sidelong on the holiday face of things, the shuttered shops, and the crowds along the pavement, much as the rider in the Tyburn cart may have observed the concourse gathering to his execution.[14]

At the station his spirits rose again; another stage of his escape was fortunately ended – he began to spy blue water. He called a railway porter, and bade him carry the portmanteau to the cloakroom: not that he had any notion of delay; flight, instant flight was his design, no matter whither; but he had determined to dismiss the cabman ere he named, or even chose his destination, thus possibly balking the Judicial Error of another link. This was his cunning aim, and now with one foot on the road-way, and one still on the coach-step, he made haste to put the thing in practice, and plunged his hand into his trousers pocket.

There was nothing there!

Oh, yes; this time he was to blame. He should have remembered, and when he deserted his blood-stained pantaloons, he should not have deserted along with them his purse. Make the most of his error, and then compare it with the punishment! Conceive his new position, for I lack words to picture it; conceive him condemned to return to that house, from the very thought of which his soul revolted, and once more to expose himself to capture on the very scene of the misdeed: conceive him linked to the mouldy cab and the familiar cabman. John cursed the cabman silently, and then it occurred to him that he must stop the incarceration of his portmanteau; that, at least, he must keep close at hand, and he turned to recall the porter. But his reflections, brief as they had appeared, must have occupied him longer than he supposed, and there was the man already returning with the receipt.

Well, that was settled; he had lost his portmanteau also; for the sixpence with which he had paid the Murrayfield Toll was one that had strayed alone into his waistcoat pocket, and unless he once more successfully achieved the adventure of the house of crime, his portmanteau lay in the cloak-room in eternal pawn, for lack of a penny fee. And then he remembered the porter, who stood suggestively attentive, words of gratitude hanging on his lips.

John hunted right and left; he found a coin – prayed God that it was a sovereign – drew it out, beheld a halfpenny, and offered it to the porter.

The man's jaw dropped.

"It's only a halfpenny!" he said, startled out of railway decency.

"I know that," said John, piteously.

And here the porter recovered the dignity of man.

"Thank you, sir," and would have returned the base gratuity. But John, too, would none of it; and as they struggled, who must join in but the cabman?

"Hoots, Mr. Baigrey," said he, "you surely forget what day it is!"

"I tell you I have no change!" cried John.

"Well," said the driver, "and what then? I would rather give a man a shillin' on a day like this than put him off with a derision like a baw-bee. I'm surprised at the like of you, Mr. Baigrey!"

"My name is not Baigrey!" broke out John, in mere childish temper and distress.

"Ye told me it was yoursel'," said the cabman.

"I know I did; and what the devil right had you to ask?" cried the unhappy one.

"Oh, very well," said the driver. "I know my place, if you know yours – if you know yours!" he repeated, as one who should imply grave doubt; and muttered inarticulate thunders, in which the grand old name of gentleman was taken seemingly in vain.

Oh, to have been able to discharge this monster, whom John now perceived, with tardy clear-sightedness, to have begun betimes the festivities of Christmas! But far from any such ray of consolation visiting the lost, he stood bare of help and helpers, his portmanteau sequestered in one place, his money deserted in another and guarded by a corpse; himself, so sedulous of privacy, the cynosure of all men's eyes about the station; and, as if these were not enough mischances, he was now fallen in ill-blood with the beast to whom his poverty had linked him! In ill-blood, as he reflected dismally, with the witness who perhaps might hang or save him. There was no time to be lost; he durst not linger any longer in that public spot; and whether he had recourse to dignity or conciliation, the remedy must be applied at once. Some happily surviving element of manhood moved him to the former.

"Let us have no more of this," said he, his foot once more upon the step. "Go back to where we came from."

He had avoided the name of any destination, for there was now quite a little band of railway folk about the cab, and he still kept an eye upon the Court of Justice, and laboured to avoid concentric evidence. But here again the fatal jarvey out-man-oeuvred him.

"Back to the Ludge?" cried he, in shrill tones of protest.

"Drive on at once!" roared John, and slammed the door behind him, so that the crazy chariot rocked and jingled.

Forth trundled the cab into the Christmas streets, the fare within plunged in the blackness of despair that neighboured on unconsciousness, the driver on the box digesting his rebuke and his customer's duplicity. I would not be thought to put the pair in competition; John's case was out of all parallel. But the cabman, too, is worth the sympathy of the judicious; for he was a fellow of genuine kindliness and a high sense of personal dignity incensed by drink; and his advances had been cruelly and publicly rebuffed. As he drove, therefore, he counted his wrongs, and thirsted for sympathy and drink. Now, it chanced he had a friend, a publican, in Queensferry Street, from whom, in view of the sacredness of the occasion, he thought he might extract a dram. Queensferry Street lies something off the direct road to Murrayfield. But then there is the hilly cross-road that passes by the valley of the Leith and the Dean Cemetery; and Queensferry Street is on the way to that. What was to hinder the cabman, since his horse was dumb, from choosing the cross-road, and calling on his friend in passing? So it was decided; and the charioteer, already somewhat mollified, turned aside his horse to the right.

John, meanwhile, sat collapsed, his chin sunk upon his chest, his mind in abeyance. The smell of the cab was still faintly present to his senses, and a certain leaden chill about his feet; all else had disappeared in one vast oppression of calamity and physical faintness. It was drawing on to noon – two-and-twenty hours since he had broken bread; in the interval, he had suffered tortures of sorrow and alarm, and been partly tipsy; and though it was impossible to say he slept, yet when the cab stopped and the cabman thrust his head into the window, his attention had to be recalled from depths of vacancy.

"If you'll no' *stand* me a dram," said the driver, with a well-merited severity of tone and manner, "I daresay ye'll have no objection to my taking one mysel'?"

"Yes – no – do what you like," returned John; and then, as he watched his tormenter mount the stairs and enter the whisky-shop, there floated into his mind a sense as of something long ago familiar. At that he started fully awake, and stared at the shop-fronts. Yes, he knew them; but when? and how? Long since, he thought; and then, casting his eye through the front glass, which had been recently occluded by the figure of the jarvey, he beheld the tree-tops of the rookery in Randolph Crescent. He was close to home – home, where he had thought, at that hour, to be sitting in the well-remembered drawing-room in friendly converse; and, instead –!

It was his first impulse to drop into the bottom of the cab; his next, to cover his face with his hands. So he sat, while the cabman toasted the publican, and the publican toasted the cab-man, and both reviewed the affairs of the nation; so he still sat, when his master condescended to return, and drive off at last down-hill, along the curve of Lynedoch Place; but even so sitting, as he passed the end of his father's street, he took one glance from between shielding fingers, and beheld a doctor's carriage at the door.

"Well, just so," thought he; "I'll have killed my father! and this is Christmas Day!"

If Mr. Nicholson died, it was down this same road he must journey to the grave; and down this road, on the same errand, his wife had preceded him years before; and many other leading citizens, with the proper trappings and attendance of the end. And now, in that frosty, ill-smelling, straw-carpeted, and ragged-cushioned cab, with his breath congealing on the glasses, where else was John himself advancing to?

The thought stirred his imagination, which began to manufacture many thousand pictures, bright and fleeting, like the shapes in a kaleidoscope; and now he saw himself, ruddy and comfortered, sliding in the gutter; and, again, a little woe-begone, bored urchin tricked forth in crape and weepers, descending this same hill at the foot's-pace of mourning coaches, his mother's body just preceding him; and yet again, his fancy, running far in front, showed him the house at Murrayfield – now standing solitary in the low sunshine, with the sparrows hopping on the threshold and the dead man within staring at the roof – and now, with a sudden change, thronged about with white-faced, hand-uplifting neighbours, and doctor bursting through their midst and fixing his stethoscope as he went, the policeman shaking a sagacious head beside the body. It was to this he feared that he was driving; in the midst of this he saw himself arrive, heard himself stammer faint explanations, and felt the hand of the constable upon his shoulder. Heavens! how he wished he had played the manlier part; how he despised himself that he had fled that fatal neighbourhood when all was quiet, and should now be tamely travelling back when it was thronging with avengers!

Any strong degree of passion lends, even to the dullest, the forces of the imagination. And so now as he dwelt on what was probably awaiting him at the end of this distressful drive – John, who saw things little, remembered them less, and could not have described them at all, beheld in his mind's eye the garden of the Lodge, detailed as in a map; he went to and fro in it, feeding his terrors; he saw the hollies, the snowy borders, the paths where he had sought Alan, the high, conventual walls, the shut door – what! was the door shut? Ay, truly, he had shut it – shut in his money, his escape, his future life – shut it with these hands, and no one could now open it! He heard the snap of the spring-lock like something bursting in his brain, and sat astonied.

And then he woke again, terror jarring through his vitals. This was no time to be idle; he must be up and doing, he must think. Once at the end of this ridiculous cruise, once at the Lodge door, there would be nothing for it but to turn the cab and trundle back again. Why, then, go so far? why add another feature of suspicion to a case already so suggestive? why not turn at once? It was easy to say, turn; but whither? He had nowhere now to go to; he could never – he saw it in letters of blood – he could never pay that cab; he was saddled with that cab for ever. Oh, that cab! his soul yearned to be rid of it. He forgot all other cares. He must first quit himself and this ill-smelling vehicle and of the human beast that guided it – first do that; do that at least; do that at once.

And just then the cab suddenly stopped, and there was his persecutor rapping on the front glass. John let it down, and beheld the port-wine countenance inflamed with intellectual triumph.

"I ken wha ye are!" cried the husky voice. "I mind ye now. Ye're a Nucholson. I drove ye to Hermiston to a Christmas party, and ye came back on the box, and I let ye drive."

It is a fact. John knew the man; they had been even friends. His enemy, he now remembered, was a fellow of great good-nature – endless good-nature – with a boy; why not with a man? Why not appeal to his better side? He grasped at the new hope.

"Great Scott! and so you did," he cried, as if in a transport of delight, his voice sounding false in his own ears. "Well, if that's so, I've something to say to you. I'll just get out, I guess. Where are we, anyway?"

The driver had fluttered his ticket in the eyes of the branch toll-keeper, and they were now brought to on the highest and most solitary part of the by-road. On the left, a row of fieldside trees beshaded it; on the right, it was bordered by naked fallows, undulating down-hill to the Queensferry Road; in front, Corstorphine Hill raised its snow-bedabbled, darkling woods against the sky. John looked all about him, drinking the clear air like wine; then his eyes returned to the cabman's face as he sat, not ungleefully, awaiting John's communication, with the air of one looking to be tipped.

The features of that face were hard to read, drink had so swollen them, drink had so painted them, in tints that varied from brick red to mulberry. The small grey eyes blinked, the lips moved, with greed; greed was the ruling passion; and though there was some good-nature, some genuine kindliness, a true human touch, in the old toper, his greed was now so set afire by hope, that all other traits of character lay dormant. He sat there a monument of gluttonous desire.

John's heart slowly fell. He had opened his lips, but he stood there and uttered naught. He sounded the well of his courage, and it was dry. He groped in his treasury of words, and it was vacant. A devil of dumbness had him by the throat; the devil of terror babbled in his ears; and suddenly, without a word uttered, with no conscious purpose formed in his will, John whipped about, tumbled over the road-side wall, and began running for his life across the fallows.

He had not gone far, he was not past the midst of the first field, when his whole brain thundered within him, "Fool! You have your watch!" The shock stopped him, and he faced once more towards the cab. The driver was leaning over the wall, brandishing his whip, his face empurpled, roaring like a bull. And John saw (or thought) that he had lost the chance. No watch would pacify the man's resentment now; he would cry for vengeance also. John would be under the eye of the police; his tale would be unfolded, his secret plumbed, his destiny would close on him at last, and for ever.

He uttered a deep sigh; and just as the cabman, taking heart of grace, was beginning at last to scale the wall, his defaulting customer fell again to running, and disappeared into the farther fields.

CHAPTER VIII

Singular instance of the utility of pass-keys

Where he ran at first, John never very clearly knew; nor yet how long a time elapsed ere he found himself in the by-road near the lodge of Ravelston, propped against the wall, his lungs heaving like bellows, his legs leaden-heavy, his mind possessed by one sole desire – to lie down and be unseen. He remembered the thick coverts round the quarry-hole pond, an untrodden corner of the world where he might surely find concealment till the night should fall. Thither he passed down the lane; and when he came there, behold! he had forgotten the frost, and the pond was alive with young people skating, and the pond-side coverts were thick with lookers-on. He looked on a while himself. There was one tall, graceful maiden, skating hand in hand with a youth, on whom she bestowed her bright eyes perhaps too patently; and it was strange with what anger John beheld her. He could have broken forth in curses; he could have stood there, like a mortified tramp, and shaken his fist and vented his gall upon her by the hour – or so he thought; and the next moment his heart bled for the girl. "Poor creature, it's little she knows!" he sighed. "Let her enjoy herself while she can!" But was it possible, when Flora used to smile at him on the Braid ponds, she could have looked so fulsome to a sick-hearted bystander?

The thought of one quarry, in his frozen wits, suggested another; and he plodded off towards Craig Leith. A wind had sprung up out of the north-west; it was cruel keen, it dried him like a fire, and racked his finger-joints. It brought clouds, too; pale, swift, hurrying clouds, that blotted heaven and shed gloom upon the earth. He scrambled up among the hazelled rubbish heaps that surround the caldron of the quarry, and lay flat upon the stones. The wind searched close along the earth, the stones were cutting and icy, the bare hazels wailed about him; and so the air of the afternoon began to be vocal with those strange and dismal harpings that herald snow. Pain and misery turned in John's limbs to a harrowing impatience and blind desire of change; now he would roll in his harsh lair, and when the flints abraded him, was almost pleased; now he would crawl to the edge of the huge pit and look dizzily down. He saw the spiral of the descending roadway, the steep crags, the clinging bushes, the peppering of snow-wreaths, and far down in the bottom the diminished crane. Here, no doubt, was a way to end it. But it somehow did not take his fancy.

And suddenly he was aware that he was hungry; ay, even through the tortures of the cold, even through the frosts of despair, a gross, desperate longing after food, no matter what, no matter how, began to wake and spur him. Suppose he pawned his watch? But no, on Christmas Day – this was Christmas Day! – the pawn-shop would be closed. Suppose he went to the public-house close by at Blackhall, and offered the watch, which was worth ten pounds, in payment for a meal of bread and cheese? The incongruity was too remarkable; the good folks would either put him to the door, or only let him in to send for the police. He turned his pockets out one after another; some San Franscisco tram-car checks, one cigar, no lights, the pass-key to his father's house, a pocket-handkerchief with just a touch of scent: no, money could be raised on none of these. There was nothing for it but to starve; and after all, what mattered it? That also was a door of exit.

He crept close among the bushes, the wind playing round him like a lash; his clothes seemed thin as paper, his joints burned, his skin curdled on his bones. He had a vision of a high-lying cattle-drive in California, and the bed of a dried stream with one muddy pool, by which the vaqueros had encamped: splendid sun over all, the big bonfire blazing, the strips of cow browning and smoking on a skewer of wood; how warm it was, how savoury the steam of scorching meat! And then again he remembered his manifold calamities, and burrowed and wallowed in the sense of his disgrace and shame. And next he was entering Frank's restaurant in Montgomery Street, San Francisco; he had ordered a pan-stew and venison chops, of which he was immoderately fond, and as he sat waiting, Munroe, the good attendant, brought him a whisky punch; he saw the strawberries float on the delectable cup, he heard the ice chink about the straws. And then he woke again to his detested fate, and found himself sitting, humped together in a windy combe of quarry refuse – darkness thick about him, thin flakes of snow flying here and there like rags of paper, and the strong shuddering of his body clashing his teeth like a hiccough.

We have seen John in nothing but the stormiest condition; we have seen him reckless, desperate, tried beyond his moderate powers; of his daily self, cheerful, regular, not unthrifty, we have seen nothing; and it may thus be a surprise to the reader, to learn that he was studiously careful of his health. This favourite pre-occupation now awoke. If he were to sit here and die of cold, there would be mighty little gained; better the police cell and the chances of a jury trial, than the miserable certainty of death at a dike-side before the next winter's dawn, or death a little later in the gas-lighted wards of an infirmary.

He rose on aching legs, and stumbled here and there among the rubbish-heaps, still circumvented by the yawning crater of the quarry; or perhaps he only thought so, for the darkness was already dense, the snow was growing thicker, and he moved like a blind man, and with a blind man's terrors. At last he climbed a fence, thinking to drop into the road, and found himself staggering, instead, among the iron furrows of a ploughland, endless, it seemed, as a whole county. And next he was in a wood, beating among young trees; and then he was aware of a house with many lighted windows, Christmas carriages waiting at the doors, and Christmas drivers (for Christmas has a double edge) becoming swiftly hooded with snow. From this glimpse of human cheerfulness, he fled like Cain; wandered in the night, unpiloted, careless of whither he went; fell and lay, and then rose again and wandered farther; and at last, like a transformation scene, behold him in the lighted jaws of the city, staring at a lamp which had already donned the tilted night-cap of the snow. It came thickly now, a "Feeding Storm"; and while he yet stood blinking at the lamp, his feet were buried. He remembered something like it in the past, a street-lamp crowned and caked upon the windward side with snow, the wind uttering its mournful hoot, himself looking on, even as now; but the cold had struck too sharply on his wits, and memory failed him as to the date and sequel of the reminiscence.

His next conscious moment was on the Dean Bridge; but whether he was John Nicholson of a bank in a California street, or some former John, a clerk in his father's office, he had now clean forgotten. Another blank, and he was thrusting his pass-key into the door-lock of his father's house.

Hours must have passed. Whether crouched on the cold stones or wandering in the fields among the snow, was more than he could tell; but hours had passed. The finger of the hall clock was close on twelve; a narrow peep of gas in the hall-lamp shed shadows; and the door of the back room – his father's room – was open and emitted a warm light. At so late an hour, all this was strange; the lights should have been out, the doors locked, the good folk safe in bed. He marvelled at the irregularity, leaning on the hall table; and marvelled to himself there; and thawed and grew once more hungry, in the warmer air of the house.

The clock uttered its premonitory catch; in five minutes Christmas Day would be among the days of the past – Christmas! – what a Christmas! Well, there was no use waiting; he had come into that house, he scarce knew how; if they were to thrust him forth again, it had best be done at once; and he moved to the door of the back room and entered.

Oh, well, then he was insane, as he had long believed.

There, in his father's room, at midnight, the fire was roaring and the gas blazing; the papers, the sacred papers – to lay a hand on which was criminal – had all been taken off and piled along the floor; a cloth was spread, and a supper laid, upon the business table; and in his father's chair a woman, habited like a nun, sat eating. As he appeared in the doorway, the nun rose, gave a low cry, and stood staring. She was a large woman, strong, calm, a little masculine, her features marked with courage and good sense; and as John blinked at her, a faint resemblance dodged about his memory, as when a tune haunts us, and yet will not be recalled.

"Why, it's John!" cried the nun.

"I daresay I'm mad," said John, unconsciously following King Lear; "but, upon my word, I do believe you're Flora."

"Of course I am," replied she.

And yet it is not Flora at all, thought John; Flora was slender, and timid, and of changing colour, and dewy-eyed; and had Flora such an Edinburgh accent? But he said none of these things, which was perhaps as well. What he said was, "Then why are you a nun?"

"Such nonsense!" said Flora. "I'm a sick-nurse; and I am here nursing your sister, with whom, between you and me, there is precious little the matter. But that is not the question. The point is: How do you come here? and are you not ashamed to show yourself?"

"Flora," said John, sepulchrally, "I haven't eaten anything for three days. Or, at least, I don't know what day it is; but I guess I'm starving."

"You unhappy man!" she cried. "Here, sit down and eat my supper; and I'll just run upstairs and see my patient, not but what I doubt she's fast asleep; for Maria is a *malade imaginaire.*"

With this specimen of the French, not of Stratford-atte-Bowe, but of a finishing establishment in Moray Place, she left John alone in his father's sanctum. He fell at once upon the food; and it is to be supposed that Flora had found her patient wakeful, and been detained with some details of nursing, for he had time to make a full end of all there was to eat, and not only to empty the teapot, but to fill it again from a kettle that was fitfully singing on his father's fire. Then he sat torpid, and pleased, and bewildered; his misfortunes were then half forgotten; his mind considering, not without regret, this unsentimental return to his old love.

He was thus engaged, when that bustling woman noiselessly re-entered.

"Have you eaten?" said she. "Then tell me all about it."

It was a long and (as the reader knows) a pitiful story; but Flora heard it with compressed lips. She was lost in none of those questionings of human destiny that have, from time to time, arrested the flight of my own pen; for women, such as she, are no philosophers, and behold the concrete only. And women, such as she, are very hard on the imperfect man.

"Very well," said she, when he had done; "then down upon your knees at once, and beg God's forgiveness."

And the great baby plumped upon his knees, and did as he was bid; and none the worse for that! But while he was heartily enough requesting forgiveness on general principles, the rational side of him distinguished, and wondered if, perhaps, the apology were not due upon the other part. And when he rose again from that becoming exercise, he first eyed the face of his old love doubtfully, and then, taking heart, uttered his protest.

"I must say, Flora," said he, "in all this business, I can see very little fault of mine."

"If you had written home," replied the lady, "there would have been none of it. If you had even gone to Murrayfield reasonably sober, you would never have slept there, and the worst would not have happened. Besides, the whole thing began years ago. You got into trouble, and when your father, honest man, was disappointed, you took the pet, or got afraid, and ran away from punishment. Well, you've had your own way of it, John, and I don't suppose you like it."

"I sometimes fancy I'm not much better than a fool," sighed John.

"My dear John," said she, "not much!"

He looked at her, and his eye fell. A certain anger rose within him; here was a Flora he disowned; she was hard; she was of a set colour; a settled, mature, undecorative manner; plain of speech, plain of habit – he had come near saying, plain of face. And this changeling called herself by the same name as the many-coloured, clinging maid of yore; she of the frequent laughter, and the many sighs, and the kind, stolen glances. And to make all worse, she took the upper hand with him, which (as John knew well) was not the true relation of the sexes. He steeled his heart against this sick-nurse.

"And how do you come to be here?" he asked.

She told him how she had nursed her father in his long illness, and when he died, and she was left alone, had taken to nurse others, partly from habit, partly to be of some service in the world; partly, it might be, for amusement. "There's no accounting for taste," said she. And she told him how she went largely to the houses of old friends, as the need arose; and how she was thus doubly welcome, as an old friend first, and then as an experienced nurse, to whom doctors would confide the gravest cases.

"And, indeed, it's a mere farce my being here for poor Maria," she continued; "but your father takes her ailments to heart, and I cannot always be refusing him. We are great friends, your father and I; he was very kind to me long ago – ten years ago."

A strange stir came in John's heart. All this while had he been thinking only of himself? All this while, why had he not written to Flora? In penitential tenderness, he took her hand, and, to his awe and trouble, it remained in his, compliant. A voice told him this was Flora, after all – told him so quietly, yet with a thrill of singing.

"And you never married?" said he.

"No, John, I never married," she replied.

The hall clock striking two recalled them to the sense of time.

"And, now," said she, "you have been fed and warmed, and

I have heard your story, and now it's high time to call your brother."

"Oh!" cried John, chap-fallen; "do you think that absolutely necessary?"

"*I* can't keep you here; I'm a stranger," said she. "Do you want to run away again? I thought you had enough of that."

He bowed his head under the reproof. She despised him, he reflected, as he sat once more alone; a monstrous thing for a woman to despise a man; and strangest of all, she seemed to like him. Would his brother despise him, too? And would his brother like him?

And presently the brother appeared, under Flora's escort; and, standing afar off beside the door-way, eyed the hero of this tale.

"So this is you?" he said, at length.

"Yes, Alick, it's me – it's John," replied the elder brother, feebly.

"And how did you get in here?" inquired the younger.

"Oh, I had my pass-key," says John.

"The deuce you had!" said Alexander. "Ah, you lived in a better world! There are no pass-keys going now."

"Well, father was always averse to them," sighed John.

And the conversation then broke down, and the brothers looked askance at one another in silence.

"Well, and what the devil are we to do?" said Alexander. "I suppose if the authorities got wind of you, you would be taken up?"

"It depends on whether they've found the body or not," returned John. "And then there's that cabman, to be sure!"

"Oh, bother the body!" said Alexander. "I mean about the other thing. That's serious."

"Is that what my father spoke about?" asked John. "I don't even know what it is."

"About your robbing your bank in California, of course," replied Alexander.

It was plain from Flora's face, that this was the first she had heard of it; it was plainer still, from John's, that he was innocent.

"I!" he exclaimed. "I rob my bank! My God! Flora, this is too much; even you must allow that."

"Meaning you didn't?" asked Alexander.

"I never robbed a soul in all my days," cried John: "except my father, if you call that robbery; and I brought him back the money in this room, and he wouldn't even take it!"

"Look here, John," said his brother; "let us have no misunderstanding upon this. McEwen saw my father; he told him a bank you had worked for in San Francisco was wiring over the habitable globe to have you collared – that it was supposed you had nailed thousands; and it was dead certain you had nailed three hundred. So MacEwen said, and I wish you would be careful how you answer. I may tell you also, that your father paid the three hundred on the spot."

"Three hundred?" repeated John. "Three hundred pounds you mean? That's fifteen hundred dollars. Why, then, it's Kirkman!" he broke out. "Thank Heaven! I can explain all that. I gave them to Kirkman to pay for me the night before I left – fifteen hundred dollars, and a letter to the manager. What do they suppose I would steal fifteen hundred dollars for? I'm rich; I struck it rich in stocks. It's the silliest stuff I ever heard of. All that's needful is to cable to the manager: Kirkman has the fifteen hundred – find Kirkman. He was a fellow-clerk of mine, and a hard case; but to do him justice, I didn't think he was as hard at this."

"And what do you say to that, Alick?" asked Flora.

"I say the cablegram shall go to-night!" cried Alexander, with energy. "Answer prepaid, too. If this can be cleared away – and upon my word I do believe it can – we shall all be able to hold up our heads again. Here, you John, you stick down the address of your bank manager. You, Flora, you can pack John into my bed, for which I have no further use to-night. As for me, I am off to the post office, and thence to the High Street about the dead body. The police ought to know, you see, and they ought to know through John; and I can tell them some rigmarole about my brother being a man of highly nervous organisation, and the rest of it. And then, I'll tell you what, John – did you notice the name upon the cab?"

John gave the name of the driver, which, as I have not been able to commend the vehicle, I here suppress.

"Well," resumed Alexander, "I'll call round at their place before I come back, and pay your shot for you. In that way, before breakfast-time, you'll be as good as new."

John murmured inarticulate thanks. To see his brother thus energetic in his service moved him beyond expression; if he could not utter what he felt, he showed it legibly in his face; and Alexander read it there, and liked it the better in that dumb delivery.

"But there's one thing," said the latter, "cablegrams are dear;

and I daresay you remember enough of the governor to guess the state of my finances."

"The trouble is," said John, "that all my stamps are in that beastly house."

"All your what?" asked Alexander.

"Stamps – money," explained John. "It's an American expression; I'm afraid I contracted one or two."

"I have some," said Flora. "I have a pound-note upstairs."

"My dear Flora," returned Alexander, "a pound note won't see us very far; and besides, this is my father's business, and I shall be very much surprised if it isn't my father who pays for it."

"I would not apply to him yet; I do not think that can be wise," objected Flora.

"You have a very imperfect idea of my resources, and none at all of my effrontery," replied Alexander. "Please observe."

He put John from his way, chose a stout knife among the supper things, and with surprising quickness broke into his father's drawer.

"There's nothing easier when you come to try," he observed, pocketing the money.

"I wish you had not done that," said Flora. "You will never hear the last of it.

"Oh, I don't know," returned the young man; "the governor is human after all. And now, John, let me see your famous pass-key. Get into bed, and don't move for anyone till I come back. They won't mind you not answering when they knock; I generally don't myself."

CHAPTER IX

*In which Mr. Nicholson concedes the
principle of an allowance*

In spite of the horrors of the day and the tea-drinking of the night, John slept the sleep of infancy. He was awakened by the maid, as it might have been ten years ago, tapping at the door. The winter sunrise was painting the east; and as the window was to the back of the house, it shone into the room with many strange colours of refracted light. Without, the houses were all cleanly roofed with snow; the garden walls were coped with it a foot in height; the greens lay glittering. Yet strange as snow had grown to John during his years upon the Bay of San Francisco, it was what he saw within that most affected him. For it was to his own room that Alexander had been promoted; there was the old paper with the device of flowers, in which a cunning fancy might yet detect the face of Skinny Jim, of the Academy, John's former dominie; there was the old chest of drawers; there were the chairs – one, two, three – three as before. Only the carpet was new, and the litter of Alexander's clothes and books and drawing materials, and a pencil-drawing on the wall, which (in John's eyes) appeared a marvel of proficiency.

He was thus lying, and looking, and dreaming, hanging, as it were, between two epochs of his life, when Alexander came to the door, and made his presence known in a loud whisper. John let him in, and jumped back into the warm bed.

"Well, John," said Alexander, "the cablegram is sent in your name, and twenty words of answer paid. I have been to the cab-office and paid your cab, even saw the old gentleman himself, and properly apologised. He was mighty placable, and indicated his belief you had been drinking. Then I knocked up old MacEwen out of bed, and explained affairs to him as he sat and shivered in a dressing-gown. And before that I had been to the High Street, where they have heard nothing of your dead body, so that I incline to the idea that you dreamed it."

"Catch me!" said John.

"Well, the police never do know anything," assented Alexander; "and at any rate, they have dispatched a man to inquire and to recover your trousers and your money, so that really your bill is now fairly clean; and I see but one lion in your path – the governor."

"I'll be turned out again, you'll see," said John, dismally.

"I don't imagine so," returned the other; "not if you do what Flora and I have arranged; and your business now is to dress, and lose no time about it. Is your watch right? Well, you have a quarter of an hour. By five minutes before the half-hour you must be at table, in your old seat, under Uncle Duthie's picture. Flora will be there to keep you countenance; and we shall see what we shall see."

"Wouldn't it be wiser for me to stay in bed?" said John.

"If you mean to manage your own concerns, you can do precisely what you like," replied Alexander; "but if you are not in your place five minutes before the half-hour I wash my hands of you, for one."

And thereupon he departed. He had spoken warmly, but the truth is, his heart was somewhat troubled. And as he hung over the banisters, watching for his father to appear, he had hard ado to keep himself braced for the encounter that must follow.

"If he takes it well, I shall be lucky," he reflected. "If he takes it ill, why it'll be a herring across John's tracks, and perhaps all for the best. He's a confounded muff, this brother of mine, but he seems a decent soul."

At that stage a door opened below with a certain emphasis, and Mr. Nicholson was seen solemnly to descend the stairs, and pass into his own apartment. Alexander followed, quaking inwardly, but with a steady face. He knocked, was bidden to enter, and found his father standing in front of the forced drawer, to which he pointed as he spoke.

"This is a most extraordinary thing," said he; "I have been robbed!"

"I was afraid you would notice it," observed his son; "it made such a beastly hash of the table."

"You were afraid I would notice it?" repeated Mr. Nicholson. "And, pray, what may that mean?"

"That I was a thief, sir," returned Alexander. "I took all the money in case the servants should get hold of it; and here is the change, and a note of my expenditure. You were gone to bed, you see, and I did not feel at liberty to knock you up; but I think when you have heard the circumstances, you will do me justice. The fact is, I have reason to believe there has been some dreadful error about my brother John; the sooner it can be cleared up the better for all parties; it was a piece of business, sir – and so I took it, and decided, on my own responsibility, to send a telegram to San Francisco. Thanks to my quickness we may hear to-night. There appears to be no doubt, sir, that John has been abominably used."

"When did this take place?" asked the father.

"Last night, sir, after you were asleep," was the reply.

"It's most extraordinary," said Mr. Nicholson. "Do you mean to say you have been out all night?"

"All night, as you say, sir. I have been to the telegraph and the police-office, and Mr. MacEwen's. Oh, I had my hands full," said Alexander.

"Very irregular," said the father. "You think of no one but yourself."

"I do not see that I have much to gain in bringing back my elder brother," returned Alexander, shrewdly.

The answer pleased the old man; he smiled. "Well, well, I will go into this after breakfast," said he.

"I'm sorry about the table," said the son.

"The table is a small matter; I think nothing of that," said the father.

"It's another example," continued the son, "of the awkwardness of a man having no money of his own. If I had a proper allowance, like other fellows of my own age, this would have been quite unnecessary."

"A proper allowance!" repeated his father, in tones of blighting sarcasm, for the expression was not new to him. "I have never grudged you money for any proper purpose."

"No doubt, no doubt," said Alexander, "but then you see you ar'n't always on the spot to have the thing explained to you. Last night for instance – "

"You could have wakened me last night," interrupted his father.

"Was it not some similar affair that first got John into a mess?" asked the son, skilfully evading the point.

But the father was not less adroit. "And pray, sir, how did you come and go out of the house?" he asked.

"I forgot to lock the door, it seems," replied Alexander.

"I have had cause to complain of that too often," said Mr. Nicholson. "But still I do not understand. Did you keep the servants up?"

"I propose to go into all that at length after breakfast," returned Alexander. "There is the half-hour going? We must not keep Miss Mackenzie waiting."

And greatly daring, he opened the door.

Even Alexander, who it must have been perceived, was on terms of comparative freedom with his parent; even Alexander had never before dared to cut short an interview in this high-handed fashion. But the truth is the very mass of his son's delinquencies daunted the old gentleman. He was like the man with the cart of apples – this was beyond him! That Alexander should have spoiled his table, taken his money, stayed out all night, and then coolly acknowledged all, was something undreamed of in the

Nicholsonian philosophy, and transcended comment. The return of the change, which the old gentleman still carried in his hand, had been a feature of imposing impudence; it had dealt him a staggering blow. Then there was the reference to John's original flight – a subject which he always kept resolutely curtained in his own mind; for he was a man who loved to have made no mistakes, and when he feared he might have made one kept the papers sealed. In view of all these surprises and reminders, and of his son's composed and masterful demeanour, there began to creep on Mr. Nicholson a sickly misgiving. He seemed beyond his depth; if he did or said anything, he might come to regret it. The young man, besides, as he had pointed out himself, was playing a generous part. And if wrong had been done – and done to one who was, after, and in spite of, all, a Nicholson – it should certainly be righted.

All things considered, monstrous as it was to be cut short in his inquiries, the old gentleman submitted, pocketed the change, and followed his son into the dining-room. During these few steps he once more mentally revolted, and once more, and this time finally, laid down his arms: a still, small voice in his bosom having informed him authentically of a piece of news; that he was afraid of Alexander. The strange thing was that he was pleased to be afraid of him. He was proud of his son; he might be proud of him; the boy had character and grit, and knew what he was doing.

These were his reflections as he turned the corner of the dining-room door. Miss Mackenzie was in the place of honour, conjuring with a teapot and a cozy; and, behold! there was another person present, a large, portly, whiskered man of a very comfortable and respectable air, who now rose from his seat and came forward, holding out his hand.

"Good-morning, father," said he.

Of the contention of feeling that ran high in Mr. Nicholson's starched bosom, no outward sign was visible; nor did he delay long to make a choice of conduct. Yet in that interval he had reviewed a great field of possibilities both past and future; whether it was possible he had not been perfectly wise in his treatment of John; whether it was possible that John was innocent; whether, if he turned John out a second time, as his outraged authority suggested, it was possible to avoid a scandal; and whether, if he went to that extremity, it was possible that Alexander might rebel.

"Hum," said Mr. Nicholson, and put his hand, limp and

dead, into John's.

And then, in an embarrassed silence, all took their places; and even the paper – from which it was the old gentleman's habit to suck mortification daily, as he marked the decline of our institutions – even the paper lay furled by his side.

But presently Flora came to the rescue. She slid into the silence with a technicality, asking if John still took his old inordinate amount of sugar. Thence it was but a step to the burning question of the day; and in tones a little shaken, she commented on the interval since she had last made tea for the prodigal, and congratulated him on his return. And then addressing Mr. Nicholson, she congratulated him also in a manner that defied his ill-humour; and from that launched into the tale of John's misadventures not without some suitable suppressions.

Gradually Alexander joined; between them, whether he would or no, they forced a word or two from John; and these fell so tremulously, and spoke so eloquently of a mind oppressed with dread, that Mr. Nicholson relented. At length even he contributed a question: and before the meal was at an end all four were talking even freely.

Prayers followed, with the servants gaping at this newcomer whom no one had admitted; and after prayers there came that moment on the clock which was the signal for Mr. Nicholson's departure.

"John," said he, "of course you will stay here. Be very careful not to excite Maria, if Miss Mackenzie thinks it desirable that you should see her. – Alexander, I wish to speak with you alone." And then, when they were both in the back-room: "You need not come to the office to-day," said he; "you can stay and amuse your brother, and I think it would be respectful to call on Uncle Greig. And by-the-by" (this spoken with a certain – dare we say? – bashfulness), "I agree to concede the principle of an allowance; and I will consult with Dr. Durie, who is quite a man of the world and has sons of his own, as to the amount. And, my fine fellow, you may consider yourself in luck!" he added, with a smile.

"Thank you," said Alexander.

Before noon a detective had restored to John his money, and brought news, sad enough in truth, but perhaps the least sad possible. Alan had been found in his own house in Regent's Terrace, under care of the terrified butler. He was quite mad, and instead of going to prison, had gone to Morningside Asylum. The murdered man, it appeared, was an evicted tenant who had for nearly a year pursued his late landlord with threats and insults; and beyond this, the cause and details of the tragedy were lost.

When Mr. Nicholson returned for dinner they were able to put a dispatch into his hands: "John V. Nicholson, Randolph Crescent, Edinburgh. – Kirkman has disappeared; police looking for him. All understood. Keep mind quite easy. – Austin." Having had this explained to him, the old gentleman took down the cellar key and departed for two bottles of 1820 port. Uncle Greig dined there that day, and Cousin Robina, and, by an odd chance, Mr. MacEwen; and the presence of these strangers relieved what might have been otherwise a somewhat strained relation. Ere they departed, the family was welded once more into a fair semblance of unity.

In the end of April John led Flora – or, let us say, as more descriptive, Flora led John – to the altar, if altar that may be called which was indeed the drawing-room mantel-piece in Mr. Nicholson's house, with the Reverend Dr. Durie posted on the hearth-rug in the guise of Hymen's priest.

The last I saw of them, on a recent visit to the north, was at a dinner-party in the house of my old friend Gellatly Macbride; and after we had, in classic phrase, "rejoined the ladies," I had an opportunity to overhear Flora conversing with another married woman on the much canvassed matter of a husband's tobacco.

"Oh, yes!" said she; "I only allow Mr. Nicholson four cigars a day. Three he smokes at fixed times – after a meal, you know, my dear; and the fourth he can take when he likes with any friend."

"Bravo!" thought I to myself; "this is the wife for my friend John!"

The Tale of Tod Lapraik[1]

✳

My faither, Tam Dale, peace to his banes, was a wild, sploring
lad in his young days, wi' little wisdom and less grace. He was
fond of a lass and fond of a glass, and fond of a ran-dan; but I
could never hear tell that he was muckle use for honest employment. Frae ae thing to anither, he listed at last for a sodger and
was in the garrison of this fort, which was the first way that ony
of the Dales cam to set foot upon the Bass.[2] Sorrow upon that
service! The governor brewed his ain ale; it seems it was the warst
conceivable. The rock was proveesioned frae the shore with vivers,
the thing was ill-guided, and there were whiles when they but to
fish and shoot solans for their diet. To crown a', thir was the Days
of the Persecution.[3] The perishin' cauld chalmers were all occupeed
wi' sants and martyrs, the saut of the yearth, of which it wasnae
worthy. And though Tam Dale carried a firelock there, a single
sodger, and liked a lass and a glass, as I was sayin', the mind of
the man was mair just than set with his position. He had glints
of the glory of the kirk; there were whiles when his dander rase
to see the Lord's sants misguided, and shame covered him that he
should be haulding a can'le (or carrying a firelock) in so black a
business. There were nights of it when he was here on sentry, the
place a' wheesht, the frosts o' winter maybe riving in the wa's,
and he would hear ane o' the prisoners strike up a psalm, and the
rest join in, and the blessed sounds rising from the different chalmers – or dungeons, I would raither say – so that this auld craig
in the sea was like a pairt of Heev'n. Black shame was on his saul;
his sins hove up before him muckle as the Bass, and above a', that
chief sin, that he should have a hand in hagging and hashing at
Christ's Kirk. But the truth is that he resisted the spirit. Day cam,
there were the rousing compainions, and his guid resolves depair-
tit.

In thir days, dwalled upon the Bass a man of God, Peden the
Prophet was his name.[4] Ye'll have heard tell of Prophet Peden.
There was never the wale of him sinsyne, and it's a question wi'

mony if there ever was his like afore. He was wild 's a peat-hag, fearsome to look at, fearsome to hear, his face like the day of judgment. The voice of him was like a solan's and dinnle'd in folks' lugs, and the words of him like coals of fire.

Now there was a lass on the rock, and I think she had little to do, for it was nae place far dacent weemen; but it seems she was bonny, and her and Tam Dale were very well agreed. It befell that Peden was in the gairden his lane at the praying when Tam and the lass cam by; and what should the lassie do but mock with laughter at the sant's devotions? He rose and lookit at the twa o' them, and Tam's knees knoitered thegether at the look of him. But when he spak, it was mair in sorrow than in anger. "Poor thing, poor thing!" says he, and it was the lass he lookit at, "I hear you skirl and laugh," he says, "but the Lord has a deid shot prepared for you, and at that surprising judgment ye shall skirl but the ae time!" Shortly thereafter she was daundering on the craigs wi' twa-three sodgers, and it was a blawy day. There cam a gwost of wind, claught her by the coats, and awa' wi' her bag and baggage. And it was remarked by the sodgers that she gied but the ae skirl.

Nae doubt this judgment had some weicht upon Tam Dale; but it passed again and him none the better. Ae day he was flyting wi' anither sodger-lad. "Deil hae me!" quo' Tam, for he was a profane swearer. And there was Peden glowering at him, gash an' waefu'; Peden wi' his lang chafts an' luntin' een, the maud happed about his kist, and the hand of him held out wi' the black nails upon the finger-nebs – for he had nae care of the body. "Fy, fy, poor man!" cries he, "the poor fool man! *Deil hae me*, quo' he; an' I see the deil at his oxter." The conviction of guilt and grace cam in on Tam like the deep sea; he flang doun the pike that was in his hands – "I will nae mair lift arms against the cause o' Christ!" says he, and was as gude's word. There was a sair fyke in the beginning, but the governor, seeing him resolved, gied him his dischairge, and he went and dwallt and married in North Berwick, and had aye a gude name with honest folk frae that day on.[5]

It was in the year seeventeen hunner and sax that the Bass cam in the hands o' the Da'rymples,[6] and there was twa men soucht the chairge of it. Baith were weel qualified, for they had baith been sodgers in the garrison, and kent the gate to handle solans, and the seasons and values of them. Forby that they were baith – or they baith seemed – earnest professors and men of comely conversation. The first of them was just Tam Dale, my faither. The second was ane Lapraik, whom the folk ca'd Tod Lapraik maistly, but whether for his name or his nature I could never hear tell.[7] Weel, Tam gaed to see Lapraik upon this business, and took me, that was a toddlin' laddie, by the hand. Tod had his dwallin' in the lang loan benorth the kirkyaird. It's a dark uncanny loan, forby that the kirk has aye had an ill name since the days o' James the Saxt and the deevil's cantrips played therein when the Queen was on the seas; and as for Tod's house, it was in the mirkest end, and was little liked by some that kenned the best. The door was on the sneck that day, and me and my faither gaed straucht in. Tod was a wabster to his trade; his loom stood in the but. There he sat, a muckle fat, white hash of a man like creish, wi' a kind of a holy smile that gart me scunner. The hand of him aye cawed the shuttle, but his een was steeked. We cried to him by his name, we skirled in the deid lug of him, we shook him by the shou'ther. Nae mainner o' service! There he sat on his dowp, an' cawed the shuttle and smiled like creish.

"God be guid to us," says Tam Dale, "this is no canny!"

He had jimp said the word, when Tod Lapraik cam to himsel'.

"Is this you, Tam?" says he. "Haith, man! I'm blythe to see ye. I whiles fa' into a bit dwam like this," he says; "it's frae the stamach."

Weel, they began to crack about the Bass and which of them twa was to get the warding o't, and by little and little cam to very ill words, and twined in anger. I mind weel, that as my faither and me gaed hame again, he cam ower and ower the same expression, how little he likit Tod Lapraik and his dwams.

"Dwam!" says he. "I think folk hae brunt far dwams like yon."

Aweel, my faither got the Bass and Tod had to go wantin'. It was remembered sinsyne what way he had ta'en the thing. "Tam," says he, "ye hae gotten the better o' me aince mair, and I hope," says he, "ye'll find at least a' that ye expeckit at the Bass." Which have since been thought remarkable expressions. At last the time came for Tam Dale to take young solans. This was a business he was weel used wi', he had been a craigsman frae a laddie, and trustit nane but himsel'. So there was he hingin' by a line an' speldering on the craig face, whaur it's hieest and steighest. Fower tenty lads were on the tap, hauldin' the line and mindin' for his signals. But whaur Tam hung there was naething but the craig, and the sea belaw, and the solans skirling and flying. It was a braw spring morn, and Tam whustled as he claught in the young geese. Mony's the time I heard him tell of this experience, and aye the swat ran upon the man.

It chanced, ye see, that Tam keeked up, and he was awaur of a muckle solan, and the solan pyking at the line. He thocht this by-ordinar and outside the creature's habits. He minded that ropes was unco saft things, and the solan's neb and the Bass Rock unco hard, and that twa hunner feet were raither mair than he would care to fa'.

"Shoo!" says Tam. "Awa', bird! Shoo, awa' wi' ye!" says he.

The solan keekit daun into Tam's face, and there was something unco in the creature's ee. Just the ae keek it gied, and back to the rope. But now it wroucht and warstl't like a thing dementit. There never was the solan made that wroucht as that solan wroucht; and it seemed to understand it's employ brawly, birzing the saft rope between the neb of it and a crunkled jag o' stane.

There gaed a cauld stend o' fear into Tam's heart.

"This thing is nae bird," thinks he. His een turnt backward in his heid and the day gaed black about him.

"If I get a dwam here," he thoucht, "it's by wi' Tam Dale." And he signalled for the lads to pu' him up.

And it seemed the solan understood about signals. For nae sooner was the signal made than he let be the rope, spried his wings, squawked out loud, took a turn flying, and dashed straucht at Tam Dale's een. Tam had a knife, he gart the cauld steel glitter. And it seemed the solan understood about knives, for nae suner did the steel glint in the sun than he gied the ae squawk, but laigher, like a body disappointit, and flegged aff about the roundness of the craig, and Tam saw him nae mair. And as sune as that thing was gane, Tam's heid drapt upon his shouther, and they pu'd him up like a deid corp, dadding on the craig.

A dram of brandy (which he went never without) broucht him to his mind, or what was left of it. Up he sat.

"Rin, Geordie, rin to the boat, mak' sure of the boat, man – rin!" he cries, "or yon solan 'll have it awa'," says he.

The fower lads stared at ither, an' tried to whilly-wha him to be quiet. But naething would satisfy Tam Dale, till ane o' them had startit on aheid to stand sentry on the boat. The ithers askit if he was for down again.

"Na," says he, "and neither you nor me," says he, "and as sune as I can win to stand on my twa feet we'll be aff frae this craig o' Sawtan."

Sure eneuch, nae time was lost, and that was ower muckle; for before they won to North Berwick Tam was in a crying fever. He lay a' the simmer; and wha was sae kind as come speiring for him, but Tod Lapraik! Folk thocht afterwards that ilka time Tod cam near the house the fever had worsened. I kenna for that; but what I ken the best, that was the end of it.

It was about this time o' the year; my grandfaither was out at the white fishing; and like a bairn, I but to gang wi' him. We had a grand take, I mind, and the way that the fish lay broucht us near in by the Bass, whaur we forgaithered wi' anither boat that belanged to a man Sandie Fletcher in Castleton. He's no lang deid neither, or ye could speir at himsel'. Weel, Sandie hailed.

"What's yon on the Bass?" says he.

"On the Bass?" says grandfaither.

"Ay," says Sandie, "on the green side o't."

"Whatten kind of a thing?" says grandfaither. "There cannae be naething on the Bass but just the sheep."

"It looks unco like a body," quo' Sandie, who was nearer in.

"A body!" says we, and we nane of us likit that. For there was nae boat that could have broucht a man, and the key o' the prison yett hung ower my faither's heid at hame in the press bed.

We keepit the twa boats closs for company, and crap in nearer hand. Grandfaither had a gless, for he had been a sailor, and the captain of a smack, and had lost her on the sands of Tay. And when we took the gless to it, sure eneuch there was a man. He was in a crunkle o' green brae, a wee below the chaipel, a' by his lee lane, and lowped and flang and danced like a daft quean at a waddin'.

"It's Tod," says grandfaither, and passed the gless to Sandie.

"Ay, it's him," says Sandie.

"Or ane in the likeness o' him," says grandfaither.

"Sma' is the differ," quo' Sandie. "De'il or warlock, I'll try the gun at him," quo' he, and broucht up a fowling-piece that he aye carried, for Sandie was a notable famous shot in all that country.

"Haud your hand, Sandie," says grandfaither; "we maun see clearer first," says he, "or this may be a dear day's wark to the baith of us."

"Hout!" says Sandie, "this is the Lord's judgments surely, and be damned to it!" says he.

"Maybe ay, and maybe no," says my grandfaither, worthy

man! "But have you a mind of the Procurator Fiscal, that I think ye'll have forgaithered wi' before," says he.

This was ower true, and Sandie was a wee thing set ajee. "Aweel, Edie," says he, "and what would be your way of it?"

"Ou, just this," says grandfaither. "Let me that has the fastest boat gang back to North Berwick, and let you bide here and keep an eye on Thon. If I cannae find Lapraik, I'll join ye and the twa of us'll have a crack wi' him. But if Lapraik's at hame, I'll rin up the flag at the harbour, and ye can try Thon Thing wi' the gun."

Aweel, so it was agreed between them twa. I was just a bairn, an' clum in Sandie's boat, whaur I thoucht I would see the best of the employ. My grandsire gied Sandie a siller tester to pit in his gun wi' the leid draps, bein' mair deidly again bogles. And then the ae boat set aff for North Berwick, an' the tither lay whaur it was and watched the wanchancy thing on the brae-side.

A' the time we lay there it lowped and flang and capered and span like a teetotum, and whiles we could hear it skelloch as it span. I hae seen lassies, the daft queans, that would lowp and dance a winter's nicht, and still be lowping and dancing when the winter's day cam in. But there would be folk there to hauld them company, and the lads to egg them on; and this thing was its lee-lane. And there would be a fiddler diddling his elbock in the chimney-side; and this thing had nae music but the skirling of the solans. And the lassies were bits o' young things wi' the reid life dinnling and stending in their members; and this was a muckle, fat, crieshy man, and him fa'n in the vale o' years. Say what ye like, I maun say what I believe. It was joy was in the creature's heart; the joy o' hell, I daursay: joy whatever. Mony a time I have askit mysel', why witches and warlocks should sell their sauls (whilk are their maist dear possessions) and be auld, duddy, wrunkl't wives or auld, feckless, doddered men; and then I mind upon Tod Lapraik dancing a' they hours by his lane in the black glory of his heart. Nae doubt they burn for it in muckle hell, but they have a grand time here of it, whatever! – and the Lord forgie us!

Weel, at the hinder end, we saw the wee flag yirk up to the mast-heid upon the harbour rocks. That was a' Sandie waited for. He up wi' the gun, took a deleeberate aim, an' pu'd the trigger. There cam' a bang and then ae waefu' skirl frae the Bass. And there were we rubbin' our een and lookin' at ither like daft folk. For wi' the bang and the skirl the thing had clean disappeared. The sun glintit, the wund blew, and there was the bare yaird whaur the Wonder had been lowping and flinging but ae second syne.

The hale way hame I roared and grat wi' the terror of that dispensation. The grawn folk were nane sae muckle better; there was little said in Sandie's boat but just the name of God; and when we won in by the pier, the harbour rocks were fair black wi' the folk waitin' us. It seems they had fund Lapraik in ane of his dwams, cawing the shuttle and smiling. Ae lad they sent to hoist the flag, and the rest abode there in the wabster's house. You may be sure they liked it little; but it was a means of grace to severals that stood there praying in to themsel's (for nane cared to pray out loud) and looking on thon awesome thing as it cawed the shuttle. Syne, upon a suddenty, and wi' the ae dreidfu' skelloch, Tod sprang up frae his hinderlands and fell forrit on the wab, a bluidy corp.

When the corp was examined the leid draps hadnae played buff upon the warlock's body; sorrow a leid drap was to be fund; but there was grandfaither's siller tester in the puddock's heart of him.[8]

III ESSAYS

*

The Pentland Rising:
A page of history   1666[1]

"A cloud of witnesses ly here,
Who for Christ's interest did appear."
Inscription on Battle-field at Rullion Green.[2]

I

The Causes of the Revolt

"Halt, passenger; take heed what thou dost see,
This tomb doth show for what some men did die."
Monument, Greyfriars' Churchyard, Edinburgh, 1661-1668.[3]

Two hundred years ago a tragedy was enacted in Scotland, the memory whereof has been in great measure lost or obscured by the deeper tragedies which followed it. It is, as it were, the evening of the night of persecution – a sort of twilight, dark indeed to us, but light as the noonday when compared with the midnight gloom which followed. This fact, of its being the very threshold of persecution, lends it, however, an additional interest.

The prejudices of the people against Episcopacy were "out of measure increased," says Bishop Burnet, "by the new incumbents, who were put in the place of the ejected preachers, and were generally very mean and despicable in all respects. They were the worst preachers I ever heard; they were ignorant to a reproach; and many of them were openly vicious. They were indeed the dregs and refuse of the northern parts. Those of them who rose above contempt or scandal were men of such violent tempers that they were as much hated as the others were despised."[4] It was little to be wondered at, from this account, that the countryfolk refused to go to the parish church, and chose rather to listen to outed ministers in the field. But this was not to be allowed, and their persecutors at last fell on the method of calling a roll of the parishioners' names every Sabbath and marking a fine of twenty shillings Scots to the name of each absenter. In this way very large debts were incurred by persons altogether unable to pay. Besides this, landlords were fined for their tenants' absences, tenants for their landlords', masters for their servants', servants for their masters', even though they themselves were perfectly regular in their attendance. And as the curates were allowed to fine with the sanction of any common soldier, it may be imagined that often the pretexts were neither very sufficient nor well proven.

When the fines could not be paid at once, bibles, clothes, and household utensils were seized upon, or a number of soldiers, proportionate to his wealth, were quartered on the offender. The coarse and drunken privates filled the houses with woe; snatched the bread from the children to feed their dogs; shocked the principles, scorned the scruples and blasphemed the religion of their humble hosts; and when they had reduced them to destitution, sold the furniture, and burned down the roof-tree, which was consecrated to the peasants by the name of Home. For all this attention each of these soldiers received from his unwilling landlord a certain sum of money per day – three shillings sterling, according to "Naphtali."[5] And frequently they were forced to pay quartering money for more men than were in reality "cessed" on them. At that time it was no strange thing to behold a strong man begging for money to pay his fines, and many others who were deep in arrears, or who had attracted attention in some other way, were forced to flee from their homes, and take refuge from arrest and imprisonment among the wild mosses of the uplands.[6]

One example in particular we may cite:–

John Nielson, the Laird of Corsack, a worthy man, was, unfortunately for himself, a Nonconformist. First he was fined in four hundred pounds Scots, and then through cessing he lost nineteen hundred and ninety-three pounds Scots. He was next obliged to leave his house and flee from place to place, during which wanderings he lost his horse. His wife and children were turned out of doors, and then his tenants were fined till they too were almost all ruined. As a final stroke, they drove away all his cattle to Glasgow and sold them.[7] Surely it was time that something were done to alleviate so much sorrow, to overthrow such tyranny.

About this time too there arrived in Galloway a person calling himself Captain Andrew Gray, and advising the people to revolt. He displayed some documents purporting to be from the northern Covenanters, and stating that they were prepared to join in any enterprise commenced by their southern brethren. The leader of the persecutors was Sir James Turner, an officer afterwards degraded for his share in the matter. "He was naturally fierce, but was mad when he was drunk, and that was very often," said Bishop Burnet. "He was a learned man, but had always been in armies, and knew no other rule but to obey orders. He told me he had no regard to any law, but acted, as he was commanded, in a military way."[8]

This was the state of matters, when an outrage was committed which gave spirit and determination to the oppressed countrymen, lit the flame of insubordination, and for the time at least recoiled on those who perpetrated it with redoubled force.

II

The Beginning

I love no warres,
I love no jarres,
   Nor strife's fire,
May discord cease,
Let's live in peace:
   This I desire.

If it must be,
Warre we must see
   (So fates conspire),
May we not feel
The force of steel:
   This I desire.

T. Jackson, 1651.[9]

Upon Tuesday, November 13th, 1666, Corporal George Deanes and three other soldiers set upon an old man in the Clachan of Dalry, and demanded the payment of his fines. On the old man's refusing to pay, they forced a large party of his neighbours to go with them and thresh his corn. The field was a certain distance out of the clachan, and four persons, disguised as countrymen, who had been out on the moors all night, met this mournful drove of slaves, compelled by the four soldiers to work for the ruin of their friend. However, chilled to the bone by their night on the hills, and worn out by want of food, they proceeded to the village inn to refresh themselves. Suddenly some people rushed into the room where they were sitting, and told them that the soldiers were about to roast the old man, naked, on his own girdle. This was too much for them to stand, and they repaired immediately to the scene of this gross outrage, and at first merely requested that the captive should be released. On the refusal of the two soldiers who were in the front room, high words were given and taken on both sides, and the other two rushed forth from an adjoining chamber and made at the countrymen with drawn swords. One of the latter, John M'Lellan of Barskob, drew a pistol and shot the corporal in the body. The pieces of tobacco pipe with which it was loaded, to the number of ten at least, entered him, and he was so much disturbed that he never appears to have recovered, for we find long afterwards a petition to the Privy Council requesting a pension for him. The other soldiers then laid down their arms, the old man was rescued, and the rebellion was commenced.[10]

And now we must turn to Sir James Turner's memoirs of himself;[11] for, strange to say, this extraordinary man was remarkably fond of literary composition, and wrote, besides the amusing account of his own adventures just mentioned, a large number of essays and short biographies, and a work on war, entitled "Pallas Armata."[12] The following are some of the shorter pieces: *Magick, Friendship, Imprisonment, Anger, Revenge, Duells, Cruelty, A Defence of some of the Ceremonies of the English Liturgie, to wit – Bowing at the Name of Jesus, The frequent repetition of the Lord's Prayer and Good Lord deliver us, Of the Doxolgie, Of Surplesses, Rotchets, Cannonicall Coats*, etc.[13] From what we know of his character we should expect *Anger* and *Cruelty* to be very full and instructive. But what earthly right he had to meddle with ecclesiastical subjects it is hard to see.

Upon the 12th of the month he had received some information concerning Gray's proceedings, but as it was excessively indefinite in its character, he paid no attention to it. On the evening of the 13th, Corporal Deanes was brought into Dumfries, who affirmed stoutly that he had been shot while refusing to sign the Covenant – a story rendered singularly unlikely by the after conduct of the rebels. Sir James instantly despatched orders to the cessed soldiers either to come to Dumfries, or meet him on the way to Dalry, and commanded the thirteen or fourteen men in the town with him to come at nine next morning to his lodging for supplies.

On the morning of Thursday the rebels arrived at Dumfries with 50 horse and 150 foot. Nielson of Corsack, and Gray, who commanded, with a considerable troop, entered the town, and surrounded Sir James Turner's lodging. Though it was between eight and nine o'clock, that worthy, being unwell, was still in bed, but rose at once and went to the window.

Nielson and some others cried – "You may have fair quarter."
"I need no quarter," replied Sir James; "nor can I be a prisoner,
seeing there is no war declared." On being told, however, that he
must either be a prisoner, or die, he came down and went into
the street in his night-shirt. Here Gray showed himself very desirous of killing him, but he was overruled by Corsack. However,
he was taken away a prisoner, Captain Gray mounting him on his
own horse, though, as Turner naïvely remarks, "there was a good
reason for it, for he mounted himself on a farre better one of mine."
A large coffer containing his clothes and money, together with
all his papers, were taken away by the rebels. They robbed Master
Chalmers, the Episcopalian minister of Dumfries, of his horses,
drank the King's health at the market-cross, and then left Dumfries.[14]

III

The March of the Rebels

"Stay, passenger, take notice what thou reads,
At Edinburgh lie our bodies, here our heads:
Our right hands stood at Lanark, these we want,
Because with them we signed the Covenant."

Epitaph on a Tombstone at Hamilton.[15]

On Friday the 16th, Bailie Irvine of Dumfries came to the Council
at Edinburgh, and gave information concerning this "horrid rebellion." In the absence of Rothes, Sharpe presided – much to the
wrath of some members; and as he imagined his own safety
endangered, his measures were most energetic. Dalzell was ordered
away to the west, the guards round the city were doubled, officers
and soldiers were forced to take the oath of allegiance, and all
lodgers were commanded to give in their names. Sharpe, surrounded with all these guards and precautions, trembled – trembled
as he trembled when the avengers of blood drew him from his
chariot on Magus Muir,[16] – for he knew how he had sold his trust,
how he had betrayed his charge, and he felt that against him must
their chiefest hatred be directed, against him their direst thunder-

bolts be forged. But even in his fear the apostate Presbyterian was unrelenting, unpityingly harsh; he published in his manifesto no promise of pardon, no inducement to submission. He said, "If you submit not you must die," but never added, "If you submit you may live!"[17]

Meantime the insurgents proceeded on their way. At Carsphairn they were deserted by Captain Gray, who, doubtless in a fit of oblivion, neglected to leave behind him the coffer containing Sir James's money. Who he was is a mystery, unsolved by any historian; his papers were evidently forgeries – that, and his final flight, appear to indicate that he was an agent of the Royalists, for either the King or the Duke of York was heard to say – "That, if he might have his wish, he would have them all turn rebels and go to arms."[18]

Upon the 18th day of the month they left Carsphairn and marched onwards.

Turner was always lodged by his captors at a good inn, frequently at the best of which their halting-place could boast. Here many visits were paid to him by the ministers and officers of the insurgent force. In his description of these interviews he displays a vein of satiric severity, admitting any kindness that was done to him with some qualifying souvenir of former harshness, and gloating over any injury, mistake, or folly which it was his chance to suffer or to hear. He appears, notwithstanding all this, to have been on pretty good terms with his cruel "phanaticks," as the following extract sufficiently proves: –

"Most of the foot were lodged about the church or churchyard, and order given to ring bells next morning for a sermon to be preached by Mr. Welch. Maxwell of Morith, and Major M'Cullough invited me to heare 'that phanatick sermon' (for soe they merrilie called it). They said that preaching might prove an effectual meane to turne me, which they heartilie wished. I answered to them that I was under guards, and that if they intended to heare that sermon it was probable I might likewise, for it was not like my guards wold goe to church and leave me alone at my lodgeings. Bot to what they said of my conversion, I said, it wold be hard to turne a Turner. Bot because I founde them in a merrie humour, I said, if I did not come to heare Mr. Welch preach, then they might fine me in fortie shillings Scots, which was duoble the suome of what I had exacted from the phanatics."[19] This took place at Ochiltree, on the 22nd day of the month. The following is recounted by this personage with malicious glee, and certainly, if authentic, it is a sad proof of how chaff is mixed with wheat, and how ignorant, almost impious, persons were engaged in this movement; nevertheless we give it, for we wish to present with impartiality all the alleged facts to the reader: –

"Towards the evening Mr. Robinsone and Mr. Crukshank gaue me a visit; I called for some ale purposelie to heare one of them blesse it. It fell Mr. Robinsone to seeke the blessing, who said one of the most bombastick graces that ever I heard in my life. He summoned God Allmightie very imperiouslie to be their secondarie (for that was his language). 'And if,' said he, 'thou wilt not be our Secondarie, we will not fight for thee at all, for it is not our cause bot thy cause; and if thou wilt not fight for our cause and thy oune cause, then we are not obliged to fight for it. They say,' said he, 'that Dukes, Earles and Lords are coming with the King's General against us, bot they shall be nothing bot a threshing to us.' This grace did more fullie satisfie me of the folly and injustice of their cause, than the ale did quench my thirst."[20]

Frequently the rebels made a halt near some roadside ale-house, or in some convenient park, where Colonel Wallace, who had now taken the command, would review the horse and foot, during which time Turner was sent either into the ale-house or round the shoulder of a hill, to prevent him from seeing the disorders which were likely to arise. He was, at last, in the 25th day of the month, between Douglas and Lanark, permitted to behold their evolutions. "I found their horse did consist of four hundreth and fortie and the foot of five hundreth and upwards. . . The horsemen were armed for most part with suord and pistoll some onlie with suord. The foot with musket, pike, sith [scythe], forke, and suord; and some with suords great and long." He admired much the proficiency of their cavalry, and marvelled how they had attained to it in so short a time.[21]

At Douglas, which they had just left on the morning of this great wapinschaw, they were charged – awful picture of depravity! – with the theft of a silver spoon and a night-gown. Could it be expected that while the whole country swarmed with robbers of every description, such a rare opportunity for plunder should be lost by rogues – that among a thousand men, even though fighting for religion, there should not be one Achan in the camp? At Lanark a declaration was drawn up and signed by the chief rebels. In it occurs the following:–

"The just sense whereof" – the sufferings of the country – "made us choose, rather to betake ourselves to the fields for self-defence, than to stay at home burdened daily with the calamities of others, and tortured with the fears of our own approaching misery."[22]

The whole body, too, swore the Covenant, to which ceremony the epitaph at the head of this chapter seems to refer.

A report that Dalzell was approaching drove them from Lanark to Bathgate, where, on the evening of Tuesday the 26th, the wearied army stopped. But at twelve o'clock the cry which served them for a trumpet of, "Horse! horse!" and "Mount the prisoner!" resounded through the night-shrouded town, and called the peasants from their well-earned rest to toil onwards in their march. The wind howled fiercely over the moorland; a close, thick, wetting rain descended. Chilled to the bone, worn out with long fatigue, sinking to the knees in mire, onward they marched to destruction. One by one the weary peasants fell off from their ranks to sleep, and die in the rain-soaked moor, or to seek some house by the wayside wherein to hide till daybreak. One by one at first, then in gradually increasing numbers, till at last, at every shelter that was seen, whole troops left the waning squadrons, and rushed to hide themselves from the ferocity of the tempest. To right and left nought could be descried but the broad expanse of the moor, and the figure of their fellow-rebels, seen dimly through the murky night, plodding onwards through the sinking moss. Those who kept together – a miserable few – often halted to rest themselves, and to allow their lagging comrades to overtake them. Then onward they went again, still hoping for assistance, reinforcement, and supplies; onward again, through the wind, and the rain, and the darkness – onward to their defeat at Pentland, and their scaffold at Edinburgh. It was calculated that they lost one half of their army on that disastrous night march.

Next night they reached the village of Colinton, four miles from Edinburgh, where they halted for the last time.[23]

IV

Rullion Green

"From Covenanters with uplifted hands,
From remonstrators with associate bands,
Good Lord, deliver us."

Royalist Rhyme, Kirkton, p. 127.[24]

Late on the fourth night of November, exactly twenty-four days before Rullion Green, Richard and George Chaplain, merchants in Haddington, beheld four men clad like west country Whigamores, standing round some object on the ground. It was at the two-mile cross, and within that distance from their homes. At last, to their horror, they discovered that the recumbent figure was a livid corpse swathed in a blood-stained winding-sheet.[25] Many thought that this apparition was a portent of the deaths connected with the Pentland Rising.

On the morning of Thursday, the 28th of November, 1666, they left Colinton and marched to Rullion Green. There they arrived about sunset. The position was a strong one. On the summit of a bare heathery spur of the Pentlands are two hillocks, and between them lies a narrow band of flat marshy ground. On the highest of the two mounds – that nearest the Pentlands, and on the left hand of the main body – was the greater part of the cavalry, under Major Learmont; on the other Barskob and the Galloway gentlemen; and in the centre Colonel Wallace and the weak half-armed infantry. Their position was further strengthened by the depth of the valley below, and the deep chasm-like course of the Rullion Burn.

The sun, going down behind the Pentlands, cast golden lights and blue shadows on their snow-clad summits, slanted obliquely into the rich plain before them, bathing with rosy splendour the leafless, snow-sprinkled trees, and fading gradually into shadow in the distance. To the south, too, they beheld a deep-shaded amphitheatre of heather and bracken; the course of the Esk, near Penicuik, winding about at the foot of its gorge; the broad, brown expanse of Maw moss; and, fading into blue indistinctness in the south, the wild heath-clad Peeblesshire hills. In sooth, that scene was fair, and many a yearning glance was cast over that peaceful evening scene from the spot where the rebels awaited their defeat; and when the fight was over, many a noble fellow lifted his head from the blood-stained heather to strive with darkening eyeballs to behold that landscape, over which, as o'er his life and his cause, the shadows of night and of gloom were falling and thickening.

It was while waiting on this spot that the fear-inspiring cry was raised, "The enemy! – Here comes the enemy!"

Unwilling to believe their own doom – for our insurgents still hoped for success in some negotiations for peace which had been carried on at Colinton – they called out, – "They are some other of our own."

"They are too blacke" (i.e. too numerous), "fie! fie! for ground to draw up on," cried Wallace, fully realising the want of space for his men, and proving that it was not till after this time that his forces were finally arranged.[26]

First of all the battle was commenced by fifty royalist horse sent obliquely across the hill to attack the left wing of the rebels. An equal number of Learmont's men met them, and, after a struggle, drove them back. The course of the Rullion Burn prevented almost all pursuit, and Wallace, on perceiving it, despatched a body of foot to occupy both the burn and some ruined sheep walls on the farther side.

Dalzell changed his position and drew up his army at the foot of the hill, on the top of which were his foes. He then despatched a mingled body of infantry and cavalry to attack Wallace's outpost, but they also were driven back. A third charge produced a still more disastrous effect, for Dalzell had to check the pursuit of his men by a reinforcement.

These repeated checks bred a panic in the lieutenant-general's ranks, for several of his men flung down their arms. Urged by such fatal symptoms, and by the approaching night, he deployed his men and closed in overwhelming numbers on the centre and right flank of the insurgent army. In the increasing twilight the burning matches of the fire-locks, shimmering on barrel, halbert, and cuirass, lent to the approaching army a picturesque effect, like a huge many-armed giant breathing flame into the darkness.

Placed on an overhanging hill, Welch and Semple cried aloud, "The God of Jacob! The God of Jacob!" and prayed with uplifted hands for victory.[27]

But still the royalist troops closed in.

Captain John Paton was observed by Dalzell, who determined

to capture him with his own hands. Accordingly, he charged forward presenting his pistols. Paton fired, but the balls hopped off Dalzell's buff coat and fell into his boot. With the superstition peculiar to his age, the Nonconformist concluded that his adversary was rendered bullet-proof by enchantment, and pulling some small silver coins from his pocket, charged his pistol therewith. Dalzell, seeing this and supposing, it is likely, that Paton was putting in larger balls, hid behind his servant, who was killed.[28]

Meantime the outposts were forced, and the army of Wallace was enveloped in the embrace of a hideous boa-constrictor – tightening, closing, crushing every semblance of life from the victim enclosed in his toils. The flanking parties of horse were forced in upon the centre, and though, as even Turner grants, they fought with desperation, a general flight was the result.

But when they fell there was none to sing their coronach or wail the death-wail over them. Those who sacrificed themselves for the peace, the liberty, and the religion of their fellow- countrymen, lay bleaching in the field of death for long, and when at last they were buried by charity, the peasants dug up their bodies, desecrated their graves, and cast them once more upon the open heath for the sorry value of their winding sheets!

Inscription on stone at Rullion Green:

Here
and near to
this place lyes the
reuerend Mr. John Crookshanks
and Mr. Andrew M'Cormock
ministers of the Gospel, and
about fifty other true covenanted Presbyterians who were
killed in this place in their own
innocent self-defence and defence of the Covenanted
Work of Reformation by
Thomas Dalzel of Bins
Upon 28 November
1666. Rev. 12. 11. Erected
September 28, 1738.

Back of stone:
    A Cloud of Witnesses ly here,
    Who for Christ's Interest did appear,
    For to restore true Liberty,
    O'erturned then by tyranny;
    And by proud Prelates who did Rage
    Against the Lords own heritage;
    They sacrific'd were for the laws
    Of Christ their King, his noble cause,
    These heroes fought with great renown
    By falling got the Martyr's crown.[29]

V

A Record of Blood

> "They cut his hands ere he was dead,
> And after that struck off his head.
> His blood under the altar cries,
> For vengeance on Christ's enemies."
>
> *Epitaph on Tomb at Longcross of Clermont.*[30]

Master Andrew Murray, an outed minister, residing in the Potter-row, on the morning after the defeat, heard the sounds of cheering and the march of many feet beneath his window. He gazed out. With colours flying, and with music sounding, Dalzell victorious entered Edinburgh. But his banners were dyed in blood, and a band of prisoners were marched within his ranks. The old man knew it all. That martial and triumphant strain was the death-knell of his friends and of their cause, the rust-hued spots upon the flags were the tokens of their courage and their death, and the prisoners were the miserable remnant spared from death in battle to die upon the scaffold. Poor old man! he had outlived all joy. Had he lived longer he would have seen increasing torment and increasing woe; he would have seen the clouds, then but gathering in the mist, cast a more than midnight darkness o'er his native hills, and have fallen a victim to those bloody persecutions which, later, sent their red memorials to the sea by many a burn. By a merciful Providence all this was spared to him – he fell beneath the first blow: and ere four days had passed since Rullion Green, the aged minister of God was gathered to his fathers.[31]

When Sharpe first heard of the rebellion, he applied to Sir Alexander Ramsay, the Provost, for soldiers to guard his house. Disliking their occupation, the soldiers gave him an ugly time of it. All the night through they kept up a continuous series of "alarms and incursions," cries of "Stand!" "Give fire!" etc., which forced the prelate to flee to the castle in the morning, hoping there to find the rest which was denied him at home.[32] Now, however, when all danger to himself was past, Sharpe came out in his true colours, and scant was the justice likely to be shown to the foes of Scotch Episcopacy when the Primate was by. The prisoners were lodged in Haddo's Hole, a part of St. Giles's Cathedral, where, by the kindness of Bishop Wishart, to his credit be it spoken, they were amply supplied with food.[33]

Some people urged, in the council, that the promise of quarter which had been given on the field of battle should protect the lives of the miserable men. Sir John Gilmore, the greatest lawyer, gave no opinion – certainly a suggestive circumstance, – but Lord Lee declared that this would not interfere with their legal trial; so "to bloody executions they went."[34] To the number of thirty they were condemned and executed; while two of them, Hugh M'Kail, a young minister, and Nielson of Corsack, were tortured with the boots.[35]

The goods of those who perished were confiscated, and their bodies were dismembered and distributed to different parts of the country; "the heads of Major M'Culloch and the two Gordons," it was resolved, says Kirkton, "should be pitched on the gate of Kirkcudbright; the two Hamiltons and Strong's head should be affixed at Hamilton, and Captain Arnot's sett on the Watter Gate at Edinburgh. The armes of all the ten, because they hade with uplifted hands renewed the Covenant at Lanark, were sent to the people of that town to expiate that crime, by placing these armes on the top of the prison."[36] Among these was John Nielson, the Laird of Corsack, who saved Turner's life at Dumfries; in return for which service, Sir James attempted, though without success, to get the poor man reprieved. One of the condemned died of his wounds between the day of condemnation and the day of execution. "None of them," says Kirkton, "would save their life by taking the declaration and renouncing the Covenant, though it was offered to them. . . But never men died in Scotland so much lamented by the people, not only spectators, but those in the country. When Knockbreck and his brother were turned over, they clasped each other in their armes, and so endured the pangs of death. When Humphrey Colquhoun died, he spoke not like an ordinary citizen, but like a heavenly minister, relating his comfortable Christian experiences, and called for his Bible, and laid it on his wounded arm, and read John iii. 8,[37] and spoke upon it to the admiration of all. But most of all, when Mr. M'Kail died, there was such a lamentation as was never known in Scotland before; not one dry cheek upon all the street, or in all the numberless windows in the mercate place."[38]

The following passage from this speech speaks for itself and its author:–

"Hereafter I will not talk with flesh and blood, nor think on the world's consolations. Farewell to all my friends, whose company hath been refreshful to me in my pilgrimage. I have done with the light of the sun and the moon; welcome eternal light, eternal life, everlasting love, everlasting praise, everlasting glory. Praise to Him that sits upon the throne, and to the Lamb for ever! Bless the Lord, O my soul, that hath pardoned all my iniquities in the blood of His Son, and healed all my diseases. Bless Him, oh! all ye His angels, that excel in strength, ye ministers that do His pleasure. Bless the Lord, O my soul!"[39]

After having ascended the gallows-ladder he again broke forth in the following words of touching eloquence:

"And now I leave off to speak any more to creatures, and begin my intercourse with God, which shall never be broken off. Farewell father and mother, friends and relations! Farewell the world and all delights! Farewell meat and drink! Farewell sun, moon, and stars! Welcome God and Father! Welcome sweet Jesus Christ, the Mediator of the new covenant! Welcome blessed Spirit of grace, and God of all consolation! Welcome glory! Welcome eternal life! Welcome Death!"[40]

At Glasgow, too, where some were executed, they caused the soldiers to beat the drums and blow the trumpets on their closing ears. Hideous refinement of revenge! Even the last words which drop from the lips of a dying man – words surely the most sincere and the most unbiassed which mortal mouth can utter – even these were looked upon as poisoned and as poisonous. "Drown their last accents," was the cry, "lest they should lead the crowd to take their part, or at least to mourn their doom!"[41] But, after all, perhaps it was more merciful than one would think – unintentionally so, of course; perhaps the storm of harsh and fiercely jubilant noises, the clanging of trumpets, the rattling of drums, and the hootings and jeerings of an unfeeling mob, which were the last they heard on earth, might, when the mortal fight was over, when the river of death was passed, add tenfold sweetness to the hymning of the angels, tenfold peacefulness to the shores which they had reached.

Not content with the cruelty of these executions, some even of the peasantry, though these were confined to the shire of Mid-Lothian, pursued, captured, plundered, and murdered the miserable fugitives who fell in their way. One strange story have we of these times of blood and persecution: Kirkton, the historian, and popular tradition tell us alike, of a flame which often would arise from the grave, in a moss near Carnwath, of some of those poor rebels; of how it crept along the ground; of how it covered the house of their murderer; and of how it scared him with its lurid glare.

Hear Daniel Defoe:[42]

"If the poor people were by these insupportable violences made desperate, and driven to all the extremities of a wild despair, who can justly reflect on them when they read in the word of God 'That oppression makes a wise man mad'? And therefore were there no other original of the insurrection known by the name of the Rising of Pentland, it was nothing but what the intolerable oppressions of those times might have justified to all the world, nature having dictated to all people a right of defence when illegally and arbitrarily attacked in a manner not justifiable either by the laws of nature, the laws of God, or the laws of the country."

Bear this remonstrance of Defoe's in mind, and though it is the fashion of the day to jeer and to mock, to execrate and to contemn the noble band of Covenanters, though the bitter laugh at their old-world religious views, the curl of the lip at their merits, and the chilling silence on their bravery and their determination, are but too rife through all society; be charitable to what was evil, and honest to what was good about the Pentland insurgents, who fought for life and liberty, for country and religion, on the 28th of November, 1666, now just two hundred years ago.

An Old Scots Gardener[1]

❋

I think I might almost have said the last: somewhere, indeed, in the uttermost glens of the Lammermuir or among the south-western hills there may yet linger a decrepit representative of this bygone good fellowship; but as far as actual experience goes, I have only met one man in my life who might fitly be quoted in the same breath with Andrew Fairservice[2] – though without his vices. He was a man whose very presence could impart a savour of quaint antiquity to the baldest and most modern flowerplots. There was a dignity about his tall stooping form, and an earnestness in his wrinkled face that recalled Don Quixote; but a Don Quixote who had come through the training of the Covenant, and been nourished in his youth on *Walker's Lives* and *The Hind let Loose*.[3]

Now, as I could not bear to let such a man pass away with no sketch preserved of his old-fashioned virtues, I hope the reader will take this as an excuse for the present paper, and judge as kindly as he can the infirmities of my description. To me, who find it so difficult to tell the little that I know, he stands essentially as a *genius loci*. It is impossible to separate his spare form and old straw hat from the garden in the lap of the hill, with its rocks over-grown with clematis, its shadowy walks, and the splendid breadth of champaign that one saw from the north-west corner. The garden and gardener seem part and parcel of each other. When I take him from his right surroundings and try to make him appear for me on paper, he looks unreal and phantasmal: the best that I can say may convey some notion to those that never saw him, but to me it will be ever impotent.

The first time that I saw him, I fancy Robert[4] was pretty old already: he had certainly begun to use his years as a stalking-horse. Latterly he was beyond all the impudences of logic, considering a reference to the parish register worth all the reasons in the world. *"I am old and well stricken in years,"* he was wont to say; and I never found any one bold enough to answer the argument. Apart from this vantage that he kept over all who were not yet octogenarian, he had some other drawbacks as a gardener. He shrank the very place he cultivated. The dignity and reduced gentility of his appearance made the small garden cut a sorry figure. He was full of tales of greater situations in his younger days. He spoke of castles and parks with a humbling familiarity. He told of places where under-gardeners had trembled at his looks, where there were meres and swanneries, labyrinths of walk and wildernesses of sad shrubbery in his control, till you could not help feeling that it was condescension on his part to dress your humbler garden plots. You were thrown at once into an invidious position. You felt that you were profiting by the needs of dignity, and that his poverty and not his will consented to your vulgar rule. Involuntarily you compared yourself with the swineherd that made Alfred watch his cakes, or some bloated citizen who may have given his sons and his condescension to the fallen Dionysius. Nor were the disagreeables purely fanciful and metaphysical, for the sway that he exercised over your feelings he extended to your garden, and, through the garden, to your diet. He would trim a hedge, throw away a favourite plant, or fill the most favoured and fertile section of the garden with a vegetable that none of us could eat, in supreme contempt for our opinion. If you asked him to send you in one of your own artichokes, *"That I wull, mem,"* he would say, *"with pleasure, for it is mair blessed to give than to receive."* Ay, and even when, by extra twisting of the screw, we prevailed on him to prefer our commands to his own inclination, and he went away, stately and sad, professing that *"our wull was his pleasure,"* but yet reminding us that he would do it *"with feelin's"* – even then, I say, the triumphant master felt humbled in his triumph, felt that he ruled on sufferance only, that he was taking a mean advantage of the other's low estate, and that the whole scene had been one of those "slights that patient merit of the unworthy takes."[5]

In flowers his taste was old-fashioned and catholic; affecting sunflowers and dahlias, wallflowers and roses, and holding in supreme aversion whatsoever was fantastic, new-fashioned or wild. There was one exception to this sweeping ban. Foxgloves, though undoubtedly guilty on the last count, he not only spared, but loved; and when the shrubbery was being thinned, he stayed his hand and dexterously manipulated his bill in order to save every stately stem. In boyhood, as he told me once, speaking in that tone that only actors and the old-fashioned common folk can use nowadays, his heart grew *"proud"* within him when he came on a burn-course among the braes of Manor that shone purple with their graceful trophies; and not all his apprenticeship and practice for so many years of precise gardening had banished these boyish recollections from his heart. Indeed, he was a man keenly alive to the beauty of all that was bygone. He abounded in old stories of his boyhood, and kept pious account of all his former pleasures; and when he went (on a holiday) to visit one of the fabled great places of the earth where he had served before, he came back full of little pre-Raphaelite reminiscences that showed real passion for the past, such as might have shaken hands with Hazlitt or Jean-Jacques.[6]

But however his sympathy with his old feelings might affect his liking for the foxgloves, the very truth was that he scorned all flowers together. They were but garnishings, childish toys, trifling ornaments for ladies' chimney-shelves. It was towards his cauliflowers and peas and cabbage that his heart grew warm. His preference for the more useful growths was such that cabbages were found invading the flower-plots, and an outpost of savoys was once discovered in the centre of the lawn. He would prelect over some thriving plant with wonderful enthusiasm, piling reminiscence on reminiscence of former and perhaps yet finer specimens. Yet even then he did not let the credit leave himself. He had, indeed, raised *"finer o' them;"* but it seemed that no one else had been favoured with a like success. All other gardeners, in fact, were mere foils to his own superior attainments; and he would recount, with perfect soberness of voice and visage, how so and so had wondered, and such another could scarcely give credit to his eyes. Nor was it with his rivals only that he parted praise and blame. If you remarked how well a plant was looking he would gravely touch his hat and thank you with solemn unction; all credit in the matter falling to him. If, on the other hand, you called his attention to some back-going vegetable, he would quote Scripture: *"Paul may plant and Apollos may water;"*[7] all blame being left to Providence, on the score of deficient rain or untimely frosts.

There was one thing in the garden that shared his preference with his favourite cabbages and rhubarb, and that other was the bee-hive. Their sound, their industry, perhaps their sweet product also, had taken hold of his imagination and heart, whether by way of memory or no I cannot say, although perhaps the bees too were linked to him by some recollection of Manor braes and his country childhood. Nevertheless, he was too chary of his personal safety or (let me rather say) his personal dignity to mingle in any active office towards them. But he could stand by while one of the contemned rivals did the work for him, and protest that it was quite safe in spite of his own considerate distance and the cries of the distressed assistant. In regard to bees, he was rather a man of word than deed, and some of his most striking sentences had the bees for text. *"They are indeed wonderfu' creatures, mem,"* he said once. *"They just mind me o' what the Queen of Sheba said to Solomon – and I think she said it wi' a sigh – 'The half of it hath not been told unto me.'"*[8]

As far as the Bible goes, he was deeply read. Like the old Covenanters, of whom he was the worthy representative, his mouth was full of sacred quotations; it was the book that he had studied most and thought upon most deeply. To many people in his station the Bible, and perhaps Burns, are the only books of any vital literary merit that they read, feeding themselves, for the rest, on the draff of country newspapers, and the very instructive but not very palatable pabulum of some cheap educational series. This was Robert's position. All day long he had dreamed of the Hebrew stories, and his head had been full of Hebrew poetry and Gospel ethics; until they had struck deep root into his heart, and the very expressions had become a part of him; so that he rarely spoke without some antique idiom or Scripture mannerism that gave a raciness to the merest trivialities of talk. But the influence of the Bible did not stop here. There was more in Robert than quaint phrase and ready store of reference. He was imbued with a spirit of peace and love: he interposed between man and wife: he threw himself between the angry, touching his hat the while with all the ceremony of an usher: he protected the birds from everybody but himself, seeing, I suppose, a great difference between official execution and wanton sport. His mistress telling him one day to put some ferns into his master's particular corner, and adding, "Though, indeed, Robert, he doesn't deserve them, for he wouldn't help me to gather them," "Eh, mem," replies Robert, *"but I wouldnae say that, for I think he's just a most deservin' gentleman."* Again, two of our friends, who were on intimate terms, and accustomed to use language to each other somewhat without the bounds of the parliamentary, happened to differ about the position of a seat in the garden. The discussion, as was usual when these two were at it, soon waxed tolerably insulting on both sides. Every one accustomed to such controversies several times a day was quietly enjoying this prize-fight of somewhat abusive wit – every one but Robert, to whom the perfect good faith of the whole quarrel seemed unquestionable, and who, after having waited till his conscience would suffer him to wait no more, and till he expected every moment that the disputants would fall to blows, cut suddenly in with tones of almost tearful entreaty: *"Eh, but, gentlemen, I wad hae nae mair words about it!"* One thing was noticeable about Robert's religion: it was neither dogmatic nor sectarian. He never expatiated (at least, in my hearing) on the doctrines of his creed, and he never condemned anybody else. I have no doubt that he held all Roman Catholics, Atheists, and Mahometans as considerably out of it; I don't believe he had any sympathy for Prelacy; and the natural feelings of man must have made him a little sore about Free-Churchism; but at least, he never talked about these views, never grew controversially noisy, and never openly aspersed the belief or practice of anybody. Now all this is not generally characteristic of Scots piety; Scots sects being churches militant with a vengeance, and Scots believers perpetual crusaders the one against the other, and missionaries the one to the other. Perhaps Robert's originally tender heart was what made the difference; or, perhaps, his solitary and pleasant labour among fruits and flowers had taught him a more sunshiny creed than those whose work is among the tares of fallen humanity; and the soft influences of the garden had entered deep into his spirit,

"Annihilating all that's made

To a green thought in a green shade."[9]

But I could go on for ever chronicling his golden sayings or telling of his innocent and living piety. I had meant to tell of his cottage, with the German pipe hung reverently above the fire, and the shell box that he had made for his son, and of which he would say pathetically: *"He was real pleased wi' it at first, but I think he's got a kind o' tired o' it now"* – the son being then a man of about forty. But I will let all these pass. "'Tis more significant: he's dead."[10] The earth, that he had digged so much in his life, was dug out by another for himself; and the flowers that he had tended drew their life still from him, but in a new and nearer way. A bird flew about the open grave, as if it too wished to honour the obsequies of one who had so often quoted Scripture in favour of its kind: "Are not two sparrows sold for one farthing? and yet not one of them falleth to the ground."[11]

Yes, he is dead. But the kings did not rise in the place of

death to greet him "with taunting proverbs" as they rose to greet the haughty Babylonian,[12] for in his life he was lowly, and a peacemaker and a servant of God.

A Winter's Walk in Carrick and Galloway

(A Fragment: 1876)[1]

✳

At the famous bridge of Doon, Kyle, the central district of the shire of Ayr, marches with Carrick, the most southerly. On the Carrick side of the river rises a hill of somewhat gentle conformation, cleft with shallow dells, and sown here and there with farms and tufts of wood. Inland, it loses itself, joining, I suppose, the great herd of similar hills that occupies the centre of the Lowlands. Towards the sea, it swells out the coastline into a protuberance, like a bay-window in a plan, and is fortified against the surf behind bold crags. This hill is known as the Brown Hill of Carrick, or, more shortly, Brown Carrick.

It had snowed overnight. The fields were all sheeted up; they were tucked in among the snow, and their shape was modelled through the pliant counterpane, like children tucked in by a fond mother. The wind had made ripples and folds upon the surface, like what the sea, in quiet weather, leaves upon the sand. There was a frosty stifle in the air. An effusion of coppery light on the summit of Brown Carrick showed where the sun was trying to look through; but along the horizon clouds of cold fog had settled down, so that there was no distinction of sky and sea. Over the white shoulders of the headlands, or in the opening of bays, there was nothing but a great vacancy and blackness; and the road as it drew near the edge of the cliff seemed to skirt the shores of creation and void space.

The snow crunched underfoot, and at farms all the dogs broke out barking as they smelt a passer-by upon the road. I met a fine old fellow, who might have sat as the father in "The Cottar's Saturday Night,"[2] and who swore most heathenishly at a cow he was driving. And a little after I scraped acquaintance with a poor body tramping out to gather cockles. His face was wrinkled by exposure; it was broken up into flakes and channels, like mud beginning to dry, and weathered in two colours, an incongruous pink and grey. He had a faint air of being surprised – which, God knows, he might well be – that life had gone so ill with him. The shape of his trousers was in itself a jest, so strangely were they bagged and ravelled about his knees; and his coat was all bedaubed with clay as though he had lain in a rain-dub during the New Year's festivity. I will own I was not sorry to think he had had a merry New Year, and been young again for an evening; but I was sorry to see the mark still there. One could not expect such an old gentleman to be much of a dandy, or a great student of respectability in dress; but there might have been a wife at home, who had brushed out similar stains after fifty New Years, now become old, or a round-armed daughter, who would wish to have him neat, were it only out of self-respect and for the ploughman sweetheart when he looks round at night. Plainly there was nothing of this in his life, and years and loneliness hung heavily on his old arms. He was seventy-six, he told me; and nobody would give a day's work to a man that age: they would think he couldn't do it. "And, 'deed," he went on, with a sad little chuckle, "'deed, I doubt if I could." He said good-bye to me at a footpath, and crippled wearily off to his work. It will make your heart ache if you think of his old fingers groping in the snow.

He told me I was to turn down beside the schoolhouse for Dunure. And so, when I found a lone house among the snow, and heard a babble of childish voices from within, I struck off into a steep road leading downwards to the sea. Dunure lies close under the steep hill: a haven among the rocks, a breakwater in consummate disrepair, much apparatus for drying nets, and a score or so of fishers' houses. Hard by, a few shards of ruined castle overhang the sea, a few vaults, and one tall gable honey-combed with windows. The snow lay on the beach to the tide-mark. It was daubed on to the sills of the ruin; it roosted in the crannies of the rock like white sea-birds; even on outlying reefs there would be a little cock of snow, like a toy lighthouse. Everything was grey and white in a cold and dolorous sort of shepherd's plaid. In the profound silence, broken only by the noise of oars at sea, a horn was sounded twice; and I saw the postman, girt with two bags, pause a moment at the end of the clachan for letters. It is, perhaps, characteristic of Dunure that none were brought to him.

The people at the public-house did not seem well pleased to see me, and though I would have stayed by the kitchen fire, sent me "ben the hoose" into the guest-room. This guest-room at

Dunure was painted in quite aesthetic fashion. There are rooms in the same taste not a hundred miles from London, where persons of an extreme sensibility meet together without embarrassment. It was all in a fine dull bottle-green and black; a grave harmonious piece of colouring with nothing, so far as coarser folk can judge, to hurt the better feelings of the most exquisite purist. A cherry-red half window-blind kept up an imaginary warmth in the cold room, and threw quite a glow on the floor. Twelve cockle-shells and a halfpenny china figure were ranged solemnly along the mantel-shelf. Even the spittoon was an original note, and instead of saw-dust contained sea-shells. And as for the hearth-rug, it would merit an article to itself, and a coloured diagram to help the text. It was patchwork, but the patchwork of the poor: no glowing shreds of old brocade and Chinese silk, shaken together in the kaleidoscope of some tasteful housewife's fancy; but a work of art in its own way, and plainly a labour of love. The patches came exclusively from people's raiment. There was no colour more brilliant than a heather mixture; "My Johnnie's grey breeks,"[3] well polished over the oar on the boat's thwart, entered largely into its composition. And the spoils of an old black cloth coat, that had been many a Sunday to church, added something (save the mark!) of preciousness to the material.

While I was at luncheon four carters came in – long-limbed, muscular Ayrshire Scots, with lean, intelligent faces. Four quarts of stout were ordered; they kept filling the tumbler with the other hand as they drank; and in less time than it takes me to write these words the four quarts were finished – another round was proposed, discussed, and negatived – and they were creaking out of the village with their carts.

The ruins drew you towards them. You never saw any place more desolate from a distance, nor one that less belied its promise near at hand. Some crows and gulls flew away croaking as I scrambled in. The snow had drifted into the vaults. The clachan dabbled with snow, the white hills, the black sky, the sea marked in the coves with faint circular wrinkles, the whole world, as it looked from a loophole in Dunure, was cold, wretched, and out-at-elbows. If you had been a wicked baron and compelled to stay there all the afternoon, you would have had a rare fit of remorse. How you would have heaped up the fire and gnawed your fingers! I think it would have come to homicide before the evening – if it were only for the pleasure of seeing something red! And the masters of

Dunure, it is to be noticed, were remarkable of old for inhumanity. One of these vaults where the snow had drifted was that "black voute" where "Mr. Alane Stewart, Commendatour of Cross-raguel," endured his fiery trials. On the 1st and 7th of September, 1570 (ill dates for Mr. Alan!), Gilbert, Earl of Cassilis, his chaplain, his baker, his cook, his pantryman, and another servant, bound the poor Commendator "betwix an iron chimlay and a fire," and there cruelly roasted him until he signed away his abbacy. It is one of the ugliest stories of an ugly period, but not, somehow, without such a flavour of the ridiculous as makes it hard to sympathise quite seriously with the victim. And it is consoling to remember that he got away at last, and kept his abbacy, and, over and above, had a pension from the Earl until he died.[4]

Some way beyond Dunure a wide bay, of somewhat less unkindly aspect, opened out. Colzean plantations lay all along the steep shore, and there was a wooded hill towards the centre, where the trees made a sort of shadowy etching over the snow. The road went down and up, and past a blacksmith's cottage that made fine music in the valley. Three compatriots of Burns drove up to me in a cart. They were all drunk, and asked me jeeringly if this was the way to Dunure. I told them it was; and my answer was received with unfeigned merriment. One gentleman was so much tickled he nearly fell out of the cart; indeed, he was only saved by a companion who either had not so fine a sense of humour or had drunken less.

"The toune of Mayboll," says the inimitable Abercrummie,[5] "stands upon an ascending ground from east to west, and lyes open to the south. It hath one principall street, with houses upon both sides, built of free-stone; and it is beautifyed with the situation of two castles, one at each end of this street. That on the east belongs to the Erle of Cassilis. On the west end is a castle, which belonged sometime to the laird of Blairquan, which is now the tolbuith, and is adorned with a pyremide [conical roof], and a row of ballesters round it raised from the top of the staircase, into which they have mounted a fyne clock. There be four lanes which pass from the principall street; one is called the Black Vennel, which is steep, declining to the south-west, and leads to a lower street, which is far larger than the high chiefe street, and it runs from the Kirkland to the Well Trees, in which there have been many pretty buildings, belonging to the severall gentry of the countrey, who were wont to resort thither in winter, and divert themselves in converse together at their owne houses. It was once the principall street of the town; but many of these houses of the gentry having been decayed and ruined, it has lost much of its ancient beautie. Just opposite to this vennel, there is another that leads north-west, from the chiefe street to the green, which is a pleasant plott of ground, enclosed round with an earthen wall, wherein they were wont to play football, but now at the Gowff and byasse-bowls. The houses of this toune, on both sides of the street, have their several gardens belonging to them; and in the lower street there be some pretty orchards, that yield store of good fruit." As Patterson says,[6] this description is near enough even to-day, and is mighty nicely written to boot. I am bound to add, of my own experience, that Maybole is tumbledown and dreary. Prosperous enough in reality, it has an air of decay, and though the population has increased, a roofless house every here and there seems to protest the contrary. The women are more than well-favoured, and the men fine tall fellows; but they look slipshod and dissipated. As they slouched at street corners, or stood about gossiping in the snow, it seemed they would have been more at home in the slums of a large city than here in a country place betwixt a village and a town. I heard a great deal about drinking, and a great deal about religious revivals: two things in which the Scottish character is emphatic and most unlovely. In particular, I heard of clergymen who were employing their time in explaining to a delighted audience the physics of the Second Coming. It is not very likely any of us will be asked to help. If we were, it is likely we should receive instructions for the occasion, and that on more reliable authority. And so I can only figure to myself a congregation truly curious in such flights of theological fancy, as one of veteran and accomplished saints, who have fought the good fight to an end and outlived all worldly passion, and are to be regarded rather as a part of the Church Triumphant than the poor, imperfect company on earth. And yet I saw some young fellows about the smoking-room who seemed, in the eyes of one who cannot count himself strait-laced, in need of some more practical sort of teaching. They seemed only eager to get drunk, and to do so speedily. It was not much more than a week after the New Year; and to hear them return on their past bouts with a gusto unspeakable was not altogether pleasing. Here is one snatch of talk, for the accuracy of which I can vouch –

"Ye had a spree here last Tuesday?"

"We had that!"

"I wasna able to be oot o' my bed. Man, I was awful bad on Wednesday."

"Ay, ye were gey bad."

And you should have seen the bright eyes, and heard the sensual accents! They recalled their doings with devout gusto and a sort of rational pride. Schoolboys, after their first drunkenness, are not more boastful; a cock does not plume himself with a more unmingled satisfaction as he paces forth among his harem; and yet these were grown men, and by no means short of wit. It was hard to suppose they were very eager about the Second Coming: it seemed as if some elementary notions of temperance for the men and seemliness for the women would have gone nearer the mark. And yet, as it seemed to me typical of much that is evil in Scotland, Maybole is also typical of much that is best. Some of the factories, which have taken the place of weaving in the town's economy, were originally founded and are still possessed by self-made men of the sterling, stout old breed – fellows who made some little bit of an invention, borrowed some little pocketful of capital, and then, step by step, in courage, thrift, and industry, fought their way upwards to an assured position.

Abercrummie has told you enough of the Tolbooth; but, as a bit of spelling, this inscription on the Tolbooth bell seems too delicious to withhold: "This bell is founded at Maiboll Bi Danel Geli, a Frenchman, the 6th November, 1696, Bi appointment of the heritors of the parish of Maiyboll". The Castle deserves more notice. It is a large and shapely tower, plain from the ground upwards, but with a zone of ornamentation running about the top. In a general way this adornment is perched on the very summit of the chimney-stacks; but there is one corner more elaborate than the rest. A very heavy string-course runs round the upper story, and just above this, facing up the street, the tower carries a small oriel window, fluted and corbelled and carved about with stone heads. It is so ornate it has somewhat the air of a shrine. And it was, indeed, the casket of a very precious jewel, for in the room to which it gives light lay, for long years, the heroine of the sweet old ballad of "Johnnie Faa" – she who, at the call of the gipsies' songs, "came tripping down the stair, and all her maids before her."[7] Some people say the ballad has no basis in fact, and have written, I believe, unanswerable papers to the proof. But in the face of all that, the very look of that high oriel window convinces

the imagination, and we enter into all the sorrows of the imprisoned dame. We conceive the burthen of the long, lack-lustre days,
when she leaned her sick head against the mullions, and saw the
burghers loafing in Maybole High Street, and the children at play,
and ruffling gallants riding by from hunt or foray. We conceive
the passion of odd moments, when the wind threw up to her some
snatch of song, and her heart grew hot within her, and her eyes
overflowed at the memory of the past. And even if the tale be not
true of this or that lady, or this or that old tower, it is true in the
essence of all men and women: for all of us, some time or other,
hear the gipsies singing, over all of us is the glamour cast. Some
resist and sit resolutely by the fire. Most go and are brought back
again, like Lady Cassilis. A few, of the tribe of Waring, go and
are seen no more; only now and again, at spring-time, when the
gipsies' song is afloat in the amethyst evening, we can catch their
voices in the glee.[8]

By night it was clearer, and Maybole more visible than during
the day. Clouds coursed over the sky in great masses; the full moon
battled the other way, and lit up the snow with gleams of flying
silver; the town came down the hill in a cascade of brown gables,
bestridden by smooth white roofs, and spangled here and there
with lighted windows. At either end the snow stood high up in
the darkness, on the peak of the Tolbooth and among the chimneys
of the Castle. As the moon flashed a bull's-eye glitter across the
town between the racing clouds, the white roofs leaped into relief
over the gables and the chimney-stacks, and their shadows over
the white roofs. In the town itself the lit face of the clock peered
down the street; an hour was hammered out on Mr. Geli's bell,
and from behind the red curtains of a public-house some one
trolled out – a compatriot of Burns, again! – "The saut tear blin's
my e'e."[9]

Next morning there was sun and a flapping wind. From the
street corners of Maybole I could catch breezy glimpses of green
fields. The road underfoot was wet and heavy – part ice, part
snow, part water; and any one I met greeted me, by way of saluta-
tion, with "A fine thowe" (thaw). My way lay among rather bleak
hills, and past bleak ponds and dilapidated castles and monasteries,
to the Highland-looking village of Kirkoswald. It has little claim
to notice, save that Burns came there to study surveying in the
summer of 1777, and there also, in the kirkyard, the original of
"Tam o' Shanter" sleeps his last sleep.[10] It is worth noticing, how-

ever, that this was the first place I thought "Highland-looking". Over the hill from Kirkoswald a farm-road leads to the coast. As I came down above Turnberry, the sea view was indeed strangely different from the day before. The cold fogs were all blown away; and there was Ailsa Craig, like a refraction, magnified and deformed, of the Bass Rock; and there were the chiselled mountain-tops of Arran, veined and tipped with snow; and behind, and fainter, the low, blue land of Cantyre. Cottony clouds stood, in a great castle, over the top of Arran, and blew out in long streamers to the south. The sea was bitten all over with white; little ships, tacking up and down the Firth, lay over at different angles in the wind. On Shanter they were ploughing lea; a cart foal, all in a field by himself, capered and winnied as if the spring were in him.

The road from Turnberry to Girvan lies along the shore, among sand-hills and by wildernesses of tumbled bent. Every here and there a few cottages stood together beside a bridge. They had one odd feature, not easy to describe in words: a triangular porch projected from above the door, supported at the apex by a single upright post; a secondary door was hinged to the post, and could be hasped on either cheek of the real entrance ; so, whether the wind was north or south, the cottar could make himself a triangular bight of shelter where to set his chair and finish a pipe with comfort. There is one objection to this device: for, as the post stands in the middle of the fairway, anyone precipitately issuing from the cottage must run his chance of a broken head. So far as I am aware, it is peculiar to the little corner of country about Girvan. And that corner is noticeable for more reasons: it is certainly one of the most characteristic districts in Scotland. It has this movable porch by way of architecture; it has, as we shall see, a sort of remnant of provincial costume, and it has the handsomest population in the Lowlands. . .

The Foreigner at Home[1]

"This is no' my ain house;
I ken by the biggin' o't."[2]

Two recent books, one by Mr. Grant White on England, one on France by the diabolically clever Mr. Hillebrand,[3] may well have set people thinking on the divisions of races and nations. Such thoughts should arise with particular congruity and force to inhabitants of that United Kingdom, peopled from so many different stocks, babbling so many different dialects, and offering in its extent such singular contrasts, from the busiest over-population to the unkindliest desert, from the Black Country to the Moor of Rannoch. It is not only when we cross the seas that we go abroad; there are foreign parts of England; and the race that has conquered so wide an empire has not yet managed to assimilate the islands whence she sprang. Ireland, Wales, and the Scottish mountains still cling, in part, to their old Gaelic speech. It was but the other day that English triumphed in Cornwall, and they still show in Mousehole, on St. Michael's Bay, the house of the last Cornish-speaking woman. English itself, which will now frank the traveller through the most of North America, through the greater South Sea Islands, in India, along much of the coast of Africa, and in the ports of China and Japan, is still to be heard, in its home country, in half a hundred varying stages of transition. You may go all over the States, and – setting aside the actual intrusion and influence of foreigners, negro, French, or Chinese – you shall scarce meet with so marked a difference of accent as in the forty miles between Edinburgh and Glasgow, or of dialect as in the hundred miles between Edinburgh and Aberdeen. Book English has gone round the world, but at home we still preserve the racy idioms of our fathers, and every county, in some parts every dale, has its own quality of speech, vocal or verbal. In like manner, local custom and prejudice, even local religion and local law, linger on into the latter end of the nineteenth century – *imperia*

in imperio,[4] foreign things at home.

In spite of these promptings to reflection, ignorance of his neighbours is the character of the typical John Bull. His is a domineering nature, steady in fight, imperious to command, but neither curious nor quick about the life of others. In French colonies, and still more in the Dutch, I have read that there is an immediate and lively contact between the dominant and the dominated race, that a certain sympathy is begotten, or at the least a transfusion of prejudices, making life easier for both. But the Englishman sits apart, bursting with pride and ignorance. He figures among his vassals in the hour of peace with the same disdainful air that led him on to victory. A passing enthusiasm for some foreign art or fashion may deceive the world, it cannot impose upon his intimates. He may be amused by a foreigner as by a monkey, but he will never condescend to study him with any patience. Miss Bird,[5] an authoress with whom I profess myself in love, declares all the viands of Japan to be uneatable – a staggering pretension. So, when the Prince of Wales's marriage was celebrated at Mentone by a dinner to the Mentonese, it was proposed to give them solid English fare – roast beef and plum pudding, and no tomfoolery. Here we have either pole of the Britannic folly. We will not eat the food of any foreigner; nor, when we have the chance, will we suffer him to eat of it himself. The same spirit inspired Miss Bird's American missionaries, who had come thousands of miles to change the faith of Japan, and openly professed their ignorance of the religions they were trying to supplant.

I quote an American in this connection without scruple. Uncle Sam is better than John Bull, but he is tarred with the English stick. For Mr. Grant White the States are the New England States and nothing more. He wonders at the amount of drinking in London; let him try San Francisco. He wittily reproves English ignorance as to the status of women in America; but has he not himself forgotten Wyoming? The name Yankee, of which he is so tenacious, is used over the most of the great Union as a term of reproach. The Yankee States, of which he is so staunch a subject, are but a drop in the bucket. And we find in his book a vast virgin ignorance of the life and prospects of America; every view partial, parochial, not raised to the horizon; the moral feeling proper, at the largest, to a clique of States; and the whole scope and atmosphere not American, but merely Yankee. I will go far beyond him in reprobating the assumption and the incivility of my country-folk to their cousins from beyond the sea; I grill in my blood over the silly rudeness of our newspaper articles; and I do not know where to look when I find myself in company with an American and see my countrymen unbending to him as to a performing dog. But in the case of Mr. Grant White example were better than precept. Wyoming is, after all, more readily accessible to Mr. White than Boston to the English, and the New England self-sufficiency no better justified than the Britannic.

It is so, perhaps, in all countries; perhaps in all, men are most ignorant of the foreigners at home. John Bull is ignorant of the States; he is probably ignorant of India; but considering his opportunities, he is far more ignorant of countries nearer his own door. There is one country, for instance – its frontier not so far from London, its people closely akin, its language the same in all essentials with the English – of which I will go bail he knows nothing. His ignorance of the sister kingdom cannot be described; it can only be illustrated by anecdote. I once travelled with a man of plausible manners and good intelligence – a University man, as the phrase goes – a man, besides, who had taken his degree in life and knew a thing or two about the age we live in. We were deep in talk, whirling between Peterborough and London; among other things, he began to describe some piece of legal injustice he had recently encountered, and I observed in my innocence that things were not so in Scotland. "I beg your pardon," said he, "this is a matter of law." He had never heard of the Scots law; nor did he choose to be informed. The law was the same for the whole country, he told me roundly; every child knew that. At last, to settle matters, I explained to him that I was a member of a Scottish legal body, and had stood the brunt of an examination in the very law in question. Thereupon he looked me for a moment full in the face and dropped the conversation. This is a monstrous instance, if you like, but it does not stand alone in the experience of Scots.

England and Scotland differ, indeed, in law, in history, in religion, in education, and in the very look of nature and men's faces, not always widely, but always trenchantly. Many particulars that struck Mr. Grant White, a Yankee, struck me, a Scot, no less forcibly; he and I felt ourselves foreigners on many common provocations. A Scotsman may tramp the better part of Europe and the United States, and never again receive so vivid an impression of foreign travel and strange lands and manners as on his first excursion into England. The change from a hilly to a level country strikes him with delighted wonder. Along the flat horizon there arise the frequent venerable towers of churches. He sees at the end of airy vistas the revolution of the windmill sails. He may go where he pleases in the future; he may see Alps, and Pyramids, and lions; but it will be hard to beat the pleasure of that moment. There are, indeed, few merrier spectacles than that of many windmills bickering together in a fresh breeze over a woody country; their halting alacrity of movement, their pleasant business, making bread all day with uncouth gesticulations, their air, gigantically human, as of a creature half alive, put a spirit of romance into the tamest landscape. When the Scottish child sees them first he falls immediately in love; and from that time forward windmills keep turning in his dreams. And so in their degree, with every feature of the life and landscape. The warm, habitable age of towns and hamlets, the green, settled, ancient look of the country; the lush hedgerows, stiles, and privy pathways in the fields; the sluggish, brimming rivers; chalk and smock-frocks; chimes of bells and the rapid, pertly-sounding English speech – they are all new to the curiosity; they are all set to English airs in the child's story that he tells himself at night. The sharp edge of novelty wears off; the feeling is scotched, but I doubt whether it is ever killed. Rather it keeps returning, ever the more rarely and strangely, and even in scenes to which you have been long accustomed suddenly awakes and gives a relish to enjoyment or heightens the sense of isolation.

One thing especially continues unfamiliar to the Scotsman's eye – the domestic architecture, the look of streets and buildings; the quaint, venerable age of many, and the thin walls and warm colouring of all. We have, in Scotland, far fewer ancient buildings, above all in country places; and those that we have are all of hewn or harled masonry. Wood has been sparingly used in their construction; the window-frames are sunken in the wall, not flat to the front, as in England; the roofs are steeper-pitched; even a hill farm will have a massy, square, cold and permanent appearance. English houses, in comparison, have the look of cardboard toys, such as a puff might shatter. And to this the Scotsman never becomes used. His eye can never rest consciously on one of these brick houses – rickles of brick, as he might call them – or on one of these flat-chested streets, but he is instantly reminded where he is, and instantly travels back in fancy to his home. "This is no' my ain house; I ken by the biggin' o't." And yet perhaps it is his own, bought with his own money, the key of it long polished in his pocket; but it has not yet, and never will be, thoroughly adopted by his imagination; nor does he cease to remember that, in the whole length and breadth of his native country, there was no building even distantly resembling it.

But it is not alone in scenery and architecture that we count England foreign. The constitution of society, the very pillars of the empire, surprise and even pain us. The dull, neglected peasant, sunk in matter, insolent, gross and servile, makes a startling contrast with our own long-legged, long-headed, thoughtful, Bible-quoting ploughman. A week or two in such a place as Suffolk leaves the Scotsman gasping. It seems incredible that within the boundaries of his own island a class should have been thus forgotten. Even the educated and intelligent who hold or own opinions and speak in our own words, yet seem to hold them with a difference or from another reason, and to speak on all things with less interest and conviction. The first shock of English society is like a cold plunge. It is possible that the Scot comes looking for too much, and to be sure his first experiment will be in the wrong direction. Yet surely his complaint is grounded; surely the speech of Englishmen is too often lacking in generous ardour, the better part of the man too often withheld from the social commerce, and the contact of mind with mind evaded as with terror. A Scottish peasant will talk more liberally out of his own experience. He will not put you by with conversational counters and small jests; he will give you the best of himself, like one interested in life and man's chief end. A Scotsman is vain, interested in himself and others, eager for sympathy, setting forth his thoughts and experience in the best light. The egoism of the Englishman is self-contained. He does not seek to proselytise. He takes no interest in Scotland or the Scots, and, what is the unkindest cut of all, he does not care to justify his indifference. Give him the wages of going on and being an Englishman, that is all he asks; and in the meantime, while you continue to associate, he would rather not be reminded of your baser origin. Compared with the grand, tree-like self-sufficiency of his demeanour, the vanity and curiosity of the Scot seem uneasy, vulgar and immodest. That you should continually try to establish human and serious relations, that you should actually feel an interest in John Bull, and desire and invite a return of interest from him, may argue something more awake and lively in your mind, but it still puts you in the attitude of a suitor and a poor relation. Thus even the lowest class of the educated English towers over a Scotsman by the head and shoulders.

Different indeed is the atmosphere in which Scottish and English youth begin to look about them, come to themselves in life, and gather up those first apprehensions which are the material of future thought and, to a great extent, the rule of future conduct. I have been to school in both countries, and I found, in the boys of the North, something at once rougher and more tender, at once more reserve and more expansion, a greater habitual distance chequered by glimpses of a nearer intimacy, and on the whole wider extremes of temperament and sensibility. The boy of the South seems more wholesome, but less thoughtful; he gives himself to games as to a business, striving to excel, but is not readily transported by imagination; the type remains with me as cleaner in mind and body, more active, fonder of eating, endowed with a lesser and a less romantic sense of life and of the future, and more immersed in present circumstances. And certainly, for one thing, English boys are younger for their age. Sabbath observance makes a series of grim, and perhaps serviceable, pauses in the tenor of Scottish boyhood – days of great stillness and solitude for the rebellious mind, when in the dearth of books and play, and in the intervals of studying the Shorter Catechism, the intellect and senses prey upon and test each other. The typical English Sunday, with the huge midday dinner and the plethoric afternoon, leads perhaps to different results. About the very cradle of the Scot there goes a hum of metaphysical divinity; and the whole of two divergent systems is summed up, not merely speciously, in the two first questions of the rival catechisms, the English tritely inquiring, "What is your name?" the Scottish striking at the very roots of life with, "What is the chief end of man?" and answering nobly, if obscurely, "To glorify God and to enjoy Him for ever." I do not wish to make an idol of the Shorter Catechism; but the fact of such a question being asked opens to us Scots a great field of speculation; and the fact that it is asked of all of us, from the peer to the ploughboy, binds us more nearly together. No Englishman of Byron's age, character and history, would have had patience for long theological discussions on the way to fight for Greece; but the daft Gordon blood and the Aberdonian schooldays kept their influence to the end. We have spoken of the material conditions; nor need much more be said of these: of the land lying everywhere more exposed, of the wind always louder and bleaker, of the black, roaring winters, of the gloom of high-lying, old stone cities, imminent on the windy seaboard; compared with the level streets, the warm colouring of the brick, the domestic quaintness of the architecture, among which English children begin to grow up and come to themselves in life. As the stage of the University approaches, the contrast becomes more express. The English lad goes to Oxford or Cambridge; there, in an ideal world of gardens, to lead a semi-scenic life, costumed, disciplined and drilled by proctors. Nor is this to be regarded merely as a stage of education; it is a piece of privilege besides, and a step that separates him further from the bulk of his compatriots. At an earlier age the Scottish lad begins his greatly different experience of crowded class-rooms, of a gaunt quadrangle, of a bell hourly booming over the traffic of the city to recall him from the public-house where he has been lunching, or the streets where he has been wandering fancy-free. His college life has little of restraint, and nothing of necessary gentility. He will find no quiet clique of the exclusive, studious and cultured; no rotten borough of the arts. All classes rub shoulders on the greasy benches. The raffish young gentleman in gloves must measure his scholarship with the plain, clownish laddie from the parish school. They separate, at the session's end, one to smoke cigars about a watering-place, the other to resume the labours of the field beside his peasant family. The first muster of a college class in Scotland is a scene of curious and painful interest; so many lads, fresh from the heather, hang round the stove in cloddish embarrassment, ruffled by the presence of their smarter comrades, and afraid of the sound of their own rustic voices. It was in these early days, I think, that Professor Blackie[6] won the affection of his pupils, putting these uncouth unbrageous students at their ease with ready human geniality. Thus, at least, we have a healthy democratic atmosphere to breathe in while at work; even when there is no cordiality there is always a juxtaposition of the different classes, and in the competition of study the intellectual power of each is plainly demonstrated to the other. Our tasks ended, we of the North go forth as free-men into the humming, lamplit city. At five o'clock you may see the last of us hiving from the college gates, in the glare of the shop windows, under the green glimmer of the winter sunset. The frost tingles in our blood, no proctor lies in wait to intercept us; till the bell sounds again, we are the masters of the world; and some portion of our lives is always Saturday, *la trève de Dieu.*[7]

Nor must we omit the sense of the nature of his country and his country's history gradually growing in the child's mind from story and from observation. A Scottish child hears much of shipwreck, outlying iron skerries, pitiless breakers, and great sealights; much of heathery mountains, wild clans, and hunted Covenanters. Breaths come to him in song of the distant Cheviots and the ring of foraying hoofs. He glories in his hard-fisted forefathers, of the iron girdle and the handful of oatmeal, who rode so swiftly and lived so sparely on their raids. Poverty, ill-luck, enterprise, and constant resolution are the fibres of the legend of his country's history. The heroes and kings of Scotland have been tragically fated; the most marking incidents in Scottish history – Flodden, Darien, or the Forty-five – were still either failures or defeats; and the fall of Wallace and the repeated reverses of the Bruce combine with the very smallness of the country to teach rather a moral than a material criterion for life. Britain is altogether small, the mere taproot of her extended empire; Scotland, again, which alone the Scottish boy adopts in his imagination, is but a little part of that, and avowedly cold, sterile and unpopulous. It is not so for nothing. I once seemed to have perceived in an American boy a greater readiness of sympathy for lands that are great, and rich, and growing, like his own. It proved to be quite otherwise: a mere dumb piece of boyish romance, that I had lacked penetration to divine. But the error serves the purpose of my argument; for I am sure, at least, that the heart of young Scotland will be always touched more nearly by paucity of number and Spartan poverty of life.

So we may argue, and yet the difference is not explained. That Shorter Catechism which I took as being so typical of Scotland, was yet composed in the city of Westminster. The division of races is more sharply marked within the borders of Scotland itself than between the countries. Galloway and Buchan, Lothian and Lochaber, are like foreign parts; yet you may choose a man from any of them, and, ten to one, he shall prove to have the headmark of a Scot. A century and a half ago the Highlander wore a different costume, spoke a different language, worshipped in another church, held different morals, and obeyed a different social constitution from his fellow-countrymen either of the south or north. Even the English, it is recorded, did not loathe the Highlander and the Highland costume as they were loathed by the remainder of the Scots. Yet the Highlander felt himself a Scot. He would willingly raid into the Scottish lowlands; but his courage failed him at the border, and he regarded England as a perilous, unhomely land. When the Black Watch, after years of foreign service, returned to Scotland, veterans leaped out and kissed the earth at Port Patrick. They had been in Ireland, stationed among men of their own race and language, where they were well liked and treated with affection; but it was the soil of Galloway that they kissed at the extreme end of the hostile lowlands, among a people who did not understand their speech, and who had hated, harried, and hanged them since the dawn of history. Last, and perhaps most curious, the sons of chieftains were often educated on the continent of Europe. They went abroad speaking Gaelic; they returned speaking not English, but the broad dialect of Scotland. Now, what idea had they in their minds when they thus, in thought, identified themselves with their ancestral enemies? What was the sense in which they were Scottish and not English, or Scottish and not Irish? Can a bare name be thus influential on the minds and affections of men, and a political aggregation blind them to the nature of facts? The story of the Austrian Empire would seem to answer, No; the far more galling business of Ireland clenches the negative from nearer home. Is it common education, common morals, a common language or a common faith, that join men into nations? There were practically none of these in the case we are considering.

The fact remains: in spite of the difference of blood and language, the Lowlander feels himself the sentimental countryman of the Highlander. When they meet abroad, they fall upon each other's necks in spirit; even at home there is a kind of clannish intimacy in their talk. But from his compatriot in the south the Lowlander stands consciously apart. He has had a different training; he obeys different laws; he makes his will in other terms, is otherwise divorced and married; his eyes are not at home in an English landscape or with English houses; his ear continues to remark the English speech; and even though his tongue acquire the Southern knack, he will still have a strong Scots accent of the mind.

Pastoral[1]

✳

To leave home in early life is to be stunned and quickened with novelties; but when years have come, it only casts a more endearing light upon the past. As in those composite photographs of Mr. Galton's,[2] the image of each new sitter brings out but the more clearly the central features of the race; when once youth has flown, each new impression only deepens the sense of nationality and the desire of native places. So may some cadet of Royal Écossais or the Albany Regiment, as he mounted guard about French citadels, so may some officer marching his company of the Scots-Dutch among the polders, have felt the soft rains of the Hebrides upon his brow, or started in the ranks at the remembered aroma of peat-smoke. And the rivers of home are dear in particular to all men. This is as old as Naaman, who was jealous for Abana and Pharpar;[3] it is confined to no race nor country, for I know one of Scottish blood but a child of Suffolk, whose fancy still lingers about the lilied lowland waters of that shire. But the streams of Scotland are incomparable in themselves – or I am only the more Scottish to suppose so – and their sound and colour dwell for ever in the memory. How often and willingly do I not look again in fancy on Tummel, or Manor, or the talking Airdle, or Dee swirling in its Lynn; on the bright burn of Kinnaird, or the golden burn that pours and sulks in the den behind Kingussie! I think shame to leave out one of these enchantresses, but the list would grow too long if I remembered all; only I may not forget Allan Water, nor birch-wetting Rogie, nor yet Almond; nor, for all its pollutions, that Water of Leith of the many and well-named mills – Bell's Mills, and Canon Mills, and Silver Mills; nor Redford Burn of pleasant memories; nor yet, for all its smallness, that nameless trickle that springs in the green bosom of Allermuir, and is fed from Halkerside with a perennial teacupful, and treads the moss under the Shearer's Knowe, and makes one pool there, overhung by a rock, where I loved to sit and make bad verses, and is then kidnapped in its infancy by subterranean pipes for the service of the sea-beholding city in the plain. From many points in the moss you may see at one glance its whole course and that of all its tributaries; the geographer of this Lilliput may visit all its corners without sitting down, and not yet begin to be breathed; Shearer's Knowe and Halkerside are but names of adjacent cantons on a single shoulder of a hill, as names are squandered (it would seem to the inexpert, in superfluity) upon these upland sheepwalks; a bucket would receive the whole discharge of the toy river; it would take it an appreciable time to fill your morning bath; for the most part, besides, it soaks unseen through the moss; and yet for the sake of auld lang syne, and the figure of a certain *genius loci*, I am condemned to linger awhile in fancy by its shores; and if the nymph (who cannot be above a span in stature) will but inspire my pen, I would gladly carry the reader along with me.

John Todd, when I knew him, was already "the oldest herd on the Pentlands," and had been all his days faithful to that curlew-scattering, sheep-collecting life. He remembered the droving days, when the drove roads, that now lie green and solitary through the heather, were thronged thoroughfares. He had himself often marched flocks into England, sleeping on the hillsides with his caravan; and by his account it was a rough business not without danger. The drove roads lay apart from habitation; the drovers met in the wilderness, as to-day the deep-sea fishers meet off the banks in the solitude of the Atlantic; and in the one as in the other case rough habits and fist-law were the rule. Crimes were committed, sheep filched, and drovers robbed and beaten; most of which offences had a moorland burial and were never heard of in the courts of justice. John, in those days, was at least once attacked – by two men after his watch – and at least once, betrayed by his habitual anger, fell under the danger of the law and was clapped into some rustic prison-house, the doors of which he burst in the night and was no more heard of in that quarter. When I knew him, his life had fallen in quieter places, and he had no cares beyond the dulness of his dogs and the inroads of pedestrians from town. But for a man of his propensity to wrath these were enough; he knew neither rest nor peace, except by snatches; in the gray of the summer morning and already from far up the hill, he would wake the "toun" with the sound of his shoutings; and in the lambing time, his cries were not yet silenced late at night. This wrathful voice of a man unseen might be said to haunt that quarter of the Pentlands, an audible bogie; and no doubt it added to the fear in which men stood of John a touch of something legendary. For my own part, he was at first my enemy, and I, in my character of a rambling boy, his natural abhorrence. It was long before I saw him near at hand, knowing him only by some sudden blast of bellowing from far above, bidding me "c'way oot amang the sheep." The quietest recesses of the hill harboured this ogre; I skulked in my favourite wilderness like a Cameronian of the Killing Time, and John Todd was my Claverhouse,[4] and his dogs my questing dragoons. Little by little we dropped into civilities; his hail at sight of me began to have less of the ring of a war-slogan; soon, we never met but he produced his snuff-box, which was with him, like the calumet with the Red Indian, a part of the heraldry of peace; and at length, in the ripeness of time, we grew to be a pair of friends, and when I lived alone in these parts in the winter, it was a settled thing for John to "give me a cry" over the garden wall as he set forth upon his evening round, and for me to overtake and bear him company.

That dread voice of his that shook the hills when he was angry, fell in ordinary talk very pleasantly upon the ear, with a kind of honied, friendly whine, not far off singing, that was eminently Scottish. He laughed not very often, and when he did, with a sudden, loud haw-haw, hearty but somehow joyless, like an echo from a rock. His face was permanently set and coloured; ruddy and stiff with weathering; more like a picture than a face; yet with a certain strain and threat of latent anger in the expression, like that of a man trained too fine and harassed with perpetual vigilance. He spoke in the richest dialect of Scots I ever heard; the words in themselves were a pleasure and often a surprise to me, so that I often came back from one of our patrols with new acquisitions; and this vocabulary he would handle like a master, stalking a little before me, "beard on shoulder," the plaid hanging loosely about him, the yellow staff clapped under his arm, and guiding me uphill by that devious, tactical ascent which seems peculiar to men of his trade. I might count him with the best talkers; only that talking Scots and talking English seem incomparable acts. He touched on nothing at least, but he adorned it; when he narrated, the scene was before you; when he spoke (as he did mostly) of his own antique business, the thing took on a colour of romance and curiosity that was surprising. The clans of sheep with their particular territories on the hill, and how, in the yearly killings and purchases, each must be proportionally thinned and strengthened; the midnight busyness of animals, the signs of the weather, the cares of the snowy season, the exquisite stupidity of sheep, the exquisite cunning of dogs; all these he could present so humanly, and with so much old experience and living gusto, that weariness was excluded. And in the midst he would suddenly straighten his bowed back, the stick would fly abroad in demonstration, and the sharp thunder of his voice roll out a long itinerary for the dogs, so that you saw at last the use of that great wealth of names for every knowe and howe upon the hillside; and the dogs, having hearkened with lowered tails and raised faces, would run up their flags again to the masthead and spread themselves upon the indicated circuit. It used to fill me with wonder how they could follow and retain so long a story. But John denied these creatures all intelligence; they were the constant butt of his passion and contempt; it was just possible to work with the like of them, he said – not more than possible. And then he would expand upon the subject of the really good dog that he had himself possessed. He had been offered forty pounds for it; but a good collie was worth more than that, more than anything, to a "herd"; he did the herd's work for him. "As for the like of them!" he would cry, and scornfully indicate the scouring tails of his assistants.

Once – I translate John's Lallan, for I cannot do it justice, being born *Britannis in montibus*, indeed, but alas! *inerudito saeculo*[5] – once, in the days of his good dog, he had bought some sheep in Edinburgh, and on the way out, the road being crowded, two were lost. This was a reproach to John, and a slur upon the dog; and both were alive to their misfortune. Word came, after some days, that a farmer about Braid had found a pair of sheep; and thither went John and the dog to ask for restitution. But the farmer was a hard man and stood upon his rights. "How were they marked?" he asked; and since John had bought right and left from many sellers and had no notion of the marks – "Very well," said the farmer, "then it's only right that I should keep them." – "Well," said John, "it's a fact that I cannae tell the sheep; but if my dog can, will ye let me have them?" The farmer was honest as well as hard, and besides I daresay he had little fear of the ordeal; so he had all the sheep upon his farm into one large park, and turned John's dog into their midst. That hairy man of business knew his errand well; he knew that John and he had bought two sheep and (to their shame) lost them about Boroughmuirhead; he knew besides (the Lord knows how, unless by listening) that they were come to Braid for their recovery; and without pause or blunder singled out, first one and then another, the two waifs. It was that afternoon the forty pounds were offered and refused. And the shepherd and his dog – what do I say? the true shepherd and his man – set off together by Fairmilehead in jocund humour, and "smiled to ither" all the way home, with the two recovered ones before them. So far, so good; but intelligence may be abused. The dog, as he is by little man's inferior in mind, is only by little his superior in virtue; and John had another collie tale of quite a different complexion. At the foot of the moss behind Kirk Yetton (Caer Ketton, wise men say)[6] there is a scrog of low wood and a pool with a dam for washing sheep. John was one day lying under a bush in the scrog, when he was aware of a collie on the far hillside skulking down through the deepest of the heather with obtrusive stealth. He knew the dog; knew him for a clever, rising practitioner from quite a distant farm; one whom perhaps he had coveted as he saw him masterfully steering flocks to market. But what did the practitioner so far from home? and why this guilty and secret manoeuvring towards the pool? – for it was towards the pool that he was heading. John lay the closer under his bush, and presently saw the dog come forth upon the margin, look all about to see if he were anywhere observed, plunge in and repeatedly wash himself over head and ears, and then (but now openly and with tail in air) strike homeward over the hills. That same night word was sent his master, and the rising practitioner, shaken up from where he lay, all innocence before the fire, was had out to a dykeside and promptly shot; for alas! he was that foulest of criminals under trust, a sheep-eater; and it was from the maculation of sheep's blood that he had come so far to cleanse himself in the pool behind Kirk Yetton.

A trade that touches nature, one that lies at the foundations of life, in which we have all had ancestors employed, so that on a hint of it ancestral memories revive, lends itself to literary use, vocal or written. The fortune of a tale lies not alone in the skill of him that writes, but as much, perhaps, in the inherited experience of him who reads; and when I hear with a particular thrill of things that I have never done or seen, it is one of that innumerable army of my ancestors rejoicing in past deeds. Thus novels begin to touch not the fine *dilettanti* but the gross mass of mankind, when they leave off to speak of parlours and shades of manner and still-born niceties of motive, and begin to deal with fighting sailor-ing, adventure, death or child-birth; and thus ancient outdoor crafts and occupations, whether Mr. Hardy wields the shepherd's crook or Count Tolstoi swings the scythe, lift romance into a near neighbourhood with epic. These aged things have on them the dew of man's morning; they lie near, not so much to us, the semi-artificial flowerets, as to the trunk and aboriginal taproot of the race. A thousand interests spring up in the process of the ages, and a thousand perish; that is now an eccentricity or a lost art which was once the fashion of an empire; and those only are perennial matters that rouse us to-day, and that roused men in all epochs of the past. There is a certain critic, not indeed of execution but of matter, whom I dare be known to set before the best: a certain low-browed, hairy gentleman, at first a percher in the fork of trees, next (as they relate) a dweller in caves, and whom I think I see squatting in cave-mouths, of a pleasant afternoon, to munch his berries – his wife, that accomplished lady, squatting by his side: his name I never heard, but he is often described as Probably Arboreal, which may serve for recognition. Each has his own tree of ancestors, but at the top of all sits Probably Arboreal; in all our veins there run some minims of his old, wild, tree-top blood; our civilised nerves still tingle with his rude terrors and pleasures; and to that which would have moved our common ancestor, all must obediently thrill.

We have not so far to climb to come to shepherds; and it may be I had one for an ascendant who has largely moulded me. But yet I think I owe my taste for that hill-side business rather to the art and interest of John Todd. He it was that made it live for me, as the artist can make all things live. It was through him the simple strategy of massing sheep upon a snowy evening, with its attendant scampering of earnest, shaggy aides-de-camp, was an affair that I never wearied of seeing, and that I never weary of recalling to mind: the shadow of the night darkening on the hills, inscrutable black blots of snow shower moving here and there like night already come, huddles of yellow sheep and dartings of black dogs upon the snow, a bitter air that took you by the throat, unearthly harpings of the wind along the moors; and for centre-piece to all these features and influences, John winding up the brae, keeping his captain's eye upon all sides, and breaking, ever and again, into a spasm of bellowing that seemed to make the evening bleaker. It is thus that I still see him in my mind's eye, perched on a hump of the declivity not far from Halkerside, his staff in airy flourish, his great voice taking hold upon the hills and echoing terror to the lowlands; I, meanwhile, standing somewhat back, until the fit should be over,* and, with a pinch of snuff, my friend relapse into his easy, even conversation.

The Manse[1]

✳

I have named, among many rivers that make music in my memory, that dirty Water of Leith. Often and often I desire to look upon it again; and the choice of a point of view is easy to me. It should be at a certain water-door, embowered in shrubbery. The river is there dammed back for the service of the flour-mill just below, so that it lies deep and darkling, and the sand slopes into brown obscurity with a glint of gold; and it has but newly been recruited by the borrowings of the snuff-mill just above, and these, tumbling merrily in, shake the pool to its black heart, fill it with drowsy eddies, and set the curded froth of many other mills solemnly steering to and fro upon the surface. Or so it was when I was young; for change, and the masons, and the pruning-knife, have been busy; and if I could hope to repeat a cherished experience, it must be on many and impossible conditions. I must choose, as well as the point of view, a certain moment in my growth, so that the scale may be exaggerated, and the trees on the steep opposite side may seem to climb to heaven, and the sand by the water-door, where I am standing, seem as low as Styx. And I must choose the season also, so that the valley may be brimmed like a cup with sunshine and the songs of birds – and the year of grace, so that when I turn to leave the river-side I may find the old manse and its inhabitants unchanged.

It was a place in that time like no other: the garden cut into provinces by a great hedge of beech, and overlooked by the church and the terrace of the churchyard, where the tombstones were thick, and after nightfall "spunkies" might be seen to dance at least by children; flower-plots lying warm in sunshine; laurels and the great yew making elsewhere a pleasing horror of shade; the smell of water rising from all round, with an added tang of paper-mills; the sound of water everywhere, and the sound of mills – the wheel and the dam singing their alternate strain; the birds on every bush and from every corner of the over-hanging woods pealing out their notes until the air throbbed with them; and in the midst of this, the manse. I see it, by the standard of my childish stature, as a great and roomy house. In truth, it was not so large as I supposed, nor yet so convenient, and, standing where it did, it is difficult to suppose that it was healthful. Yet a large family of stalwart sons and tall daughters was housed and reared, and came to man and womanhood in that nest of little chambers; so that the face of the earth was peppered with the children of the manse, and letters with outlandish stamps became familiar to the local postman, and the walls of the little chambers brightened with the wonders of the East. The dullest could see this was a house that had a pair of hands in divers foreign places: a well-beloved house – its image fondly dwelt on by many travellers.

Here lived an ancestor of mine, who was a herd of men.[2] I read him, judging with older criticism the report of childish observation, as a man of singular simplicity of nature; unemotional, and hating the display of what he felt; standing contented on the old ways; a lover of his life and innocent habits to the end. We children admired him: partly for his beautiful face and silver hair, for none more than children are concerned for beauty and, above all, for beauty in the old; partly for the solemn light in which we beheld him once a week, the observed of all observers, in the pulpit. But his strictness and distance, the effect, I now fancy, of old age, slow blood, and settled habit, oppressed us with a kind of terror. When not abroad he sat much alone, writing sermons or letters to his scattered family in a dark and cold room with a library of bloodless books – or so they seemed in those days, although I have some of them now on my own shelves and like well enough to read them; and these lonely hours wrapped him in the greater gloom for our imaginations. But the study had a redeeming grace in many Indian pictures, gaudily coloured and dear to young eyes. I cannot depict (for I have no such passions now) the greed with which I beheld them; and when I was once sent in to say a psalm to my grandfather, I went, quaking indeed with fear, but at the same time glowing with hope that, if I said it well, he might reward me with an Indian picture.

"Thy foot He'll not let slide, nor will
      He slumber that thee keeps,"[3]
it ran: a strange conglomerate of the unpronounceable, a sad model to set in childhood before one who was himself to be a versifier, and a task in recitation that really merited reward. And I must suppose the old man thought so too, and was either touched or

amused by the performance; for he took me in his arms with most unwonted tenderness, and kissed me, and gave me a little kindly sermon for my psalm; so that for that day, we were clerk and parson. I was struck by this reception into so tender a surprise that I forgot my disappointment. And indeed the hope was one of those that childhood forges for a pastime, and with no design upon reality. Nothing was more unlikely than that my grandfather should strip himself of one of those pictures, love-gifts and reminders of his absent sons; nothing more unlikely than that he should bestow it upon me. He had no idea of spoiling children, leaving all that to my aunt; he had fared hard himself, and blubbered under the rod in the last century; and his ways were still Spartan for the young. The last word I heard upon his lips was in this Spartan key. He had overwalked in the teeth of an east wind, and was now near the end of his many days. He sat by the dining-room fire, with his white hair, pale face and bloodshot eyes, a somewhat awful figure; and my aunt had given him a dose of our good old Scots medicine, Dr. Gregory's powder. Now that remedy, as the work of a near kinsman of Rob Roy himself, may have a savour of romance for the imagination;[4] but it comes uncouthly to the palate. The old gentleman had taken it with a wry face; and that being accomplished, sat with perfect simplicity, like a child's, munching a "barley-sugar kiss." But when my aunt, having the canister open in her hands, proposed to let me share in the sweets, he interfered at once. I had had no Gregory; then I should have no barley-sugar kiss: so he decided with a touch of irritation. And just then the phaeton coming opportunely to the kitchen door – for such was our unlordly fashion – I was taken for the last time from the presence of my grandfather.

Now I often wonder what I have inherited from this old minister. I must suppose, indeed, that he was fond of preaching sermons, and so am I, though I never heard it maintained that either of us loved to hear them. He sought health in his youth in the Isle of Wight, and I have sought it in both hemispheres; but whereas he found and kept it, I am still on the quest. He was a great lover of Shakespeare, whom he read aloud, I have been told, with taste; well, I love my Shakespeare also, and am persuaded I can read him well, though I own I never have been told so. He made embroidery, designing his own patterns; and in that kind of work I never made anything but a kettle-holder in Berlin wool, and an odd garter of knitting, which was as black as the chimney before I had done with it. He loved port, and nuts, and porter; and so do I, but they agreed better with my grandfather, which seems to me a breach of contract. He had chalk-stones in his fingers; and these, in good time, I may possibly inherit, but I would much rather have inherited his noble presence. Try as I please, I cannot join myself on with the reverend doctor; and all the while, no doubt, and even as I write the phrase, he moves in my blood, and whispers words to me, and sits efficient in the very knot and centre of my being. In his garden, as I played there, I learned the love of mills – or had I an ancestor a miller? – and a kindness for the neighbourhood of graves, as homely things not without their poetry – or had I an ancestor a sexton? But what of the garden where he played himself? – for that, too, was a scene of my education. Some part of me played there in the eighteenth century, and ran races under the green avenue at Pilrig; some part of me trudged up Leith Walk, which was still a country place, and sat on the High School benches, and was thrashed, perhaps, by Dr. Adam. The house where I spent my youth was not yet thought upon; but we made holiday parties among the cornfields on its site, and ate strawberries and cream near by at a gardener's. All this I had forgotten; only my grandfather remembered and once reminded me. I have forgotten, too, how we grew up, and took orders, and went to our first Ayrshire parish, and fell in love with and married a daughter of Burns's Dr. Smith – "Smith opens out his cauld harangues."[5] I have forgotten, but I was there all the same, and heard stories of Burns at first hand.

And there is a thing stranger than all that; for this *homunculus* or part-man of mine that walked about the eighteenth century with Dr. Balfour[6] in his youth, was in the way of meeting other *homunculos* or part-men, in the persons of my other ancestors. These were of a lower order, and doubtless we looked down upon them duly. But as I went to college with Dr. Balfour, I may have seen the lamp and oil man taking down the shutters from his shop beside the Tron[7] – we may have had a rabbit-hutch or a bookshelf made for us by a certain carpenter in I know not what wynd of the old, smoky city; or, upon some holiday excursion, we may have looked into the windows of a cottage in a flower-garden and seen a certain weaver plying his shuttle. And these were all kinsmen of mine upon the other side; and from the eyes of the lamp and oil man one-half of my unborn father, and one-quarter of myself, looked out upon us as we went by to college. Nothing of all this would cross the mind of the young student, as he posted up the Bridges with trim, stockinged legs, in that city of cocked hats and good Scots still unadulterated. It would not cross his mind that he should have a daughter; and the lamp and oil man, just then beginning, by a not unnatural metastasis, to bloom into a lighthouse-engineer, should have a grandson; and that these two, in the fulness of time, should wed; and some portion of that student himself should survive yet a year or two longer in the person of their child.

But our ancestral adventures are beyond even the arithmetic of fancy; and it is the chief recommendation of long pedigrees, that we can follow backward the careers of our *homunculos* and be reminded of our antenatal lives. Our conscious years are but a moment in the history of the elements that build us. Are you a bank-clerk, and do you live at Peckham? It was not always so. And though to-day I am only a man of letters, either tradition errs or I was present when there landed at St. Andrews a French barber-surgeon, to tend the health and the beard of the great Cardinal Beaton;[8] I have shaken a spear in the Debateable Land and shouted the slogan of the Elliots;[9] I was present when a skipper, plying from Dundee, smuggled Jacobites to France after the '15;[10] I was in a West India merchant's office, perhaps next door to Bailie Nicol Jarvie's, and managed the business of a plantation in St. Kitt's;[11] I was with my engineer-grandfather (the son-in-law of the lamp and oil man)[12] when he sailed north about Scotland on the famous cruise that gave us the *Pirate* and the *Lord of the Isles;*[13] I was with him, too, on the Bell Rock, in the fog, when the *Smeaton* had drifted from her moorings, and the Aberdeen men, pick in hand, had seized upon the only boats, and he must stoop and lap sea-water before his tongue could utter audible words;[14] and once more with him when the Bell Rock beacon took a "thawe," and his workmen fled into the tower, then nearly finished, and he sat unmoved reading in his Bible – or affecting to read – till one after another slunk back with confusion of countenance to their engineer.[15] Yes, parts of me have seen life, and met adventures, and sometimes met them well. And away in the still cloudier past, the threads that make me up can be traced by fancy into the bosoms of thousands and millions of ascendants: Picts who rallied round Macbeth and the old (and highly preferable) system of descent by females, fleërs from before the legions of Agricola, marchers in Pannonian morasses, star-gazers on Chaldaean plateaus; and furthest of all, what face is this that fancy can see peering through the disparted branches? What sleeper in green tree-tops, what muncher of nuts, concludes my pedigree? Probably Arboreal in his habits. . .

And I know not which is the more strange, that I should carry about with me some fibres of my minister-grandfather; or that in him, as he sat in his cool study, grave, reverend, contented gentleman, there was an aboriginal frisking of the blood that was not his; tree-top memories, like undeveloped negatives, lay dormant in his mind; tree-top instincts awoke and were trod down; and Probably Arboreal (scarce to be distinguished from a monkey) gambolled and chattered in the brain of the old divine.

Memoirs of an Islet[1]

✳

Those who try to be artists use, time after time, the matter of their recollections, setting and resetting little coloured memories of men and scenes, rigging up (it may be) some especial friend in the attire of a buccaneer, and decreeing armies to manoeuvre, or murder to be done, on the playground of their youth. But the memories are a fairy gift which cannot be worn out in using. After a dozen services in various tales, the little sunbright pictures of the past still shine in the mind's eye with not a lineament defaced, not a tint impaired. *Glück und Unglück wird Gesang,* if Goethe pleases;[2] yet only by endless avatars, the original re-embodying after each. So that a writer, in time, begins to wonder at the perdurable life of these impressions; begins, perhaps, to fancy that he wrongs them when he weaves them in with fiction; and looking back on them with ever-growing kindness, puts them at last, substantive jewels, in a setting of their own.

One or two of these pleasant spectres I think I have laid. I used one but the other day: a little eyot of dense, freshwater sand, where I once waded deep in butterburrs, delighting to hear the song of the river on both sides, and to tell myself that I was indeed and at last upon an island. Two of my puppets lay there a summer's day, hearkening to the shearers at work in riverside fields and to the drums of the gray old garrison upon the neighbouring hill. And this was, I think, done rightly: the place was rightly peopled – and now belongs not to me but to my puppets – for a time at least. In time, perhaps, the puppets will grow faint; the original memory swim up instant as ever; and I shall once more lie in bed, and see the little sandy isle in Allan Water as it is in nature, and the child (that once was me) wading there in butterburrs; and wonder at the instancy and virgin freshness of that memory; and be pricked again in season and out of season, by the desire to weave it into art.

There is another isle in my collection, the memory of which besieges me. I put a whole family there, in one of my tales;[3] and later on, threw upon its shores, and condemned to several days of rain and shellfish on its tumbled boulders, the hero of another.[4] The ink is not yet faded; the sound of the sentences is still in my mind's ear; and I am under a spell to write of that island again.

I

The little isle of Earraid lies close in to the south-west corner of the Ross of Mull: the sound of Iona on one side, across which you may see the isle and church of Columba; the open sea to the other, where you shall be able to mark, on a clear, surfy day, the breakers running white on many sunken rocks. I first saw it, or first remember seeing it,[5] framed in the round bull's-eye of a cabin port, the sea lying smooth along its shores like the waters of a lake, the colourless, clear light of the early morning making plain its heathery and rocky hummocks. There stood upon it, in these days, a single rude house of uncemented stones, approached by a pier of wreckwood. It must have been very early, for it was then summer, and in summer, in that latitude, day scarcely withdraws; but even at that hour the house was making a sweet smoke of peats which came to me over the bay, and the bare-legged daughters of the cotter were wading by the pier. The same day we visited the shores of the isle in the ship's boats; rowed deep into Fiddler's Hole, sounding as we went; and having taken stock of all possible accommodation, pitched on the northern inlet as the scene of operations. For it was no accident that had brought the lighthouse steamer to anchor in the Bay of Earraid. Fifteen miles away to seaward, a certain black rock stood environed by the Atlantic rollers, the outpost of the Torran reefs. Here was a tower to be built, and a star lighted, for the conduct of seamen. But as the rock was small, and hard of access, and far from land, the work would be one of years; and my father was now looking for a shore station, where the stones might be quarried and dressed, the men live, and the tender, with some degree of safety, lie at anchor.

I saw Earraid next from the stern thwart of an Iona lugger, Sam Bough[6] and I sitting there cheek by jowl, with our feet upon our baggage, in a beautiful, clear, northern summer eve. And behold! there was now a pier of stone, there were rows of sheds, railways, travelling-cranes, a street of cottages, an iron house for the resident engineer, wooden bothies for the men, a stage where the courses of the tower were put together experimentally, and behind the settlement a great gash in the hillside where granite was quarried. In the bay, the steamer lay at her moorings. All day long there hung about the place the music of chinking tools; and even in the dead of night, the watchman carried his lantern to and fro in the dark settlement, and could light the pipe of any midnight muser. It was, above all, strange to see Earraid on the Sunday, when the sound of the tools ceased and there fell a crystal quiet. All about the green compound men would be sauntering in their Sunday's best, walking with those lax joints of the reposing toiler, thoughtfully smoking, talking small, as if in honour of the stillness, or hearkening to the wailing of the gulls. And it was strange to see our Sabbath services, held, as they were, in one of the bothies, with Mr. Brebner reading at a table, and the congregation perched about in the double tier of sleeping bunks; and to hear the singing of the psalms, "the chapters," the inevitable Spurgeon's sermon, and the old, eloquent lighthouse prayer.

In fine weather, when by the spy-glass on the hill the sea was observed to run low upon the reef, there would be a sound of preparation in the very early morning; and before the sun had risen from behind Ben More, the tender would steam out of the bay. Over fifteen sea-miles of the great blue Atlantic rollers she ploughed her way, trailing at her tail a brace of wallowing stone-lighters. The open ocean widened upon either board, and the hills of the mainland began to go down on the horizon, before she came to her unhomely destination, and lay-to at last where the rock clapped its black head above the swell, with the tall iron barrack on its spider legs, and the truncated tower, and the cranes waving their arms, and the smoke of the engine-fire rising in the mid-sea. An ugly reef is this of the Dhu Heartach; no pleasant assemblage of shelves, and pools, and creeks, about which a child might play for a whole summer without weariness, like the Bell Rock or the Skerryvore, but one oval nodule of black-trap, sparsely bedabbled with an inconspicuous fucus, and alive in every crevice with a dingy insect between a slater and a bug. No other life was there but that of sea-birds, and of the sea itself, that here ran like a mill-race, and growled about the outer reef for ever, and ever and again, in the calmest weather, roared and spouted on the rock itself. Times were different upon Dhu Heartach when it blew, and the night fell dark, and the neighbour lights of Skerryvore and Rhu-val were quenched in fog, and the men sat prisoned high up in their iron drum, that then resounded with the lashing of the sprays. Fear sat with them in their sea-beleaguered dwelling; and the colour changed in anxious faces when some greater billow struck the barrack, and its pillars quivered and sprang under the blow. It was then that the foreman builder, Mr. Goodwillie, whom I see before me still in his rock-habit of undecipherable rags, would get his fiddle down and strike up human minstrelsy amid the music of the storm. But it was in sunshine only that I saw Dhu Heartach; and it was in sunshine, or the yet lovelier summer afterglow, that the steamer would return to Earraid, ploughing an enchanted sea; the obedient lighters, relieved of their deck cargo, riding in her wake more quietly; and the steersman upon each,, as she rose on the long swell, standing tall and dark against the shining west.

II

But it was in Earraid itself that I delighted chiefly. The lighthouse settlement scarce encroached beyond its fences; over the top of the first brae the ground was all virgin, the world all shut out, the face of things unchanged by any of man's doings. Here was no living presence, save for the limpets on the rocks, for some old, gray, rain-beaten ram that I might rouse out of a ferny den betwixt two boulders, or for the haunting and the piping of the gulls. It was older than man; it was found so by incoming Celts and seafaring Norsemen, and Columba's priests. The earthy savour of the bog plants, the rude disorder of the boulders, the inimitable seaside brightness of the air, the brine and the iodine, the lap of the billows among the weedy reefs, the sudden springing up of a great run of dashing surf along the sea-front of the isle, all that I saw and felt my predecessors must have seen and felt with scarce a difference. I steeped myself in open air and in past ages.

> "Delightful would it be to me to be in *Uchd Ailiun*
>> On the pinnacle of a rock,
> That I might often see
>> The face of the ocean;
> That I might hear the song of the wonderful birds,
>> Source of happiness;
> That I might hear the thunder of the crowding waves
>> Upon the rocks:
> At times at work without compulsion –
>> This would be delightful;
> At times plucking dulse from the rocks;
>> At times at fishing."

So, about the next island of Iona, sang Columba himself twelve hundred years before.[7] And so might I have sung of Earraid.

And all the while I was aware that this life of sea-bathing and sun-burning was for me but a holiday. In that year cannon were roaring for days together on French battle-fields;[8] and I would sit in my isle (I call it mine, after the use of lovers) and think upon the war, and the loudness of these far-away battles, and the pain of the men's wounds, and the weariness of their marching. And I would think too of that other war which is as old as mankind, and is indeed the life of man: the unsparing war, the grinding slavery of competition; the toil of seventy years, dear-bought bread, precarious honour, the perils and pitfalls, and the poor rewards. It was a long look forward; the future summoned me as with trumpet calls, it warned me back as with a voice of weeping and beseeching; and I thrilled and trembled on the brink of life, like a childish bather on the beach.

There was another young man on Earraid in these days, and we were much together, bathing, clambering on the boulders, trying to sail a boat and spinning round instead in the oily whirlpools of the roost. But the most part of the time we spoke of the great uncharted desert of our futures; wondering together what should there befall us; hearing with surprise the sound of our own voices in the empty vestibule of youth. As far, and as hard, as it seemed then to look forward to the grave, so far it seems now to look backward upon these emotions; so hard to recall justly that loath submission, as of the sacrificial bull, with which we stooped our necks under the yoke of destiny. I met my old companion but the other day; I cannot tell of course what he was thinking; but, upon my part, I was wondering to see us both so much at home, and so composed and sedentary in the world; and how much we had gained, and how much we had lost, to attain to that composure; and which had been upon the whole our best estate: when we sat there prating sensibly like men of some experience, or when we shared our timorous and hopeful counsels in a western islet.

The Coast of Fife[1]

✳

Many writers have vigorously described the pains of the first day or the first night at school; to a boy of any enterprise, I believe, they are more often agreeably exciting. Misery – or at least misery unrelieved – is confined to another period, to the days of suspense and the "dreadful looking-for" of departure; when the old life is running to an end, and the new life, with its new interests, not yet begun; and to the pain of an imminent parting, there is added the unrest of a state of conscious pre- existence. The area-railings, the beloved shop-window, the smell of semi-suburban tanpits, the song of the church bells upon a Sunday, the thin, high voices of compatriot children in a playing-field – what a sudden, what an overpowering pathos breathes to him from each familiar circumstance! The assaults of sorrow come not from within, as it seems to him, but from without. I was proud and glad to go to school; had I been let alone, I could have borne up like any hero; but there was around me, in all my native town, a conspiracy of lamentation: "Poor little boy, he is going away – unkind little boy, he is going to leave us"; so the unspoken burthen followed me as I went, with yearning and reproach. And at length, one melancholy afternoon in the early autumn, and at a place where it seems to me, looking back, it must be always autumn and generally Sunday, there came suddenly upon the face of all I saw – the long empty road, the lines of the tall houses, the church upon the hill, the woody hillside garden – a look of such a piercing sadness that my heart died; and seating myself on a door-step, I shed tears of miserable sympathy. A benevolent cat cumbered me the while with consolations – we two were alone in all that was visible of the London Road: two poor waifs who had each tasted sorrow – and she fawned upon the weeper, and gambolled for his entertainment, watching the effect, it seemed, with motherly eyes.

For the sake of the cat, God bless her! I confessed at home the story of my weakness; and so it comes about that I owed a certain journey, and the reader owes the present paper, to a cat

in the London Road. It was judged, if I had thus brimmed over
on the public highway, some change of scene was (in the medical
sense) indicated; my father at the time was visiting the harbour
lights of Scotland; and it was decided he should take me along
with him around a portion of the shores of Fife; my first professional
tour, my first journey in the complete character of man, without
the help of petticoats.[2]

The kingdom of Fife (that royal province)[3] may be observed
by the curious on the map, occupying a tongue of land between
the firths of Forth and Tay. It may be continually seen from many
parts of Edinburgh (among the rest, from the windows of my
father's house) dying away into the distance and the easterly *haar*
with one smoky sea-side town beyond another, or in winter print-
ing on the grey heaven some glittering hill-tops. It has no beauty
to recommend it, being a low, sea-salted, wind-vexed promontory;
trees very rare, except (as common on the east coast) along the
dens of rivers; the fields well cultivated, I understand, but not
lovely to the eye. It is of the coast I speak: the interior may be
the garden of Eden. History broods over that part of the world
like the easterly *haar*. Even on the map, its long row of Gaelic
place-names bear testimony to an old and settled race. Of these
little towns, posted along the shore as close as sedges, each with
its bit of harbour, its old weather-beaten church or public building,
its flavour of decayed prosperity and decaying fish, not one but
has its legend, quaint or tragic: Dunfermline, in whose royal towers
the king may be still observed (in the ballad) drinking the blood-
red wine;[4] somnolent Inverkeithing, once the quarantine of Leith;[5]
Aberdour, hard by the monastic islet of Inchcolm, hard by Donibristle where the "bonny face was spoiled";[6] Burntisland, where,
when Paul Jones was off the coast, the Reverend Mr. Shirra had
a table carried between tide-marks, and publicly prayed against
the rover at the pitch of his voice and his broad lowland dialect;[7]
Kinghorn, where Alexander "brak's neckbane"[8] and left Scotland
to the English wars; Kirkcaldy, where the witches once prevailed
extremely and sank tall ships and honest mariners in the North
Sea;[9] Dysart, famous – well famous at least to me for the Dutch
ships that lay in its harbour, painted like toys and with pots of
flowers and cages of song birds in the cabin windows, and for one
particular Dutch skipper who would sit all day in slippers on the
break of the poop, smoking a long German pipe;[10] Wemyss (pro-
nounce Weems) with its bat-haunted caves, where the Chevalier

Johnstone, on his flight from Culloden, passed a night of superstitious terrors;[11] Leven, a bald, quite modern place, sacred to summer visitors, whence there has gone but yesterday the tall figure and the white locks of the last Englishman in Delhi, my uncle Dr. Balfour, who was still walking his hospital rounds, while the troopers from Meerut clattered and cried "Deen, Deen" along the streets of the imperial city, and Willoughby mustered his handful of heroes at the magazine, and the nameless brave one in the telegraph office was perhaps already fingering his last despatch;[12] and just a little beyond Leven, Largo Law and the smoke of Largo town mounting about its feet, the town of Alexander Selkirk, better known under the name of Robinson Crusoe.[13] So on, the list might be pursued (only for private reasons, which the reader will shortly have an opportunity to guess) by St. Monans, and Pittenweem, and the two Anstruthers, and Cellardyke, and Crail, where Primate Sharpe was once a humble and innocent country minister:[14] on to the heel of the land, to Fife Ness, overlooked by a seawood of matted elders, and the quaint old mansion of Balcomie, itself overlooking but the breach or the quiescence of the deep – the Carr Rock beacon rising close in front, and as night draws in, the star of the Inchcape reef springing up on the one hand, and the star of the May Island on the other, and farther off yet a third and a greater on the craggy foreland of St. Abb's. And but a little way round the corner of the land imminent itself above the sea, stands the gem of the province and the light of mediaeval Scotland, St. Andrews, where the great Cardinal Beaton held garrison against the world, and the second of the name and title perished (as you may read in Knox's jeering narrative) under the knives of true-blue Protestants,[15] and to this day (after so many centuries) the current voice of the professor is not hushed.

Here it was that my first tour of inspection began, early on a bleak easterly morning. There was a crashing run of sea upon the shore, I recollect, and my father and the man of the harbour light must sometimes raise their voices to be audible. Perhaps it is from this circumstance, that I always imagine St. Andrews to be an ineffectual seat of learning, and the sound of the east wind and the bursting surf to linger in its drowsy class-rooms and confound the utterance of the professor, until teacher and taught are alike drowned in oblivion, and only the sea-gull beats on the windows and the draught of the sea-air rustles in the pages of the open lecture. But upon all this, and the romance of St. Andrews in general, the reader must consult the works of Mr. Andrew Lang; who has written of it but the other day in his dainty prose and with his incommunicable humour, and long ago in one of his best poems, with grace, and local truth and a note of unaffected pathos.[16] Mr. Lang knows all about the romance, I say, and the educational advantages, but I doubt if he had turned his attention to the harbour lights; and it may be news even to him, that in the year 1863 their case was pitiable. Hanging about with the east wind humming in my teeth, and my hands (I make no doubt) in my pockets, I looked for the first time upon that tragi-comedy of the visiting engineer which I have seen so often re-enacted on a more important stage. Eighty years ago, I find my grandfather writing: "It is the most painful thing that can occur to me to have a correspondence of this kind with any of the keepers, and when I come to the Light House, instead of having the satisfaction to meet them with approbation and welcome their Family, it is distressing when one is obliged to put on a most angry countenance and demeanour."[17] This painful obligation has been hereditary in my race. I have myself, on a perfectly amateur and unauthorised inspection of Turnberry Point, bent my brows upon the keeper on the question of storm-panes; and felt a keen pang of self-reproach, when we went downstairs again and I found he was making a coffin for his infant child; and then regained my equanimity with the thought that I had done the man a service, and when the proper inspector came he would be readier with his panes. The human race is perhaps credited with more duplicity than it deserves. The visitation of a lighthouse at least is a business of the most transparent nature. As soon as the boat grates on the shore, and the keepers step forward in their uniformed coats, the very slouch of the fellows' shoulders tells their story, and the engineer may begin at once to assume his "angry countenance." Certainly the brass of the hand-rail will be clouded; and if the brass be not immaculate, certainly all will be to match – the reflectors scratched, the spare lamp unready, the storm-panes in the storehouse. If a light is not rather more than middling good, it will be radically bad. Mediocrity (except in literature) appears to be unattainable by man. But of course the unfortunate of St. Andrews was only an amateur, he was not in the Service, he had no uniform coat, he was (I believe) a plumber by his trade and stood (in the mediaeval phase) quite out of the danger of my father; but he had a painful interview for all that, and perspired extremely.

From St. Andrews, we drove over Magus Muir. My father had announced we were "to post," and the phrase called up in my hopeful mind visions of top-boots and the pictures in Rowlandson's *Dance of Death;*[18] but it was only a jingling cab that came to the inn door, such as I had driven in a thousand times at the low price of one shilling on the streets of Edinburgh. Beyond this disappointment, I remember nothing of that drive. It is a road I have often travelled, and of not one of these journeys do I remember any single trait. The fact has not been suffered to encroach on the truth of the imagination. I still see Magus Muir two hundred years ago; a desert place, quite unenclosed; in the midst, the primate's carriage fleeing at the gallop; the assassins loose-reined in pursuit, Burley Balfour, pistol in hand, among the first. No scene of history has ever written itself so deeply on my mind; not because Balfour, that questionable zealot, was an ancestral cousin of my own;[19] not because of the pleadings of the victim and his daughter; not even because of the live bum-bee that flew out of Sharpe's 'bacco-box, thus clearly indicating his complicity with Satan;[20] nor merely because, as it was after all a crime of a fine religious flavour, it figured in Sunday books and afforded a grateful relief from *Ministering Children* or the *Memoirs of Mrs. Katherine Winslowe.*[21] The figure that always fixed my attention is that of Hackston of Rathillet,[22] sitting in the saddle with his cloak about his mouth, and through all that long, bungling, vociferous hurly-burly, revolving privately a case of conscience. He would take no hand in the deed, because he had a private spite against the victim, and "that action" must be sullied with no suggestion of a worldly motive;[23] on the other hand, "that action" in itself was highly justified, he had cast in his lot with "the actors," and he must stay there, inactive but publicly sharing the responsibility. "You are a gentleman – you will protect me!" cried the wounded old man, crawling towards him. "I will never lay a hand on you," said Hackston, and put his cloak about his mouth.[24] It is an old temptation with me, to pluck away that cloak and see the face – to open that bosom and to read the heart. With incomplete romances about Hackston, the drawers of my youth were lumbered.[25] I read him up in every printed book that I could lay my hands on. I even dug among the Wodrow manuscripts,[26] sitting shamefaced in the very room where my hero had been tortured two centuries before, and keenly conscious of my youth in the midst of other and (as I fondly thought) more gifted students. All was vain: that he had passed a riotous nonage, that he was a zealot, that he twice displayed (compared with his grotesque companions) some tincture of soldierly resolution and even of military common-sense, and that he figured memorably in the scene of Magus Muir, so much and no more could I make out. But whenever I cast my eyes backward, it is to see him like a landmark on the plains of history, sitting with his cloak about his mouth, inscrutable. How small a thing creates an immortality! I do not think he can have been a man entirely commonplace; but had he not thrown his cloak about his mouth, or had the witnesses forgot to chronicle the action, he would not thus have haunted the imagination of my boyhood, and to-day he would scarce delay me for a paragraph. An incident, at once romantic and dramatic, which at once awakes the judgment and makes a picture for the eye, how little do we realise its perdurable power! Perhaps no one does so but the author, just as none but he appreciates the influence of jingling words; so that he looks on upon life, with something of a covert smile, seeing people led by what they fancy to be thoughts and what are really the accustomed artifices of his own trade, or roused by what they take to be principles and are really picturesque effects. In a pleasant book about a school-class club, Colonel Fergusson has recently told a little anecdote.[27] A "Philosophical Society" was formed by some Academy boys – among them, Colonel Fergusson himself, Fleeming Jenkin, and Andrew Wilson, the Christian Buddhist and author of *The Abode of Snow*.[28] Before these learned pundits, one member laid the following ingenious problem: "What would be the result of putting a pound of potassium in a pot of porter?" "I should think there would be a number of interesting bi-products," said a smatterer at my elbow; but for me the tale itself was a bi-product, and stands as a type of much that is most human. For this inquirer who conceived himself to burn with a zeal entirely chemical, was really immersed in a design of a quite different nature; unconsciously to his own recently breeched intelligence, he was engaged in literature. Putting, pound, potassium, pot, porter; initial p, mediant t – that was his idea, poor little boy! So with politics and that which excites men in the present, so with history and that which rouses them in the past: there lie at the root of what appears most serious unsuspected elements. The triple town of Anstruther Wester, Anstruther Easter, and Cellardyke, all three Royal Burghs – or two Royal Burghs and a less distinguished suburb, I forget which – lies continuously along the seaside, and boasts of either two or three separate parish churches, and either two or three separate harbours. These ambiguities are painful; but the fact is (although it argue me uncultured), I am but poorly posted upon Cellardyke. My business lay in the two Anstruthers. A tricklet of a stream divides them, spanned by a bridge; and over the bridge at the time of my knowledge, the celebrated Shell House stood outpost on the west. This has been the residence of an agreeable eccentric; during his fond tenancy, he had illustrated the outer walls, as high (if I remember rightly) as the roof, with elaborate patterns and pictures, and snatches of verse in the vein of *exegi monumentum;* shells and pebbles, artfully contrasted and conjoined, had been his medium; and I like to think of him standing back upon the bridge, when all was finished, drinking in the general effect and (like Gibbon) already lamenting his employment.

The same bridge saw another sight in the seventeenth century. Mr. Thomson, the "curat" of Anstruther Easter, was a man highly obnoxious to the devout: in the first place, because he was a "curat"; in the second place, because he was a person of irregular and scandalous life; and in the third place, because he was generally suspected of dealings with the Enemy of Man. These three disqualifications, in the popular literature of the time, go hand in hand; but the end of Mr. Thomson was a thing quite by itself, and in the proper phrase, a manifest judgment. He had been at a friend's house in Anstruther Wester, where (and elsewhere, I suspect), he had partaken of the bottle; indeed, to put the thing in our cold modern way, the reverend gentleman was on the brink of *delirium tremens.* It was a dark night, it seems; a little lassie came carrying a lantern to fetch the curate home; and away they went down the street of Anstruther Wester, the lantern swinging a bit in the child's hand, the barred lustre tossing up and down along the front of slumbering houses, and Mr. Thomson not altogether steady on his legs nor (to all appearance) easy in mind. The pair had reached the middle of the bridge when (as I conceive the scene) the poor tippler started in some baseless fear and looked behind him; the child, already shaken by the minister's strange behaviour, started also; in so doing, she would jerk the lantern; and for the space of a moment the lights and the shadows would be all confounded. Then it was that to the unhinged toper and the twittering child, a huge bulk of blackness seemed to sweep down, to pass them close by as they stood upon the bridge, and to vanish on the farther side in the general darkness of the night. "Plainly the devil came for Mr. Thomson!" thought the child. What Mr. Thomson thought himself, we have no ground of knowledge; but he fell upon his knees in the midst of the bridge like a man praying. On the rest of the journey to the manse, history is silent; but when they came to the door, the poor caitiff, taking the lantern from the child, looked upon her with so lost a countenance that her little courage died within her, and she fled home screaming to her parents. Not a soul would venture out; all that night, the minister dwelt alone with his terrors in the manse; and when the day dawned, and men made bold to go about the streets, they found the devil had come indeed for Mr. Thomson.[29]

This manse of Anstruther Easter has another and more cheerful association. It was early in the morning, about a century before the days of Mr. Thomson, that his predecessor was called out of bed to welcome a Grandee of Spain, the Duke of Medina Sidonia, just landed in the harbour underneath.[30] But sure there was never seen a more decayed grandee; sure there was never a duke welcomed from a stranger place of exile. Half-way between Orkney and Shetland, there lies a certain isle; on the one hand the Atlantic, on the other the North Sea, bombard its pillared cliffs; sore-eyed, short-living, inbred fishers and their families herd in its few huts; in the grave-yard pieces of wreck-wood stand for monuments; there is nowhere a more inhospitable spot. *Belle-Isle-en-Mer* – Fair-Isle-at-Sea – that is a name that has always rung in my mind's ear like music; but the only "Fair Isle" on which I ever set my foot, was this unhomely, rugged turret-top of submarine sierras. Here, when his ship was broken, my lord Duke joyfully got ashore; here for long months he and certain of his men were harboured; and it was from this durance that he landed at last to be welcomed (as well as such a papist deserved, no doubt) by the godly incumbent of Anstruther Easter; and after the Fair Isle, what a fine city must that have appeared! and after the island diet, what a hospitable spot the minister's table! And yet he must have lived on friendly terms with his outlandish hosts. For to this day there still survives a relic of the long winter evenings when the sailors of the great Armada crouched about the hearths of the Fair Islanders, the planks of their own lost galleon perhaps lighting up the scene, and the gale and the surf that beat about the coast contributing their melancholy voices. All the folk of the north isles are great artificers of knitting: the Fair-Islanders alone dye their fabrics in the Spanish manner. To this day, gloves and nightcaps, innocently decorated, may be seen for sale in the Shetland warehouse at Edinburgh, or on the Fair Isle itself in the catechist's house; and to this day, they tell the story of the Duke of Medina Sidonia's adventure.

It would seem as if the Fair Isle had some attraction for "persons of quality". When I landed there myself, an elderly gentleman, unshaved, poorly attired, his shoulders wrapped in a plaid, was seen walking to and fro, with a book in his hand, upon the beach. He paid no heed to our arrival, which we thought a strange thing in itself; but when one of the officers of the *Pharos*, passing narrowly by him, observed his book to be a Greek Testament, our wonder and interest took a higher flight. The catechist was cross-examined; he said the gentleman had been put across some time before in Mr. Bruce of Sumburgh's schooner, the only link between the Fair Isle and the rest of the world; and that he held services and was doing "good". So much came glibly enough; but when pressed a little further, the catechist displayed embarrassment. A singular diffidence appeared upon his face: "They tell me," said he, in low tones, "that he's a lord." And a lord he was, a peer of the realm pacing that inhospitable beach with his Greek Testament, and his plaid about his shoulders, set upon doing good, as he understood it, worthy man! And his grandson, a good-looking little boy, much better dressed than the lordly evangelist, and speaking with a silken English accent very foreign to the scene, accompanied me for a while in my exploration of the island. I suppose this little fellow is now my lord, and wonder how much he remembers of the Fair Isle. Perhaps not much; for he seemed to accept very quietly his savage situation; and under such guidance, it is like that this was not his first nor yet his last adventure.

The Education of an Engineer[1]

✳

Anstruther is a place sacred to the Muse; she inspired (really to a considerable extent) Tennant's vernacular poem *Anster Fair;*[2] and I have there waited upon her myself with much devotion. This was when I came as a young man to glean engineering experience from the building of the breakwater.[3] What I gleaned, I am sure I do not know; but in deed I had already my own private determination to be an author; I loved the art of words and the appearances of life; and *travellers*, and *headers*, and *rubble*, and *polished ashlar*, and *pierres perdues*, and even the thrilling question of the *string-course*, interested me only (if they interested me at all) as properties for some possible romance or as words to add to my vocabulary. To grow a little catholic is the compensation of years; youth is one-eyed; and in those days, though I haunted the breakwater by day, and even loved the place for the sake of the sunshine, the thrilling sea-side air, the wash of waves on the sea-face, the green glimmer of the divers' helmets far below, and the musical chinking of the masons, my one genuine preoccupation lay elsewhere, and my only industry was in the hours when I was not on duty. I lodged with a certain Bailie Brown, a carpenter by trade; and there, as soon as dinner was despatched, in a chamber scented with dry rose-leaves, drew in my chair to the table and proceeded to pour forth literature, at such a speed, and with such intimations of early death and immortality, as I now look back upon with wonder. Then it was that I wrote *Voces Fidelium*, a series of dramatic monologues in verse; then that I indited the bulk of a covenanting novel – like so many others, never finished.[4] Late I sat into the night, toiling (as I thought) under the very dart of death, toiling to leave a memory behind me. I feel moved to thrust aside the curtain of the years, to hail that poor feverish idiot, to bid him go to bed and clap *Voces Fidelium* on the fire before he goes; so clear does he appear before me, sitting there between his candles in the rose-scented room and the late night; so ridiculous a picture (to my elderly wisdom) does the fool present! But he was driven to his bed at last without miraculous intervention; and the manner of his driving sets the last touch upon this eminently youthful business. The weather was then so warm that I must keep the windows open; the night without was populous with moths. As the late darkness deepened, my literary tapers beaconed forth more brightly; thicker and thicker came the dusty night-fliers, to gyrate for one brilliant instance round the flame and fall in agonies upon my paper. Flesh and blood could not endure the spectacle; to capture immortality was doubtless a noble enterprise, but not to capture it at such a cost of suffering; and out would go the candles, and off would I go to bed in the darkness, raging to think that the blow might fall on the morrow, and there was *Voces Fidelium* still incomplete. Well, the moths are all gone, and *Voces Fidelium* along with them; only the fool is still on hand and practises new follies.

Only one thing in connection with the harbour tempted me, and that was the diving, an experience I burned to taste of. But this was not to be, at least in Anstruther; and the subject involves a change of scene to the subarctic town of Wick.[5] You can never have dwelt in a country more unsightly than that part of Caithness, the land faintly swelling, faintly falling, not a tree, not a hedgerow, the fields divided by single slate stones set upon their edge, the wind always singing in your ears and (down the long road that led nowhere) thrumming in the telegraph wires. Only as you approached the coast was there anything to stir the heart. The plateau broke down to the North Sea in formidable cliffs, their tall out-stacks rose like pillars ringed about with surf, the coves were over-brimmed with clamorous froth, the sea-birds screamed, the wind sang in the thyme on the cliff's edge; here and there, small ancient castles toppled on the brim; here and there, it was possible to dip into a dell of shelter, where you might lie and tell yourself you were a little warm, and hear (near at hand) the whin-pods bursting in the afternoon sun, and (farther off) the rumour of the turbulent sea,. As for Wick itself, it is one of the meanest of man's towns, and situate certainly on the baldest of God's bays. It lives for herring, and a strange sight it is to see (of an afternoon) the heights of Pulteney blackened by seaward-looking fishers, as when a city crowds to a review – or, as when bees have swarmed, the ground is horrible with lumps and clusters; and a strange sight, and a beautiful, to see the fleet put silently out against a rising moon, the sea-line rough as a wood with sails, and even and again and one after another, a boat flitting swiftly by the silver disk. This mass of fishers, this great fleet of boats, is out of all proportion to the town itself; and the oars are manned and the nets hauled by immigrants from the Long Island (as we call the outer Hebrides), who come for that season only, and depart again, if "the take" be poor, leaving debts behind them. In a bad year, the end of the herring fishery is therefore an exciting time; fights are common, riots often possible; an apple knocked from a child's hand was once the signal for something like a war; and even when I was there, a gunboat lay in the bay to assist the authorities. To contrary interests, it should be observed, the curse of Babel is here added: the Lews men are Gaelic speakers, those of Caithness have adopted English; an odd circumstance, if you reflect that both must be largely Norsemen by descent. I remember seeing one of the strongest instances of this division: a thing like a Punch-and-Judy box erected on the flat grave-stones of the church-yard; from the hutch or proscenium – I know not what to call it – an eldritch-looking preacher laying down the law in Gaelic about some one of the name of *Powl*, whom I at last divined to be the apostle to the Gentiles; a large congregation of the Lews men very devoutly listening; and on the outskirts of the crowd, some of the town's children (to whom the whole affair was Greek and Hebrew) profanely playing tigg. The same descent, the same country, the same narrow sect of the same religion, and all these bonds made very largely nugatory by an accidental difference of dialect!

Into the bay of Wick stretched the dark length of the unfinished breakwater, in its cage of open staging; the travellers (like frames of churches) over-plumbing all; and away at the extreme end, the divers toiling unseen on the foundation. On a platform of loose planks, the assistants turned their air-mills; a stone might be swinging between wind and water; underneath the swell ran gaily; and from time to time, a mailed dragon with a window-glass snout came dripping up the ladder. Youth is a blessed season after all; my stay at Wick was in the year of *Voces Fidelium* and the rose-leaf room at Bailie Brown's; and already I did not care two straws for literary glory. Posthumous ambition perhaps requires an atmosphere of roses; and the more rugged excitant of Wick east winds had made another boy of me. To go down in the diving-dress, that was my absorbing fancy; and with the countenance of a certain handsome scamp of a diver, Bob Bain by name, I gratified the whim.

It was grey, harsh, easterly weather, the swell ran pretty high, and out in the open there were "skipper's daughters," when I found myself at last on the diver's platform, twenty pounds of lead upon each foot and my whole person swollen with ply and ply of woollen underclothing. One moment, the salt wind was whistling round my nightcapped head; the next, I was crushed almost double under the weight of the helmet. As that intolerable burthen was laid upon me, I could have found it in my heart (only for shame's sake) to cry off from the whole enterprise. But it was too late. The attendants began to turn the hurdy-gurdy, and the air to whistle through the tube; some one screwed in the barred window of the vizor; and I was cut off in a moment from my fellow-men; standing there in their midst, but quite divorced from intercourse: a creature deaf and dumb, pathetically looking forth upon them from a climate of his own. Except that I could move and feel, I was like a man fallen in a catalepsy. But time was scarce given me to realise my isolation; the weights were hung upon my back and breast, the signal-rope was thrust into my unresisting hand; and setting a twenty-pound foot upon the ladder, I began ponderously to descend.

Some twenty rounds below the platform, twilight fell. Looking up, I saw a low green heaven mottled with vanishing bells of white; looking around, except for the weedy spokes and shafts of the ladder, nothing but a green gloaming, somewhat opaque but very restful and delicious. Thirty rounds lower, I stepped off on the *pierres perdues* of the foundation; a dumb helmeted figure took me by the hand, and made a gesture (as I read it) of encouragement; and looking in at the creature's window, I beheld the face of Bain. There we were, hand to hand and (when it pleased us) eye to eye; and either might have burst himself with shouting, and not a whisper come to his companion's hearing. Each, in his own little world of air, stood incommunicably separate.

Bob had told me ere this a little tale, a five minutes' drama at the bottom of the sea, which at that moment possibly shot across my mind. He was down with another, settling a stone of the sea-wall. They had it well adjusted, Bob gave the signal, the scissors were slipped, the stone set home; and it was time to turn to something else. But still his companion remained bowed over the block like a mourner on a tomb, or only raised himself to make absurd contortions and mysterious signs unknown to the vocabulary of the diver. There, then, these two stood for a while, like

the dead and the living; till there flashed a fortunate thought into
Bob's mind, and he stooped, peered through the window of that
other world, and beheld the face of its inhabitant wet with streaming tears. Ah! the man was in pain! And Bob, glancing downward,
saw what was the trouble: the block had been lowered on the foot
of that unfortunate – he was caught alive at the bottom of the sea
under fifteen tons of rock.

That two men should handle a stone so heavy, even swinging
in the scissors, may appear strange to the inexpert. These must
bear in mind the great density of the water of the sea, and the
surprising results of transplantation to that medium. To understand
a little what these are, and how a man's weight, so far from being
an encumbrance, is the very ground of his agility, was the chief
lesson of my submarine experience. The knowledge came upon
me by degrees. As I began to go forward with the hand of my
estranged companion, a world of tumbled stones was visible, pillared with the weedy uprights of the staging: overhead, a flat roof
of green: a little in front, the sea-wall, like an unfinished rampart.
And presently in our upward progress, Bob motioned me to leap
upon a stone. I looked to see if he were possibly in earnest, and
he only signed to me the more imperiously. Now the block stood
six feet high; it would have been quite a leap to me unencumbered;
with the breast and back weights, and the twenty pounds upon
each foot, and the staggering load of the helmet, the thing was
out of reason. I laughed aloud in my tomb; and to prove to Bob
how far he was astray, I gave a little impulse from my toes. Up I
soared like a bird, my companion soaring at my side. As high as
to the stone, and then higher, I pursued my impotent and empty
flight. Even when the strong arm of Bob had checked my shoulders,
my heels continued their ascent; so that I blew out sideways like
an autumn leaf, and must be hauled in, hand over hand, as sailors
haul in the slack of a sail, and propped upon my feet again like
an intoxicated sparrow. Yet a little higher on the foundation, and
we began to be affected by the bottom of the swell, running there
like a strong breeze of wind. Or so I must suppose; for, safe in my
cushion of air, I was conscious of no impact; only swayed idly like
a weed, and was now borne helplessly abroad, and now swiftly –
and yet with dream-like gentleness – impelled against my guide.
So does a child's balloon divagate upon the currents of air, and
touch and slide off again from every obstacle. So must have inef-
fectually swung, so resented their inefficiency, those light clouds

that followed the Star of Hades, and uttered exiguous voices in the land beyond Cocytus.

There was something strangely exasperating, as well as strangely wearying, in these uncommanded evolutions. It is bitter to return to infancy, to be supported, and directed, and perpetually set upon your feet, by the hand of someone else. The air besides, as it is supplied to you by the busy millers on the platform, closes the eustachian tubes and keeps the neophyte perpetually swallowing, till his throat is grown so dry that he can swallow no longer. And for all these reasons – although I had a fine, dizzy, muddleheaded joy in my surroundings, and longed, and tried, and always failed, to lay hands on the fish that darted here and there about me, swift as humming-birds – yet I fancy I was rather relieved than otherwise when Bain brought me back to the ladder, and signed to me to mount. And there was one more experience before me even then. Of a sudden, my ascending head passed into the trough of a swell. Out of the green, I shot at once into a glory of rosy, almost of sanguine light – the multitudinous seas incarnadined, the heaven above a vault of crimson. And then the glory faded into the hard, ugly daylight of a Caithness autumn, with a low sky, a grey sea, and a whistling wind.

Bob Bain had five shillings for his trouble, and I had done what I desired. It was one of the best things I got from my education as an engineer: of which however, as a way of life, I wish to speak with sympathy. It takes a man into the open air; it keeps him hanging about harbour-sides, which is the richest form of idling; it carries him to wild islands; it gives him a taste of the genial dangers of the sea; it supplies him with dexterities to exercise; it makes demands upon his ingenuity; it will go far to cure him of any taste (if ever he had one) for the miserable life of cities. And when it has done so it carries him back and shuts him in an office! From the roaring skerry and the wet thwart of the tossing boat, he passes to the stool and desk; and with a memory full of ships, and seas, and perilous headlands, and the shining pharos, he must apply his long-sighted eyes to the petty niceties of drawing, or measure his inaccurate mind with several pages of consecutive figures. He is a wise youth, to be sure, who can balance one part of genuine life against two parts of drudgery between four walls, and for the sake of the one, manfully accept the other.

Wick was scarce an eligible place of stay. But how much better it was to hang in the cold wind upon the pier, to go down with Bob Bain among the roots of the staging, to be all day on a boat coiling a wet rope and shouting orders – not always very wise – than to be warm and dry, and dull, and dead-alive, in the most comfortable office. And Wick itself had in those days a note of originality. It may have still, but I misdoubt it much. The old minister of Keiss would not preach, in these degenerate times, for an hour and a half upon the clock. The gipsies must be gone from their caverns; where you might see, from the mouth, the women tending their fire, like Meg Merrilies,[6] and the men sleeping off their coarse potations; and where in winter gales, the surf would beleaguer them closely, bursting in their very door. A traveller to-day upon the Thurso coach would scarce observe a little cloud of smoke among the moorlands, and be told, quite openly, it marked a private still. He would not indeed make that journey, for there is now no Thurso coach. And even if he could, one little thing that happened to me could never happen to him, or not with the same trenchancy of contrast.

We had been upon the road all evening; the coach-top was crowded with Lews fishers going home, scarce anything but Gaelic had sounded in my ears; and our way had lain throughout over a moorish country very modern to behold. Latish at night, though it was still broad day in our subarctic latitude, we came down upon the shores of the roaring Pentland Firth, that grave of mariners; on one hand, the cliffs of Dunnet Head ran seaward; in front was the little bare, white town of Castleton, its streets full of blowing sand; nothing beyond, but the North Islands, the great deep, and the perennial ice-fields of the Pole. And here, in the last imaginable place, there sprang up young outlandish voices and a chatter of some foreign speech; and I saw, pursuing the coach with its load of Hebridean fishers – as they had pursued *vetturini* up the passes of the Apennines or perhaps along the grotto under Virgil's tomb – two little dark-eyed, white-toothed Italian vagabonds, of twelve to fourteen years of age, one with a hurdy-gurdy, the other with a cage of white mice. The coach passed on, and their small Italian chatter died in the distance; and I was left to marvel how they had wandered into that country, and how they fared in it, and what they thought of it, and when (if ever) they should see again the silver wind-breaks run among the olives, and the stone-pine stand guard upon Etruscan sepulchres.

Upon any American, the strangeness of this incident is some-what lost. For as far back as he goes in his own land, he will find some alien camping there; the Cornish miner, the French or Mexican half-blood, the negro in the south, these are deep in the woods and far among the mountains. But in an old, cold, and rugged country such as mine, the days of immigration are long at an end; and away up there, which was at that time far beyond the northernmost extreme of railways, hard upon the shore of that ill-omened strait of whirlpools, in a land of moors where no stranger came, unless it should be a sportsman to shoot grouse or an antiquary to decipher runes, the presence of these small pedestrians struck the mind as though a bird of paradise had risen from the heather or an albatross come fishing in the Bay of Wick. They were as strange to their surroundings as my lordly evangelist or the old Spanish grandee on the Fair Isle.[7]

Years after, I read in the papers that some defaulting banker had been picked up by a yacht upon the coast of Wales; the two vagabonds of Castleton (I know not why) rose instantly before my fancy; and that same night I had made the framework of a blood-and-thunder tale, which perhaps the reader may have dipped through under the name of *The Pavilion on the Links*. But how far more picturesque is the plain fact!

IV APPENDIX

✳

Scott's Voyage in the Lighthouse Yacht. Note[1]

Writing from Abbotsford on July 24, 1814, Scott announced to Morrit his voyage in the lighthouse tender. "I should have mentioned," he adds, "that we have the celebrated engineer, Stevenson, along with us. I delight in these professional men of talent: they always give some new lights by the peculiarity of their habits and studies, so different from people who are rounded, and smoothed, and ground down for conversation, and who can say all that every other person says, and nothing more".[2] The anticipation expressed in this slipshod passage appears to have been partly realized. My grandfather was a man in whom Scott could hardly fail to have been interested and from whom he could scarce help but profit. Romantically minded, he had led a life of some romance. Two years before he had brought to an end the unique adventure of the Bell Rock Lighthouse;[3] he had moved since boyhood as a pioneer among secluded and barbarous populations; his knowledge of the islands and their inhabitants was probably unrivalled; and his memory was rich in strange incidents and traits of manners, some of which have been preserved by Sir Walter in substance, while many others were doubtless boiled down into the general impression of "The Pirate".[4]

The anticipations of my grandfather would scarce be raised so high. He would have a proper respect for the sheriff of Selkirkshire as he had for all authorities. He would be prepared to sympathize with any Tory. He had a passion for the sea, the open air, wild scenery, and strange places. He was a reader, too, and a reader of poetry; doubtless he read Scott's poems as they appeared; and it will be seen that he spoke of them with their author. But in all this, there was perhaps something of effort, while his taste for the Waverley Novels was genuine and deep. I think it is so we must construe some of the expressions in the following paper: that he was not very much moved by the occasion of sailing shipmates with the author of "Marmion",[5] but had he been able to foresee in him the author of "Rob Roy", he would have kept a diary and begged for "one of the crook-headed hazel sticks".[6]

Scott and he had been acquainted before the cruise; I find them in correspondence as early as 1809; from 1814 on, they seem to have maintained the touch-and-go intimacy of neighbours and old shipmates; and upon one occasion Robert Stevenson applied to the great man for literary council. It took my grandfather four years to build the Bell Rock – and fourteen to prepare his quarto narrative of the achievement.[7] The book was dedicated to that majestic sovereign George the Fourth, a step which probably seemed to its author the most formidable of his life. All his friends wagged their Scots heads over the dedication, and it was submitted in proof to Sir Walter. *"It is with much diffidence that the author now lays before your majesty an Account of the arduous national undertaking of erecting a Lighthouse on the Bell Rock – a sunk reef lying about eleven miles from the shore and situate"* – thus the text began, and here on the proof sheet (which is now in my possession) we find Sir Walter substituting *situated* for *situate*, his only emendation.[8] This my grandfather dutifully accepted; he knew better in his heart and adhered elsewhere to the much more elegant *situate*; but if the other were the more proper wear for royalty, he was never the man to appear conspicuous at court. The concession was made in vain; in vain was the quarto spread in the sight of the King. I cannot find that the dedication was ever even formally acknowledged; but I do find Dr. Patrick Neill writing shortly after to congratulate my grandfather on his majesty's *"silent approbation"*. Dr. Neill is portrayed in the "Chaldee Manuscript" with a "rotten calabash" on his head;[9] he walks in my mind's eye with a scroll issuing from his mouth and the words *silent approbation* in the scroll. But such were manners in 1824, such the bland light that beat in these days on the occupant of a throne.

In 1850 my grandfather began to fail early in the year, and chafed for the period of the annual voyage which was his medicine and delight. In vain his sons dissuaded him from the adventure. The day approached, the obstinate old gentleman was found in his room furtively packing a portmanteau, and the truth had to be told him ere he would desist: that he was stricken with a malignant malady, and before the yacht should have completed her circuit of the lights, must have himself started on a more distant cruise.[10] My father has more than once told me of the scene with emotion. The old man was intrepid; he had faced death before with a firm countenance; and I do not suppose he was much dashed at the nearness of our common destiny. But there was something else that would cut him to the quick: the loss of the cruise, the end of all his cruising; the knowledge that he looked his last on Sumburgh, and the wild crags of Skye, and that Sound of Mull with the praise of which his letters were so often occupied; that he was never again to hear the surf break in Clashcarnock; never again to see lighthouse after lighthouse (all younger than himself and the more part of his own device) open in the hour of the dusk their flowers of fire, or the topaz and the ruby interchange on the summit of the Bell Rock. To a life of so much activity and danger, a life's work of so much interest and essential beauty, here came the long farewell.

It was in this spring and summer – at first impatiently expecting to revisit the scenes commemorated, and afterwards awaiting death in his own house and following with his mind's eye the course of the yacht now gone without him – that he returned with a memory already dim on the details of a former voyage, and wrote with a hand already failing his reminiscences of Scott. On June 28th he sent them to his favourite child Mrs. Warden,[11] with a note (not very coherently expressed) in which he proposes that she or "one of the misses" should "continue" them. Fourteen days later, on July 12th, Scott's shipmate followed him to the dark shore.

Two and forty years have passed. Mrs. Warden and "the misses" were alike forgetful, and still the memoranda have lain upon one side. I believe it would have pleased the old man to know that another of his descendants, on whose face he never looked but who shares with him in his love of Sir Walter, of the sea, and of wild islands, should prepare them at last for publication in an isle beyond the farthest cruising of the lighthouse tender.

Robert Stevenson has shown elsewhere that he could hold a pen. His *Account* of the Bell Rock is of its sort a masterpiece, and has been so recognized by judges: "the romance of stone and lime", it has been called, and "the *Robinson Crusoe* of engineering", both happy and descriptive phrases.[12] Even in his letters, though he cannot always be trusted for the construction of his sentences, the same literary virtues are apparent, a strong sense of romance and reality and an almost infallible instinct for the right detail. So much it is only fair to premise; for the present paper is strikingly inferior, and I am here exhibiting my grandfather in the weakness of his approaching death. This is his "Count Robert of Paris", if not his "Siege of Malta".[13] Two fair copies, both written with his own hand, both with corrections interlined, and yet with scarce a difference, show that he had not spared for vain pains; – and his recommendation to Mrs. Warden, that he was partly conscious of his failure. "Continue", the word that he has written, was plainly not the word that he intended. Plainly what he hoped was that someone else should take his material, and do it that justice in the presentment of which he felt he was himself no longer capable. But I have preferred to leave it, with a few suppressions, as it stood. Such as they are, it seems worth while (for the love of Sir Walter) to give these notes the commemoration of type. Once again, on the faith of a new witness, we find the same Scott represented, healthy, happy, regardful, intrepid and enthusiastic, a man of ten millions. His abstraction at Corriskin,[14] his pleasure in the company of seamen and pilots, his manly delight in danger, these are traits it is worth while to preserve or to confirm. And the paper offers besides, as through the chink of a door, one glimpse of Mrs. Lockhart, charming as usual. There is perhaps no one in story of whom we know so little and whom we love so well; she only shows at the wing, but with so taking a grace, that we are apt, when she appears, to forget the leading actors; and I have at times a hallucination (which I daresay I share with a thousand rivals) that I courted her when I was young, and "carried her books" along George Street, and was rejected in favour of *The Scorpion*, to my lasting sorrow.[15]

One thing I beg of my readers, that they will take down the fourth volume of Lockhart and read over again the *Voyage in the Lighthouse Yacht to Nova Zembla and the Lord knows where*, one of the most delightful passages in one of the most delightful of books.[16]

V EXPLANATORY NOTES

*

I INTRODUCTION

1   Recent collections include Binding, 1979, Calder, 1979, Campbell, 1980 and Calder, 1987. Stevenson's own collections of stories were themselves often miscellaneous in character: *New Arabian Nights*, 1882, included 'Bohemian', French and one Scottish story; *The Merry Men*, 1887, included several European fables, a French comic story and two Scottish stories.

2   See especially Jenni Calder's two anthologies, cited above: her edition of *Dr Jekyll and Mr Hyde* contains two South Pacific short stories.

3   See Swearingen, 1980, pp. 6-7.

II STORIES
The Plague-Cellar

1   Swearingen, 1980, p. 3, suggests this story was written 'Summer 1864, possibly later'. Since it deals with the Pentland insurrection of 1666, it seems probable that the story was written around the same time as Stevenson's essay 'The Pentland Rising', that is, late 1866, when Stevenson was fifteen or sixteen. The story mentions, in particular, the martyred Covenanter John Neilson of Corsack: Stevenson draws attention to him too in 'The Pentland Rising': see p. 205 and note 35. Both 'The Plague-Cellar' and 'The Pentland Rising' share the same historical site: the short story may have even been lifted from Stevenson's work on a novel about the Pentland insurrection at this time: see 'The Pentland Rising', note 1. The story seems to be set in early 1667, a month or two after the Pentland insurrection. It has not been published before in book form : it appeared, however, in *The Weekend Scotsman*, 24 August 1985. The manuscript of 'The Plague-Cellar' is held at Princeton University Library.

2   The first of the Pentland insurgents were executed in Edinburgh on 7 December 1666; the last on 22 December: see Kirkton, 1817, pp. 248-9. But the story is set in 1667 (see p. 19), clearly at the very beginning of that year.

3   Ravenswood, like Martext, is a fictional character. His name may well have been lifted from the protagonist of Sir Walter Scott's *The Bride of Lammermoor*, 1819. 'The Council' is of course the Privy Council of Scotland, presided over at this time by James Sharp: see note 10 below.

4   John Neilson of Corsack was an actual Covenanter, arrested and tortured in Edinburgh and executed on 14 December 1666: see 'The Pentland Rising', p. 205, 216 and note 35.

5   I do not know who 'Donald' could be; the well-known Cameronian Donald Cargill was in Glasgow at the time of the Pentland insurrection.

6   The last recorded outbreak of bubonic plague in Edinburgh was in 1645. Stevenson's plague of 1661 is fictional; possibly he meant it to coincide with the restoration

of Charles II in 1660 and the beginning of the days of the Persecution. See also *Edinburgh: Picturesque Notes*, xxvi, pp. 156-7.

7 See note 4.

8 I.e. referring to the persecution of nonconformist ministers at this time. See Introduction; see also 'The Pentland Rising', p. 204 and notes 23, 35.

9 Ravenswood's account neatly reverses a popular story about an attempt on the persecutor Tom Dalyell's life. See 'The Pentland Rising', p. 214: a bullet is deflected by Dalyell's 'buff-coat'. In Ravenswood's case, the Bible itself deflects the bullet, providing some claim for divine intervention where the Covenanters are concerned.

10 James Sharp (1613-1679). Sharp was appointed minister of Crail in 1649; however, some time later, in 1659, he began scheming for the Restoration and the introduction of episcopacy. See *DNB*, xvii, p. 1344: 'he afterwards excused himself for betraying his trust on the ground that no effort of his could have prevented the introduction of episcopacy. . . he seems to have had no scruples in playing what was beyond doubt a double part': it is in this sense that Ravenswood calls him 'apostate'. Sharp presided over the trials of the Pentland insurgents; he was particularly severe on the Covenanters, and several attempts were made on his life. He was murdered at Magus Muir in Fife on 3 May 1679 by a group of Covenanters led by David Hackston of Rathillet: see 'The Coast of Fife', p. 264, and notes 20, 22-25.

11 Dr Zophar Cant is fictional: his surname may be a parodic reference to the overblown style of the story. Compare the fate of Martext with Rev. Mr Soulis at the end of 'Thrawn Janet'.

The Pavilion on the Links

1 Probably begun in late 1878, but not completed until October 1879 when Stevenson was in Monterey, California. It was first published serially in *Cornhill Magazine*, 42 (September 1880) and 42 (October 1880), the first number breaking the story at the end of chapter IV. It was included in Stevenson's first book of fiction, the short story collection *New Arabian Nights*, 1882.

The *Cornhill* version differs from the final *New Arabian Nights* version in a number of small but significant ways: Stevenson must have revised the story for *New Arabian Nights* between the end of 1880 and 1882. The *Cornhill* version begins with a long introductory paragraph (left out of the final version) that shows the narrator, Frank Cassilis, directly addressing his children with the intention of revealing through the story that follows the 'long-kept secret' of how he had met their mother Clara, who is now dead. Narrating to his children in this way, this earlier version of the story is more personal and exclamatory than the final version (which dropped Cassilis's frequent emotional outbursts and all his references to 'my dear children', but left in occasional references to 'your mother': see, for example, p. 41). The long opening paragraph in the *Cornhill* version does, however, underline the essentially restorative role Clara has in the story – the way she changes Cassilis's gypsy life for the better, and so on. In this earlier version, Cassilis also tells his children that the story will contain a number of 'lessons', one of them being that 'it should teach in our family a spirit of great charity to the unfortunate and all those who are externally dishonoured.' The reference here is to Clara's father, the defaulting banker Huddlestone, who is presented in more detail – and even less favourably – in the *Cornhill* version.

2 In the Tusitala Edition of the story, an introductory note says 'The scenery

was suggested by Dirleton in East Lothian, near North Berwick, and midway between Tantallon and Gillane [*sic.*], haunts of his [Stevenson's] boyhood to which he returned in *Catriona', New Arabian Nights*, i, p. 158. However, the description of Graden Easter suggests a location further north. Swearingen, 1980, has drawn attention to Stevenson's remarks in the final sentences of 'The Education of an Engineer' as that essay appeared in *Scribner's Magazine*, 4 (November 1888) – sentences that were dropped when the essay was collected in *Across the Plains*, 1892, but which are restored in this edition: see p. 276. Here, Stevenson recalls his trip to the north-east tip of Scotland in September and October 1868, remarking on Wick and Castleton (or Castletown) in particular, and explicitly linking the location and events there with his 'blood-and-thunder tale' 'The Pavilion on the Links'.

3 Compare Stevenson's description of Aros in 'The Merry Men', p. 101: 'On calm days you can go wandering between them in a boat for hours. . . but when the sea is up, Heaven help the man that hears that caldron boiling. . . The homelessness of men, and even of inanimate vessels, cast away upon strange shores, came strongly in upon my mind'. 'The Pavilion on the Links' and 'The Merry Men' have a number of things in common. Both stories present a young man's account of his unusual experiences with a father and daughter. In both cases, the fathers are morally degraded or deteriorated. And both narrators, Cassilis and Charles Darnaway, approach the daughters with romantic intentions. The locations for both stories are bleak, isolated and windswept coastal places. See also note 5.

4 On Italians at Castleton, see 'The Education of an Engineer', pp. 275-6.

5 Compare Cassilis's experience here with Charles Darnaway in 'The Merry Men' as he dives for treasure and grasps an old shoe buckle from the *Espirito Santo*, p. 118: 'I held it in my hand, and the thought of its owner appeared before me like the presence of an actual man. . . The grave, the wreck of the brig, and the rusty shoe-buckle were surely plain advertisements. A child might have read their dismal story, and yet it was not until I touched that actual piece of mankind that the full horror of the charnel ocean burst upon my spirit'. The shoe-buckle, like the Italian's hat in 'The Pavilion on the Links', calls up before the narrator the foreign culture to which it once belonged.

6 The Carbonari or Charcoal-burners began as a secret sect, not unlike the Freemasons, in Italy in the early 19th century, soon rising to power. See Woolf, 1979, pp. 219-24, 252-64.

7 Giuseppe Garibaldi (1807-82) was a famous Italian freedom fighter. He led a volunteer army to the Tyrol, unsuccessfully, in Summer 1866 during the war with Austria.

Thrawn Janet

1 Completed in June 1881 and first published in *Cornhill Magazine*, 44 (October 1881). It was first collected in *The Merry Men and Other Tales*, 1887. Stevenson may have worked on the story as early as 1868: it is listed as one of the titles for his 'A Covenanting Story-Book' planned at this time: see Swearingen, 1980, p. 6.

2 The parish of Balweary is fictional but may be intended to recall the 'ruinous tower of Balwearie' in Fife, once belonging to the magician Sir Michael Scott. See Sibbald, 1803, p. 316. For further remarks on the connections between Stevenson's Balweary and Fife, see Parsons, 1946, pp. 551-2.

3 *I Peter*, v, 8: 'Be sober, be vigilant; because your adversary the devil, as a

roaring lion, walketh about, seeking whom he may devour.'

4   Stevenson took up the character of Janet M'Clour again in his unfinished novel *Heathercat*, begun in 1893 – twelve years after 'Thrawn Janet'. *Heathercat* is, however, set 30 years before the short story, taking place towards the end of the 'Killing Time' in 1682. Here, Janet is young and carefree and mixes with a drunken and 'incumbent' curate nicknamed 'Hell Haddo': 'This Janet M'Clour was a big lass, being taller than the curate; and what made her look the more so, she was kilted very high. . . the pair sat, drinking of the bottle, and daffing and laughing together, on a mound of heather,' *Weir of Hermiston*, pp. 149-50. Janet's irresponsible liaison with the curate at this time is certainly central to the fate in store for her in 'Thrawn Janet'. Note too that Stevenson adds in the short story that Janet has not 'come forrit' (i.e. taken holy communion) for 'thretty year' – that is, since the events in *Heathercat*.

5   *I Samuel*, xxviii, 3-25. Saul employs a woman at Endor to call up Samuel from the dead, even though he had earlier exiled all those 'that had familiar spirits, and. . . wizards'.

6   I.e. before the 'Glorious Revolution' of 1689.

7   Law, 1818, contains a number of examples of the devil appearing as a 'black man'.

The Body Snatcher

1   Begun in June 1881; but in July Stevenson wrote to Sidney Colvin that he had laid it aside 'in a justifiable disgust, the tale being horrid', *Letters*, ii, p. 158. It finally appeared in the *Pall Mall Christmas 'Extra'*, 13 (December 1884), but was not published in book form until its inclusion in the (posthumous) Edinburgh Edition of his complete works.

2   The 'extramural teacher of anatomy' is clearly a reference to Dr Robert Knox (1791-1862), who took control of the anatomical school at Edinburgh University in 1826: 'He at once took first rank as an anatomical lecturer, and his classes increased until his students numbered 504 in 1828-9, when he lectured for three hours daily. . . Knox, who was an enthusiast for practical dissection, was the best customer of the "resurrectionists", from whom alone "subjects" for dissection could be procured. He gave higher prices than others, and consequently offered a tempting market in 1828 for the victims of Burke and Hare', *DNB*, xi, p. 331.

3   The 'body-snatcher' William Burke (1792-1829) was hanged in Edinburgh on 28 January 1829.

4   William Burke and William Hare emigrated from Ireland to Scotland around 1818; they were both 'Ulster Catholics of the agricultural labourer class', Edwards, 1980, p. i.

5   The passage concerning Jane Galbraith is interestingly adapted from William Burke's confession, printed in the *Edinburgh Evening Courant*, 21 January 1829, a week before he was hanged. Burke's fourth murder victim, Mary Paterson, was delivered to the anatomists for dissection after being 'only four hours dead'. As the confession expressed it, 'One of the students said she was like a girl he had seen in the Canongate as one pea is like to another.' Edwards, 1980, p. 89, has remarked on Stevenson's adaptation of Burke's confession here: noting that 'as many as three of the assistants and students may have had previous carnal knowledge of Mary Paterson', he considers Stevenson's representation of Fettes' recognition of 'the girl he had jested with the day before' as one of his 'happiest euphemisms'. However, Fettes does later add, 'She was as well known as the Castle

Rock'. Fettes' response in this scene may have been modelled on an account given by one of Knox's keepers, David Paterson: see *West Port Murders* (Edinburgh, 1829), iv, p. 7. Paterson received the body of Mary Paterson (no relation) from Burke and Hare. He recognised the body but added, 'Now, as I remembered that I had positive orders from the Doctor not to interfere at all with these men, I was content to be silent'.

6 It may be worth asking why Stevenson sent his anatomists/body snatchers out to Glencorse. Burke and Hare, by contrast, did not go outside Edinburgh to procure their bodies. Stevenson was familiar with Glencorse: his grandfather Lewis Balfour was minister at Colinton, and Stevenson has recalled that as a child he once imagined there 'some dead man. . . sitting up in his coffin and watching us with that strange fixed eye', Balfour, 1901, i, p. 43. The Stevenson's Swanston Cottage was also nearby, and, staying there in 1872, Stevenson recalled 'a pit-worker from mid-Calder' who 'told me some curious stories of body-snatching from the lonely little burying-ground at Old Pentland, and spoke with the exaggerated horror that I have always observed in common people of this very excusable misdemeanour', *ibid.*, pp. 108-9. For an interesting parallel to the end of 'The Body-Snatcher', see the Ettrick Shepherd on Burke and Hare and 'ghosts in the Kintra' (country), *Blackwood's Magazine*, 41 (March 1829), p. 382.

The Merry Men

1 Begun in Summer 1881; revised in Winter 1881-2 and first published serially in *Cornhill Magazine*, 45 (June 1882) and 46 (July 1882), the first number containing the first three chapters. Collected in *The Merry Men and Other Tales*, 1887.

As with 'The Pavilion on the Links', 'The Merry Men' was revised for publication in book form at some time between mid-1882 and early 1887 – probably mid-1884 (see *Letters*, ii, p. 303). The revisions to the *Cornhill* version are significant and all of them are listed in Gelder, 1986, pp. 262-87. In particular, the revisions involve changes in the representation of the negro in the last chapter. In the *Cornhill* version, he is an animated and simple figure, a lost 'Man Friday'; while in the later book version (given here) he has a more solemn and symbolic role as an emblem of the 'black man' (as a 'fallen king', and so on).

2 See *Letters*, ii, p. 160: 'Aros is Earraid, where I lived lang syne; the Ross of Grisapol is the Ross of Mull'. Earraid is a small island off the south-west coast of Mull: Stevenson had stayed there in August 1870, and the story itself is set in July and August; see his essay 'Memoirs of an Islet'.

3 Compare the description of the waves on the Bass Rock by David Balfour's Highland companions in *Catriona*, p. 127: 'When the waves were anyway great they roared about the rock like thunder. . . dreadful but merry to hear'. Stevenson's description of the Merry Men at Aros Roost may have been influenced by Scott's descriptions of Sumburgh Roost on the southern tip of the Shetlands in his 'Voyage in the Lighthouse Yacht to Nova Zembla, and the Lord Knows Where', 1814: looking down at Sumburgh Roost, Scott observed, 'he must have a stouter heart than mine, who can contemplate without horror the situation of a vessel of an inferior description caught among these headlands and reefs of rock, in the long and dark winter nights of these regions. Accordingly, wrecks are frequent', Lockhart, 1902, iv, p. 229. Scott visited the Shetlands with Stevenson's grandfather, Robert Stevenson: see Stevenson's 'Scott's Voyage in the Lighthouse Yacht. Note', included here as an appendix. Scott also described Sumburgh Roost in *The Pirate*, 1822, which Stevenson knew well: see 'The Manse', note 13. In *The Pirate*, Basil

Merton and his son Mordaunt watch a ship come to grief in the 'huge swelling waves' of Sumburgh Roost that follow a recent storm: the scene is parallelled in 'The Merry Men'. Stevenson has almost certainly taken his title from Scott's introduction to *The Pirate* where Scott recalls the tour of the northern islands with Robert Stevenson and the other lighthouse commissioners, and remarks, 'for a time we might have adopted the lines of Allan Cunningham's fine sea-song,

> The world of waters was our home,
> And merry men were we!'

4   St Columba came to Iona in 563: see 'Memoirs of an Islet', note 7.

5   Possibly William Robertson (1721-1793), a prolific historian, created *D.D.* by Edinburgh University in 1758 and Principal of Edinburgh University from 1762 to 1792: see *DNB*, xvi, pp. 1311-6. This would set 'The Merry Men' in the mid-1790s, not long after Robertson had ceased as Principal.

6.   Train, 1814, pp. 217-8, remarks on a line from the ballad 'Elcine de Aggart', 'The last ship has sunk by our good Lady's Isle', explaining, 'It is reported, that the ship which carried the Vice-Admiral Alcarede, after being nearly dashed to pieces, went down by this rocky islet, about two leagues from the bar of Ayr'. Stevenson's Ross of Grisapol/Ross of Mull is some distance from Lady Isle, but Stevenson may have drawn on Train's further notes for a later scene in 'The Merry Men' involving sunken treasure from a ship from the Spanish Armada: see note 13. On Stevenson's fascination with the Armada presence in Scotland, see 'The Coast of Fife', p. 267 and note 30.

7   I.e. James VI, King of Scotland (1567-1603) when the Armada came to grief around the coast of Britain in 1588.

8   The Cameronians or Society Folk were militant Covenanters who took their name from Richard Cameron, a young field preacher who on 22 June 1680 declared war on King Charles II and the government at the market cross of Sanqhuar in Dumfries. See Howie, 1807, pp.421-9.

9   The first chosen title of 'The Merry Men' was 'The Wreck of the *Susanna*': see *Letters*, ii, p. 151. The change in the ship's name to *Christ-Anna* obviously gives it a Christian significance it previously lacked.

10   Metrical Psalm 65.

11   Metrical Psalm 107.

12   Christiania was the earlier name of Norway's capital, Oslo.

13   It is worth quoting the rest of Train's account of the sunken Spanish ship cited above, note 6, since it provides an interesting source for Charles' diving experience: 'Many articles of immense value, particularly a golden chair, intended as a throne for the personage who was to be the viceroy of his Catholic Majesty in England, was said to have been lost in this man of war; to recover which, two celebrated divers were brought, at the public expence [*sic.*], from the coast of Holland, who succeeded in stripping the bodies of the grandees and their ladies of such an amazing variety of jewellry, on deck, as really to justify the expectation that vast treasure would be found on searching the state rooms; but one of them, on his attempting to enter the cabin, had heard such an unearthly voice issue from within, that he never could be prevailed upon to descend again. The other, although more robust, was so much intimidated by the assurances of his companion, that it was not until he had received the grant of some crown-lands in Carrick, that he would venture on the dangerous enterprise. Agreeable to his contract, he entered by a hatchway at the forecastle, and, with the intention of rummaging the whole ship as he passed along the different wards, neither soldier, sailor, nor

galley-slave, escaped the rifling hand of the amphibious Hollander. Here he drew the silver-hilted sword which once dangled at the side of a proud Castilian, and there he snatched the crucifix from the hand of a military monk, whose sightless eye was still fixed on the idolatrous image. Thus performing the object of his mission, he went on, although he was often startled by the sudden appearance of angry-looking spirits, that seemed to take particular persons under their protection, yet he had the courage to proceed to the very door of the great cabin, where his countryman had been so awfully alarmed. To fortify his mind, he there put up a short ejaculation, and stepped forward; but as he crossed the threshold, a very ordinary looking gentleman, who was sitting in the golden chair, rose to salute him, presenting, at the same time, his *cloven hoof*, the sight of which so terrified the Dutchman, that he retreated in the utmost confusion, so that he was nearly drowned ere he could find his way to the surface of the water.' This account is also generally interesting, given uncle Gordon's superstitions concerning 'folk in the sea'. On Stevenson's own diving experiences, see 'The Education of an Engineer', pp. 270-4.

14 Metrical Psalm 93. Stevenson had quoted this same verse in a letter to his mother while he stayed at Wick in 1868, experiencing a violent storm; see *Letters*, i, p. 25.

15 On the 'black man' as a representation of the Devil, see 'Thrawn Janet', p. 75 and note 7.

The Misadventures of John Nicholson

1 Begun in late October 1885, but laid aside; continued in December 1886, but by January 1887 it still had not been published and Stevenson wrote to Henry James complaining about his 'silly Xmas story (with some larks in it) which won't be out till I don't know when', *Letters*, iii, p. 115. As Swearingen, 1980, p. 103, notes, Stevenson probably left the story with his publishers Cassell and Co. 'for publication at their pleasure', and it finally appeared under the full title 'The Misadventures of John Nicholson. A Christmas Story' in *Yule Tide, 1887; being Cassell's Christmas Annual*. The story was not published in book form until its inclusion in the (posthumous) Edinburgh Edition of Stevenson's complete works.

2 On 18 May 1843, some 470 ministers popularly known as Evangelicals broke away from the establishment Church of Scotland to form the Free Church. See Drummond *et al.*, 1975, p. 5: 'the Evangelicals who abandoned the Establishment would have been seen, not as the Free Church nor as a new denomination, but as the Church of Scotland, the Church of the Reformers and Covenanters, in her rightful freedom'.

3 Robert Candlish (1806-73), minister of St George's Free Church, Edinburgh, who led the organisation of the Free Church; James Begg (1808-83), after the Disruption minister of Newington Free Church, Edinburgh.

4 I.e. those ministers who remained with the establishment Church of Scotland.

5 John Lee (1779-1859), elected Principal of Edinburgh University in 1840 and shortly afterwards made Professor of Divinity; after the Disruption he remained faithful to the Church of Scotland; elected Moderator of the General Assembly in 1844.

6 This description of Mr Nicholson's stately home (in the stateliest part of Edinburgh's new town) – 'unassailable by right-hand defections or left-hand extremes' – is a discreet allusion to the Covenanter historian Patrick Walker, *Biographia Presbyteriana*; see i, p.iv: 'When I travelled many Miles, enquiring for my old

Acquaintances of the Gleanings of that unheard-of Persecution, it was for the most part answered. . . Others of them, whom I found alive. . . were obliged to say, that then it was better with them than now; especially these who have got the World in their Arms, and too much of it in their Hearts, and lost Sight of both their Eyes, and fallen in contentedly with this backsliding and upsitten Church. . . Others, upon the Right-Hand, of the bigot Dissenters, looking upon me with an evil Eye, and constructing all to the worst about me, gave me indiscreet, upbraiding Language, calling me a vile *old Apostate*. But these were no new things to me, being Weather-beaten, having been in the Midst of these Fires of Division, *between the Left-hand Defections and Right-hand Extreams*, upwards of Forty years' (my italics, except for 'old Apostate'). I am indebted to Dr Graham Tulloch of Flinders University, South Australia, for pointing out this reference to me. The allusion to Walker here certainly underscores the connections between the Free Churchmen and (in Drummond's phrase) 'the Church of the Reformers and Covenanters'.

7   Binding, 1979, pp. 28-31, argues that Mr Nicholson is a 'portrait' of Stevenson's father Thomas Stevenson. However, Stevenson's essay 'Thomas Stevenson' offers little specific grounds for comparison. Binding does not seem to take into account the representation of Mr Nicholson as a Free Churchman, sympathetic to the traditions the Free Church was trying to revive; by contrast, as Stevenson notes, Thomas Stevenson 'bore a clansman's loyalty' to the more moderate Church of Scotland, *Memories and Portraits*, xxix, p. 69.

8   On parallels here with Stevenson's youthful nocturnal escapades, see Balfour, 1901, i, pp. 79-84 and Furnas, 1952, p. 54.

9   Compare the Parable of the Prodigal Son, *Luke*, xv, 13: 'And not many days after, the younger son gathered all together, and took his journey into a far country, and there wasted his substance with riotous living'. In this passage, John leaves his father's house and the house of God at the same time, as in the parable. The title to chapter V is 'the Prodigal's Return'. Stevenson certainly alludes to this parable a number of times in his story. Ernest J. Mehew has noted that Stevenson's Vailima Library contained J. Goodman's *The Penitent Pardoned: or, a Discourse of the Nature of Sin, and the Efficacy of Repentance, under the Parable of the Prodigal Son*, 1679, a religious tract that discusses the implications of the Parable and the notion of penitence – also important in Stevenson's story.

10   Stevenson himself left Scotland for California at the beginning of August 1879.

11   Contrast the Parable of the Prodigal Son, *Luke*, xv, 20: 'his father saw him, and had compassion and ran, and fell on his neck, and kissed him'. Mr Nicholson's inability to forgive his son – on Christmas Eve – may be a comment on the severity or intransigence of the Free Church position.

12   On a source for Alan Houston's house at Murrayfield, see *Letters*, iv, p. 56.

13   Stevenson was born at 8 Howard Place.

14   I do not know the reference here.

The Tale of Tod Lapraik

1   Written in February 1892 and included in chapter iv of the novel *Catriona*, 1893. The story is told to David Balfour while he is kept prisoner on the Bass Rock. The narrator, named Black Andie Dale, is 'Prefect' of the rock, 'being at once the shepherd and the gamekeeper of that small and rich estate', *Catriona*, p. 119; Balfour describes him as 'a long-headed, sensible man, and a good Whig and

Presbyterian; read daily in a pocket Bible, and. . . both able and eager to converse seriously on religion, leaning more than a little towards the Cameronian extremes', p. 120. Andie's Presbyterian background and Cameronian 'leanings' are important to the story.

2   The Bass Rock was bought in 1671 by Charles II and turned into a garrison with 'eighteen soldiers, besides officers. . . placed in it', Wodrow, ii, p. 190. Covenanter prisoners were held there.

3   The story at this time is probably set in the mid-1670s: see note 4 below.

4   Alexander Peden (1626?-1686) was 'the most famed and revered of all Scottish covenanting preachers', *DNB*, xv, p. 651. In 1660 he was ordained minister of New Luce, Galloway, 'but having refused to comply with the acts of parliament, 11 June, and of the privy council, 1 Oct. 1662, requiring all who had been inducted since 1649 to obtain a new presentation from the lawful patron and have collation from the bishop of the diocese, letters were directed against him and twenty other ministers of Galloway, 24 Feb. 1663, for "labouring to keep the hearts of the people from the present government in church and state",' *ibid.*, p. 650. Peden was out-lawed or 'outed' from his ministry, but continued field-preaching. He was arrested and imprisoned on the Bass Rock on 26 June 1673, then removed on 9 October 1677 and later ordered to be transported to Virginia; but he managed to return to Scotland the following year. 'Peden's fame as a prophet was perpetuated among the peasants of the south of Scotland, by the collection of his prophecies, with instances of their fulfilment, made by Patrick Walker', *ibid.*, p. 651. See Walker, 1827, i, especially p. 43 (see note 5 below). See also Anderson, 1847.

5   The last two paragraphs (from 'Now there was a lass' to 'frae that day on') are in fact adapted from events in Walker, 1827, i, p. 43: 'While Prisoner in the *Bass*, one Sabbath Morning, being about the publick Worship of God, a young Lass, about the Age of Thirteen or Fourteen Years, came to the Chamber-door, mocking with loud Laughter: He said, Poor Thing, thou mocks and laughs at the Worship of God; but ere long, God shall write such a sudden, surprising Judgement on thee, that shall stay thy Laughing, and thou shalt not escape it. Very shortly thereafter, she was walking upon the Rock, and there came a Blast of Wind, and sweeped her off the Rock into the Sea where she was lost.

While prisoner there, one Day walking upon the Rock, some Soldiers passing by him, one of them cried, The Devil take Him; He said, Fy, fy, poor Man, thou knowest not what thou'rt saying, but thou wilt repent that: At which Words the Soldier stood astonished, and went to the Guard distracted, crying aloud for Mr *Peden*, saying, The Devil would immediately take him away. He came and spoke to him, and prayed for him; The next Morning he came to him again, and found him in his Right Mind, under Deep Convictions of great Guilt. The Guard being to change, they desired him to go to his Arms; he refused, and said, He would lift no Arms against Jesus Christ his Cause, and persecute his People, I've done that too long: The Governor threatened him with Death to Morrow at Ten a Clock; he confidently said Three Times, Tho' he should tear all his Body in Pieces, he should never lift Arms that Way. About three Days after the Governor put him out of the Garrison, setting him ashore; he having Wife and Children, took a House in *East-Lothian*, where he became a singular Christian.'

The conversion of the soldier (Tam Dale in Stevenson's story) away from his role as a persecutor of the Covenanters is made clear in Walker's account; Steven-son's story also shows the fate of a soldier who is not converted away from this role, Tod Lapraik.

6   Probably referring to Sir Hew Dalrymple (1652-1737), Lord North Berwick, 3rd son of James Dalrymple, first Viscount Stair.

7   The name Tod Lapraik may allude to a character from Scott's 'Wandering Willie's Tale', *Redgauntlet*, 1824; London, 1978, p. 115: here Steenie Steenson's neighbour is 'Laurie Lapraik – a sly tod'. Stevenson's tale has much in common with Scott's: both are set inside novels; the events they describe take place in the days of the persecution and end in the early 18th century some time after the Glorious Revolution; both narrators are devout Presbyterians, supporters of Kirk and Covenant; and both tales show wild young characters who are converted and restrained by their experiences. Compare the description of Steenie Steenson in Scott's tale, as a 'rambling, rattling chiel'. . . in his young days' (p. 113), with the description of Tam Dale, 'a wild sploring lad in his young days'; and compare the end of the stories, where Steenie 'held a circumspect walk' and 'of his ain accord, lang forswore baith the pipes and the brandy' (p. 129), and Tam Dale similarly 'had aye a gude name with honest folk frae that day on'.

8   The superstition that 'bogles' can only be killed with silver bullets or silver coins (testers) surely arises out of Covenanter mythology. Compare, for example, the view of Sir Robert Redgauntlet, a fierce persecutor of the Covenanters, in Scott's 'Wandering Willie's Tale': he is thought to have entered into 'a direct compact with Satan – that he was proof against steel – and that bullets happed aff his buff-coat like hailstanes from a hearth', *Redgauntlet*, p. 113; see also p. 124, 'And there was Claverhouse. . . his left hand always on his right spule-blade, to hide the wound that the silver bullet had made'. Scott's *Old Mortality*, 1816, also describes the superstition that Claverhouse could only be killed with 'a silver bullet'. See also Stevenson's account of Thomas Dalyell, 'The Pentland Rising', p. 214 and note 28.

III ESSAYS
The Pentland Rising

1   This essay is dated 28 November 1866 and was written to mark the bicentenary of the Pentland insurrection. One hundred copies of the essay were printed (as a sixteen-page pamphlet), at Stevenson's father's expense. Balfour, 1901, i, p. 67, notes that Stevenson had at this time originally begun to write a novel on the 1666 Pentland insurrection, but soon abandoned it: 'though the novel was destroyed, his studies issued in a small green pamphlet, entitled, *The Pentland Rising: a Page of History, 1666*, published anonymously, in 1866, by Andrew Elliot in Edinburgh'. See also Stevenson's essay, 'My First Book', *Treasure Island*, ii, p. xxiii; and Swearingen, 1980, p. 4.

2   For the complete verse, see p. 215 and note 29 below.

3   *Theatre of Mortality*, p. 10, Edin. 1713 [R.L.S.]. Monteith, 1713, p.10. The inscription, from Martyrs Monument in Greyfriars Kirk, Edinburgh, is cited in full here.

4   *History of my Own Times, beginning 1660*, by Bishop Gilbert Burnet, p. 158 [R.L.S.]. Burnet, 1724, p. 158. Stevenson misquotes in part, omitting a sentence: the passage should read, '. . .vicious. They were a disgrace to their orders, and the sacred functions; and were indeed. . .'

5   Stewart and Stirling, 1721, p. 123.

6   Wodrow's *Church History*, book ii, chapter 1, sect. I [R.L.S.]. Wodrow, 1829-30, ii, Book ii, chapter 1, p. 202.

7   Crookshank's *Church History*, 1751, 2nd edit., p. 202 [R.L.S.]. Crookshank,

1751, p. 202, adds 'and all this for nothing but non-conformity'.

8 Burnet, p. 348 [R.L.S.]. Actually, Burnet, 1724, p. 211.

9 Fuller's *Historie of the Holy Warre.* 4th edit., 1651 [R.L.S.]. Fuller, 1651, epigraph, n.p. This short poem, by 'Tho. Jackson' and titled 'To his old Friend M. FULLER', has three verses. The last, not quoted by Stevenson, reads

> But in thy Book
> When I do look
>   And it admire;
> Let *Warre* be there
> But Peace elsewhere;
>   This I desire.

10 Wodrow, vol. ii, p. 17 [R.L.S.]. Wodrow, 1829-30, ii, Book ii, chapter 1, section 1, pp. 17-8.

11 Turner, 1829.

12 Turner, 1683.

13 For a complete list of Turner's 'shorter pieces', see Turner, 1829, p. xiii, 'Appendix: Analysis of the Contents of the Manuscript from which Sir James Turner's Memoirs have been extracted'.

14 Sir J. Turner's *Memoirs*, pp. 148-150 [R.L.S.]. Actually, *ibid.*, p. 149.

15 *A Cloud of Witnesses*, p. 376 [R.L.S.]. Thomson, 1765, p. 376. Actually, 'Inscription upon a grave-stone in the church-yard of Hamilton, lying on the heads of John Parker, Gavin Hamilton, James Hamilton, and Christopher Strang, who suffered at Edinburgh, Dec. 7. 1666'.

16 James Sharp was murdered at Magus Muir on 3 May 1679. See 'The Plague-Cellar', note 10, and 'The Coast of Fife', pp. 264 and notes 20, 22-25.

17 Wodrow, pp. 19-20 [R.L.S.]. Wodrow, 1829-30, ii, Book ii, chapter 1, section 2, pp. 20-1. Stevenson dramatises the position here. Wodrow quotes Sharp's proclamation against the rebels on 21 November 1666, and summarises, 'such a proclamation could have little other effect, but to imbolden the poor men, and let them see they must either go through what they had begun, or die', p. 21.

18 *A Hind Let Loose*, p. 123 [R.L.S.]. Shields, 1744, p. 123: 'it is known how desirous they have been of an Insurrection, when they thought themselves sure to suppress it, that they might have a vent for their Cruelty; and how one of the Brothers hath been heard say, *That if he might have his wish, he would have them all turn Rebels, and go to arms*'.

19 Sir J. Turner, p. 163 [R.L.S.]. Actually, Turner, 1829, pp. 163-4.

20 Turner, p. 198 [R.L.S.]. Actually, *ibid.*, pp. 158-9.

21 *Ibid.*, p. 167 [R.L.S.].

22 Wodrow, p. 29 [R.L.S.]. Actually, Wodrow, 1829-30, ii, Book ii, chapter 1, section 2, p. 25. Stevenson is quoting the 'Declaration of those in arms for the covenant, 1666'.

23 Turner, Wodrow, and *Church History*, by James Kirkton, an outed minister of the period [R.L.S.]. Actually, Turner, 1829, p. 177; Wodrow 1829-30, i, Book ii, chapter 1, section 2, p. 29; Kirkton, 1817, p. 241. Like Stevenson's fictional minister Martext in 'The Plague-Cellar', Kirkton was 'an outed minister'. See Kirkton, 1817, p. ix: on '11th June, 1674, the council gave out a decreet against the heritors of Cramond, because, "notwithstanding the acts against conventicles, in April or May last, . . . Mr. James Kirktoun kept a conventicle in the kirk and kirk-yard of Cramond;" and on the 16th of July, Kirkton, with many of his brethren, was denounced rebel, and put to the horn, for holding these unlawful meetings'.

24 Kirkton, 1817, p. 127. The 'rhyme' reads, in full,

> From Covenants with uplifted hands,
> From Remonstrators with associate bands,
> From such Committees as govern'd this nation,
> From Church Commissioners and their protestation,
>   Good Lord deliver us.

25 Kirkton, p. 244 [R.L.S.]. *Ibid.*, pp. 244-5n.

26 Kirkton [R.L.S.]. *Ibid.*, pp. 242-3. Stevenson is dramatising here: the exclamations are his.

27 Turner [R.L.S.]. Turner, 1829, p. 186.

28 Kirkton, p. 244 [R.L.S.]. Kirkton, 1817, p. 244n. Stevenson drew on this story in 'The Plague-Cellar' (see p. 19 and note 9) and 'The Tale of Tod Lapraik' (see p. 202 and note 8).

29 Kirkton, p. 246 [R.L.S.]. Actually, Thomson, 1765, p. 389. Stevenson may have confused his references here. The first two lines of the verse form the epigraph to Stevenson's essay. The verse is also cited in Howie, 1870, p. 356 (in Howie's account of Hugh M'Kail).

30 *Cloud of Witnesses*, p. 389. Edin. 1765 [R.L.S.]. Thomson, 1765, p. 389. The subject here is Andrew Guilline, 'who suffered at the Gallowlee of Edinburgh, July 20, 1681, and afterwards was hung on a pole in Magus-muir, and lieth buried in the Long-cross of Clermont, near Magus-muir'. The verse reads, in full,

> A faithful martyr here doth lie,
> A witness against perjury;
> Who cruelly was put to death,
> To gratify proud Prelates wrath;
> They cut his hands ere he was dead.
> And after that struck off his head.
> To Magus-muir then did him bring,
> His body on a pole did hing.
> His blood under the alter cries,
> For vengeance on Christ's enemies.

31 Kirkton, p. 247 [R.L.S.]. Kirkton, 1817, p. 247: 'But up and down the countrey many grew sick of grief, and some died. Particularly Mr Arthure Murray, ane honest outed minister, dwelling in a suburb of Edinburgh, by which Dalyell's men entered the city after the victory. He hearing they were passing by, opened his window to view them, where he saw them display their banners tainted in the blood of these innocent people, and heard them shout victory, upon which he took to his bed and died within a few dayes'.

32 *Ibid.*, p. 254 [R.L.S.]. *Ibid.*, pp. 254-5.

33 *Ibid.*, p. 247 [R.L.S.]. *Ibid.*, pp. 247 and 247n. Kirkton calls this prison 'Haddock's-hole'. He suggests Wishart (or 'Wisheart') kept the prisoners well supplied with food because he himself 'well knew the horrors of incarceration, having himself been immured by the covenanters for seven months in a dark, loathsome dungeon, where he was allowed only once to change his linen, and had like to have been devoured by rats, the marks of whose voracity he bore on his face to his grave', p. 247n.

34 *Ibid.*, p. 247, 248 [R.L.S.]. *Ibid.*, p. 248.

35 See *ibid.*, pp. 250-2. Neilson of Corsack is mentioned in Stevenson's story 'The Plague-Cellar': see p. 18 and note 4. Kirkton notes, 'The executioner favoured Mr McKaill, but Corsack was cruelly tormented, and screight for pain in terrible

manner, so as to have moved a heart of stone', p. 252. On Corsack's life, see especially Wodrow, 1829-30, ii, Book ii, chapter 1, section 2, pp. 50-1. Wodrow notes that 'The Sufferings of. . . John Neilson of Corsack, in the parish of Parton in Galloway, and those of his lady and children, are so remarkable that they deserve a room in this collection', p. 50. Corsack was declared a non-conformist by the curate of Parton, Mr Dalgliesh, and was often harrassed by Sir James Turner and his soldiers, being at length 'imprisoned for some time', p. 50. However (as Steven- son notes below in 'The Pentland Rising'), while Corsack was imprisoned in Edin- burgh, Sir James Turner 'used his interest to get his life spared, because Corsack, out of his truly Christian temper, saved Sir James when some were seeking to take his life, both at Dumfries and afterwards, though few had felt more of his severity than this gentleman', p. 50. But curate Dalgliesh persuaded the bishops that Cor- sack 'was a ringleader to the fanatics in Galloway': 'This went further than Sir James his interest could go, and so he was executed', p. 50 – on 14 December 1666. See also Stewart *et al.*, 1721, pp. 196-8, 'The Testimony of John Neilson of Corsack who died at Edinburgh, Dec. 14. 1666'.

36 Kirkton, p. 248 [R.L.S.]. Kirkton, 1817, p.248.

37 *1 John*, iii, 8: 'He that committeth sin is of the devil; for the devil sinneth from the beginning. For this purpose the Son of God was manifested, that he might destroy the works of the devil'.

38 Kirkton, p. 249 [R.L.S.]. Kirkton, 1817, p. 249.

39 *Naphtali*, Glas. 1721, p. 205 [R.L.S.]. Stewart *et al.*, 1721, pp. 205-6.

40 Wodrow, p. 59 [R.L.S.]. Wodrow, 1829-30, ii, Book ii, chapter 1, section 3, p. 59n. Wodrow is probably quoting Stewart *et al.*, p. 234.

41 Kirkton, p. 246 [R.L.S.]. Actually, Kirkton, 1817, p. 252. Again, Stevenson is dramatising the occurrence: the exclamation is his, not Kirkton's.

42 Defoe's *Hist. of the Church* [R.S.L.]. Defoe, 1717, p. 159.

An Old Scots Gardener

1 Probably written in early 1871; it was first published in *The Edinburgh University Magazine* (March 1871), and collected in *Memories and Portraits*, 1887. Stevenson attached the following preface to the essay in *Memories and Portraits*, actually the last paragraph from his essay on *The Edinburgh University Magazine*, 'A College Magazine': 'From this defunct periodical I am going to reprint one of my own papers. The poor little piece is all tail-foremost. I have done my best to straighten its array, I have pruned it fearlessly, and it remains invertebrate and wordy. No self-respecting magazine would print the thing; and here you behold it in a bound volume, not for any worth of its own, but for the sake of the man whom it purports dimly to represent and some of whose sayings it preserves; so that in this volume of Memories and Portraits, Robert Young, the Swanston gardener, may stand alongside of John Todd, the Swanston shepherd [the subject of Stevenson's essay 'Pastoral']. Not that John and Robert drew very close together in their lives; for John was rough, he smelt of the windy brae; and Robert was gentle, and smacked of the garden in the hollow. Perhaps it is to my shame that I liked John the better of the two; he had grit and dash, and that salt of the old Adam that pleases men with any savage inheritance of blood; and he was a wayfarer besides, and took my gipsy fancy. But however that may be, and however Robert's profile may be blurred in the boyish sketch that follows, he was a man of a most quaint and beautiful nature, whom, if it were possible to recast a piece of work so old, I should like well to draw again with a maturer touch. And as I think of him and of John, I

wonder in what other country two such men would be found dwelling together, in a hamlet of some twenty cottages, in the woody fold of a green hill', *Memories and Portraits*, xxix, p. 36.

2   Andrew Fairservice is the gardener in Scott's *Rob Roy*, 1817.

3   Both texts are Covenanting histories: see Walker, 1827, and Shields, 1744.

4   Robert Young: see note 1.

5   *Hamlet*, III, i, ll.73-4:actually, 'spurns/That patient merit of th'unworthy takes'.

6   I.e. William Hazlitt (1778-1830) and Jean-Jacques Rousseau (1712-78).

7   *I Corinthians*, iii, 6: 'I have planted, Apollos watered; but God gave the increase'.

8   *I Kings*, x, 7: 'and, behold, the half was not told me'.

9   Andrew Marvell, 'The Garden', 1681, verse 6.

10   Andrew Marvell, 'An Epitaph upon – '. The poem is dated after the Restoration of Charles II. The last line actually reads, "Twere more significant, *She's Dead*'.

11   *St Matthew*, x, 29: 'Are not two sparrows sold for a farthing? / One of them shall not fall on the ground without your Father'.

12   *Isaiah*, xiv, 4-21: 'thou shalt take up this proverb against the king of Babylon, and say, How hath the oppressor ceased! the golden city ceased!', and so on. The context is that the king of Babylon, after he dies, goes down to hell and is greeted mockingly by all those he had earlier sent there.

A Winter's Walk in Carrick and Galloway

1   Dated by Swearingen, 1980, 'After 17 January 1876', p. 22. It was first published after Stevenson's death, in *The Illustrated London News* (Summer 1896), pp. 13-5.

2   Robert Burns, 'The Cotter's Saturday Night', 1784-5. Stevenson probably has in mind l. 14, 'The toil-worn *Cotter* frae his labour goes'.

3   The reference is to a traditional Scottish song, 'Johnie's Gray Breeks': see Cunningham, 1825, ii, pp. 284-6. In the song, the narrator, Johnie's lover, connects the shabby state of his trousers ('now they're threadbare worn') with the state of his love for her; but she ends, 'We'll make them hale between us yet', p. 286.

4   This account of Gilbert, fourth Earl of Cassilis, and Alane Stewart, was taken from Paterson, 1852, ii, p. 284: 'It was this Earl who was guilty of roasting the Commendator of Crossraguel in "the black vout" of Dunure. On the 1st and 7th of September 1570 he carried Allan Stewart, the Commendator, to the castle of Dunure, where he presented to him for signature various deeds, conveying to the Earl the lands belonging to the abbacy, upon his refusing to sign which the Earl placed him over a large fire in one of the vaults of Dunure to compel him to do so. Kennedy of Bargany, hearing of his position, came to the assistance of the Commendator with a large force, and took the castle of Dunure. The Commendator lodged a complaint with the Privy Council against his Earl, who alleged, in defence, that the complaint was neither civil or criminal, and that he ought not answer thereto to the Privy Council. The Privy Council, however, sent him to Dumbarton Castle until he found security not to molest the Commendator, in £2000'.

5   William Abercrombie. See *Fasti Ecclesiae Scoticanae,* under 'Maybole'(Part iii) [R.L.S.]. William Abercrombie was minister at Maybole from 1673 to 1690. The reference is to Scott, 1915-28, iii, 'Synod of Glasgow and Ayr'. But in fact the passage is cited in Paterson, 1852, ii, pp. 343-4: see note 6.

6   Paterson, 1852, ii, pp. 343-4. Paterson, p. 344, actually says, 'The description thus given by Abercrummie, nearly two hundred years ago, presents a minute picture of Maybole even at the present time'.

7 'Johnie Faa, The Gypsy Laddie', a ballad; see Chambers, 1829, p. 144: 'And she cam tripping down the stair,/And all her maids before her'.

8 The story of 'Johnie Faa' concerns the seduction of Lady Cassilis by Johnie Faa, a wandering gypsy. The ballad is supposed to have some basis in fact, involving the wife of John, sixth Earl of Cassilis – 'a stern Covenanter', according to the description cited in Chambers, 1829, p. 143n. Chambers continues: 'She had previously been beloved by a gallant young knight, a Sir John Faa of Dunbar. . . When several years were spent and gone, and Lady Cassilis had brought her husband three children, this passion led to a dreadful catastrophe. Her youthful lover, seizing an opportunity when the Earl was attending the Assembly of Divines at Westminster, came to Cassilis Castle, a massive old tower on the banks of the Doon, four miles from Maybole, then the principal residence of the family. . . He was disguised as a gypsy, and attended by a band of these desperate outcasts. In the words of the ballad. . ."They cuist the glamourye owere her".

Alas! love has a glamourye for the eyes much more powerful than that supposed of old to be practised by wandering gypsies, and which must have been the only magic used on this occasion. The Countess right soon condescended to elope with her lover. Most unfortunately, ere they had proceeded very far, the Earl came home, and, learning the fact, immediately set out in pursuit. . . He brought them back to Cassilis, and there hanged all the gypsies, including the hapless Sir John.' Stevenson's narrator in 'The Pavilion on the Links' is named Cassilis, and describes himself as a kind of gypsy; see also Stevenson's reference to his own 'gipsy fancy', 'An Old Scots Gardener', note 1.

9 'Sir Patrick Spens', a ballad: see verse 4, 'The teir blinded his ee'.

10 Douglas Graham (1738?-1811) was the 'original' of Burns' poem 'Tam o' Shanter. A Tale', 1790. See Robert Chambers, n.d., iii, pp. 152-3: 'The country-people in Ayrshire, contrary to their wont, unmythicise the narrations of Burns, and point both to a real Tam and Souter Johnny. . . The hero was an honest farmer named Douglas Graham, who lived at Shanter, between Turnberry and Colzean. . . Douglas Graham and John Davidson, the supposed originals of Tam o' Shanter and Souter Johnny, have long reposed in the church-yard of Kirkoswald, where the former has a handsome monument, bearing a pious inscription.'

The Foreigner at Home

1 Swearingen, 1980, p. 76, suggests this essay was written over Winter 1881-2 and 'probably finished January or February 1882'. It was first published in *Cornhill Magazine*, 45 (April 1881), pp. 410-8, and collected in *Memories and Portraits*, 1887.

2 A Scottish song: see Ramsay, 1876, i, pp. 93-4. The song begins,

> This is no mine ain house,
> I ken by the rigging o't;
> Since with my love I've changed vows,
> I dinna like the bigging o't.

See also Whitelaw, 1844, p. 413. Whitelaw quotes a 'ditty' he says existed before the song given in Ramsey:

> This is no my ain house,
> My ain house, my ain house,
> This is no my ain house,
> I ken by the biggin' o't.

Whitelaw also quotes an early Jacobite version of the song:

> O, This is no my ain house,

>   I ken by the biggin' o't;
> For bow-kail thrave at my door check,
>   And thristles on the riggin' o't.

Stevenson cites his epigraph again below in the essay.

3 Richard Grant White, *England Without and Within* (Cambridge, Mass., 1881); Karl Hillebrand, *France and the French in the Second Half of the Nineteenth Century* (Paris, 1880; trans. 1881).

4 Literally, 'a realm within a realm'.

5 The reference is to Mrs Isabella Lucy Bishop (née Bird), *Unbeaten Tracks in Japan*, 2 vols (London, 1880).

6 John Stuart Blackie (1809-95), Professor of Greek at Edinburgh University from 1852.

7 Literally, 'the truce of God'; a ceasefire; a holiday.

Pastoral

1 Written around Spring 1887 and first published in *Longman's Magazine*, 9 (April 1887). It was collected in *Memories and Portraits*, 1887.

2 Francis Galton (1822-1911). The reference is probably to Galton's composite photographs of different species or races in *Inquiries into Human Faculty and its Development*, 1883. Galton is generally taken as the inventor of eugenics, a science concerned with evidence of evolution and heredity and the improvement of the human race. See also Furnas, 1952, pp. 241-2, 'like most of his contemporaries, he [Stevenson] had been greatly taken by the "eugenics" that Galton had popularised for fifteen years.'

3 *II Kings*, v, 12: 'Are not Abana and Pharpar, rivers of Damascus, better than all the waters of Israel? may I not wash in them, and be clean? So he turned and went away in a rage'. The passage concerns Naaman, a leper, advised to wash seven times in the river Jordan: by 'jealous for', Stevenson probably means 'nostalgic for'.

4 John Graham of Claverhouse, first Viscount Dundee (1649-1689). Claverhouse was an enemy and persecutor of the Covenanters and was present at the famous Covenanter defeat at Bothwell Bridge on 22 June 1679. He supported the Stuarts against William of Orange, and led an army of Jacobites against an army of Williamites twice the size at Killiecrankie on 27 July 1689, where he was killed. He was often the subject of Covenanter histories and narratives: he is mentioned in Scott's 'Wandering Willie's Tale' in *Redgauntlet*: see 'The Tale of Tod Lapraik', note 8.

5 Literally, 'being born in the mountains of Britain (i.e. Scotland), indeed, but alas! of an ignorant century (or age)'.

6 Caer Ketton Hill is in the Pentland Hills; Stevenson possibly means that educated people or those 'in the know' call it by this name: see *Edinburgh: Picturesque Notes*, p. 195: 'Kirk Yetton forms the north-eastern angle of the range; thence, the Pentlands trend off to south and west'.

The Manse

1 Written in Spring 1887 and first published in *Scribner's Magazine*, 1 (May 1887), pp. 611-4; it was first collected in *Memories and Portraits*, 1887. See also Balfour, 1901, i, pp. 40-7.

2 Stevenson's maternal grandfather, Rev. Lewis Balfour (1777-1860). His daughter Margaret Isabella was Stevenson's mother.

3   Metrical Psalm 121.

4   See Stevenson's *A Family of Engineers*, xix, pp. 160-2; and on the probable Gregory/MacGregor links, see Scott's introduction to *Rob Roy*, p. xxxix: 'Dr James MacGregor (by descent a MacGregor). . . Professor of Medicine in King's College, Aberdeen. . . Dr Gregory thought it a point of prudence to claim a kindred. . . with a man so formidable and influential'.

5   See Burns' 'The Holy Fair', 1784-5, verse 14: 'xxxx opens out his cauld harangues,/On *practice* and on *morals*'. See also Balfour, 1901, i, p. 11: at 'about the age of twenty', Lewis Balfour 'went to his first Ayrshire parish, and there fell in love with and married a daughter of Dr Smith of Galston, the Dr Smith. . . in Burns' *Holy Fair*'.

6   I. e. Stevenson's grandfather, Rev. Lewis Balfour: see note 2 above.

7   Actually, Thomas Smith: see *A Family of Engineers*, p. 166: 'He founded a solid business in lamps and oils. . . April, 1786, was the date of his chief advancement, when, having designed a system of oil lights to take the place of the primitive coal fires before in use, he was dubbed engineer to the newly-formed Board of Northern Lighthouses'. Thomas Smith was the stepfather of Robert Stevenson, Stevenson's paternal grandfather.

8   See *A Family of Engineers*, p. 162: 'To one more tradition I may allude, that we are somehow descended from a French barber-surgeon who came to St. Andrews in the service of one of the Cardinal Beatons. No details were added. But the very name of France was so detested in my family for three generations, that I am tempted to suppose there may be something in it'. The latter reference is probably to Cardinal David Beaton of St Andrews, murdered in 1546; see also 'The Coast of Fife', note 15.

9   See Balfour, 1901, i, p.11: Stevenson is referring to a remote connection to 'Sir John Elphinstone of Logie and. . . Sir Gilbert Elliot, known as Lord Minto, a judge of the Court of Sessions'.

10   See *A Family of Engineers*, p. 165, on Thomas Smith's ancestry: 'The Smith pedigree has been traced a little more particularly than the Stevensons', with a similar dearth of illustrious names. One character seems to have appeared, indeed, for a moment at the wings of history: a skipper of Dundee who smuggled over some Jacobite big-wig at the time of the Fifteen, and who was afterwards drowned in Dundee harbour while going on board his ship'.

11   *Ibid.*, pp. 163-4. Stevenson refers to his great-grandfather Alan Stevenson (1752-1774). Alan and his brother Hugh 'were owners of an islet near St. Kitts; and it is certain that they had risen to be at the head of considerable interests in the West Indies, which Hugh managed abroad and Alan at home, at an age when others are still curveting a clerk's stool', p.164. Alan's death, struck down after being 'exposed to the pernicious dews of the tropics', p.164, may have inspired Stevenson's 'Story of the Fair Cuban' in *More New Arabian Nights. The Dynamiter*, 1885. Bailie Nicol Jarvie is a merchant in Scott's *Rob Roy*.

12   Robert Stevenson (1772-1850) was Alan Stevenson's son. Alan's widow later married Thomas Smith, 'the lamp and oil man': see note 7 above. Stevenson means that Robert Stevenson, his paternal grandfather, was Thomas Smith's stepson.

13   Robert Stevenson, with other lighthouse commissioners, sailed to the northern islands of Scotland (and then down the west coast), accompanied by Sir Walter Scott, from 29 July to 8 September 1814. The trip to the northern islands inspired Scott's *The Pirate*, 1822, and his long poem *Lord of the Isles*, 1815. See Appendix,

'Scott's Voyage in the Lighthouse Yacht. Note'.

14 From 1807-1812, Robert Stevenson supervised the building of the Bell Rock lighthouse; he sailed there in a 'sloop of forty tons' named the *Smeaton*, *A Family of Engineers*, p. 221. On the passage, see *ibid.*, pp. 239-43.

15 *Ibid.*, p. 282: 'the beacon had an *ill-faured twist*'.

Memoirs of an Islet

1 Written around Spring-Summer 1887 and published for the first time in *Memories and Portraits*, 1887.

2 Literally, 'happiness and unhappiness become song (or, are transformed into art)? I am unable to find the source of this quotation; it is likely that it is not Goethe at all.

3 I.e. 'The Merry Men'.

4 David Balfour in *Kidnapped*, 1886.

5 Stevenson first visited the island of Earraid in August 1870 with his father, chief engineer of the nearby Dhu Heartach lighthouse.

6 Shortly after staying at Earraid with his father, Stevenson toured the western islands with (among others) Sam Bough (1822-1878), the landscape painter and 'thorough Bohemian', *DNB*, ii, p. 913. See *Letters*, i, pp. 29-35; see also Stevenson's eulogy, 'The Late Sam Bough, R.S.A.', *Essays Literary and Critical*, xxviii, pp. 135-7.

7 St Columba's poem is cited in full in Skene, 1876-80, ii, pp. 92-3. Skene notes, 'The original of this interesting poem is in one of the Irish MSS. in the Burgundian Library at Brussels. It was transcribed and translated for the late Dr Todd by the late Professor O'Curry, and was kindly given to the author by Dr Reeves, now Dean of Armagh, in 1866', p. 93n. Skene says, of Iona, 'the rocky heights which bound the central plain on the south-west are termed *Uchdachan*, or breasts', p. 91. St Columba (521-597) went to Iona in 563.

8 I.e. the Franco-Prussian War (1870-1871).

The Coast of Fife

1 Written in Spring 1888 and first published in *Scribner's Magazine*, 4 (October 1888), pp. 507-12. It was first collected in *Across the Plains*, 1892.

2 Stevenson first visited Fife with his father in Summer 1863, when he was twelve.

3 See Chambers, 1827, ii, p. 164: 'There can be no doubt, moreover, that the common epithet, "The Kingdom of Fife", took its rise in the idea which the neighbouring people had at an early period of its eminent wealth and isolated and independent character'. Stevenson's description of the coast of Fife seems influenced by and indebted to Sibbald, 1803, 'Description of the East Coast', pp. 302-43.

4 'Sir Patrick Spens', a ballad: verse 1, 'The King sits in Dumferling toune,/ Drinking the blude-red wine'. The king is Alexander III.

5 See Chambers, 1827, ii, p. 167n: 'the magistrates of Inverkeithing had a power of pit and gallows, and a right to levy customs, – at all fairs and markets, upon goods and cattle, – at all harbours upon ships – and at all ferries upon whatever crossed over'.

6 'The Bonnie Earl of Moray', a ballad: see Child, 1882-98, iii, pp. 447-9. The Earl of Moray was murdered by the Earl of Huntly and a number of soldiers on 7 February 1592 at Donibristle.

7 John Paul Jones (1747-1792), born at Kirkbean, Kirkcudbright, was a naval commander during the American revolution in the 1770s. Rev. Mr Shirra was a

minister of the Secession church at Kirkcaldy when Jones took part in a raid on his home country in September 1778. See Taylor, 1869, pp. 39-40: 'Mr Shirra knelt on the wet sands, and prayed fervently to the Lord that He would interpose on behalf of the defenceless towns, and send Paul Jones and his privateers by the way by which they had come. The prayer was visibly and speedily answered. The wind veered round, and blew freshly from the west. The hostile ships hovered about for a time, uncertainly, and then, turning their prows, bore down the Forth, and outwards to the ocean'. See also Sibbald, 1803, pp. 337-8.

8   See Robert Burns, 'Tam o' Shanter. A Tale', l. 92: 'Whare drunken *Charlie* brak's neck-bane'. But Stevenson is actually referring to Alexander III who, one night in March 1286, fell from his horse while riding from Inverkeithing to Kinghorn. His death was apparently prophesied by Thomas the Rhymer. See Sibbald, 1803, p. 311.

9   See Law, 1818, pp. xxxvi-xxxvii: in the late 16th century, Agnis Sampson and other witches were supposedly responsible for raising 'a tempest in the sea. . . the cause of a perishing of a boat or vessell coming over from the towne of Brunt Island to the towne of Leith, wherein was sundrie jewelles'.

10   See Chambers, 1827, p. 218: Dysart 'was formerly so prosperous and so busy a place, as to get the popular name of "Little Holland". The port had no fewer than thirty-six brigs belonging to it; and it was the custom to expose prodigious quantities of merchandise for sale, under the piazzas which then pervaded the central street'. I do not know the identity of the 'particular Dutch skipper' Stevenson refers to.

11   See Johnstone, 1870-1, ii, pp. 70-3. Johnstone went to Wemyss ('that execrable town', p. 59) after Culloden in 1745, hiding a number of times in a cave along the coast inhabited by 'owls and other innumerable birds of prey', p. 72: 'The frightful noise of these animals could not be compared to any sound I had ever heard. . . If I had not examined to the bottom, with coolness, the cause of an effect so singular, I never could have known to what to attribute it, and doubt not that an anchorite saint, had he been in my place, would have found supernatural miracles, in this adventure, and would have made romantic stories, as good as St. Anthony, – for enthusiasm is always closely allied to credulity and childishness', pp. 72-3.

12   See Furnas, 1952, p. 24: 'John Balfour, high in the medical service of the East India Company, was last man out of Delhi when the Mutiny broke'. Stevenson refers to the Mutiny in Delhi in May 1857. Lt George Willoughby blew up a magazine near the Kashmir Gate, killing himself and a group of British soldiers under his command barricaded inside, but also killing hundreds of mutineers trying to get in. See Harris, 1973, pp. 46-7: although the Postmaster had been killed, 'two young Eurasian signallers, William Brendish and J. W. Pilkington. . . had the sense to send a signal to the Commander-in-Chief at Simla. . . It was said later that the telegraph saved India'.

13   Alexander Selkirk (1676-1721), the prototype for Defoe's Robinson Crusoe, was born in Largo. See Howell, 1829.

14   See 'The Plague Cellar', note 10.

15   Cardinal David Beaton was murdered at St Andrews on 29 May 1546. Beaton had fortified the old castle of St Andrews, also storing his treasure there. Knox, 1949, orig. 1586-7, i, pp. 76-9, described the murder of Beaton in detail. Knox's 'jeering narrative' refers to his closing remarks about the murder: 'How miserably lay David Beaton, careful Cardinal! . . . These things we write merrily', pp. 78-9.

16 Andrew Lang's *St. Andrews* was not published until 1903. The poem is probably 'Alme Matres' (1862-1865), which begins, 'St. Andrews by the northern sea,/ A haunted town it is to me': see Mrs Lang ed., *The Poetical Works of Andrew Lang* (London, 1923), i, pp. 3-5.

17 See *A Family of Engineers*, pp. 204-5. Stevenson notes of his grandfather Robert Stevenson, 'he was well qualified to inspire a salutary terror in the service', p. 204.

18 Thomas Rowlandson, *The English Dance of Death*, 2 vols (1815-1816). Rowlandson was a caricaturist.

19 See Howie, 1870, p. 622: 'John Balfour of Kinloch, sometimes called Burley, was a gentleman in the north of Fife'. Balfour was also a commanding officer in the Covenanter battles at Drumclog and Bothwell Bridge in June 1679. He may or may not have been Stevenson's maternal 'ancestral cousin': Furnas, 1952, p. 41, says he was. The 'primate' is Archbishop Sharpe: see note 20 below.

20 James Sharp was murdered while travelling in a coach through Magus Muir with his eldest daughter Isabel. See 'James Russell's Account of the Murder of Archbishop Sharp. 1679', in Kirkton, 1817, pp. 420-1n: the assassins 'took nothing from him but his tobacco-box and Bible, and a few papers. With these they went to a barn near by. Upon the opening of his tobacco-box, a living humming bee flew out. This either Rathillet or Balfour called his familiar, and some in the company not understanding the term, they explained it to be a devil'.

21 Maria Louisa Charlesworth, *Ministering Children: a tale dedicated to childhood* (London, 1856); Octavius Winslow, *Life in Jesus. A Memoir of Mrs Mary Winslow, Arranged from her Correspondence, Diary and Thoughts* (London, 1856).

22 See Howie, 1870, pp. 430-5, on David Hackston of Rathillet. Hackston also fought at Drumclog and Bothwell Bridge in June 1679; he was arrested the following year and executed and dismembered in a particularly bloodthirsty way in Edinburgh on 20 July 1680. Howie, p. 435, remarks, 'his head was fixed on the Nether Bow, one of his quarters, with his hands, at St Andrews, another at Glasgow, a third at Leith, and the fourth at Burntisland'.

23 See 'James Russell's Account. . .', Kirkton, 1817, pp. 415-6: 'But Rathillet answered, that the Lord was his witness he was willing to venture all he had for the interest of Christ, yet he durst not lead them on to that action, there being a known prejudice betwixt the bishop and him, which would mar the glory of the action, for it would be imputed to his particular revenge and that God was his witness he did nothing on that account; but he would not hinder them from what God had called them to, and that he should not leave them. . . and James [Russell] riding towards the coach, to be sure, seeing the bishop looking out at the door, cast away his cloak and. . . crying to the rest to come up, and the rest throwing away their cloaks except Rathillet.'

24 *Ibid.*, p. 421n: Sharp 'creeped on hand and foot toward Rathillet, crying, Sir, you are a gentleman, you will protect me. To which he replied, Sir, I shall never lay a hand on you'.

25 Stevenson mentions his early attempt at writing a novel based on Hackston of Rathillet in 'My First Book': 'Reams upon reams must have gone into the making of *Rathillet* . . . *Rathillet* was attempted before fifteen', *Treasure Island*, p. xxiii.

26 See Wodrow, 1829-30.

27 Fergusson, 1887, pp. 56-60.

28 Andrew Wilson, *The Abode of Snow: Observations on a Journey from Chinese Tibet to the Indian Caucasus, through the Upper Valleys of the Himalaya* (Edinburgh,

1875). See Fergusson, 1887, p. 57, on the 'Philosophical Society': 'the President was poor "Skinny Wilson" – that is to say, Andrew Wilson, whose *Abode of Snow* is not likely to be forgotten'.

29   On 'curat' Thomson, see Scott, 1915-28, p. 180, 'Anstruther Easter': '*Edward Thomson*, said to be the son of a min. by whom he was "bred in the knowledge of the truth and profession of godliness", and who on his death-bed abjured him not to disown the Covenant; studied at St. Andrews; M.A. (about 1658); was regent in Old College, St. Andrews; had a testimonial for licence from Presb. of St. Andrews 24th Oct., ord. 11th, and adm. 14th Nov. 1677. After the death of his wife he became "very sad and heavy", and on Saturday, 19 Dec. 1685, he went to make a visit at night and stayed late. "As he returned, the servant girl that bore his lantern affirmed it shook as they passed a bridge, and that she saw something like a black beast pass before him". He rose early next morning and threw himself in to the Dreel, where he was found dead, aged about 44. He marr. 25th April 1673, Mary Balfour, and had issue – James; Philip; Mary; Susanna; Helen; Christian'. The story of Thomson's death is lifted from Kirkton, 1817, pp. 188-90, as one of a number of examples of the fates that befell those who had lapsed from the Covenanting position during the days of the Persecution in the 1670s and 1680s: 'But the most sad of all was that of Mr Edward Thomson, curat of Anstrudder; this man was the son of a godly father, a minister, who bred his son in the knowledge of the truth and profession of godliness; and when the honest father died, he straitly charged this his son to follow his father's way, and in any case to beware of conforming to the course of the bishops. This course he followes for some time, but wearying of the poverty of non-conformists, he went to one of their mock presbytries, and there entered upon his tryals. The report went, that when he was upon his tryals, his father appeared to him and threatened him for engadging in such a course, whereupon he desisted for some time; but the same tentation returning, he once more engadged with the bishops, entered upon his tryals, and having passed, settled at Anstrudder. He hade while he was there wife and children; afterwards, being a widow, he continued in his ministry, but at length became very sad and heavy. One Saturday, at night, he went to make a visit, and stayed out very late, and as he returned homeward, the wench that bare his lanthron, as they past a bridge, affirmed the bridge trembled and shoke, also that she saw something like a black beast pass the bridge before him. This made some suspect he medled with the devil, and he was known to have a brother that was a diabolick man. However, home he came very late, and after he had lyen a while in bed, rose early upon Sabbath morning, and threw himself into the river, where he was taken up dead, to the great astonishment of his poor neighbours.' Stevenson dramatises this story in 'The Coast of Fife'; its interest for him as a Covenanting tale and its similarities to events in 'Thrawn Janet' and 'The Tale of Tod Lapraik' are discussed in the Introduction.

30   For an account of the arrival at Anstruther of Jon Gomaz de Medina of the Spanish Armada in 1588, and his reception by the minister James Melville, see Sibbald, 1803, Appendix No. X, pp. 460-1; see also Conolly, 1869, pp. 183-5. Stevenson's fascination with the presence of the Spanish Armada off the coast of Scotland is also apparent in 'The Merry Men': see notes 6 and 13.

The Education of an Engineer

1   This essay was written in Spring 1888 and first published in *Scribner's Magazine*, 4 (November 1888). It was first collected in *Across the Plains*, 1892. The *Scribner's*

version has two sentences at the end that were, for some reason, dropped from the collected versions, which end 'on the Fair Isle'. The two sentences are included here.

2 William Tennant, *Anster Fair. Poem* (Edinburgh, 1812).

3 Stevenson stayed at Anstruther in July 1868.

4 Swearingen, 1980, does not list *Voces Fidelium*, written (according to Stevenson) in the late 1860s; but see Balfour, 1901, i, p. 104, and Furnas, 1952, p. 48. On Stevenson's early attempts at writing Covenanting fiction, see 'My First Book', *Treasure Island*, p. xxiii.

5 After staying at Anstruther, Stevenson went on to Wick: he stayed there in September and October 1868.

6 A gypsy character in Scott's *Guy Mannering*, 1815.

7 See 'The Coast of Fife', pp. 267-8. The collected version of the essay ends here.

IV APPENDIX
Scott's Voyage in the Lighthouse Yacht. Note

1 Stevenson's 'Note' introduces his grandfather Robert Stevenson's 'Reminiscences of Sir Walter Scott, Baronet', which Stevenson published in *Scribner's Magazine*, 14 (October 1893), pp. 492-4. The 'Note' is dated and signed 'Vailima Upalu, Samoa, July 31, 1892'. It is collected in book form here for the first time.

2 Actually, Scott's letter to Miss Clephane, 23 July 1814, Abbotsford: see Grierson, 1932, p. 470. Stevenson seems to have confused this with Scott's letter to J. B. S. Morritt, 24 July 1814, cited in Lockhart, 1902, iv, pp. 152-7: no mention is made here of Robert Stevenson, although Scott does refer to the tour with the lighthouse commissioners.

3 I.e. by 1812: see 'The Manse', note 14.

4 See 'The Manse', note 13.

5 Scott's *Marmion* was published in 1808.

6 Stevenson seems to be referring here to the story that Scott used notched sticks to help him remember things. See Wilson, 1932, p. 281. Wilson presents J. E. Shortreed's 'Conversations with my Father on the subject of his Tours with Sir Walter Scott in Liddesdale. Written in June, 1824' (National Library of Scotland, MS.921, f.78). At one point, Shortreed asks his father Robert S. Shortreed if Scott ever kept a memorandum-book during their tours of Liddesdale together. His father replies, 'None that I ever saw. We had neither pens, or ink, nor paper. But we had *knives* and they served the turn just as weel, for we took bits o' Cuttings wi' them, frae a broom Cowe, or an aller, or a hazel-bush, or whatever else might be at hand, and on thae bits o' stick (maybe tway or three inches lang they were) he made a variety o' notches, and these were the only memoranda I ever saw him take or have, of any of the memorable spots he wished to preserve the recollection of, or any tradition connected wi' them', p. 281. See also Pottle, 1969, pp. 242-3. Stevenson seems to mean, generally, that although his grandfather then wasn't very impressed with Scott as a famous poet (author of *Marmion*), if he had forseen the publication of *Rob Roy* he would have been impressed enough with Scott at the time to take up or imitate Scott's methods of recollection while on tour with him. I am indebted to Dr Graham Tulloch for these references.

7 I.e. Stevenson, 1824.

8 Robert Stevenson's dedication actually continues, '*and so situated as to have long proved an object of dread to mariners on the eastern coast of Scotland, especially when making for the Friths of Forth and Tay*', ibid., n.p.

9   Dr Patrick Neill (1776-1851) was a celebrated Scottish naturalist. Neill was a great introducer of exotic plants to the public, and was caricatured in the notorious 'Translation from an Ancient Chaldee Manuscript', *Blackwood's Magazine* (October 1817), p. 95, chapter IV, verses 8-13: 'Then there came into his chamber a lean man. . . One which delighteth in trees, and fruits, and flowers. . . And he had a rotten melon on his head, after the fashion of an helmet'.

10   Robert Stevenson died on 12 July 1850, four months before Stevenson was born.

11   Robert Stevenson's only surviving daughter: he dictated his *An Account of the Bell Rock Lighthouse* to her.

12   I cannot find the source of these two descriptions; but see A *Family of Engineers*, pp. 221-2.

13   Scott's *Count Robert of Paris*, 1832, was his last novel. *The Seige of Malta* was not published in Scott's lifetime.

14   See Lockhart, 1902, iv, p. 159: 'I have been often told by one of the companions of this voyage, that heartily as Scott entered throughout into their social enjoyments, they all perceived him, when inspecting for the first time scenes of remarkable grandeur, to be in such an abstracted and excited mood, that they felt it would be the kindest and discreetest plan to leave him to himself. "I often," said Lord Kinnedder, "on coming up from the cabin at night, found him pacing the deck rapidly, muttering to himself – and went to the forecastle, lest my presence should disturb him. I remember, that at Loch Corriskin, in particular, he seemed quite overwhelmed with his feelings; and we all saw it, and retiring unnoticed, left him to roam and gaze about by himself, until it was time to muster the party and be gone".' See also Scott's description of Loch Corriskin in *Lord of the Isles*, iii, verse 14.

15   'The Scorpion' was a name given to John Gibson Lockhart (1794-1854), Scott's biographer, who married Scott's daughter Sophia on 29 April 1820. See *DNB*, xii, p. 48; after Lockhart's supposed contributions to the 'Chaldee Manuscript', 'He challenged an anonymous author who had abused him as the "Scorpion" in a pamphlet called "Hypocrisy Unveiled", but his opponent declined to come forward'.

16   I.e. Scott's 'Voyage in the Lighthouse Yacht to Nova Zembla, and the Lord Knows Where', Lockhart, 1902, iv, pp. 160-324.

VI REFERENCES

✳

ANDERSON, James, 1847, *The Martyrs of the Bass*. In McCrie, Thomas ed., *The Bass Rock*, Edinburgh and London: John Greig and Hamilton, Adams & Co.

BALFOUR, Graham, 1901, *The Life of Robert Louis Stevenson*, London: Methuen

BINDING, Paul ed., 1979, *Weir of Hermiston, and other stories*, Harmondsworth: Penguin Books

BURNET, Gilbert, 1724, *History of His Own Time*, Vol.1, London: Thomas Ward

CALDER, Jenni ed., 1979, *The Strange Case of Dr Jekyll and Mr Hyde, and other stories*, Harmondsworth: Penguin Books

CALDER, Jenni ed., 1981, *Stevenson and Victorian Scotland*, Edinburgh: Edinburgh University Press

CALDER, Jenni ed., 1987, *Island Landfalls: Robert Louis Stevenson*, Edinburgh: Canongate

CAMPBELL, Ian ed., 1980, *Selected Short Stories of R.L. Stevenson*, Edinburgh: The Ramsey Head Press

CHAMBERS, Robert, 1827, *The Picture of Scotland*, Edinburgh: William Tait

CHAMBERS, Robert ed., 1829, *The Scottish Ballads*, Edinburgh: William Tait

CHAMBERS, Robert ed., n.d., *The Life and Works of Robert Burns*, Edinburgh and London

CHILD, Francis James, 1882-98, *The English and Scottish Popular Ballads*, London: H. Stevens, Son and Stiles

CONOLLY, M.F., 1869, *Fifiana: or, the Memorials of the East of Fife*, Glasgow: John Tweed

CROOKSHANK, William, 1751, *The History of the State and Sufferings of the Church of Scotland, from the Restoration to the Revolution*, 2nd edition, Edinburgh

CUNNINGHAM, Allan, 1825, *The Songs of Scotland, ancient and modern*, London: John Taylor

DEFOE, Daniel, 1717, *Memoirs of the Church of Scotland, in four periods. . . ,* London: Eman. Matthews; T. Warner

DNB: *The Dictionary of National Biography*, eds. Sir Leslie Stephen and Sir Sidney Lee, Oxford

DRUMMOND, Andrew L. and BULLOCH, James, 1975, *The Church in Victorian Scotland, 1843-1874*, Edinburgh: Saint Andrew Press

EDWARDS, Owen Dudley, 1980, *Burke and Hare*, Edinburgh: Edinburgh University Press

EIGNER, Edwin M., 1966, *Robert Louis Stevenson and Romantic Tradition*, Princeton, New Jersey: Princeton University Press

FERGUSSON, Lt Col Alexander, 1887, *Chronicles of the Cumming Club, and memories of old Academy Days*, Edinburgh: T.& A. Constable

FULLER, Thomas, 1651, *The Historie of the Holy Warre*, 4th edition, Cambridge: T. Buck

FURNAS, J. C., 1952, *Voyage to Windward: The Life of Robert Louis Stevenson*, London: Faber & Faber

GELDER, Kenneth, 1986, 'Robert Louis Stevenson's Revisions to "The Merry Men",' *Studies in Scottish Literature*, 21 (December)

GELDER, Kenneth, 1984, 'Stevenson and the Covenanters: "Black Andie's Tale of Tod Lapraik" and "Thrawn Janet",' *Scottish Literary Journal*, 11 (December)

GRIERSON, H. J. C. ed., 1932, *The Letters of Sir Walter Scott*, London: Constable & Co.

GRIEVE, C. M., 1926, *Contemporary Scottish Studies*, London: Leonard Parsons

HARRIS, John, 1973, *The Indian Mutiny*, London: Hart-Davis MacGibbon

HOWELL, John, 1829, *The life and adventures of Alexander Selkirk, containing the real incidents upon which the romance of Robinson Crusoe is founded. . .* , Edinburgh

HOWIE, John, 1870, orig. 1781-2, *Biographia Scotticana; or a brief historical account of the lives. . . of the most eminent Scots Worthies. . .* Revised by W. H. Carslaw, Edinburgh: Johnstone, Hunter & Co.

JOHNSTONE, James de, 1870-1, *Memoirs of the Chevalier de Johnstone. . .* translated by Charles Winchester, Aberdeen

KIELY, Robert, 1964, *Robert Louis Stevenson and the Fiction of Adventure*, Cambridge, Mass.: Harvard University Press

KIRKTON, James, 1817, *The Secret and True History of the Church of Scotland, from the restoration to the year 1678. . . To which is added, an account of the murder of Archbishop Sharp, by James Russell, an actor therein.* Edited from the MSS. by C. K. Sharpe, Edinburgh: J. Ballantyne

KNOX, John, 1949, orig. 1586-7, *The History of the Reformation in Scotland*, ed. W. C. Dickinson, London: Thomas Nelson and Sons

LAW, Robert, 1818, *Memorialls; or the memorable things that fell out within this island of Brittain from 1638 to 1684. . .* Edited from the MS. by C. K. Sharpe, Edinburgh: A. Constable

LOCKHART, John Gibson, 1902, orig. 1837-45, *The Life of Sir Walter Scott, Bart.*, Edinburgh: T. C. and E. C. Jack

LUKÁCS, George, 1981, orig. 1962, *The Historical Novel*, Harmondsworth: Penguin Books

MONTEITH, Robert, 1713, *An Theatre of Mortality; or, a further collection of funeral-inscriptions over Scotland, etc.*, Edinburgh: The Heirs of A. Anderson

MOORE, John Robert, 1944, 'Stevenson's Source for "The Merry Men",' *Philological Quarterly* 23 (April)

NOBLE, Andrew ed., 1983, *Robert Louis Stevenson*, London and Totowa, New Jersey: Vision and Barnes & Noble

PARSONS, Coleman O., 1946, 'Stevenson's Use of Witchcraft in "Thrawn Janet",' *Studies in Philology*, 43 (July)

PATERSON, James, 1847, 1852, *History of the County of Ayr, with a genealogical account of the Families of Ayrshire*, Paisley and Ayr: Stewart and Dick

POTTLE, Frederick A., 1969, 'The Power of Memory in Boswell and Scott'. In Jeffares, A. N. ed., *Scott's Mind and Art*, Edinburgh: Oliver and Boyd

RAMSAY, Allan, 1876, orig. 1720s, with many additions thereafter, *The Tea-Table Miscellany. A Collection of Choice Songs, Scots and English*, Glasgow: R. Forrester

REID, James Macarthur, 1960, *Kirk and Nation. The story of the Reformed Church of Scotland*, London: Skeffington

SCOTT, Hew, 1915-28, *Fasti Ecclesiae Scoticanae. The succession of ministers in the Church of Scotland from the Reformation*, Edinburgh: Oliver and Boyd

SCOTT, Sir Walter: Most works referred to in the text are given the date of publication of the first editions. However, it should be noted that Scott's own Introductions and Notes to the Waverley Novels first appeared in the Magnum Edition of 1829-33.

SHIELDS, Alexander, 1744, orig. 1687, *A Hind let loose; or, an Historical Representation of the Testimonies of the Church of Scotland for the Interest of Christ. By a Lover of True Liberty*, Edinburgh

SIBBALD, Sir Robert, 1803, orig. 1710, *The History, Ancient and Modern, of the Sherrifdoms of Fife and Kinross, and of the Firths of Forth and Tay, and of the Islands in them, etc.*, Cupar, Fife

SKENE, William F., 1876-80, *Celtic Scotland: A History of Ancient Alban*, Edinburgh

SPEIRS, John, 1962, *The Scots Literary Tradition. An Essay in Criticism*, revised 2nd edition, London: Faber & Faber

STEVENSON, Robert, 1824, *An Account of the Bell Rock Light-house...*, Edinburgh

STEVENSON, Robert Louis: Unless specified otherwise, references throughout are to the Tusitala Edition of The Works of Robert Louis Stevenson, 1923-4, 35 vols, London: William Heinemann. However, the date of first publication is added where applicable.

STEWART, Sir James and STIRLING, James, 1721, orig. 1667, *Naphtali; or, the wrestlings of the church of Scotland, etc.*, Glasgow

SWEARINGEN, Roger G., 1980, *The prose writings of Robert Louis Stevenson: a guide*, Paisley and Hamden, Connecticut: Wilfion Books and Archon Books

SWEARINGEN, Roger G. ed., 1982, *An Old Song & Edifying Letters of the Rutherford Family*, Paisley and Hamden, Connecticut: Wilfion Books and Archon Books

TAYLOR, J. W., 1869, *Some Historical Notices: Chiefly Ecclesiastical, connected with Kirkcaldy and Abbotshall*, Kirkcaldy

THOMSON, John H., 1765, orig. ?1720, *A Cloud of Witnesses, for the royal prerogatives of Jesus Christ. . . ,* Edinburgh: Duncan

TRAIN, Joseph, 1814, *Strains of the Mountain Muse*, Edinburgh

TURNER, Sir James, 1829, *Memoirs of His Own Life and Times. By Sir James Turner. MDCXXXII-MDCLXX*, ed. T. Thomson, Edinburgh

TURNER, Sir James, 1683, *Pallas Armata. Military Essays of the Ancient Grecian, Roman and Modern Art of War. Written in the Years 1670 and 1671*, London: M. W., for R. Chiswell

WALKER, Patrick, 1827, orig. ?1732, *Biographia Presbyteriana*, ed. J. Stevenson, Edinburgh: D. Speare, etc.

WHITELAW, Alexander ed., 1844, *The Book of Scottish Song. . . ,* Glasgow

WILSON, W. E., 1932, 'The Making of the "Minstrelsy". Scott and Shortreed in Liddesdale', *Cornhill Magazine*, 73 (September)

WODROW, Robert, 1829-30, orig. 1721-2, *The History of the Sufferings of the Church of Scotland, from the Restauration to the Revolution, collected from the public records. . . and. . . well attested narratives*, Glasgow and Edinburgh

WOOLFE, Stuart J., 1979, *A History of Italy, 1700-1860: the social constraints of political change*, London: Methuen

VII GLOSSARY

✳

abune: above
ae: one
ahint: behind
aik: oak
ajee: to one side, off course (*a wee thing set ajee*: a little dissuaded from his former intentions)
auld: old
aye (adverb): always, at all times
bairnly: childlike
bairns: babies
baith: both
banes: bones
bauldly: boldly
begoud: began
ben: within, inside
benorth: beneath
beild: sheltered (*bieldy bit*: sheltered part or spot)
biggin: building
birks: birch trees
birzing: *lit.* bruising, crushing
bit: little, small (*his bit denners*: his little meals)
blithe, blythe: happy, in good spirits
bogle: ugly creature, ghost
bonny: pretty, beautiful (*bonnier nor that*: better than that)
bothie, bothy: small hut
braes: hills, hillsides
braw: splendid, beautiful; splendid thing, fine thing
brawly: well
bruik: enjoy the use of
brunt: burnt (*bruntstane spunk*: *lit.* a brimstone spark or chip of wood, tinder)
buckled to: *lit.* joined to; get oneself going

buff, played buff: ie. struck or hit, with a dull or puffing sound
bullering: bellowing, roaring
but, in the but: ie. in the outer part of the house, an outer room
but: in addition to, a prelude to
callant: youth, young person (often *callan*)
caller: cool, cooler
cantrip: charm, spell, trickery
canty: pleasant
capered: tossed the head
carline: old woman, witch
cawed: kept in motion, worked
chafts: cheeks, jawbones
chalmers: prisons, dungeons; chambers
chappin': striking
cla'es: clothes
clachan: village
claps: sudden bursts
claught: caught, clutched
claverin', clavers: gossiping, chattering; gossip
clean-strae: natural; *lit.* clean-straw
click: clicking, clattering (*played click wi' her teeth*: clattered her teeth together)
clink: rhyme, jingle, to make rhyme (English)
clum: climbed
coble: a short flat-bottomed boat
collieshangie: noisy dispute, animated conversation, uproar
corbie craws: carrion crows
corp: corpse
crack wi': shoot at
crack: gossip
craig: neck; rock, crag (*craigsman*: one

who works on the rocks, rock-climber)

crap: crept

creish: grease, fat

crunkled: crinkled, wrinkled, uneven

cuist: cast off

cummers: troubles, distress

dadding: bumping, banging against

daffin': merrily, playfully

daft: foolish

daundering, dandering: strolling, aimless wandering

daunten: taunt

deave: deafen

deil: devil

diddling: fiddling, dancing (*diddling his elbock:* i.e. imitating a fiddler, with his elbow as the upraised fiddle)

dinnle'd, dinnling: shook, vibrated; shaking

dirl, dirlin': clatter; vibrating, clattering (*play dirl thegither in her chafts:* chatter or clash together in her cheeks)

doddered, doddering: tottered, tottering

door-cheeks: doorways, doorposts

dowie: sad, mournful

dowp, doup: buttocks

dozened, dozenedness: stupid, dazed; stupidity, weakness (often through age)

draps: pellets, shot

droun: drown

duddy: ragged

duds: clothes, raggedy clothes

dunt, duntin': knock, thud; knocking, beating

dwam: daydream, stupor

dwining: declining, fading (in health)

e'en: eyes

eicht: eight

eldritch: elfish, unearthly

eneuch: enough

ettling (at): driving at, referring to

Fair-guid-een: *lit.* fair-good-evening, greetings; also *Fair-guid-day*

fashed: troubled, bothered, annoyed

fause: false

fechtin': fighting, struggling

feck: a large number

feckless: weak

feesh: fish

ferlies: curiosities, marvels

fiddling: fussing

flang: flung

flegged: flew, rushed

fleyed: frightened

flyting: quarrelling, violently arguing

focht: fought

forby, forbye: besides, in addition to

forgaithered: assembled (*forgaithered wi':* assembled before)

forjeskit: exhausted

forrit: forward (*to come forrit:* to go forward, to take the sacrament)

fower: four

frae: from (*frae their ordinar:* i.e. from their normal selves)

frichit: frightened

fuff: hiss or spit

fyke: fuss (*a sair fyke:* a great fuss)

gaed, gang: go, went (*gang her ain gyte:* go her own way)

gangrel: toad

gart: made

gash: grim

gate: way, direction, course

gaun: going

girn: grin, grimace

girzie: maidservant

glamour: enchantment, magic

glebe: portion of land assigned to a parish minister in addition to his stipend

glintin': shining

glisk: glimpse, glance

gloamin': evening, twilight

glowrin': staring

goun: nightshirt

grat: wept, cried

grogram: coarse fabric of silk or mohair and wool mixed with silk (English)

grue: melting snow, slush

guid: good (*guidwives:* goodwives)

gurlin', gurled: howling, howled

gutsy: greedy

gwost: gust

gyte: mad, crazy; way, direction

hae: have

hag: ground in a moor or bog

hagging: chopping up, felling

hail, hale: whole

han'sel, handsel: gift or payment

hangit: hanged

hap-step-an'-lowp: hop-skip-and-jump

happed: wrapped around

hash: mess, contemptuous term for someone

hashing: slicing up, destroying

hasp: clasp or catch on a door or gate

haud: hold

het: hot

hinder: the rear

hinderlands: backside

hirsle, hirsled: slither or shuffle, move with difficulty

hoots! hout!: expressing dissent, remonstrance

howff: a refuge, a favourite spot

howking: poking, burrowing into

hunkers, on his hunkers: squatting down

ilka: each

ither: the other, each other (*ither whiles*: other times)

jag: sharp point

jaloosed: suspected, guessed

keeked, keekit: peeped, glanced

ken, kenned, kent: know, knew (*kent the gate*: knew the way, knew how)

kep: cap

kilted: tucked up

kist: chest

kittle: ticklish, unreliable (*a kittle bit*: a difficult or unreliable spot)

knock: clock

knoitered: knocked, beat

kye: cows

laigh: low

laird: landlord

lane: alone, (on your) own

lauchin': laughing

lee-lane: alone, (on their) own

leelang: whole, length of

leid: lead

leir: learn (English)

licht, lichtly: light, lightly

limmer: loose woman; a term of contempt for a woman

lowed: flared up, glowed

lown: still, becalmed

lowp: jump, leap

luffed: worked the luff, a contrivance for altering a ship's course

lug: ear

luntin': burning, blazing

mair: more

maned: mourned, bemoaned

maud: a checked plaid or wrap, often worn by shepherds

maun, maunna: must, must not

meddled: interfered with

mind: remember, recollect

mirk: dark, gloomy (*pit-mirk*: dark as a pit, pitch-black)

misdoobt: doubt

mistrysted: misarranged, gone against

moo: mouth

muckle: much, the most (*muckle hell*: the depths of hell: *no'. . . so muckle worth*: less in value, not worth so much)

muir: moor

mutch: nightcap

nae: no

naething: nothing

napery: table linen

nar: no

nebs: tips

neist: nearest, next

neuk: corner, end or tip (*the neuk o' a plaid*: the corner or end fold of a plaid)

nicht: night

ower lang: too long (*ower weariet*: excessively tired; *ower weel*: very well)

owercome (of a song): a refrain or chorus

oxter: armpit

partans: edible crabs

pechin': gasping

pickle: a little, a small amount

plenished: furnished

powney: pony

preen: fasten, attach

prentit: printed

puddock: toad, term of abuse

puir: poor

pyking: picking, probing

quean: young girl

rairin': roaring, weeping

ram-stam: headstrong, heedless

ran-dan: riotous behaviour, spree (English)

ratton: rat, contemptuous name for someone

reid: *lit.* red; lively, furious

reishng: rustling, clattering

rins: runs

riving: bursting, eating away, forcing into

rumm'led: rumbled, disturbed (with a noise)

sabbin': sobbing; the sound made by running water

sae: so

saft: soft, pliable

sair: sore, causing distress (*a sair wark*: a hard job, a hard time)

sang: song

sants: saints

sark: shirt

saughs: willow trees

saut: salt, bitter (*saut wilderness*: i.e. the sea)

scart: marks made by a pen, scribbles; furrows

scunner: loathing, repulsion, revulsion (*gart me scunner*: made me nauseated, nauseated me)

shouther: shoulder

shure: sure

sib: sibling, related

sic, siccan: such

siller: silver

sinsyne: some time ago, since then

skelloch: shriek, scream

skelpit: struck, hit

skirl, skirled: shriek, scream

skreighed: shrieked, screeched

slavered: chattered, talked nonsense

slockened: extinguished, soaked, quenched one's thirst

smack: single-masted sailing vessel, usually for fishing

smoored: smothered, buried; concealed, rendered useless

sneck: latch or notch on a door

sodger: soldier

solans: gannet geese

sook: flow, current

soom: swim

sowp: sip, drink

spak: spoke

spang: span, amount (*a sair spang*: a severe amount, a great deal)

spate: suddenly

speered, speiring: inquired, asked after; inquiring

speldering: stretching, sprawling

spenster: monster?

sploring: frolicking, merry, showing off

spried, spreid: spread

spunk: tinder, spark

spunkies: spirits, will-o'-the'-wisps

steekit, steeked: shut, closed

steer: disturbance

steered: frightened

steighest: stuffed full, filled up

stend: surge, thrill

stending: leaping, bounding

stramp: stamping, trampling

straucht: straight

stravaguin': roaming, aimlessly rambling

suld: shall, should

swat: sweat

syne: since, before (*lang syne*: long since)

taed: toad

tauld: told

teetotum: small four-sided disc with a spindle passing through it, to be spun like a top (English)

teevil: devil

tenty: attentive, watchful

tester: pellet, bullet

thegither: together

thir: this

thirled (into): subjected to, bound to (in servitude)

thocht: thought

thon: that, that thing or place (*Thon:* him; pronoun indicating a thing or person more remote from the speaker than others)

thrapples: throats, gullets

thrawn: twisted, crooked, misshapen

thraws: throws, convulsions

threep: insist, assert (*threep it doun their thrapples:* i.e. forced the point down their throats)

thretty: thirty

thrumming: strumming, purring

tint: lost

tummled: tossed, tumbled

twa: two

twined: parted, separated

tyke: dog, cur

unco: strange, uncanny (*an unco time:* an awful time)

unstreakit: not buried or laid out (*an unstreakit corp:* an unburied corpse)

upsitten: indifferent

vivers: food, provisions

wab: web, warp (of the loom)

wabster: weaver

wad: will

waefu': woeful

wale: best of, pick of

wanchancey: uncanny, deformed; unlucky or ill-omened

wark: work, job, period of time

wars'lin: struggling, wrestling

wast: west

waur: worst

wean: child, youngster

weary: dispiriting, sad (*weary fa' them:* damn them, devil take them)

wee: little

weicht: weight

whammled: overturned, turned upside down

whaur: where

wheen: few (*a wheen duds:* a few clothes, a few rags)

wheesht!: be quiet!; ejaculation suggesting impatience

wheesht: silent, quiet

whiles: sometimes, at times

whilk: which

whilly-wha: coax, cajole

won: get; succeeded, reached, arrived at

wrang: wrong

wroucht: worked

wud: white

wynd: winding lane

yam-yammered: babbled incoherently

yett: gate

yirk up: jerk up, tug up, hoist

yoke on: set on, attack

yowlin': howling